SWORDS AND PLOWSHARES

Books by Maxwell D. Taylor

Swords and Plowshares
Responsibility and Response
The Uncertain Trumpet

MAXWELL D. TAYLOR

General, U.S. Army

SWORDS AND PLOWSHARES

A DA CAPO PAPERBACK

Library of Congress Cataloging in Publication Data

Taylor, Maxwell D. (Maxwell Davenport), 1901-1987.
  Swords and plowshares / Maxwell D. Taylor.
      p.   cm. — (A Da Capo paperback)
  Reprint. Originally published: New York: W. W. Norton, 1972.
  Includes index.
  ISBN 0-306-80407-7
  1. Taylor, Maxwell D. (Maxwell Davenport), 1901-1987. 2.
Generals—United States—Biography. 3. United States. Army—
Biography. I. Title.
  [E745.T317   1990]
  355′.0092—dc20   90-3692
  [B]   CIP

This Da Capo Press paperback edition of *Swords and Plowshares* is an
unabridged republication of the edition published in New York in 1972.
It is reprinted by arrangement with W. W. Norton & Company.

Maps by Theodore R. Miller

Published by Da Capo Press, Inc.
A Subsidiary of Plenum Publishing Corporation
233 Spring Street, New York, New York 10013

To Diddy

The Best Taylor Soldier

Contents

9

CONTENTS

Illustrations

Acknowledgments

In writing this book I have been greatly indebted to my son John and his wife Priscilla for their criticisms and suggestions for its improvement. Evan Thomas, Vice President of W. W. Norton and Company, has contributed his broad experience as an editor to help me avoid at least some of the pitfalls which beset an author who ventures into the controversial fields of contemporary policy. Besides these few, I am grateful to a long line of able and loyal associates, military and civilian, too numerous to mention, who have supported me in the course of the events described herein.

Foreword

"And He shall judge between the nations and shall rebuke many people: and they shall beat their swords into plowshares, and their spears into pruning hooks: Nation shall not lift up sword against nation, neither shall they learn war anymore."

Isaiah 2:4
Micah 4:3

"Beat your plowshares into swords, and your pruning hooks into spears: let the weak say, I am strong."

Joel 3:10

While bending an arthritic back over the manuscript of this book for nearly two years, I have often wondered why I ever undertook the task. I had originally intended the book to be a summary of conclusions, which I had drawn over the years, regarding the capabilities and limitations of the power at the disposal of a great democracy. The autobiographical portion was to be limited to that necessary to remind the reader of the background and qualifications of the author. Unfortunately, I soon found it rather enjoyable to relive some of the episodes of the past and to reflect on their significance at leisure, a luxury rarely available at the time of occurrence. As a result, the personal reminiscences have far exceeded my original intention. However, this self-indulgence has allowed me a welcome opportunity to bear witness to the many facets of a military career and, in so doing, to acknowledge the debt which I owe to the Army and to the dedicated men and women with whom I worked during more than forty years of diversified government service. My old Confederate grandfather used to ask me when I was a new second lieutenant

15

"What do you Army fellows do when you're not drilling?" I hope in this book to have given one Army man's answer to that pertinent question.

My book makes no claim to being finished history, complete with footnotes and cross references. Rather, it recounts my personal involvement in a series of historic episodes and records my own impressions of what took place without attempting to reconcile them with other versions of the same events. I am thoroughly aware that contrary views worthy of high respect exist on many of the issues contained in this book; however, I do not undertake to refute them beyond exposing my own views and the reasons for them. I hope that my account, considered with those of other observers, will be of some assistance in composing the complete history of the period which remains to be written.

As a military man, I have necessarily been concerned during most of my career with the use of military power as a means to assure our national security and to advance our national interests. Although this focus of concern may suggest a narrowly professional outlook on world problems, I do not believe that this is necessarily the case. Any thoughtful consideration of the uses of military power leads to basic questions such as the meaning of national interests and the validity of the goals in which the national interest finds expression. The military profession obliges one to think deeply about the requirements of national security—what we need to protect, how, and why. It forces examination of relationships between military and nonmilitary forms of power and between the requirements of national security and those of the domestic welfare. These are some of the matters which I have undertaken to discuss in the subsequent chapters.

As the patient reader will discover, my conclusions as to our future prospects as a world power are not encouraging. While we displayed tremendous strength in waging total war against the Axis powers in World War II, as a democracy we are facing serious difficulties in coping with the lesser threats of the Cold War in their changing forms. To many of these threats, the contents of our vast military arsenal offer only a limited response. The techniques of the so-called War of National Liberation were designed by our Communist adversaries to avoid the risks of overt warfare and to substitute subversion and the exploitation of internal weaknesses as an indirect means of conquest. We are today the target of such an attack, and it is presently a question whether we can recover the unity lost during the Vietnam War and correct the defects we have demonstrated in the use of our available power. To do these things, we will have to adjust many of our ways in comparatively short order.

I am afraid that much which I have written on this subject suggests a belief that the United States is a declining power with the best of its history behind it. Actually I am a practicing optimist, having found long ago that pessimism plays into the hands of the enemy and thereby contributes

16

to defeat. I do not believe in the inevitability of any of the dire forecasts which are recorded herein as possible. However, we are running the grave risk of permitting our democracy to destroy itself through its own excesses. One way to forestall disaster is to recognize the new scope of the threats which confront us, particularly those which would subvert or destroy the sources of our national power: our unity, leadership, institutions, and economy. They are all under attack today and can be destroyed without the firing of a hostile shot.

I chose the title of my book, *Swords and Plowshares*, after meditating on the apparent conflict in the quotations from the Prophets cited at the head of this Foreword. However, a close reading of the Biblical context reveals that the Prophets are considering different times and circumstances at the Final Judgment and that their contradictions are more apparent than real. They seem to be in agreement that, while the sword will be needed to destroy the wicked on the Day of Judgment, thereafter it will have no place in the better world which follows. This will be the time for the plow and pruning hook.

Despite the origins of its title, my book makes no pretense to prophecy. For its purposes, swords and plowshares are but symbols of the recurrent and often competing needs of war and peace in a world where peoples are still obliged to learn war and the wolf still does not dwell with the lamb. My book relates episodes involving the use of the sword both in total and limited war as well as instances of Cold War hostilities conducted without resort to the sword. It contains examples—Italy, Berlin, and Korea—where warriors have taken up the plow and pruning hook to repair the devastation caused by war. Vietnam illustrates the necessity for the concurrent use of sword and plow, the one to defend the harvest of the other. In the current ordering of world affairs, both warrior and plowman must work in unity to preserve the power from which both draw their security and well-being.

M. D. T.

SWORDS AND PLOWSHARES

CHAPTER 1

~~~~~~

Gestation of a Second Lieutenant

Three factors have exercised the greatest influence on my life—my parents, my wife, and my profession. Over the choice of my parents, I could exercise no control but may claim some credit for good judgment in selecting the other two, although always conceding the ever-present factor of luck. My birthplace was a small frame house in Keytesville, Missouri, a country town with a population then of a few hundred souls, and today about the same, but always proud of being the county seat of Chariton County. The town itself was about two miles from the railway station with which it was connected by a mule-drawn street car. This car was an endless delight to ride when I returned each summer in my boyhood to visit my grandparents' farm, far more interesting than the ordinary trolley cars in Kansas City where our family had come to reside two years after my birth.

When I was born, my father was a young lawyer who had just been admitted to the bar after a period of study in the law office of a local attorney. He had not only a bride, the daughter of a neighboring farmer, but also a widowed mother to support—and now an heir. The weekly *Chariton Courier* of August 30, 1901, carried the news of the event four days later: "John E. M. Taylor, one of Keytesville's studious and promising young attorneys, is papa, his wife having presented him an 11½ pound son Monday morning at 8:30 o'clock. Mother and babe are doing nicely, while the father is conducting himself with wonderful decorum, considering the youngster is Mr. and Mrs. Taylor's firstborn." Although the child's weight must have been a press exaggeration, the facts reported were essentially correct. Father undertook his new obligations with the calm deliberateness

21

which was his manner, and his decorum was never tested again by an addition to the family until I brought him my bride, "Diddy" Happer, twenty-four years later. Oddly enough she had been born the same day as I, August 26, 1901, in Worcester, Massachusetts.

My first formal schooling began in Kansas City when Mother enrolled me at the age of six in the kindergarten of Likens Grammar School. She and Grandmother Taylor, who lived with us, had encouraged my early interest in books by reading to me and helping me to learn my letters at an early age. So I was well advanced in reading when I entered school, where I was fortunate to find excellent teachers who further stimulated my interest in books. The Kansas City public school system of that period was of very high quality, and many of my teachers in grammar school and high school remained among my best friends throughout their lives. They encouraged me to go faster than the normal rate of progression, so that I finished grammar school at eleven and graduated from Northeast High School at fifteen.

During this time Father was struggling to make ends meet on a modest salary in the law firm of New, Miller, Cammack, and Winger. The first family crisis which I remember was in the summer of 1906 when Dad and I, in succession, contracted typhoid fever. While we were not seriously ill, we required prolonged medical attention and although Mother did all the nursing, the bills accumulated. In the end, Dad owed the family doctor a hundred dollars, an enormous sum to him, which had to be paid off slowly over nearly two years. I remember the celebration when the last installment was paid, and when I now receive a hundred dollar bill as a director's fee for a couple of hours of discussion, I often think what that bill would have meant to Dad in those hard times.

Summer vacations were a period of unmitigated joy because they were the occasion to visit my maternal grandparents, Milton and Mary Eliza Davenport on their farm between Keytesville and Dalton, Missouri. I thought that Grandpa Davenport was about the greatest man in the world and spent much of the school year looking forward to being with him the next summer. Grandpa was a one-armed Confederate veteran who had fought for four years with Generals Price and Shelby in Missouri and Arkansas. He had risen to the grade of sergeant in the cavalry, but he ended in the infantry, as he explained, "after my horse died." The perfect day for me was to work with him in the field during the daylight hours, listen to his Victor phonograph after dinner, and have him refight the battles of The War. He did not glorify the war or try to make it appear other than it had been—a bitter, exhausting ordeal for soldiers and civilians alike—but his eyes would light up as he told about the "boys" in action. Since becoming a veteran myself and recognizing privately the loss in historical accuracy and the gain in dramatic quality of my own stories with the passage of time, I sometime wonder now whether Grandpa's "boys" were quite the heroes he depicted. But his tales had a gripping quality in describing how shared hardships and dangers bind men together in the camaraderie of arms.

At the feet of this old Confederate, I acquired much of my early interest in things military, an interest already whetted by early historical reading. Inquiring how I too could become a soldier, I first heard about West Point from Grandfather, where his heroes, Lee and Jackson, had prepared themselves for the battlefields of the Mexican and Civil Wars. Thereafter I read everything I could find about it and, in due course, decided that it was the place for me. On a sixth grade form, I recorded a commitment to the military life by listing as my future profession, major general. While this was a display of considerable self confidence, it also showed that at an early age I had the good fortune of knowing what I wanted to be—a great advantage to any young man.

It was one thing to decide to go to West Point, another to get there. Indeed, it took World War I to persuade my parents that their only child should "seek the bubble reputation even in the cannon's mouth." Despite the fact that the material rewards of the legal profession had been meager, Father was devoted to the law and hoped that I would follow in his footsteps. He had been encouraged by my interest in debating in high school which, he thought, augured well for success in a legal career. Indeed, the law appealed to me also but only as a second choice to the Army.

The United States entered World War I in 1917, the year I graduated from high school and entered the local junior college, Kansas City Polytechnic Institute. My high school credits for college were badly out of balance for one aspiring to West Point, comprising as they did four years of English, Latin, and Spanish and two years of Greek but minimal credits in mathematics and science. To correct the imbalance, I loaded my freshman college course with mathematics and physics and continued my favorite language studies only in Spanish. My hope was to complete two years of college in Kansas City and then, at seventeen, to obtain an appointment to the Military Academy.

But world events were on the march and disrupted the plans of many young men of that period. My contemporaries in school, all older, began to enter the Armed Forces, leaving me to a sense of humiliation at being left behind. So in 1918, in rebellion against being a stay-at-home, I falsified my age by a year and registered for the draft. In that war, the possession of a draft card was the next best thing to wearing a uniform if a young man wanted the respect of his associates.

Father, though not displeased by my action, was startled and galvanized into seeking an appointment for me to West Point. In the end he got me the privilege of taking the competitive examination for an appointment held by our Congressman, William P. Borland, of the Fifth Missouri District. Borland had a vacancy that year for both West Point and Annapolis, and I was lucky enough to win his appointment to both. The next problem was to pass the entrance examination then required for admission by both academies. The tests covered essentially the same ground, except that the Annapolis one included a geography examination where West Point had one in history.

When I took the two examinations I passed those for West Point after failing the Annapolis geography examination. In the course of taking the latter, I remember puzzling over a list of out-of-the-way places about the world whose locations had to be identified. One was the Strait of Malacca which I guessed wrongly to be in the Middle East but which I have since verified by personal inspection to be in Southeast Asia. The resulting ignominy of failure allowed me in subsequent years to compare my lot to that of the famous painter, James McNeill Whistler, at the Military Academy. Whistler had a brief career as a West Point cadet at the start of the Civil War but was dismissed before graduating for having failed chemistry. In describing the incident in later years, he reportedly said: "Had silicon been a gas, I might have been a general." So now I tell my Navy friends that, had the Strait of Malacca been in the Mediterranean, I might have been an admiral, although they are clearly unconvinced on the latter point.

On the evening of October 30, 1918, Father took me to the Kansas City Union Station and put me on the train bound for New York. It was my first trip outside Missouri if one does not count occasional visits to my cousins across the state line in Kansas City, Kansas. He explained to me how to behave on the Pullman, how to find my way to the diner, and how to tip the porter at journey's end. He told me how to get from the Pennsylvania Station in New York to the Weehawken ferry and thence to the West Shore Railway Station, places which sounded as foreign to me as the Strait of Malacca. With that we shook hands, and I left home for the Army, never to return again except as a transient visitor between military assignments.

The class which I joined upon arriving at West Point was out of phase with the normal sequence of classes, entering in early November for the purpose of graduating the following June. Unwisely, in my judgment, the authorities in Washington had decided to turn the Academy into little more than an officer candidate school in order to produce a few hundred more infantry lieutenants for the victory drive anticipated for the summer of 1919. But fortunately for all parties, as we now say at class reunions, the Kaiser and Hindenburg heard of this new threat to the armies of the Fatherland forming on the banks of the Hudson and decided to accept an armistice on November 11, nine days after I had reported for duty as a new cadet. In due time, the academic program of the Academy reverted first to a three-year course and eventually to the traditional one of four years. Thus my classmates and I became the four-year class of 1922.

Because of the short stay projected for us at the start, my class did not receive upon arrival the gray uniform which is the hallmark of the West

24

Point cadet. Instead we were issued enlisted men's uniforms differentiated only by a wide yellow band on the campaign hat, which earned for us the title of the "Oriole" class. Since there was only one other class at West Point ahead of us, our recruit training in "Beast Barracks" was conducted by young officers who were themselves very recent graduates. Although perhaps a trifle less exacting than cadet officers would have been, they appeared to have lost none of their zeal for plebe training as they toiled over us morning and night on the drill field and in the barracks, often seeming to despair of ever making acceptable cadets from such unpromising material. When the Armistice came no one took time to tell us about it; November 11 was just another day of drilling on the Plain. I found out that the war was over only by courtesy of our "barrack policeman," the janitor who looked after the division of the old South Barracks where my "beast" company was quartered, who reported the war's end a couple of days after the fact.

During my cadet years, West Point was still a military cloister, linked tenuously to the outside world by the West Shore Railway, the excursion boats on the Hudson, and a winding road leading westward into New Jersey. A cadet normally entered the Academy in July and never left it on vacation until his second Christmas. In the meantime, he led a completely regimented life, arising at six, going to bed at ten and rarely having a moment without a duty to occupy it. As a member of the Army and subject to its laws and regulations, he received a salary just sufficient to pay his essential expenses, to permit saving a few dollars monthly for his uniforms at graduation, and to give him an allowance of five dollars a month for pure dissipation at the "Boodlers" where ice cream and candy were available to a hungry cadet seeking to supplement the mess hall fare. As he could legally have no more money than this allowance, if he succeeded in enticing a young lady, properly chaperoned of course, to come to a weekend hop, she had to foot the bills for dinners shared together. These would take place only at the venerable West Point Hotel where the quality of the view up the Hudson compensated for the lack of service and central heating.

Every cadet took essentially the same academic course, which was roughly equivalent to the course of studies for a bachelor of science degree in general engineering. The scientific orientation of the curriculum went back a century to the time when West Point was the only engineering school in the country and had as its primary mission the training of engineer and artillery officers. Later, even after becoming a source of officers for all branches, the Academy continued this emphasis because of the educational value attached to training in mathematics and the growing importance of science and technology in the military profession regardless of the branch of service. There were no electives in this curriculum, although a few advanced courses were provided for cadets who were well ahead of the rest of their class in certain subjects, by virtue either of aptitude for the subject or of prior work at other schools. As I had had most of the subjects taught during the first two years, I had ample leisure to do a great deal of desultory reading in the small but well-stocked Cadet Library where I continued to indulge my interest in reading widely, if not deeply, in the fields of philosophy and military history.

Then, as now, a factor of great importance at West Point was the Cadet Honor System. A cadet could not lie, steal, or cheat and, if discovered, remain a cadet. This simple but stern ethic was inculcated into a new cadet from the day he entered and was enforced in practice largely by the cadets themselves. The role of the administration with regard to the Honor System was principally one of seeing that, in the immoderation of youth, the cadets were not too hard on one another in applying the sanctions of the code. It was a civilian, Secretary of War Newton D. Baker, who gave the best expression I know of its justification: "Men may be inexact or even untruthful in ordinary matters and suffer as a consequence only the disesteem of their associates or even the inconvenience of unfavorable litigation, but the inexact or untruthful soldier trifles with the lives of his fellowmen and the honor of his government. It is therefore no matter of idle pride but rather of stern disciplinary necessity that makes the Army require of its officers a character for trustworthiness which knows no evasion."

At the end of my plebe year in 1919, Brigadier General Douglas MacArthur, at thirty-nine the youngest general in the Army, arrived to become superintendent of the Academy bringing with him an Army-wide reputation for brilliance, a charming bride, and a new outlook on the mission of West Point. Fresh from the battlefields of Europe, he began at once to review the objectives and methods of the Academy and to require their validation against the requirements of war as he had come to know them. His innovations were many, but I remember most vividly his contributions to the modernization of the plebe system and his introduction of intramural athletics to the slogan, "Every cadet an athlete."

The treatment or mistreatment of the plebes had long been a problem at the Academy. While their training was based on the sound principle that those who aspire to command must first learn to obey, it was easy for abuses to crop up which nullified its virtues. At its worst, the plebe system led to hazing of varying degrees of severity and contributed to making martinets of the upper classmen; at its best, it taught proper methods of leadership to the upperclassmen and impressed habits of discipline and order on the plebes. MacArthur was well aware of the problem and upon arrival appealed to the upperclassmen to take the lead in rooting out the bad and in cultivating the good in the system, as it existed at the time. His personal prestige carried the day and overcame the reluctance to cooperate on the part of those cadets who would have resisted an intrusion of authority into the traditions of the Corps of Cadets of which they felt themselves the guardians.

The intramural athletic program was aimed at cadets like me, uninterested in athletics or unable to make the Corps squads, and thus consigned to cheer for the varsity teams from the grandstand. It rooted me out of my deep chair at the library and compelled me to learn something about games other than tennis, my only varsity sport. Wisely it placed emphasis on the acquisition of sports like polo, golf, tennis, and handball, which graduates in subsequent life could continue to play in order to maintain the physical condition so essential to a professional soldier.

MacArthur did one little thing which will never appear in his long list of accomplishments but which meant much to me. Traditionally, a cadet could never smoke legally at West Point during his entire four years. I arrived never having smoked, but I soon discovered the sport involved in surreptitious puffing on an occasional cigarette in my room in barracks. When we heard the inspecting officer approaching, my roommate and I would open a window, take a blanket, and fan it desperately to clear out the smoke. Then we would stand rigidly at attention during room inspection and enjoy a minor triumph if the officer departed without detecting our dereliction. MacArthur knew the ways of cadets, having been one himself only some twenty years before, and decided to stop such nonsense. One day he decreed that henceforth cadets could smoke freely in their rooms—but still not outside of barracks. That took the fun out of the game. I never smoked thereafter and remain today a nonsmoker, thanks to Douglas MacArthur.

At a Saturday evening hop in the fall of 1920, I met my future wife by the second column on the left as one enters the Cullun Hall dance floor. One of the medieval practices which survived among the cadets at that time was the custom of keeping formal dance cards for the weekly hops, something modern cadets disdain to do and thus assure dull weekends for themselves and their girls. At the start of a year, friends would trade dances by number among each other for the coming social season and thus share together the rewards and tribulations of "dragging blind," that is, inviting unknown ladies to dances. In the course of swapping such a dance with a classmate, Francis Wilson, I made the acquaintance of Lydia Happer of Washington. I pursued the lady vigorously, and with some success, from that time on, but at some cost to my standing in academics and deportment. In fact, on one occasion, she nearly cost me my diploma.

During graduation week, in June, 1922, I was walking arm-in-arm with her through a shady barracks sally-port, forgetting as we emerged into the sunlight that I was committing the offense of "showing affection to a young lady in public" in the language of the demerit book. Our arm-in-arm stroll was soon interrupted by a cadet officer of the guard who informed me that I was wanted by Major Simon Bolivar Buckner at Cadet Headquarters. Fully appreciating that I had been caught *in flagrante delicto* by one of the toughest officers of the Tactical Department, I presented myself with considerable trepidation before the redoubtable major who proceeded to expatiate on the enormity of my offense. When he had finished, he asked me whether I really thought that, under the circumstances, I should be allowed to graduate two days hence. I replied in none too confident tones that I hoped so, and was then dismissed, but I never felt entirely safe until I had my diploma in hand two days later.

In World War II, Major Buckner became a three-star Army commander and died a hero's death in the battle with the Japanese for Okinawa. One of my tasks as Superintendent of West Point after the war was to dedicate the cadet summer camp in honor of General Buckner and to pronounce a fitting eulogy for the occasion. I am afraid that my eloquence in rendering tribute to a gallant soldier was somewhat tempered by the memory of that scene in graduation week of 1922.

In spite of Major Buckner's misgivings, I graduated on June 13, number 4 in a class of 102. General MacArthur gave me my diploma and his "Congratulations, Mr. Taylor" was the last time I heard his voice until, as the new Chief of Staff of the Army, I called on him in the Waldorf Towers in 1956. Although he had done much for the Corps of Cadets during his superintendency, oddly enough he had never made an effort to impress his personality on the cadets through direct communication with them. I do not ever recall his having made a speech to us and only a few cadets were ever asked to his house. Certainly no graduate has left greater evidence of deep affection for West Point and the Corps than MacArthur, but the cadets saw little of this during his superintendency.

Upon graduation I had my choice of branch of service, and I took the engineers for two unrelated but, for me, compelling reasons. The first was that Robert E. Lee had been an engineer, and the second that the Engineer School at Camp Humphreys, Virginia, now Fort Belvoir, was conveniently near Washington where Miss Happer lived. It became the first of the long list of Army stations at which I was to serve.

CHAPTER 2

~~~~~~

Preparation for High Command

The Army which I joined in 1922 was drab and unexhilarating after West Point. Most of our citizens assumed that World War I had ended all wars and hence regarded a standing army as useful as "a chimney in summer," to use an old English phrase. Promotion was strictly by seniority, and a large bloc of temporary officers taken into the Regular Army at the end of the war constituted a discouraging "hump" in the promotion list just ahead of my contemporaries and me. As a result it took me thirteen years to become a captain, and such distinguished officers as Generals Gruenther, McAuliffe, Palmer, and Wedemeyer, who graduated a few years before me, took seventeen years.

Under such conditions of stagnation, many of the most promising young officers resigned and sought their fortune in civil life. But for some unaccountable reason a remarkable number stayed in the service to become the military leaders of World War II. In these doldrums, they were saved by some inner feeling of the importance of their profession, reinforced by the influence of the Army school system. I enjoyed the benefit both of the sense of vocation and of the school system, serving as a student officer at the Engineer School at Camp Humphreys immediately after graduation and intermittently thereafter at the Artillery School at Fort Sill, the Command and General Staff School at Fort Leavenworth, and the Army War College in Washington. Betweentimes I taught at West Point for five years as an instructor and assistant professor of French and Spanish.

Apart from my wedding to Miss Happer in 1925, my greatest bits of luck in this period were the birth of my sons Jack and Tom and my selection to the Command and General Staff School while still a first lieutenant.

29

I owed this latter break to General MacArthur, who had become Army Chief of Staff in 1930. Noting the advanced age of Leavenworth students and the slow promotion of postwar officers, he directed a widening of the field of selection for the school to allow dipping into the ranks of the senior lieutenants as a step to negate the charge that our Army had the best educated retired officer corps in the world. As a result, there were five or six lieutenants chosen for the class entering in 1933 and I was fortunate enough to be one of them.

The course at that time lasted two years. It was highly competitive, since an officer's record at the school determined whether he would ever attend the War College and thus attain elegibility for the highest assignments of the officer corps. The backbone of the course was a series of map problems and terrain exercises in which the student officers were required to solve the problems of senior commanders and staff officers in hypothetical war situations. The solutions were largely individual tasks, sometimes requiring several days of intensive work. All the solutions were carefully marked and the grades determined class standing. The pressure on the students was considerable, and, over the years, an occasional suicide had not been uncommon.

There were about 125 members in my class selected from all branches of the Army and ranging from one lieutenant colonel to the handful of lowly lieutenants I have mentioned. They turned out to be the most able group of officers of that size with whom I have even been associated. Almost all had distinguished careers in World War II, including such men as Mark Clark, Matthew Ridgway, Walter Bedell Smith, and George Stratemeyer, to mention only a few of the illustrious.

Leavenworth in that day turned out well-trained potential commanders and general staff officers, all speaking the same professional language, following the same staff procedures, schooled in the same military doctrine, and thus ready to work together smoothly in any theater of war. It taught that the purpose of war was to break the will of the enemy and that the surest way to accomplish that purpose was to destroy his armed forces through offensive operations exploiting fire power and maneuver. The tactical innovation of the day was the so-called wide envelopment, which consisted of wide turning movements around the enemy flanks directed at the vital points in his rear thus avoiding the costly frontal attacks which had characterized World War I. Although many of us thought the school carried the wide envelopment to extremes, it certainly encouraged bold maneuver and, I am sure, had a wholesome effect on the development of our tactical thinking.

As graduation day approached in June, 1935, I received startling proof of the wisdom of the Army dictum which warns against volunteering for anything. In its contravention, upon arriving at Leavenworth I had volunteered to assist the school library in translating military articles from

French, Spanish, and Italian for reproduction in the military journal published by the school. Shortly before graduation, the librarian, Major Charles Willoughby, later famous in the Korean War as General MacArthur's chief intelligence officer, informed me that, in appreciation of the help I had been rendering, he had arranged for me to be assigned to Leavenworth to serve as his assistant. I was at my wit's end to find a way to extricate myself from this dismal prospect when I was saved by the War Department through one of those quirks in the Army personnel system which, from time to time, have been a source of wonderment.

Back in 1923, just out of West Point, I had visited the Army Intelligence Section of the General Staff, in the old State, War, and Navy Building alongside the White House, to apply for a language assignment to Japan. At West Point, I had learned of the practice of sending two officers a year to Japan and China for language study and, because of my interest in languages, I decided after graduation to put my application on file in Washington. Colonel Warner McCabe, the officer in charge of the office, listened to me politely but assured me that, as an officer of the Corps of Engineers, I had no chance of getting the assignment to Japan since engineers could not be spared for such nontechnical duties. Although I had transferred to the Field Artillery in 1926, I had never repeated my request and had almost forgotten about it. Then, twelve years later, in my hour of need, someone in Washington dug it out of the files and wrote asking if I was still interested. Faced with the prospect of a translator's desk in the Leavenworth library, I was definitely interested, accepted eagerly, and shortly embarked on a four year assignment which, in a just world, should have assured me of a translator's desk in some Pacific headquarters throughout World War II.

I arrived in Yokohama in October, 1935, accompanied by my wife and our two sons. The older, Jack, had been born at West Point five years before, whereas Tom was a recent acquisition at Leavenworth. Assisted by the military attaché, Lieutenant Colonel William C. Crane, we rented and occupied a small Western-style house more promptly than we could memorize its address, Shiba-ku, Shirokanedaimachi, itchome nanabanchi. This tongue-twister meant that mine was the seventh house built in the first section of the Shirokane district of the Shiba ward of Tokyo. There was not a named street in the city and an address was a series of contracting concentric circles ending in a house or building designated by a number indicating the order in time of its construction. Thus an initial visit to an address usually called for a long reconnaissance involving consultations with the local police as well as residents of the neighborhood suspected of containing the number sought.

No sooner were we installed in our new residence, with three Japanese servants speaking no English, than I began my study of Japanese, with a zeal stimulated by the practical need to converse with our cook. The Embassy had established a tutorial system of instruction for the benefit of the language officers of the State, War, and Navy Departments assigned to it. The head instructor and director of the course was Naganuma San, a truly gifted teacher, who designed the curriculum, provided the instruction materials, and hired the tutors. The language officers worked at their homes with their tutors and were examined at the Embassy every six months to verify their progress. While the course varied somewhat according to government service, the Army course usually consisted of about two years of formal tutorial instruction followed by a six month assignment to a Japanese regiment.

I found the language fascinating and worked hard at it seven days a week for about a year and a half, by which time I could converse fairly well about the ordinary subjects of daily life, read the 4,000-odd Chinese characters found in the text of the average newspaper, and understand the radio pretty well, provided it did not deal with some esoteric subject.

I found the study of the Chinese characters, in Japanese called *kanji*, a particularly intriguing aspect of the language. The Japanese had borrowed the characters from the Chinese along with Buddhism about the eighth century and had then laboriously adapted them to their own polysyllabic, atonal language which has no kinship or similarity at all to monosyllabic, tonal Chinese. The result is the most complex system of writing which any people ever succeeded in devising for the befuddlement of themselves and of foreign scholars who try to read it.

Nevertheless, to those who become addicted to it, the Chinese character is an intellectual challenge and a source of aesthetic pleasure. The myriad characters written on flaunting banners in the streets or blinking in neon lights appear as symbols of the enigmatic Orient which, if comprehended, would reveal all its mysteries. So at the start, the eager student finds endless enjoyment in looking for the few *kanji* he can read among the thousands which he cannot. If after thousands of hours of intensive study his interest or eyesight has not flagged, he will eventually reach the stage of searching only for unknown *kanji* among the street signs, jotting down their curving strokes in his memory or in his notebook and then running them down in his *kanji* dictionary, the use of which is an achievement in itself. The moment of triumph comes when a newly learned *kanji* fills a gap in a series of characters heretofore unintelligible even though, as in the case of one of my triumphs, the enigma, when resolved, turns out to be the advertisement for a permanent wave.

I was allowed to terminate my Embassy studies after a year and a half to get an early start on a regimental assignment, which most Army students viewed as a recompense for the long months of language study. My assignment was to the Imperial Guards Artillery Regiment which, as a unit of Guards Division, had its headquarters in Tokyo. Reporting for duty was quite an ordeal as it required courtesy calls on all the senior officers beginning with the division commander and ending with a presentation to the colonel and officers of the regiment at the regimental mess. This occasion called for me to make a formal speech which I memorized so thoroughly in advance that I can still repeat most of it today. It expressed my deep honor at being attached to such a famous regiment, asked pardon for the many rudenesses I was sure to commit, and ended in a peroration, which could be roughly translated "Here standing in reverent awe I, Captain Taylor, present you my respectful greetings."

For the short time it lasted, life in the regiment was an engrossing experience. The regiment moved almost at once to the firing range at the foot of Mount Fuji where, after World War II many an American artillery unit stationed in Japan held its target practice. We officers lived in simple frame barracks where each had a small private room and an orderly to look after it. Separate buildings housed the mess and the regimental bath. Social relations were patterned after those in the Japanese family with the colonel in the role of paterfamilias. This fact was particularly apparent at the bath hour when, the colonel in the lead, we filed to the bath, which consisted of a large tank of near boiling water serving the function of the wooden *o-furo* of a Japanese family. Thereupon, in order of rank, one by one, we soaped and scrubbed ourselves outside the tank, then eased ourselves gently into the hot water to parboil, being careful not to agitate it for fear of further raising the temperature. As I had been given a courtesy ranking at the head of the captains of the regiment, I always had the good fortune to get into the tank fairly early in the sequence.

I saw little of the mess as most of our meals were eaten in the field with the troops where the simplicity of the mess arrangements was most impressive. The only mess gear carried for the officers of a battalion of artillery was a pair of metal tubs for boiling rice, and the entire mess detachment charged with feeding and serving some 400 men comprised fewer than a half dozen soldiers. When meal time came, an officer went to a nearby tree, broke off a couple of twigs to serve as chopsticks, washed out his helmet which was to serve as his plate, and went through the mess line. At the tub, he received in his helmet a large chunk of rice, a tin of canned chicken or whale meat, and some soy sauce as a condiment; and that was it. When he finished his meal, he threw away the homemade chopsticks, washed his helmet, and went back to work for the Emperor.

A novelty in my battalion was that one of the batteries was commanded by a captain who was of the Imperial family and, as a cousin of the Son of Heaven, was never known by his own name but simply as Tai-i Omiya Denka, Imperial Prince Captain. Because of the linguistic problem presented I was a bit shaken when I learned without warning that I was about to be introduced to him. A curiosity of the language is that it requires a shifting of linguistic gears in accordance with the rank and social status of the person addressed. One uses a different set of words indicating possession and relationship depending on whether one is addressing an inferior, an equal, or a superior. This system allows an ill-chosen verb to convey mortal offense and practically eliminates the need for profanity. If by chance one had the unusual honor of conversing with a member of the Imperial Family, an extremely exalted form of the language was required, which had not been included in the curriculum of Naganuma San for Embassy language officers. So when I was introduced to the captain, I had to admit to the inadequacy of my Japanese honorifics and asked to be excused for any apparent lack of respect.

Tai-i Omiya Denka turned out to be a very likeable young officer who commanded his battery well and did about the same things as his less patrician comrades. I was interested in watching his manner toward them and theirs toward him and was surprised to see how unceremonious they were. One day riding back from target practice, several of us got off our horses and raised a farmer's patch of ripe watermelons. Imperial Prince Captain was chosen to draw his samurai sword and to slice the melons which we ate with the happy conviction that the unknown owner would be honored to have his melons provide pleasure for the Imperial Army.

In one way at least Imperial Prince Captain was different from the other captains. He had a private aide-de-camp who was a lieutenant colonel. Also he did not use the regimental bath—he had a private one next to his billet.

While I was watching my associates closely and trying to evaluate them, I suspected that they were trying equally hard to size up their foreign visitor. Although our respective governments were at serious odds, I detected nothing unfriendly in their attitude toward me and eventually concluded that they probably conceded to me certain assets while charging me with certain liabilities. On the target range, they saw that I carried a .45 caliber pistol and could accomplish modest things with it, such as hitting an empty beer bottle at fifteen paces. They carried poor quality pistols, which they had purchased themselves, and with which they could hit nothing— and knew it. However, they carried family swords which their forebears had borne in the wars of the Meiji, swords which had a razor sharpness capable of flicking off a head with a casual blow. My own sword was designed primarily to draw at parade and guard mount, and had cut nothing I can remember other than our wedding cake. A final good mark for me was my ability to absorb quantities of *saké* without apparent damage, *saké* which in lesser amounts put them quickly to sleep on the *tatami* of the local restaurant. But that asset was more than offset, I fear, when they noted in Tokyo that I hurried home early from stag parties. Clearly I was afraid of my wife and did not rule my household as would befit a *danna-san* in Japan.

My regimental assignment came to a sudden end shortly after the Marco Polo Bridge incident outside Peking in the course of the Japanese invasion of North China in July, 1937. As the Japanese forces moved southward, most of our Embassy was evacuated from Peking to Chungking and I was ordered to Peking as a Japanese-speaking officer to assist the military attaché, Colonel Joseph W. Stilwell, "Vinegar Joe" of later fame, who had remained to report the war in the north. My trip to Peking allowed me my first glimpse of Korea as I traveled by rail to Mukden, and I remember the peaceful beauty of Seoul or Keijo as the Japanese called it. As the train passed through Antung on the Manchurian border at night, unbeknownst to me the local customs officials put my trunk off the train for inspection and neglected to put it back on. So at Mukden I was faced with the decision of waiting for the trunk or moving on to Peking with nothing but a briefcase and a linen summer suit. As my orders said, "proceed to Peking without delay," and as I had been trained to believe that all orders meant all they said, I chose the latter course and never saw my trunk again until November when it finally reached Peking.

My principal task in Peking was to accompany Colonel Stilwell everywhere the Japanese would allow us to go in the wake of their forces advancing south to the Yellow River. While we were anything but welcome, the Japanese were not completely uncooperative, and we did have a fair opportunity to observe something of their logistic system. Washington was screaming for the identification of troop units, but the Japanese had removed all unit designations from uniforms and equipment so that identification was very difficult. Fortunately, on my first visit to the Summer Palace outside Peking, I found written, on the back of the Great Buddha overlooking the lake, the names of three Japanese soldiers who had considerately added the numerical designations of their divisions. The urge to write one's name in public places is apparently an international weakness.

I found "Vinegar Joe" a genial travel companion, full of Chinese lore and glad to talk about the country and people to an interested listener. He had a deep affection for the Chinese, an admiration for their achievements of the past, and a faith in the promise of their future. We rambled together over a good part of North China, traveling by automobile, by crowded troop trains, and not infrequently by foot. We slept wherever night found us and led thoroughly unsanitary lives. Stilwell openly despised the rules laid down by Western doctors for staying alive in China; he loved to walk through a Chinese market and pick up fruit to eat after merely brushing off the dust with a sweaty sleeve. Though I knew it was folly, I could do no less and soon became an ambulant case of chronic diarrhea while Stilwell seemed to flourish on our regime.

As winter came on, the war moved away from us and at the end of the year I was ordered back to Tokyo. I was unhappy to return for I had begun the study of Chinese upon arrival and hoped that I might be left in China to acquire something of the language. While it is structurally dissimilar from Japanese, a knowledge of the common character gives a Japanese

35

language student an important advantage upon which I hoped to build. But Washington decided otherwise, and my request to stay in China was turned down. Possibly the fact that Stilwell had supported it may have worked against me for he had been constantly feuding with his superiors in Washington. When, upon taking leave of him to return home, I expressed the hope that I might serve under him again, he shrugged it off saying, "This is my last assignment. I'm going home to retire. You know what Washington thinks of me." He would have been right about his future or lack thereof except for something he did not know at the time—his old friend George Marshall was about to become Chief of Staff of the Army.

Back in Tokyo, I spent the remainder of my tour of duty in the office of the military attaché, Colonel Harry Creswell, working on reports of the war in China. My principal contribution was a study of Japanese military tactics based on an analysis of map problems published in Japanese military publications. Although the Japanese were extremely secretive about such matters, I found that books written to assist officers in preparing for the entrance examinations could be purchased in the bookstores around the Staff College and the Infantry School. They contained many hypothetical military situations and the approved solutions of the actions and decisions of the opposing commanders. I would stake out each situation on an appropriate map, work out my own solution without looking at that contained in the book, and then compare mine with theirs to see the difference between the working of an oriental and occidental military mind.

In general, there was no significant difference in our solutions, except in situations when one side was so hopelessly inferior that, in my judgment, it should retreat or at least dig in on a defensive position. In such cases, the Japanese solution was almost always to attack at night, a manifestation of the unshakeable faith in the Japanese *seishin*, translatable as spirit or morale, which was presumed able to overcome all material obstacles. It was much like the French faith in the *offensive à outrance* in 1914 which led to so many bloody defeats in the early years of World War I. I would say that the Japanese commanders in World War II behaved about as predicted in my study and that *seishin* proved a formidable but fortunately not an invincible force which eventually succumbed to superior American fire power.

My family and I left Yokohama in June, 1939, in time for me to enter the Army War College in what turned out to be the last class before the school closed for World War II. As we left Japan, I would have said that war between the two countries was certainly possible but I had no premonition that it was only two years away.

On the opening day of the War College, a number of senior officers from the War Department attended to welcome the new class. The first man to speak I had never seen before, but he was just as impressive at first glance as he remained in my eyes in later life—George Marshall, the new Army Chief of Staff. What he said that day I do not remember, but the way he said it, I do. General Marshall never spoke anywhere without receiving the undivided attention of every listener to the words of a man who obviously knew what he was talking about. One could never imagine questioning the accuracy of his facts or challenging the soundness of his conclusions on any subject he undertook to discuss. He did not give the impression of great brilliance of mind, as General MacArthur did, but of calm strength and unshakeable will. I was to owe much to him—my service on his staff at the outbreak of the war, later the command of a division in Europe, and assignment as Superintendent of West Point following the war. But my greatest privilege was the opportunity to see General Marshall in action at close range at the outbreak of World War II.

Whereas Leavenworth prepared its graduates for military command and staff up to the level of the field army, the Army War College concentrated on the military problems of the theater of operations and at the seat of government. It operated in the realm of military and national strategy and drew heavily for its lectures on the leaders of government, of the military services, and of the university world. There was none of the individual competition among the students which characterized Leavenworth; the year at the War College was a time for mature reflection on the broadest problems of the military profession in company with congenial fellow professionals, most of whom were destined for senior assignments in the approaching global war.

As it turned out, I was obliged to graduate from the War College in absentia. In the spring of 1940, I was taken out of school to join a group of Army and Navy officers who were sent in pairs through the countries of Central and South America to ascertain the military needs of hemispheric defense against the Nazi threat. The officer in charge of the project was Lieutenant Colonel Matthew B. Ridgway, one of my Spanish instructors at West Point as well as a Leavenworth classmate, who had asked for my assignment to the mission because of my knowledge of Spanish. It was an indication of the low ebb of language instruction in the Armed Forces that Ridgway had to raid the War College class to fill out a slate of some ten officers qualified to do serious business in Spanish.

I made two swings through Latin America: the first to Guatemala, Costa Rica, El Salvador, Honduras, and Nicaragua; the second to Peru, Bolivia, and Chile. I had never visited these countries before and enjoyed the trips from both a professional and tourist point of view even though our transportation was by a twin-motor C-47 which flew only in daylight.

Without knowing it, we officers of this mission were the pioneers of the far-flung military aid program which has resulted in the expenditure of so many billions of dollars since World War II and we had an experience

37

which should have warned us of the many pitfalls in foreign aid programs. Our procedure was to arrive as a team of two in a Latin American capital and, working through our ambassador, to open military discussions with the local Chief of Staff. The latter was encouraged to set forth his evaluation of the Nazi threat to his country and to indicate what kind of military help he would like from the United States to cope with it. We had no authority to approve or reject his requests; we were merely messengers picking up the mail for the War and Navy Departments.

As one might expect, we were received like Santa Claus on a pre-Christmas visit and were soon weighted down with the shopping lists presented by our hosts. In Bolivia, for example, I received a request for military equipment totaling over $200 million, including a small navy for Lake Titicaca, 13,000 feet up in the Andes. Upon departure, as my airplane doors were about to close, an aide rushed out with a note from the Chief of Staff asking that I add to his request for twenty fighter-bombers a factory to build them in La Paz. Under the circumstances I should not have been surprised or reproachful over such excessive requests, merely grateful for this early insight into the problems of providing military assistance to allies.

I returned from my last round of calls just in time to pack my family off for San Antonio, Texas, for a tour of badly needed troop duty. I received command almost at once of the 12th Field Artillery Battalion, the 155 mm. howitzer unit of the 2d Infantry Division and retained it for about a year. The battalion was a splendid representative of the Old Army at its best, manned by professional soldiers who had spent much of their service in it. There were five batteries, and each had a first sergeant with at least ten years in that grade. My sergeant major, Harry Robertson, took me in hand and helped a newly promoted, overschooled major to brush up on the basic facts of soldiering. As our time was spent largely on maneuvers in the field, the year was a most useful tune-up for the responsibilities which lay ahead.

In July of 1941, with little warning I was ordered back to Washington to join the military secretariat of the Chief of Staff, General Marshall. My immediate boss was the Secretary of the General Staff, Colonel Orlando Ward, who had been in charge of gunnery instruction at the Field Artillery School when I had been a student officer there. His principal assistant, soon to succeed him as Secretary, was Lieutenant Colonel Walter Bedell Smith, a Leavenworth classmate, who had been close to General Marshall in former years. "Beetle" was an unusual officer who, without benefit of a college degree, was to have a remarkable career—Chief of Staff to General Eisenhower during the war, then Director of the Central Intelligence Agency, and thereafter Undersecretary of State. He had an incisive mind, a sharp tongue, and a rugged integrity which accounted for much of his personal success. He in turn owed much to the influence of General Marshall.

The secretariat, consisting of the Secretary and about six assistant secretaries of whom I became one, served as the focal point for all important papers arriving in the office of the Chief of Staff and the Deputy Chiefs of Staff. We sorted them, determined their routing, saw that they reached the proper general for decision, and then transmitted the decisions to the agency responsible for carrying them out. After that, we kept tab on their progress to final implementation.

In dealing with those papers requiring the attention of General Marshall, the practice was for each assistant secretary, in turn, to be responsible for preparing and presenting to the Chief the accumulation of one twenty-four hour period. At 10:00 A.M., the responsible officer walked into Marshall's office with his papers, sat down in a chair facing the Chief across his desk, and awaited the word to proceed. When the Chief nodded, the secretary proceeded to explain the issues contained in each paper, gave the pros and cons of the arguments if there were different points of view within the staff, and then received the General's decision. Marshall seldom took a paper to read for himself but he often posed very searching questions about its substance to which the secretary was expected to reply. As no officer ever wanted to look stupid before the Chief of Staff, it behooved the secretaries to know their business and to try to anticipate his questions.

I can well remember my first experience in presenting papers to General Marshall because it taught me a lesson of lasting impact. It occurred a few months prior to Pearl Harbor at a time when the War Department, while very busy in preparing for possible war, was still operating largely on a peacetime basis with the authority for most decisions still retained at the level of the Chief of Staff. The papers which I was to present trickled in during the course of one working day and I had time overnight to prepare for my meeting with General Marshall the following morning. As a matter of fact, after absorbing the content of my papers, I used Mrs. Taylor as a stand-in for General Marshall and presented the issues to her in the language I planned to use on the morrow.

The first paper which I presented was typical of the minor matters which reached the Chief of Staff at the time, a proposal to increase the Alaskan National Guard by two companies. It came to Marshall for decision because two Assistant Chiefs of Staff disagreed; the G-3, the assistant chief responsible for operations was for it, whereas G-1, the assistant chief for personnel, was against it. I explained the conflict, doing meticulous justice to each side and then sat back awaiting the Chief's decision. He looked across the desk at me with cold appraising eyes and asked, "What do you think about it, Taylor?" I nearly fell off the chair in my surprise at being expected to take sides in an argument involving two august heads of General Staff divisions, and I cut a very poor figure while improvising a weak answer. But the embarrassment taught me a lesson which I never forgot; thereafter, I never took another paper on any subject to George Marshall or to any other superior in later years without having made up my mind in advance as to the decision I would take if the matter were my responsibility.

If George Marshall had a fault it was that his strong personality had such an unnerving effect on officers around him that it adversely affected the quality of their work. I have seen many a general officer in his outer office betraying a most unmilitary agitation while awaiting his turn to pass through the door of his office upon which was written, "Whoever opens this door *must* go in." The reason for the warning was this. It did not seem to disturb the Chief if anyone opened the door, but if the new arrival did not enter, take a chair, and await his turn on the hot seat opposite Marshall, the latter halted everything until the intruder was dragged in and seated. Hence, we secretaries in the anteroom always stood ready to propel inward any reluctant visitor who hesitated on the threshold.

One of General Marshall's idiosyncrasies was a notorious inability to remember correctly the names of people around him, regardless of how long they were with him. He never fully appreciated the fact that the name of his own secretary was Miss Nason, not Miss Mason. He confused me with Bob Young, another assistant secretary, for reasons neither of us could fathom. On one occasion, as Young told the story, he had met General and Mrs. Marshall at Bolling Field at a very late hour to escort them to their house at Fort Myer. When he started to take leave of them on the porch of the house, General Marshall turned to him and said in his courtly fashion, "Thank you very much, Taylor." When I escaped from the War Department ahead of him to a division headed overseas, Bob insisted that I had received the reward through a case of mistaken identity!

As Pearl Harbor day, December 7, 1941, approached, the atmosphere of General Marshall's office reflected the mounting tension of our relations with Japan. To put the office on something resembling a war footing, one of us secretaries, with his stenographer, was kept on duty around the clock to assure that an experienced officer was always present to deal with unexpected contingencies. By that time we knew pretty well the Chief's working habits and could decide whether he should be disturbed at Fort Myer when important messages arrived at night.

The attack on Pearl Harbor occurred on a Sunday afternoon, Washington time. I was working over some papers at my house while my sons, Jack and Tom, were listening in the next room to a radio broadcast of the Redskins football game. Suddenly Jack called to me that the radio had announced that Pearl Harbor was under attack.

Incredulous, I tried to telephone General Marshall's office, but every circuit was already jammed. So I jumped into my car, drove rapidly to the Munitions Building on Constitution Avenue, and rushed up to the office. There, Major William Sexton, the assistant secretary who had been on duty overnight, was ready with the available news which, as is usually the case in the first hours of a disaster, exaggerated its extent, bad as it was in fact. At first it appeared that we had lost the whole Pacific Fleet and that a Japanese landing force might be standing off Hawaii ready to come ashore. General Marshall appeared very shortly from Fort Myer, where he had been riding his horse after a morning of work at the office, and my colleagues came streaming in from their homes about town.

The first and most difficult task was to sort fact from rumor and estimate the dimensions of the disaster. Concurrently, we had to alert all our military forces at home and abroad, inform them of what we knew, and direct the level of increased readiness which they should assume.

As this terrible day drew to a close, General Marshall decided to summarize the situation, as he knew it, for President Roosevelt and called for a stenographer. Unfortunately, secretaries had been in short supply all day; only a few had come to the office at the first reports of the attack. The only one available for General Marshall was Major Sexton's secretary who, unfortunately, was new on the job and whose untested stenographic skills were suspect among us officers because of her conspicuous physical charms. To add to my doubts, she took dictation by punching keys on a little stenotype box which, like its manipulator, had not proved itself. Nonetheless it was Miss X who got the job of typing General Marshall's first communiqué of World War II.

After she had received her dictation and started to type it, I paid no further heed until General Marshall buzzed for me and asked about his dictation, for which he was waiting with visible impatience. I went out and asked the young lady how she was doing and received a momentarily reassuring reply. But as I watched her, now aware of the Chief's impatience, I saw that things were far from right; she was clearly in trouble. So I went back to her and asked her, gently I hope, for the full facts. Thereupon, those beautiful eyes, which had been the admiration of the secretariat, filled with tears and she burst out, "Major, I did not get a word of the Chief's dictation!"

I have rarely had a more unwelcome task than to go back to General Marshall and tell him that he would have to do his dictation all over again. On the bleakest day of his life, this must have seemed a final, cruel blow. But, showing a far greater restraint than would have been his wont, he wearily repeated the exercise. I sat by Miss X until the final typing was completed and carried the dog-eared, untidy sheet to General Marshall for his signature. Then I drove to the White House and delivered it to the President's military aide, General "Pa" Watson. As far as I was concerned, World War II was off to an inauspicious start.

I only got into trouble with General Marshall once—but once was enough. He was properly a great stickler for the protection of the security of military information and was ruthless in punishing officers who were

41

careless in handling classified material. Telephones were his particular aversion since he knew the American propensity to use them excessively and to forget their insecurity.

One day in the last tragic week of the defense of Bataan, General Marshall asked me to carry a paper to the White House requesting the President's approval of the evacuation of General MacArthur by submarine from Corregidor. Following our usual practice, I called on General Watson and presented to him the problem of getting the President's signature. To my surprise he told me that the President had gone to Hyde Park but that he would telephone the message. Knowing General Marshall's feelings about telephones, I objected as vigorously as a major could to a major general but without avail. Watson assured me that this was a special, secure circuit which the President used all the time for the most sensitive matters, so I had to hold my uneasy peace.

Back at the Munitions Building, I reported what had happened to Marshall. At the word telephone he was out of his chair in a dudgeon, and proceeded to express his opinion of one of his own officers who could have been so careless in such a delicate matter. There was nothing to do but weather the storm in silence, but I was soon back at the White House to tell Watson of the depth and darkness of the doghouse in which I found myself. Recognizing his share in my troubles, he agreed to have the Chief Signal Officer of the Army, who had installed the phone, prepare a paper explaining the special characteristics which had convinced the best American experts that it was safe to use for any matter. A few days later, I passed the Chief this report, which he noted without comment but which I hope set his mind at rest.

So many matters of interest, great and small, occurred during this period with Marshall that I find it difficult to choose those worthy of recording here. It was a time of rapid turnover among officers on duty in Washington, many of whom were being promoted and going to assignments in the field. The requirements for promotion to temporary brigadier general were being relaxed to allow outstanding lieutenant colonels to jump directly to that grade and one of the first to make the jump was another Leavenworth comrade, Mark Clark, later to become Commander of the Fifth Army in the invasion of Italy.

At a cocktail party at the War College in celebration of his promotion, I recall Clark's saying his only regret was that Eisenhower had not received the same recognition as he. I do not recall ever having heard that name before but obviously it was not the last time. As a matter of fact, Colonel Eisenhower was in the next list of officers promoted to brigadier general and very shortly was ordered to Washington to become the head of the War Plans Division of the General Staff. Shortly after he arrived I was assigned to escort him to the White House on the occasion of his first call on President Roosevelt. I remember being impressed at the easy and relaxed way with which he greeted the President, showing none of the uneasiness of most of the military visitors I had escorted under similar circumstances. But, as the world was to discover, Eisenhower was not easy to shake or overawe. In later years, I asked him how he had got along with the upperclassmen when he was a plebe at West Point. "No difficulty," he replied. "One of them ordered me to report to his room after taps for inspection in my full dress coat. I went in the full dress coat—nothing else. After that I wasn't bothered."

Early in 1942, General Stilwell, my superior in China five years before, was called to Washington to organize the staff of his new command which eventually became the China-Burma-India theater. We had lunch together at one of the seafood restaurants on Maine Avenue, and he asked me if I would like to join his staff. Since, in common with most of my contemporaries, escape from Washington to war was a primary objective at the moment, I accepted eagerly and verified that my name was on the list submitted for General Marshall's approval. It came out of his office the next day with all names approved except Taylor's. He never mentioned the matter to me; I wondered if it was that telephone call to Hyde Park.

But a few weeks later, my name appeared on another list for his consideration. Like Clark, Matt Ridgway had been one of the first lieutenant colonels jumped to brigadier general and then quickly to major general when he received command of the 82d Infantry Division at Camp Claiborne, Louisiana. Having need of a division chief of staff, he forwarded to Washington a list of about six officers, including myself, from which he requested the appointment to be made.

The list went to Marshall and it came back with my name approved— again with no comment. That decision destined me to fight the war in Europe instead of in Asia, notwithstanding my past experience in the Orient. But while it made no sense in terms of personnel utilization, I have always been grateful to General Marshall since it led me into airborne service and eventually to the command of the 101st Airborne Division in the decisive European theater.

CHAPTER 3

The Sicilian Campaign

I joined the 82d in Camp Claiborne in the summer of 1942, a recently made chicken colonel, happy to serve with General Ridgway for whom I had a long-standing regard and from whom I was to learn much in the art of troop leadership. We worked in the field from morning till night, seven days a week in sizzling Louisiana temperatures—which were an excellent preparation for our later service in the desert of North Africa. Matt was a stickler for physical condition and drove his men hard to reach that level of fitness necessary for combat. I often accompanied him to inspect troop training in the field, the two of us jogging briskly from site to site under the midday sun to the wonderment of the troops.

I had hardly got myself acquainted with the Division and its key officers when we received an important visitation from Washington. Brigadier Generals Floyd Parks and John Lentz arrived as emissaries of the Army Ground Forces to inform us that the 82d Infantry Division was to be split into two airborne divisions which would then move to Fort Bragg, North Carolina, to complete their training for overseas duty in Europe.

This decision was the indirect result of an event which had taken place in the Mediterranean in the spring of the previous year. On May 20, some 15,000 German parachute and glider troops had attacked and captured the island of Crete from greatly superior ground forces on the island and in the teeth of the British Navy which controlled the sea around it. It was a brilliant *coup de main* which made an enormous impression in Washington as evidence of the feasibility of division-size airborne operations in the execution of a "vertical envelopment." Oddly enough, the effect on the Germans was quite the contrary. They were impressed primarily by the cost of the operation: 4,000 soldiers killed and scores of aircraft destroyed or damaged. As a result, unbeknownst to us, Hitler vowed never again to permit another major airborne operation, and he adhered to that decision to the end of the war. But what was a red light to General Student and his German airborne colleagues was a green light to those American officers who had a vision of the possibilities of airborne warfare.

It proved an intricate job to put together two new airborne divisions from the elements of the 82d Infantry Division, supplemented by parachute units in training at Fort Benning, Georgia, the seat of the Parachute School. The new divisions were to be designated the 82d and 101st Airborne Divisions, with Ridgway commanding the 82d and Major General William C. Lee, a pioneer parachutist, commanding the 101st. Both units were activated on August 15, and moved shortly thereafter to Fort Bragg, where the parachute elements from Benning joined them.

As soon as we received the order to make this conversion, General Ridgway and I became anxious to make the acquaintance of the parachute troops in Benning destined for our division. In turn, we paid visits to them and all returned impressed by a number of things, some good, some bad. First, there was the youth of the officers; one infantry regiment, the 504th, was commanded by Lieutenant Colonel Reuben Tucker, age thirty-one, seven years out of West Point. Colonel James M. Gavin, who commanded the 505th Parachute Infantry Regiment at thirty-five with thirteen years of service, was a relatively "old soldier" among the parachute commanders, few of whom had progressed as far as Leavenworth in the school system. While the troops were plainly full of dash and enthusiasm, some of their energy had been misdirected, as the bad disciplinary record of the units attested. While their *esprit de corps* was admirable, it often seemed to express itself in assaults on nonparachute military policemen and in refusing to salute officers of units other than their own.

It was apparent to us visitors that if we were to impose our authority and the discipline needed on these troops, the first thing to do was to get a parachute jump to our credit. When my turn came, I went to the Parachute School and spent a forenoon watching the training, which was very impressive in the physical demands made on the students. At the end of the morning, I turned to the commander of the school and told him that I wanted to make a practice jump after lunch. He was clearly unhappy about allowing an officer, whom he viewed as elderly at forty-one, to jump without the benefit of school instruction. To overcome his reluctance, I turned to a jump instructor, a master sergeant who was a veteran of many jumps, and asked him if it was really necessary to go through all this preliminary training to be able to jump safely. "Hell no, colonel," he replied, "just get out of the door and hope to Christ you hit easy." Over the years, I have gibed many of my "professional" parachute friends with the sergeant's words, the wisdom of which was borne out in my subsequent jumping experience, limited though it always was to the strict requirements of training and combat. Far from getting jump-happy as some did, I viewed the parachute strictly as a vehicle to ride to the battlefield, to be used only when a better ride was not available.

My initial jump was in a way my best as, up to that time, I did not know how it felt to run into the earth at fifteen miles an hour. My jump master was an officer of the school faculty, Captain Julian Ewell, who later became one of my most valued officers in the war. We went up in a doorless C-47 jump plane and circled the Fort Benning jump field while Julian gave me final instructions. Then he had me stand in the door while he jumped to demonstrate the proper technique. I must say that his demonstration was not particularly reassuring, as I could see from the door the horrendous shock the jumper received from the quick opening of his parachute caught in the slipstream of the airplane. The next time round I went out and enjoyed a feeling of owning the world as the chute floated downward until roughly awakened by the bang of impact with Mother Earth. Fortunately, I had been trained by many a fall from a horse to hit the ground relaxed, and thus escaped the consequences which a green jumper can suffer in an awkward landing. Whatever my form lacked, the jump enabled me to return to Fort Bragg with a skinned chin and an airborne patch on my cap to show membership in the exclusive fraternity of military parachutists.

After all the units of the Division were settled in Fort Bragg in October, we began to learn for ourselves the seamy side of commanding parachute units. They were just as full of the Old Nick as their advance notices had warned, and as a result, we senior officers spent a good part of our time bailing them out of local jails and placating the civil officials of neighboring communities following their depredations. With the 82d and the 101st living side by side, a new factor was added to the prejudice of good order and discipline: the growing rivalry between the members of the divisions which, as the war went on, became famous throughout the Army. Sometimes it was wholesome and constructive, sometimes it was partisan and acrimonious, but in whatever form it created many problems in unit and individual relations. Actually it was the rivalry of twin brothers who were so much alike in temperament as to be indistinguishable to innocent bystanders who soon discovered to their sorrow how quickly they would put aside family quarrels to turn on outsiders. Having served with both divisions in the course of the war, I could never have chosen between them except for the inevitable bias which came from having commanded the 101st. One's own division is necessarily number one.

The example of their senior officers in becoming jumpers stirred up a spate of applications from the junior officers from Claiborne to take parachute training. One day in December, shortly after exchanging my job of Chief of Staff for a brigadier's star and the command of the Division Artillery, I received a call from one of our chaplains. He was a mild young man named Reed, from a small-town congregation in the South. Upon arrival in the Division, he seemed a bit confused by the rough world in which he found himself, and I doubted for a time that he would ever make an effective chaplain. But while these swaggering young parachutists used language which he had never heard before and did things he had never dreamed of, Reed soon began to recognize qualities in them which stirred his admiration and eventually his emulation.

His call on me was to request permission to take parachute training. I was amazed that he would want to do this, and tried to talk him out of it. "Worry about your men's souls, chaplain, and not about jumping out of airplanes," I advised him. When he persisted, I asked him point-blank for one good reason why he should be a parachutist. Blushing deeply, he replied, "If you'll excuse the expression, sir, just for the hell of it."

Just for the hell of it, I let him go to parachute school and he came back a changed man. Henceforth, he was one of the boys, and they accepted him as such. In the invasion of Sicily, he parachuted with his flock and was lost for three days behind the Italian lines. His life was on my conscience until he reappeared one day safe and happy with three comrades who had fought their way back to our lines. Throughout the war, he was a tower of spiritual strength among the men.

Meanwhile, American forces landed in North Africa in November 1942 —the first step down the long road leading eventually to Rome and Berlin. After some jockeying in Washington for the honor of being the first airborne division into combat in Europe, the 82d was chosen to move to the Mediterranean theater in the late spring of 1943, and the 101st was held back to go to England for the invasion of Western Europe in 1944. In March, General Ridgway sent me and a small advance party of the 82d to North Africa to prepare for the arrival of the Division in its assigned training area near Oudjda in Morocco.

My party flew the Atlantic to Dakar and then to Morocco, arriving just at the end of the spring rains. The fields around Oudjda were carpeted with wild flowers and, as we laid out the camps, I thought how happy our troops would be in such a beautiful setting. Alas, by the time they arrived in May the flowers were gone and the fields were nothing but dust and sand.

After arrival, the first combat mission of the Division was to take part in operation "Husky," the assault on Sicily in July. It was to be made by the United States Seventh Army under General Patton and the British Eighth Army under General Montgomery as a prelude to the subsequent invasion of Italy. As a result, I spent most of my time after arrival in Algiers representing the division in the planning for the operation, leaving to my capable deputy, Colonel Andrew March, the training of the division artillery.

I can recall very well my consternation when I first saw the operations map of Sicily. The island appeared completely covered with the red symbols by which intelligence officers indicate enemy defenses and troop locations. In the map wars in which I had participated at home, too many of these red marks on a hostile shore were a warning to avoid it and to land some place else. Since the British disaster at the Dardanelles in World War I, the American Army had been impressed with the heavy losses to be expected from landings in the face of fortified positions, and Sicily appeared to be one continuous fortification. My first reaction was that the invasion plan which would have never received a passing mark at Leavenworth and, if implemented, offered me the prospect of beginning and perhaps ending my active career in a bloody defeat on a most inhospitable shore. Of course, it did not turn out that way. There were strong defenses on Sicily, but few stout defenders with the resolve to hold at all costs which, in the end, determines the outcome of battles. It was my first lesson in the danger of succumbing to fears created by the industry of one's own intelligence officers.

To our disappointment, the invasion plan did not assign an airborne mission to the division. Only the 505th Parachute Combat Team, commanded by Jim Gavin, had an airborne D-day mission, that of landing north and east of Gela on the south coast during the night preceding the amphibious landing. Another combat team, the 504th, was to parachute into the beachhead after the seaborne landing as a means of introducing reinforcements quickly without using landing craft, always in short supply. The rest of the Division was to land by ship, reassemble and take part in the advance inland as a light infantry division.

On July 10, the Division moved from its camps in Morocco to the vicinity of Kairouan in Tunisia, one of the holy cities of Islam and also a center of typhus infestation. We lived in tent camps on the desert near the airfields from which we were to take off for Sicily, and trained in a furnace heat during the day which was followed by a delightful cool at night. Our only dissipation was to drink the local red wine, which we buried in water cans deep in the sand during the day and exhumed after nightfall hoping that the contents would not still be bubbling from the heat. Our only sport was volleyball, which we played before supper with a deliberate disregard for all the rules barring physical interference with opposing players and thereby improved the game remarkably, or so we thought.

During this preparatory phase, I had a number of occasions to extend my previously limited acquaintance with the Seventh Army Commander, General Patton. I had first met him in 1923 when, as a student at the Engineer School, I attended with my classmates a cavalry demonstration at Fort Myer, across the Potomac from Washington. We lieutenants were enormously impressed by the officer who demonstrated the use of the sabre on horseback, a Major George Patton. He was a magnificent rider and swordsman who, at the end of the demonstration, came over to the benches from which we were watching and regaled us with a memorably profane eulogy of the cavalry charge and the *arme blanche*. Several years later, while serving in Hawaii, I had had a few social contacts with him and his charming wife, Bea, while he was on duty as the Intelligence Officer of the Hawaiian Department.

Shortly after my arrival in North Africa, General Patton asked me to join him at dinner at his headquarters in Mostaganem, Morocco. I enjoyed the evening very much, particularly his tales of the desert campaign against Rommel which had just ended. Some brave spirit at the table interrupted to ask what he thought of General Montgomery. Patton's eyes brightened with enthusiasm. "Monty is a truly great soldier—a magnificent soldier," he said. "But he's wasted as a mere army commander. He should command a whole theater of operations—a hell of a long way from mine!"

A few days before the invasion of Sicily, Patton had all the general officers of the Seventh Army at his headquarters for a final briefing. He turned the conduct of the discussions of details over to members of his staff and took little personal part until the close of the day's work. Then he took the floor and gave us a moving address on the theme of the quality of the American soldiers whom we were leading into action, for most of us, our first action. He described their exploits in Tunisia, how well they had stood up against the German veterans of the Afrika Korps. He described with emotion the bravery of small units and there were tears rolling down his cheeks when he told of one company which had held its position until completely destroyed. It was pretty clear that with such men under our command, he considered that if anything went wrong it would be the fault of the generals. In a grand peroration he turned on us with a roar and, waving a menacing swaggerstick under our noses, concluded: "Now we'll break up, and I never want to see you bastards again unless it's at your post on the shores of Sicily." We departed, convinced that it would be well to turn up on time and at the right place on the Sicilian beaches.

In my case, I was not to make that D-day rendezvous. I had been given the job of staying behind in North Africa to supervise the launching of Colonel Tucker's 504th Combat Team on the evening of D day. Gavin's troops got off on schedule the night before D day, but his planes were badly dispersed enroute to the drop zone so that the parachutists were widely scattered on a sixty-five-mile front. Nevertheless, they created disorder and confusion in the enemy rear areas, softened up the Italian resistance, and most of them eventually worked their way back to the beachhead at Gela in the course of the next few days.

Tucker's operation was viewed as purely an airborne reinforcement of the beachhead and, as such, little more than a training exercise. That is not to say that every precaution was not taken to assure an accurate drop within friendly lines, but no resistance was expected at destination. Full information on the flight plan was disseminated to the commanders of our forces in the landing area, both Army and Navy. So I had no thought of possible disaster as I watched the 144 C-47's take off on the evening of July 11 and returned to camp expecting to pass a quiet night.

I had not been asleep long when my aide aroused me with word that some of Tucker's planes were returning to nearby airfields badly damaged and with some wounded aboard. I hurried to the nearest field and found the report only too true. There were about a dozen C-47's on this field in various states of damage. Some had great incisions down the fuselage, as if a giant can opener had ripped them. All bore marks of various calibres of gunfire. What had happened was that our planes had been mistaken for German bombers and had been made the target of every weapon in our landing force capable of shooting upward. The transports, endeavoring to maneuver to avoid the unexpected fire, often fouled neighboring planes and ripped them with their wing tips. In all, we lost twenty-three aircraft, but fortunately most of the parachutists aboard were able to jump to safety. A tragic exception was the Assistant Division Commander, Brigadier General Charles L. Keerans—aboard merely to supervise and report on the jump—who was lost with one of the aircraft.

In the returning planes, there were several dead and wounded. I talked to one of the latter with an American bullet in his shoulder as he was being taken off on a stretcher. Trying to think of something sympathetic to say, I remarked awkwardly that it must have been pretty hot over the beachhead in all that fire. "Yes, it was," he replied cheerfully, "but I was glad to see that our fellows could shoot so good."

Following Gavin's and Tucker's ill-starred parachute operations, the Division slowly assembled in reserve in the Gela area. Most of the scattered parachutists gradually rejoined their units, and the remainder of the combat elements of the Division arrived from Africa by plane and ship. The 82d, along with the 3d Division and part of the 9th, was assigned to a provisional corps under the command of Major General Geoffrey Keyes which, on July 19, moved west from Gela with the mission of attacking Palermo from the south and southwest. My light airborne artillery was reinforced by the attachment of the 155mm howitzer battalion of the 9th Division, commanded by a Lieutenant Colonel W. C. Westmoreland, whose sure-handed manner of command led to the entry of his name in a little black book I carried to record the names of exceptional young officers for future reference.

The advance led through Sciacca to Castelvetrano, then to Marsala and Trapani which the Division occupied on July 23, after a march of about 150 miles in six days. Most of the way it was as pleasant a campaign as one is likely to find in war. No one was very angry at anyone. The Italians had no desire to die for the King or Badoglio, much less for Hitler. In the towns we passed through, the villagers greeted us as liberators and many rushed up to ask in broken English about relatives in America.

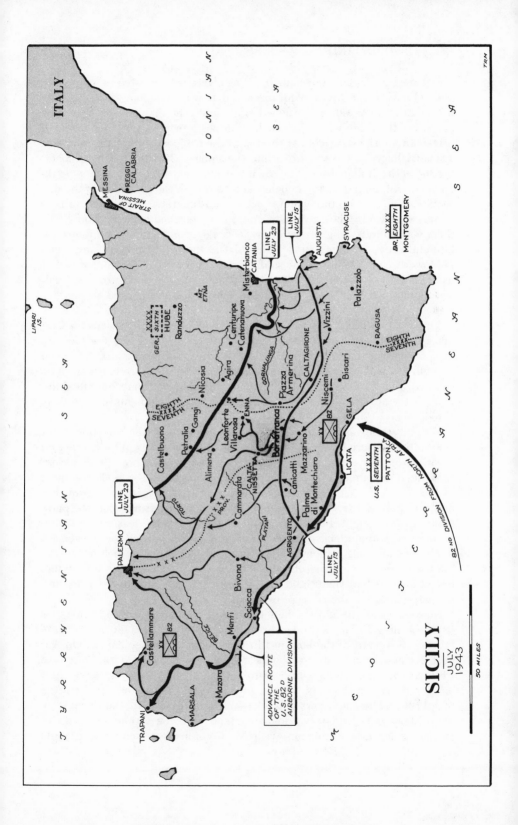

ITALY

T Y R R H E N I A N   S E A

LIPARI IS.

STRAIT OF MESSINA

MESSINA

REGGIO CALABRIA

I O N I A N   S E A

Castellammare

TRAPANI

MARSALA

Mazara

Manfi

Sciacca

Bivona

Castelbuono

Petralia

Alimena

Gangi

Nicosia

Agira

CALTA-NISSETTA

Cammarata

Canicatti

Palma di Montechiaro

AGRIGENTO

LICATA

Leonforte

Villarosa

ENNA

Barrafranca

Piazza Armerina

Mazzarino

GELA

Niscemi

Biscari

CALTAGIRONE

Vizzini

Catenanuova

Centuripe

Randazzo

MT. ETNA

Misterbianco

CATANIA

Palazzolo

RAGUSA

AUGUSTA

SYRACUSE

GER. SIXTH HUBE

XXXX

EIGHTH SEVENTH

XXXX

EIGHTH SEVENTH

XXXX

XX 82

XX 82

U.S. SEVENTH PATTON

XXXX

BR. EIGHTH MONTGOMERY

XXXX

LINE JULY 23

LINE JULY 15

LINE JULY 23

LINE JULY 15

XXX Prov.

TORTO

SALSO

BELICE

PLATANI

GORNALUNGA

PALERMO

82 ND DIVISION FROM NORTH AFRICA

ADVANCE ROUTE OF THE U.S. 82 D AIRBORNE DIVISION

SICILY
JULY 1943

50 MILES

TRM

One day in the mountains north of Castelvetrano, I wanted to move from one column of the division to another that was advancing on a parallel road on the other side of a rugged ridge line. The map showed a narrow road over the ridge which looked feasible for a jeep so, with my aide and driver, I took the short cut. At the top of the ridge we had to pass through a small village, and as we drove into the square I had the feeling of meeting the entire Italian army. The town was filled with Italian soldiers, skulkers no doubt, lolling on the benches and baking in the sun far from the discomforts of war in the valleys below. Fortunately, they were just as surprised as we by the encounter, and no one reached for a weapon. Since there was no retreating, I rose in my jeep, raised my hand in a military salute and drove by them. In a testimonial to the irresistibility of ingrained military discipline, most of the soldiers struggled to their feet and stared at us as we passed by and out the gate leading down the hill to the next valley. Not a shot was fired. That could hardly have happened in another war.

This relative quiet existed only in the west where there were no Germans; in the northeast it was a bitter struggle to clear out the German troops covering the exit from the island at the Strait of Messina. And even in a quiet war there are casualties, perhaps more to be regretted than those suffered in decisive combat. In Sicily, our division lost some 200 killed, including the airborne losses of the 504th and 505th Regiments, but, in turn, it took over 20,000 prisoners.

While Patton was most flattering in his comments on the behavior of our troops, the scattered drop of the two parachute regiments put a damper on the airborne movement both in the Army and in Air Force. It was clear that the joint training of our parachute troops with the Troop Carrier units of the Air Force had been deficient and that the navigational equipment and methods of the Air Force were inadequate to assure accurate parachute drops at night. In Washington, the issue as to the feasibility of division-size airborne attacks was reopened, and critics pressed for a reversion to the use of small parachute units primarily for sabotage behind enemy lines. Our senior airborne officers, such as Generals Ridgway and Swing, fought back as best they could and, in the end, were able to defer any immediate change in the concept of airborne missions.

No sooner had the 82d reached Trapani than Ridgway began to press for its reassembly in the Kairouan area in order to prepare for an airborne mission in support of the landings in Italy planned for September. On August 2 I flew from Sicily to Algiers to report to General Mark Clark, the Fifth Army Commander, who was to command the U.S. Army forces in a landing at Salerno south of Naples. In Algiers, with a few officers from the 82d, I set up a headquarters to work on airborne plans with the Fifth Army Staff. Meanwhile, Ridgway had to contend with the serious problems of preparing for a new mission with his division dispersed in a triangle marked by Trapani, Kairouan and Algiers, each group separated from the others by 300 to 600 miles.

August and September were a confused period of planning for missions which were always changing. In all, we drew up five plans for using all or part of the division in an airborne mission to facilitate the landing at Salerno. The projected operations extended geographically from the Salerno area to Rome, but none was carried out for a variety of reasons—usually the inability to provide the necessary air support. The most important of the cancelled missions was a plan to put a part of the Division into the Rome area to cooperate with Italian forces in seizing and defending Rome, while the Fifth Army pushed north after the Salerno landing.

On September 1 General Ridgway and I were called to General Alexander's Fifteenth Army Group headquarters near Syracuse and learned for the first time about the possible use of the Division in the Rome area. We were informed of the political developments since Mussolini's overthrow on July 25 and the King's appointment of Marshall Badoglio to succeed the Duce as prime minister. This development had caused deep concern to Hitler who began a quiet reinforcement of German troops in Italy. His fears were thoroughly justified, for by mid-August, the Badoglio government, using General Guiseppe Castellano as its agent, was in contact with the Allied high command in the Mediterranean. Castellano reached Alexander's headquarters only a short time before Ridgway and I had been summoned and conversations were in progress when we arrived over the conditions of an armistice and the passage of Italy to the side of the Allies. One condition of the Italians, we learned, was that the Allies provide troops as soon as possible to assist in defending Rome against the German reaction to the Italian defection. In response to this demand, Eisenhower had agreed to commit the 82d to the vicinity of Rome to join with the Italian divisions nearby in the defense of the city. If successful, it was estimated that this operation would materially assist the Salerno landing which had become much more difficult because of the arrival of the new German forces in Italy.

I was struck both by the attraction of the mission—the opportunity which it afforded the division to participate in a truly history-making operation—and by the many difficulties to be overcome in a short period of time. The misadventures of the airborne landings in Sicily had convinced me of the need for careful preparation with the Air Force if we were to get our forces down safely at the intended place. Also I was impressed, as was General Ridgway, with the loose undertakings into which Castellano was entering, often under considerable pressure from General Bedell Smith, General Eisenhower's Chief of Staff, who was conducting the discussion. Little as I knew of the situation in and around Rome, I could not believe that the Italians could do all the things to which Castellano was agreeing.

On September 3, Ridgway and I had a long session with the Allied Staff and Castellano to formulate the airborne plan which was to be called Giant II. In its final form, the plan called for combined parachute and air landing operations covering several days at five airfields in the vicinity of Rome and for a small seaborne force carrying artillery and antitank weapons to come up the Tiber and reinforce the airborne forces. Because of a shortage of troop carrier aircraft, our troops would necessarily arrive by increments with the first one consisting merely of a reduced regimental combat team of about 2,000 men landing on the night of September 8–9 at the Furbara and Cerveteri airfields twenty-five miles outside of Rome. The remoteness of the landings from Rome was imposed by the large number of antiaircraft batteries in the Rome area which had to be avoided by our troop-carrier aircraft.

For such a plan to have any chance of success would require close cooperation from the Italian armed forces in the Rome area. They would have to provide protection for the airfields where the landings were to take place and suppress all antiaircraft fire threatening the airborne formations. The fields would have to be illuminated in a prearranged way and navigational aids installed to guide in the troop carrier pilots to destination. Upon landing, the airborne troops would need several hundred trucks in order to move promptly on their objectives. Also they would need rations, signal and engineer supplies, and manual labor from Italian sources. Finally, the American commanders would have to be furnished with the latest intelligence regarding both the German and Italian forces.

Castellano accepted all these requirements without much hesitation, but the more we observed him and reflected on the difficulties the Italians would probably have in making good these commitments, the more apprehensive Ridgway and I became. So together we went to Generals Alexander and Smith, stated our concern, and proposed that two senior officers, one representing the 82d Division and the other the Troop Carrier Command, be sent at once to Rome to ascertain the state of things and to determine the feasibility of the operation. This proposal was accepted and, after some discussion, I was chosen to represent the 82d and Air Force Colonel William Tudor Gardiner, the Troop Carrier Command. As I learned after the war, the plan for Giant II was sent by messenger to Rome on September 5, following its approval at Cassibile.

At the time I had no particular feeling of lack of preparation for this mission, which I viewed as little more than a personal reconnaissance of the battlefield before the firing began. With the knowledge subsequently acquired, however, I am aghast at how little Gardiner and I knew of the background of the situation which awaited us in Rome and how ill-prepared we were to cope with it. Among the critical points about which we knew little or nothing were the discrepancies between the views of Castellano in Sicily and of senior officers in Rome as to the desirability of Giant

II, the mistaken impression of Badoglio and his associates that the main Allied landing would not take place until September 12 or later, their persistent hope that the landing would be near Rome, their illusion that our airborne landing at Rome would be promptly reinforced, and Badoglio's strong opposition to announcing an armistice prior to the main Allied landing. All we knew about the background of Giant II was that it had been a condition imposed by the Italians for signing an armistice. This was to be proclaimed by Eisenhower and Badoglio on the evening of September 8, in time to assure that we would not have to fight Italians as well as Germans in the landing at Salerno on the following morning. Gardiner and I were not to communicate the time or place of the landing to the Italians, although I later learned that on September 4 Castellano had been told in Sicily that the landing would take place within two weeks from that date.

On September 6, I flew to Palermo picking up Colonel Gardiner on the way. I had barely met him before and it was pure, unplanned luck that got me such an admirable partner for this adventure. Gardiner was a well-known New England lawyer of about fifty-three, a former governor of Maine who had taken up flying at the age of forty-five. Among his many attainments was a good understanding of French, which was to prove most useful since we were to do most of our business in Rome in that language.

CHAPTER 4

Missions in Italy

At General Alexander's direction, we left on our mission undesirably late in view of the many things to be done in Rome, but his injunction was justified by the danger of our capture before D day with the knowledge of the Salerno plans. But once allowed to depart we moved fast. After a few hours' sleep in Palermo, we boarded a fast British patrol boat at 2:00 A.M. which rendezvoused with an Italian corvette, the *Ibis*, at daylight off Ustica Island.

As we drew near the ship, it seemed to have broken out in a red rash, an impression caused by the red life preservers worn by the members of the crew in readiness for attack by hostile aircraft or submarines which, on this voyage, could be either Allied or German. After some difficulty with the surf, we drew alongside the *Ibis* and went aboard with our baggage which included a precious radio to reinforce the tenuous clandestine link between the Italian high command in Rome and the Allied headquarters in Algiers and Sicily. We were both in uniform, a deliberate decision taken as a possible protection against summary execution if taken by the Germans, and we carried only musette bags for our toilet articles and minor essentials.

On board we were met by Admiral Franco Maugeri, the Director of Intelligence of the Italian Navy, who had received orders on the preceding day to rendezvous with us and escort us to Gaeta harbor. He was a cordial host who, as we steamed across the sunny Tyrrhenian Sea, regaled us on deck with interesting stories about conditions in wartime Italy—and provided an excellent lunch. As we approached Gaeta at the end of the afternoon, the corvette zigzagged through the minefields outside the harbor and came to rest alongside a pier where a group of curious spectators watched the docking. It had been agreed to account for us as Allied officers picked up at sea so, for realism, our escorts prodded us into alacrity as we went down the gangplank. We were quickly put into a Navy automobile, driven

56

to the outskirts of Gaeta, and transferred to a military ambulance which awaited us on a wooded side road; then we were off for Rome seventy-five miles to the north via the Appian Way.

It was not the most comfortable ride that I had ever made, sitting in the body of the ambulance with Gardiner and Maugeri. The windows were of frosted glass with several unfrosted port holes covered only by a painted red cross. Through them we could see out fairly well but hoped that the outside world could not see in so well. Though the road was rough and the springs of the ambulance had little resilience, I was enormously interested in everything along the ancient Roman road over which so much of history had passed. The only signs of the war were occasional road blocks, where we had to stop while the driver presented his papers, and many road signs pointing the direction to military headquarters off the road, of which an increasing number were German as we moved north.

We arrived in Rome just at dusk, the advance guard of the Allied invasion which was not to reach the city until nine months later. There we were taken to the Palazzo Caprara in the Via Firenze where spacious quarters had been prepared for us on the second floor. There we were welcomed by Colonel Salvi, Chief of Staff to General Carboni commanding the Army Corps assigned to the defense of Rome, along with Major Marchesi who had been with Castellano in Sicily and an aide, Lieutenant Lanza. We learned that Carboni was our immediate host but that we were not to see him until the following morning; in the meantime we were to have dinner in our quarters and get a good night's rest. To add to our surprise, we were told that General Ambrosio, the Chief of Staff of the Armed Forces whom I had rather expected to meet us, was visiting in Turin on private business.

While this schedule might have been a considerate doctor's prescription for tired travelers, it was not the program which Gardiner and I were prepared to accept. It was unbelievable to us that the Italians would be so casual at such a critical moment when every minute counted. While not rejecting the dinner which turned out to be of quite a different quality from the field rations which had been sustaining us in Africa and Sicily, we insisted that General Carboni come to see us at once as a matter of the utmost urgency.

In response to our importunity, Carboni joined us after dinner. He has been described by our naval host of the afternoon, Admiral Maugeri, as *"un bel uomo di professione,"* a professional dandy, and in his highly decorated tunic and polished boots he lived up to this dashing description. But that evening he was not in a dashing mood; his world was black, broken only by a little gray here and there. He gave Gardiner and me a most discouraging evaluation of the situation about Rome: the Germans were reinforcing their units in the area and throttling the flow of supplies to the Italian divisions upon which we would have to depend for the support of our airborne assault. He was sure that, if Italy declared an armistice, the Germans would occupy Rome at once and there was little that his troops could do to prevent it. The proposed landing of our airborne forces, far from being indispensable to the defense of Rome as Castellano had described it, would only provoke the Germans to harsher reprisals against their late Italian allies and the ensuing combat would result in the destruction, not the salvation, of the Eternal City. The Americans would be able to accomplish little since the Italians could not give them anything like the support called for in the Giant II plan; indeed they could not even guarantee the security of the airfields which were essential to our operation. Hence, Carboni was opposed to the airborne operation, at least until the Allies were safely ashore in Italy and had approached to within supporting distance of Rome. He said that General Roatta, the Army Chief of Staff, shared this opinion.

Although I had arrived quite prepared to learn that all Castellano had promised would not be possible, the deep pessimism of this general who would be responsible for cooperating with the airborne troops was dismaying news. Rather than argue the case with him with the precious minutes flying, we demanded to be taken at once to see the Prime Minister, Marshal Badoglio.

It was not easy to arrange a meeting on such short notice with an aged soldier-politician who did not like being disturbed in the middle of the night during an air alert. Nevertheless our call was arranged by telephone, and we groped our way in Carboni's car across blacked-out Rome through sentry check points and finally reached Badoglio's villa on the edge of town around midnight. Carboni preceded us into Badoglio's study while Gardiner and I awaited outside until summoned to enter.

Badoglio, then seventy-three years of age with an eventful military career of more than a half century behind him, received us cordially, if informally, in his pajamas. Whether it was the result of his long military career or his short but wearing political stint as Prime Minister since the fall of Mussolini in July, he looked old and tired. Carboni had taken advantage of his *tête-à-tête* to inform Badoglio of our earlier discussions and the reason for our untimely call. Speaking French, Badoglio immediately plunged into a discussion of the military and political situation expressing views so similar to Carboni's that I suspected him of merely parroting his subordinate. This was not the case, as I learned later, for Badoglio had previously urged the Allies to make their landing by sea north of Rome and to mount an airborne operation near Rome only after they were ashore and near enough the city to reinforce its defenders. He and all the Italians with whom we talked were deathly afraid of the Germans, far more than of the Allies, and the preservation of Rome from German reprisals was much more important to them than participation in any military operation which, though it might facilitate the Allied landing, would endanger the city.

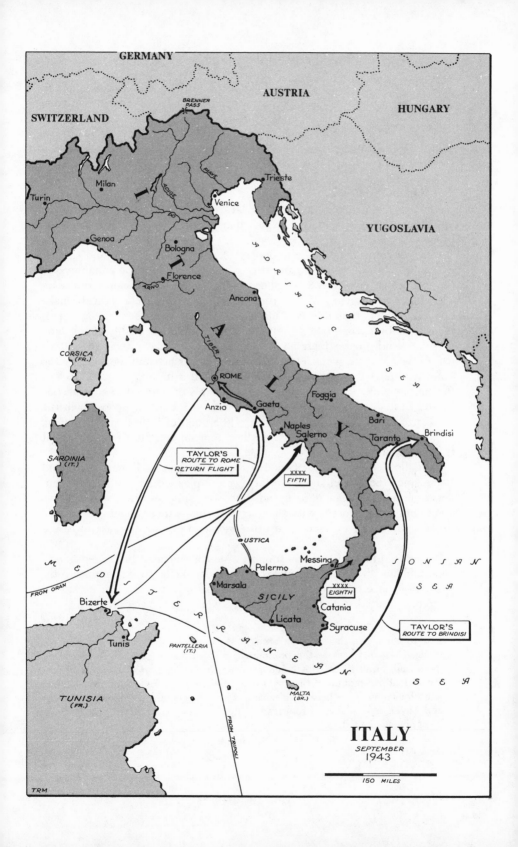

GERMANY

AUSTRIA

SWITZERLAND

HUNGARY

BRENNER
PASS

Milan

Turin

DIAVE

ADIGE

Trieste

Venice

PO

Genoa

Bologna

Florence

YUGOSLAVIA

ARNO

Ancona

CORSICA
(FR.)

A

TIBER

ROME

Anzio

Gaeta

Foggia

Naples
Salerno

Bari

SARDINIA
(IT.)

TAYLOR'S
ROUTE TO ROME
RETURN FLIGHT

XXXX
FIFTH

Taranto

Brindisi

USTICA

Palermo

Messina

T
Y
R
R
H
E
N
I
A
N
S
E
A

Marsala

FROM ORAN

Bizerte

SICILY

Licata

XXXX
EIGHTH

Catania

Syracuse

TAYLOR'S
ROUTE TO BRINDISI

I
O
N
I
A
N

S
E
A

Tunis

PANTELLERIA
(IT.)

M
E
D
I
T
E
R
R
A
N
E
A
N

S
E
A

TUNISIA
(FR.)

MALTA
(BR.)

FROM TRIPOLI

ITALY

SEPTEMBER
1943

150 MILES

TRM

With Gardiner keeping notes, I launched forth in a rhetorical effort to change his position handicapped by a lack of knowledge of what had gone on before between the Badoglio government and the Allied Command but with the conviction that some initiative had to be taken without delay. While I could not discuss with Badoglio the time or place of the American landing, it was pretty clear that the senior Italians knew that it was to be south of Rome—too far south from their point of view—but equally clear that they did not expect it for several days. This latter miscalculation explained to some extent the complete lack of preparations for our airborne operation, which was neither expected nor desired at the time when we proposed to conduct it.

After verifying that Badoglio opposed Giant II at this time and that he was not ready to declare the armistice which I knew must be announced at the end of that very day, September 8, I hinted at the imminence of the invasion and the urgency of the armistice in sufficiently clear terms to make him understand that it was a matter of hours rather than of days. This seemed to be a complete surprise to him, one which visibly shook him. Now he could procrastinate no longer. He had to make a decision, and his fear of the Germans won the day. He insisted that he could not declare the armistice under the existing conditions. I asked if he was prepared to face the consequences if, after having been so deeply committed to an armistice by the Castellano mission, he now reneged on a bargain upon which the success of our landing and the prompt liberation of Italy depended. If so, he could expect no mercy from the Allied commanders after failing them at this late hour.

Badoglio defended himself, saying that conditions had changed around Rome since the Castellano undertakings and pleaded for the Allies to understand the dilemma of a friend who was only awaiting a propitious movement to join forces with them against the German enemy. He hoped that Gardiner and I would return to Africa and present his case to Eisenhower.

We refused to give him any support or encouragement but urged him, if he would not draw back from his dangerous course, to communicate his position at once to General Eisenhower in his own words. This he agreed to do and drafted in longhand a message which in translation read:

Due to change in the situation brought about by the disposition and strength of the German forces in the Rome area, it is no longer possible to accept an immediate armistice as this could provoke the occupation of the capital and the violent assumption of the government by the Germans. Operation Giant II is no longer possible because of lack of forces to guarantee the airfields. General Taylor is available to return to Sicily to present the views of the government and awaits orders.

Badoglio asked me to concur in his evaluation and decision, but I refused to take any responsibility for the Italian interpretation of the situation or to serve as anything more than as a messenger conveying his views to the Allied authorities if they authorized it. So I prepared my own message to Algiers which read as follows:

> In view of the statement of Marshal Badoglio as to inability to declare armistice and to guarantee fields, Giant II is impossible. Reasons given for change are irreplaceable lack of gasoline and munitions and new German dispositions. Badoglio requests Taylor return to present government views. Taylor and Gardiner awaiting instructions.

I signed this message at 1:21 A.M., September 8, then took leave of Badoglio and returned with Gardiner and Carboni to our hideout in the Palazzo Caprara, running the crosstown gauntlet of sentries for a second time. Carboni took the messages for transmission over the clandestine radio, and we were informed the next morning at about 8:00 A.M. of the reception in Algiers of Badoglio's message. There had been a worrisome delay in the transmission, and it was not clear that the acknowledgement of receipt included my message as well as Badoglio's.

With an uncertain period of waiting ahead of us, Gardiner and I considered what we could do which might be useful to our chiefs in Africa, whose exasperated state of mind I could imagine. We decided to send a message giving the latest intelligence which we had received from the Italians, not knowing whether or not it would be news in Algiers. So at 8:20 A.M. I dispatched another message which amplified somewhat the views of the situation as held by Badoglio and Carboni and stressed again their rejection of Giant II.

About 11:00 A.M. Carboni called on us to say that Badoglio wished to send a senior general to Africa to intercede for his government with General Eisenhower. At first, the Italian leaders were inclined to pick Roatta, the Army Chief of Staff, but as an ex-military attaché to Germany he was considered very valuable in dealing with the German high command, and in the impending circumstances his skills were likely to be badly needed in Rome. So in the end I was asked to take Lieutenant General Francesco Rossi, the Deputy Chief of the Supreme General Staff, on my return flight to Sicily, the assumption being that I would be ordered back shortly.

Throughout the morning Gardiner and I had worried as to whether Algiers had received and was acting on our message recommending the cancellation of Giant II. We had been assured that Badoglio's message had been acknowledged by Algiers and that ours had been dispatched at the same time, but that information was not good enough to dissipate our concern. Fortunately, prior to leaving Algiers I had worked out an arrangement with the Allied Staff that any message which I might send from Rome which contained the word "innocuous" should be considered an urgent request to cancel Giant II. My thought in proposing this code word had been in anticipation of a possible contingency arising in which Gardiner and I found cause to recommend a cancellation, but the Italians, whom we supposed to be eager for the operation, might not be willing to transmit a cancellation request. Although the actual situation was nothing like the one anticipated, I sent off a message at 11:35 A.M. to Algiers containing only the word "innocuous" as a safeguard against any misunderstanding arising from the earlier messages. On the heels of this message, I sent another indicating Badoglio's desire to send Rossi with me to Africa and requesting authority to bring him. Then, hoping to probe another source of information on the situation, I asked for an interview with General Ambrosio, Chief of the Supreme General Staff, who had returned that morning from his leisurely trip by train to Turin.

The interview, scheduled for 4:30 P.M., never took place. About 3:00 P.M. we were informed that orders had been received from General Eisenhower to send us back by airplane without delay to Fairfield, his forward headquarters near Bizerte. We did not know until long after that this order was embodied in the text of a long, blistering telegram from Eisenhower to Badoglio, insisting that the latter discharge his obligation to declare the armistice but agreeing to the suspension of Giant II. Had we been aware of the context of this message, General Rossi would not have had to make his trip to Africa, and Gardiner and I would have ceased to worry about the word getting through in time to our airborne troops on the Sicilian airfields where they were waiting to take off for Rome.

As a matter of fact, the time factor involved in stopping the airborne operation turned out to be very close indeed. It required the initiative of Brigadier General Lyman Lemnitzer, the Deputy Chief of Staff to General Alexander, who, recognizing the shortness of time and fearing delay in radio communications, boarded an airplane and personally carried the message to the departure fields. Already some of the planes were in the air, but they were recalled without mishap.

Meanwhile in the Palazzo Caprara, Gardiner and I awaited the hour of our return flight, which had been set for 5:00 P.M., hoping to get a reply regarding our request for authority to bring back General Rossi. As it never came, I decided on my own initiative to take him and his interpreter with us. So gathering our overnight baggage together, still consisting of two musette bags but now including a bottle of Scotch whiskey presented to me by one of our hosts, Gardiner and I again embarked in the frosted ambulance and were driven to the Centocelli airfield on the edge of Rome where a trimotor Savoia-Marchetti bomber awaited us at the end of the runway with Rossi and his interpreter already on board. Although its external appearance was that of a bomber, inside it had been outfitted as a liaison plane with chairs and tables to facilitate staff work in flight.

The return flight to El Alouina, the airfield at Fairfield, lasted about two hours and was for me the most nerve-racking part of the entire expedition. Although our Italian hosts had assured us that our flight plan had been communicated to both the Italian and Allied air forces and that there was no danger that the Germans would intercept us, I knew the high probability of error in any quickly arranged flight in a theater of war like the Mediterranean. It needed only one inattentive fighter pilot at the morning briefing of the day's operations to get us into trouble if we flew into the airspace of his responsibility. As we were crossing the African coast line, my misgivings seemed fully justified when a high-flying U.S. attack plane spotted us and went into a power dive in the general direction of our tail. But it veered away at the last minute, and we landed shortly after at El Alouina without further incident.

Just before we entered Allied Headquarters, General Eisenhower, having heard nothing further from Badoglio, had announced the surrender of Italy over Radio Algiers and had read the text of the statement which Badoglio was supposed to have made. An hour later, Badoglio himself repeated the statement over Radio Rome. Meanwhile, the Allied convoys were converging on the Gulf of Salerno for the landing the following morning.

After making a brief report to General Eisenhower and talking to several of his staff, I sought out a bedroom to enjoy a rest at the end of a very long day. Murmuring, "Thank God, I'm home," I tossed my musette bag into a corner where the sound of the smashing glass of my forgotten bottle of Scotch provided a fitting ending to a disappointing mission.

Since the war, this mission to Rome has been a subject of controversy particularly in Italy where the principal actors have undertaken to explain their actions and motives, particularly their rejection of the American airborne landing. In America, it has been treated as just another episode of a period of history so replete with events as to divert concentrated attention upon any one. However, there has been some criticism to the effect that I opposed the mission from the outset or that I was not aggressive enough in pressing the Italians to cooperate with us. The thought seems to be that I should not have taken "no" for an answer.

On the first point, I would say that it was a great personal disappointment to me and I suspect to most of the members of the 82d Airborne Division assigned to this mission that Giant II had to be called off. What more glorious task could fighting men receive than to liberate and defend the Eternal City while easing the difficulties of our troops at Salerno? But the obstacles, then and now, seemed too great to allow any reasonable hope that the accomplishments of our airborne soldiers, heroic though they might be, could compensate for the losses to be expected.

In the light of what we know today, had we decided to go ahead with Giant II in spite of the refusal of the Italians to cooperate with us, we could never have introduced more than the first night's increment of about 2,500 troops, fewer than a full regimental combat command. They would have landed twenty-five miles from Rome with no trucks, few supplies, and limited ammunition. With surprise lost after the first night's landing, and no Italian antiaircraft defense of the airfields, the German air force would never have allowed further reinforcements to arrive from Sicily by air, and our men on the ground would have been on their own with no assurance that the Italian forces would be even friendly to them. What they could have accomplished under these circumstances I certainly do not know, but I have never regretted the decision which spared these elite troops to serve their country with distinction at Salerno, Anzio, Normandy, and elsewhere rather than end their useful days in Italian graves or German prisons.

Apart from giving these brave men the chance to fight another day on a better field, I felt that our mission had performed a service in developing the facts regarding the Italian attitude toward the armistice and the changeover to the Allied side. Castellano was telling us one thing in Sicily while Badoglio and company were of another mind in Rome. It was very late in the game when the arrival of Gardiner and me in Rome forced the moment of truth upon them barely in time to salvage the assets which the Italian surrender represented to us. Without it, the risks being run of Salerno, already high, would have correspondingly increased. So our trip to Rome was not wasted, although a mistake avoided brings none of the satisfaction of a feat achieved.

After filing a written report at Allied Headquarters covering the mission to Rome, I departed for Sicily to assemble my field equipment and rejoin the 82d Airborne in the Salerno beachhead. But before I could get a flight to the beachhead, I was recalled to Fairfield and given a new assignment which caused me to miss the Salerno show.

On the day of my departure from Rome and shortly after the proclamation of the armistice, the King, Badoglio, and several members of their entourage fled to Pescara on the Adriatic, passing German columns moving in the opposite direction on Rome. At Pescara, they embarked on an Italian corvette and steamed down the Adriatic uncertain where to seek refuge. Finally they put into Brindisi at the heel of Italy where they lived unhappily in constricted quarters until the Allies arrived to bring them help. Fortunately Badoglio had brought out his clandestine radio from Rome, so it was possible for him to communicate with General Eisenhower in North Africa, inform him of his location, and request an Allied mission to establish contact with his government-in-exile.

In response to this latter request, Eisenhower hastily put together a party to send to Brindisi. It consisted of Robert Murphy and Harold Macmillan, the American and British political advisers at Allied Headquarters, Lieutenant General Sir Noel Mason MacFarlane, the Military Governor of Gibraltar, and myself. Apparently I qualified for membership on the basis of having become an Italian expert after some twenty-four hours in Rome. We were placed aboard a B-17 bomber and flown to Taranto where the British 1st Airborne Division had landed on September 9.

As we approached the Taranto airfield which was situated well out of town, our pilot reported that he was unable to raise anyone in the control tower. So we were obliged to circle the field which, viewed from a low altitude, seemed completely deserted. Finally, we put down but found no one on the ground either to greet us or to answer our questions. Meanwhile, we could hear firing to the north, showing that some combat was still in progress.

Uncertain as to what to do next, the four of us walked out to the road running by the field and eventually found a passing car to hail. It was a tiny Fiat with an Italian soldier at the wheel. In my halting Italian, I explained that we wanted a ride to Brindisi some twenty-five miles away. The soldier objected that this was Lieutenant Colonel Bianco's car and that he could not oblige us without the colonel's permission. We then resorted to intimidation, announcing that we were the representatives of the Allies who had just won the war and we had no concern for the convenience of his colonel. We announced that his car was commandeered by our governments and proceeded to pile into the Fiat over his protest.

We were four big men, and the seams of the little car seemed to stretch as it bounced over the road toward Brindisi. We were stopped frequently at road blocks by Italian soldiers who demanded our papers, but we were gaining confidence in our role of Allied conquerors, and scorning all requests for *documenti*, brushed by the barricades. Fortunately, there was no determined sentry to challenge us with a bullet.

In the late afternoon we arrived in Brindisi, a town strange to us all. I vaguely recalled that Caesar had crossed the Adriatic here on his way to do battle with Pompey at Pharsalus but that fact seemed of little immediate relevance. Eventually we found the Albergo Internazionale, the principal hotel, where we inquired as to the whereabouts of the King and Badoglio. We learned that the royal family was lodged in the local naval commander's quarters and that the remainder of the party was scattered through several naval barracks. With that information, we proceeded to requisition the hotel as the seat of the Allied Military Mission to the Italian government and then made contact with Badoglio and his people.

Our first task was to establish order first within our own Mission, then within the Badoglio government which the Allied governments had decided to support. I undertook to act as Chief of Staff of the Mission, which

I hoped to get organized quickly so that I could return to my division. This had been the understanding arrived at with General Bedell Smith when he sent me on this mission.

Shortly after our arrival, American and British officers began to arrive from North Africa for assignment to the Mission. Most of them were reserve officers, many of whom brought important talents to contribute to the solution of the complex problems of military and civil government which were taking form in Brindisi. Samuel Reber and Harold Caccia appeared to represent the State Department and the British Foreign Office. Edward Foley was the U.S. Treasury representative and performed the indispensable function of putting the new government in funds with currency printed in the United States. Many other eminent Americans, most of them in uniform, joined the Mission to provide special skills badly needed—Charles Spofford, Ellery Stone, and Charles Poletti to mention only a few. Others came who were not so welcome, for example, the American education expert whose primary interest was in Italian methods of teaching Latin in the secondary school system. Representatives of intelligence agencies from Washington and London made their appearance, showing interest in such matters as Italian research in heavy water and the Yugoslav underground movement.

During my period of duty with the Mission, I served as Chief of Staff to two officers, Lieutenant General Mason MacFarlane and Major General Kenyon Joyce, neither of whom I had known previously. MacFarlane was a very impressive British officer with wide diplomatic and military experience in the Mediterranean whose leonine head might have served to adorn the British coat of arms. He knew a great deal about Italian politics and showed none of the bitterness toward the Italians which handicapped many British officers in their relations with their former enemies. I learned a great deal from "Mason-Mac" and regretted his departure when, as the result of some deal in Allied intramural politics, he was replaced by General Joyce.

Kenyon Joyce was a well-known American cavalry officer who, retired before the war, was recalled to active duty in 1941 and given command of the IX Corps at Fort Lewis, Washington, with Colonel Dwight D. Eisenhower as his Chief of Staff. When it became necessary to replace General MacFarlane in Brindisi, General Eisenhower chose his old commander for the assignment. While Joyce demonstrated from the start an unconcealed dislike for most of the British and State Department representatives with whom he was associated, he got along well with Badoglio and the Italians until he, in turn, fell a victim to Allied politics and was replaced by MacFarlane who returned early in 1944 after my own departure from Italy.

As might be imagined, many Allied bigwigs visisted us at Brindisi and often overtaxed our limited guest accommodations. I particularly remember a visit from Andrei Vishinsky, the notorious Soviet prosecutor who had become the Soviet representative on the Consultation Commission for Italian Affairs. In due course he decided to come to Brindisi to see what the Americans and British were up to with the Badoglio government. The passenger list, wired to us before the arrival of his plane, indicated that in addition to Vishinsky and his secretary the party included three "collaborators" of unexplained official background. Our lack of knowledge of their diplomatic standing posed us problems of protocol in the assigning of rooms in the Albergo Internazionale. It was clear that I would have to give up my room to Vishinsky and move down the hall to a closet next to the maid's dustpan and brooms. But where to put the "collaborators"? I decided to assign them a single, fair-sized room just above Vishinsky's on the next floor and then, with some misgivings, took off for the local airfield to meet the party. When the plane arrived and the party disembarked, the mystery of the "collaborators" was quickly cleared up. They had clipped heads, low foreheads, and hips made lumpy by pistol holsters bulging underneath their coats. They were plainly Vishinsky's bodyguards.

Vishinsky, a grandfather figure with silver hair and china-blue eyes, totally devoid of the manner expected of a vindictive prosecutor, proved an easy guest to entertain. At dinner, we chatted easily about generalities of the war, and when he asked to retire early, I escorted him to my old room, wished him good night, and eventually found my bed alongside the brooms.

The next morning, the Italian maid rushed to see me, hands waving, with the news that Signor Vishinsky had not slept in the room we had assigned him, and she had no idea where he had come to rest. Obviously, he had slept somewhere because he appeared at breakfast seemingly in good spirits and with no complaints concerning his accommodations. That evening, the same sequence of events took place. But this time, after I had taken Vishinsky to my old room after dinner and had wished him pleasant dreams, I set a watch on his door. What my surveillance discovered was that Vishinsky was spending each night upstairs in the room with the "collaborators," who by way of precaution had carefully filled the keyhole of their door with sealing wax. Whether Vishinsky really believed that his life was in danger from his hosts or whether he was assuring himself of witnesses should he ever have to account in Moscow for his conduct, I shall never know.

A prime duty of the Mission was to assist Badoglio in forming his government and carrying out his duties as Prime Minister. The first service which I can recall rendering him was of a personal and nonpolitical nature. A couple of days after we had joined him in Brindisi, he remarked to me that he had noticed that an Allied post exchange had been set up in town and asked if I would be good enough to buy him some underwear, as he had only the set he was wearing. "You know, we had to leave Rome in a hurry," he reminded me.

Badoglio began at once to try to form an acceptable Cabinet, and it was not an easy task. To qualify for membership in his Cabinet, a candidate must not have served Mussolini, and, if possible, should be a nationally known figure with some apparent competence for his job. To meet these requirements fully, he must have made his political reputation sometime before 1922 when Mussolini came to power and thus be on the shady side of sixty. So the first Cabinet was necessarily one of elderly men with a few relatively young technicians to bolster them.

One of the hardest positions to fill was that of Minister of Finance, and it was some time before Badoglio could find a qualified candidate approximating the criteria. Eventually Dr. Guido Jung, a well-known banker with past experience in the Finance Ministry, was located in Sicily and flown to Brindisi for consultation with Badoglio. When he called on MacFarlane and me, we were somewhat startled to meet a small elderly gentleman in the uniform of a major of artillery. Concealing our surprise, we shook hands warmly and congratulated him on having been chosen to be Finance Minister in the first government of liberated Italy.

"But, gentlemen, I do not wish to be Finance Minister," he replied in perfect Oxonian English. "I have had the position in better times, and it was never one which appealed to me." MacFarlane and I were more than a little taken back by this reluctant ministerial candidate and tried appeals to his sense of duty and patriotism to get him to change his mind. But our efforts were in vain although he freely recognized his obligation to serve his country in this crisis. Eventually, it occurred to me to ask how he would like to serve Italy if not as Finance Minister. "Gentlemen," he replied, "I would like to be a leftenant [sic] colonel of artillery." MacFarlane and I, spotting the possibility of a deal, hastened to propose that he be promoted and at the same time serve as Finance Minister. To our enormous relief he accepted and proceeded to serve in the Badoglio cabinet contentedly in uniform. In so doing, he provided me, also a dedicated artillery man, with a story which I have enjoyed telling to U.S. Secretaries of Treasury whom I have subsequently known.

One of my last acts before leaving the Mission was to participate in the plans and arrangements for moving the King, Badoglio, and the Mission to the Naples area. The hardest part of the move was to find appropriate accommodations for the King in an area in which most public buildings had been long since requisitioned for military use and where most of the villas around the Bay of Naples were filled with Allied generals or wounded soldiers. Also I soon discovered that the few Italians who had not been evicted from their properties by the war showed no enthusiasm for moving out to provide a roof for their King. Nevertheless, I eventually found a villa for him at Ravello on the south side of the Bay of Naples but, in so doing, nearly fell a victim to British understatement.

One day, while reconnoitering villas along the Sorrento peninsula by jeep, my aide and I were bouncing over a mountain road along a cliff over-looking the sea, driving a bit faster than we should have for safety. We slowed down somewhat when we noted a British Army sign alongside the road which read, "Slow. Bridge damaged." Rounding the next curve, my driver slammed on all brakes, plastering my nose on the windshield and bringing the jeep to a screaming halt on the edge of a precipice several hundred feet deep. At the bottom lay the bridge, damaged to be sure just as the sign had cautioned.

Early in December, after having rendered distinguished service in the campaign from Salerno to Naples, the 82d Airborne Division left Italy for North Ireland to prepare for Normandy. However, at General Mark Clark's insistence, it left behind the 504th Regimental Combat Team under Colonel Tucker for use in the January landing at Anzio. About the same time, Bedell Smith made good on his promise to relieve me from my duties with the Allied Control Commission in time to return with the division. General Ridgway, however, preferred for me to remain for the time being at Fifth Army Headquarters at Caserta, north of Naples, so that I could keep an eye on Tucker's troops and extricate them from the clutches of his West Point classmate, Mark Clark, just as soon as possible.

I spent several weeks at Caserta in comparative idleness except for a visit to the 504th Combat Team after its landing in the Anzio beachhead. Between times, I did what I could to press for the relief of Tucker and his men and thereby made myself a nuisance to the Fifth Army Staff, particularly to Al Gruenther, Clark's brilliant and reasonably patient Chief of Staff. They understood though that I had to satisfy a hard-driving division commander in Ireland who naturally wanted all his troops back to train for the invasion of France. Eventually, it was agreed that Tucker would be relieved at the end of March and I rejoined the Division in its training area near Belfast. I arrived just in time to participate in its movement from Ireland to the vicinity of Leicester in central England, a move occasioned by the need for airfields to support the forthcoming invasion of Normandy.

CHAPTER 5

D Day in Normandy

Shortly after the 82d Division moved to England, I became the beneficiary of a stroke of good fortune with a most unfortunate cause. In February, General Bill Lee, the idolized commander of the 101st Airborne Division, suffered a severe heart attack which ended his active service and resulted in his evacuation to the United States. Thanks largely to the intervention of Generals Bradley and Ridgway, I was chosen to replace him and took command of the Division on March 14 at its headquarters in Newbury, Berkshire.

General Lee had brought the Division into southwestern England during the fall of 1943 where a fourth regiment, the 501st Parachute Infantry, joined it in January. By the time I arrived, intensive unit training and staff planning for D day had been going on for several months in preparation for the coming operation. Under General Lee's leadership, an unusual division was being shaped to do unusual things, and it was a cruel stroke of fortune which deprived him of the privilege of leading it into battle.

Although I knew that there was some disappointment that Lee's successor had not been chosen from within the 101st, I was received warmly upon arrival. If there were any heartburns among senior officers, they were never visible, but my pleasure in receiving the command was tempered by the knowlwdge of the highly qualified men over whom I had been advanced. In a perfect world, it would have gone to the Division Artillery Commander, Brigadier General Anthony McAuliffe, of later Bastogne fame, and I would have been left to take my chances in the 82d.

There were many things to do to catch up with the requirements of the new job. I had to become acquainted with my officers, particularly the regimental and battalion commanders who would bear the brunt of the coming battle. There was the need to supervise the training programs and verify their quality and realism. In this task I had the assistance of many able

70

officers: Tony McAuliffe, Brigadier General Don F. Pratt, the Assistant Division Commander; Colonel G. J. Higgins, the Chief of Staff; and Lieutenant Colonel Raymond D. Millener, the Assistant Chief of Staff for Operations. Also, I had to represent the Division at the many planning sessions at higher headquarters in and around London, and adjust the division plans to the changing decisions of the higher commanders.

I was most fortunate in being under two senior officers for whom I had the greatest respect, Lieutenant General J. Lawton Collins, commanding the VII Corps and General Omar Bradley, commanding the First Army. Collins had been brought from the Pacific, where he had commanded the 25th Infantry Division at Guadalcanal and had won the nickname of "Lightning Joe," to provide experienced leadership to the Corps which would make the initial landing on Utah Beach. As a major, he had been one of my instructors at the Army War College where he had impressed the class with his clarity of thought and expression as well as by the evidence he gave of being a profound student of the art and science of war.

General Bradley I had first known as a major at West Point when I was a cadet. It was his departure from command of the 82d Infantry Division in 1942 which set in motion the chain of events which carried me from Washington to England by way of the Mediterranean. As a corps commander in Sicily, Bradley had confirmed his peacetime reputation for leadership and now was about to lead the U.S. Army forces into Normandy alongside Montgomery's British divisions.

Both Bradley and Collins understood the need of rigorous training for combat and left no stone unturned to assure the success of the operations ahead of them. They believed, as I did, that there was no operation in war worth undertaking which was not worth rehearsing in advance. In preparation for D day, General Collins organized two large corps exercises which simulated the amphibious landings at Utah Beach as faithfully as could be done on the coast of the English Channel. The 101st participated in both, bringing parachutists to the beach by truck to imitate their advance from the Normandy drop zones to contact with the American troops landing on Utah beach. At my insistence, from May 9 to 12, Exercise Eagle was conducted by the 101st and the Troop Carrier Command to rehearse the movement of our airborne troops to their departure airfields in England, the marshaling in the air of the troop-carrier squadrons and the dropping of our parachutists by night on drop zones laid out to simulate those in Normandy. The final phase of the exercise was the assembly of our men in the darkness and their movement toward terrain objectives similar to those in France.

Commanders and soldiers alike learned a great deal from each of these rehearsals. Some of the lessons were major, some relatively trivial but still important. Exercise Eagle impressed me with the unresolved problems of finding in the darkness equipment bundles dropped by parachute and of

71

distinguishing friend from foe. As a result, we got an expedited delivery from the United States of luminous cord which glowed in the darkness for use in securing our equipment bundles, as well as thousands of toy crickets which when squeezed emitted a popping sound for identification at night. Such small things do not win battles but they often help.

Naturally, we had many visitors during the final weeks of our preparations, the most notable being Prime Minister Churchill accompanied by General Eisenhower at the end of March. The Division put on a demonstration parachute jump for the visitors in the afternoon, and the Prime Minister and Eisenhower reciprocated with a dinner on board their special train for the American division commanders stationed in that part of England. Churchill was just getting up from a nap when we arrived at the train, and he appeared tired and a bit grumpy. However, drinks were soon passed, and he seized upon a large glass of cognac. Soon the color was back in his jowls and the sparkle in his eyes. He began to reminisce about the Boer War, and by the time dinner was served, he had us in the midst of World War I. He remained in superb form throughout the evening, keeping us early-rising soldiers well beyond our normal bedtime. But it was a grand evening for the visitors although, I suspect, rather hard on General Eisenhower who had to bear up under many such long evenings of conviviality. However, one of the notable observations during the evening was the evidence of a warm informal relationship between Churchill and Eisenhower, an asset of priceless value for the Allied cause during the war.

One of the great problems of the invasion was how to keep secret the place and time of the landings. As to place, there were only two plausible areas, the vicinity of the only two ports large enough to support such an operation, Cherbourg and Le Havre. After Cherbourg was chosen, every conceivable device was used on our side to create the impression in the minds of the German High Command that the main landing would be directed at Le Havre. As we know, this deception was surprisingly successful whether because of our cleverness or of Hitler's fixed idea that we were sure to land at Le Havre, I am not sure.

In any case, we certainly had no complacent feeling that all was well as D day approached, particularly after we discovered in the bookstalls of London a book called *Paratroopers* written by a Czechoslovak captain named Mitske. It was a résumé of the German airborne operations up to that time and included a study of the possible uses of airborne forces by the Allies in invading Europe. As a matter of fact, it contained a hypothetical plan for the employment of parachutists in a cross-Channel operation with the Cherbourg peninsula for the landing area, and with drop zones which almost coincided with those which my division planned to use on D day.

To protect the secrecy of both time and place, the knowledge of these two bits of information—for a time about the most important secrets in the world—was initially limited to a handful of senior officers whose names were recorded in the so-called "Bigot" registry. As time went on and D day approached, the number in the know was gradually expanded following a "need-to-know" principle. It was not until mid-May that I could reveal the division plan, but not the time, to my regimental and battalion commanders. They could brief only a few of their staff officers who then worked on the plans in carefully secured war rooms. The troops themselves never learned of the plan or of their unit mission until they were locked in the marshaling areas near the airfields or ports from which they would depart for France. There they had sandtables and maps reproducing the whole Cherbourg peninsula which each man was required to study, giving particular but not exclusive attention to the area in which he expected to fight. Remembering the scattering of our parachutists in Sicily, I insisted that our men not only know the task of their own unit but the tasks of the others around them. On the sand tables, they were required to reproduce from memory the location of the key terrain features and tactical objectives over the entire Cherbourg peninsula—a bit of precautionary training which was to stand them in good stead on D day.

While one might assume that such secrecy measures would have retarded our final preparations, actually they did not, since our division plan was constantly being revised in step with the changing decisions of higher headquarters. For example, the number of gliders which we were to be allotted to carry heavy equipment was at issue until mid-May. From the outset, Air Chief Marshal Leigh-Mallory had been deeply pessimistic regarding the outcome of the airborne operations and, as late as May 30, expressed his forebodings to General Eisenhower. He was particularly dubious about the wisdom of using gliders in the hedgerow country of Normandy and exerted all his influence to hold down the number authorized for our use. As a result, our D-day glider lift was sufficient for only about 300 men, and most of our glider regiment, the 327th, had to be brought into the beachhead by sea.

In its final form, the invasion plan called for the parachute elements of the 101st Airborne Division, some 6,600 men, to land under cover of darkness preceding the seaborne assault and to seize the exits of four causeways leading inland from Utah Beach for use by the 4th Infantry Division which spearheaded the landing forces. We were given this mission because of the anticipated difficulties of the landing forces in moving inland across the extensive inundations just behind the beach, which the Germans had created and then covered by minefields. In so doing, they had limited the exits from the three mile beach to four roads elevated on causeways that constituted easily defended defiles through which our troops must pass. Hence, the primary mission of the parachutists of the 101st on landing was to seize and defend the inland exits of these defiles. Thereafter we were to regroup our faces to the south, seize the town of Carentan, the communications center at the base of the Cherbourg peninsula, and protect the south flank of the VII Corps as its units landed and turned north to take Cherbourg.

Our parachute troops were to land on three drop zones and the gliders on one, located three to four miles behind the beach. Parachute-pathfinder teams carrying lights and radar beacons for guiding in the planes were to drop shortly ahead of the main body and mark the landing areas. Theirs was the unenviable task of dropping in darkness into enemy-infested territory and announcing their own presence to the Germans by turning on their lights and beacon signals. These pathfinders were among the real heroes of D day.

With the invasion set for June 5, I began on May 28 to make the rounds of the seventeen marshaling areas scattered over Wales and southern England where my troops were sealed up and receiving their final instructions. Standing on the top of a jeep, I addressed every unit in the Division, trying to communicate to the men my feeling of the historic significance of the drama in which we were to be key actors, and the pride we would feel someday in telling our children and grandchildren that we had been in Normandy on D day. Henry V had said it much better on St. Crispin's Day, but I was encouraged by the bright-eyed attention of the men and their visible eagerness to get on with the hazardous business which seemed to hold no terrors for them.

My soldiers were always like that throughout the war—an unfailing tonic for senior officers condemned to spend most of their time in planning and making the decisions upon which the lives of these men depended. In my experience the history books that depicted the role of the general as being that of galvanizing his men into action were all wrong. I found more often than not that I went up to the front lines not to urge on the troops but to escape the worries of the command post where all battle noises sounded like the doings of the enemy and where it was easy for the commander to give way to dire imaginings. A visit to the men of the 101st under fire never failed to send me back to the command post, assured that the situation was well in hand, and that there was no cause for worry.

In the course of taking final leave of the troops, I was called to Bristol, where General Bradley wished to hold a similar leave-taking with the corps and division commanders of the First Army. Elsewhere I have described a similar session with General Patton on the eve of the invasion of Sicily; the meeting in Bristol was a study in contrasts with that at Mostaganem. Here General Bradley, the old school teacher from West Point and the Infantry School, personally conducted the class of generals. Each of us stepped up to the operation map of France, pointer in hand, and described in detail the scheme of maneuver of his corps or division. When my turn came, I found that Bradley knew as much about what my battalions were supposed to do as I did. I sat down wondering like a cadet how many "tenths" I had lost by my recitation and whether, indeed, I had made a passing mark for the day.

When the discussion was over, like General Patton in North Africa, Bradley felt the need to say something appropriate to this occasion, something to rouse these commanders upon whom the success of his Army depended. But General Bradley, although a wonderfully inspiring leader in most ways, is a quiet man of few words and not a fluent speaker. Seeming to sense his rhetorical inadequacies at this critical moment, he folded his hands behind his back, his eyes got a little moist, and in lieu of a speech he simply said, "Good luck, men." We left without the smart of Patton's blistering farewell but with the feeling that we had a commander worth all we could give.

Meanwhile General Eisenhower, as the soldiers would say, was sweating out the decision of the date of D day in company with those augurs of a modern commander, the meteorologists. The landing had been set for June 5, but the weather had become so unfavorable that, after hearing all the evidence and listening to all those qualified to advise, Eisenhower postponed it twenty-four hours to June 6. A coded message indicating the change reached our division headquarters early on June 4.

The delay was a disappointment because we were all set to go and this meant a break in the momentum. For me, it presented an unusual problem —what to do with a day with no work scheduled. This enforced idleness proved almost my undoing. Among the visitors from London to see us off was an old friend, Colonel Frank Reed, familiarly known as "Froggie." As we had played a great deal of squash racquets together in former years, I suggested a game on an Air Force court at a nearby field. When we got into action, I was surprised to discover that "Froggie" knew a lot more about the English version of squash than I did and was about to give me a firstclass licking, something I had not anticipated. Making a maximum effort to stave off defeat, I suddenly pulled a leg tendon with an audible pop, and I was obliged to stop. Though I escaped the ignominy of defeat through default the price was high. By evening I could hardly walk, and when I finally parachuted into Normandy the following morning, I instinctively pulled up my game leg and landed with all my weight on the other. It didn't break, but it was a torture to walk for the first week in France, ample time to curse myself for this self-inflicted wound and "Froggie" for his surprising skill with the squash racquet.

Many other visitors filled our headquarters by the end of June 5. The most important one was Ike himself who, with several of his staff, was our guest for an early dinner at our headquarters' mess. After dinner we drove to several nearby airfields where our parachutists, many in Indian warpaint and with freakish haircuts, were getting into their equipment. Paraphrasing Wellington's feelings about his peninsular troops, General Eisenhower whispered to me that they might not scare the Germans, but they would certainly scare him. He went from plane to plane talking to the men in that wonderfully friendly, man-to-man way which was one of the strengths of his personality, and the men glowed with pride that the Supreme Commander himself had come to see them off. When the round of visits was over, still in the daylight of the English double summer time, he shook hands, wished me luck, and returned to the manor house at the Greenham Common airfield which served as the division command post. From the roof he watched the airborne squadrons form, straighten out in column, and head for the Channel and Normandy.

Once the visitors had gone, the jumpmaster of my stick of parachutists, Major Laurence Legere, helped me into my parachute and suspended from me all the paraphernalia which made parachutists into pack mules: emergency parachute, pistol, jump knife, hand grenades, field rations, canteen, first-aid kit, gas mask, maps, and a leg bag in which I had prudentially stored a bottle of Irish whisky. When everything was in place, a brawny sergeant proceeded to tighten the straps of my parachute to the point that breath came hard, reminding me that the tighter the straps the less the shock of opening when I left the plane.

The parachutists in a plane, about a dozen in number, constituted a "stick" which was under the supervision of the jumpmaster, always a picked man and an experienced parachutist. For the moment, he was an autocrat with unchallenged authority somewhat like that of the skipper of a ship. Regardless of the rank of the members of his stick, he was responsible for them for the duration of the flight and could give whatever orders were necessary to carry out his duties. Larry Legere, four years out of West Point, performed that role for our stick, checking our equipment, reminding us of exit procedures, and getting us into the proper bucket seat. My fellow passengers included my aide, personal bodyguards, several communications personnel, and Robert Reuben, a Reuters correspondent. Lieutenant Colonel Frank McNeese, one of the most experienced pilots of the Troop Carrier Command, was our pilot, and I had every confidence that, if anyone could, he would get our plane to the drop zone.

Promptly at 11:00 P.M., our plane placed itself at the head of the squadron departing from the field. McNeese gunned the engines, we hurtled down the runway, and we were off on what was to be, for most of us, our greatest adventure. To me it was a moment of relief to be off after so many months of laborious preparation. I was content in the feeling that I could think of nothing which we had left undone to assure success. Now it only remained to go into action in the spirit of the verse of Montrose which Montgomery had quoted to the Allied commanders at their last conference:

> He either fears his fate too much
> Or his deserts are small,
> That dares not put it to the touch
> To gain or lose it all.

Our parachute planes circled in the dusk over England for more than an hour as the successive squadrons rose from the airfields to join the airborne caravan which now included not only the planes of the 101st but also those of the 82d arriving from their fields in central England. In all there were over 800 transport planes in the formation as it turned toward France carrying about 13,000 parachutists of the two divisions.

By the time my plane reached the Channel it was dark with a faint moon showing. We were flying very low in a tight V of V's formation to keep below the vision of the German radars on the French coast. As I stood in the open door of the plane, I felt that I could touch the sparkling waves of the Channel so close below. The men were strangely quiet, some seeming to doze on their hard metal seats in spite of the load of their equipment. They, too, seemed to have left their cares behind.

Our route was across the Channel from Portsmouth to an air corridor between the islands of Guernsey and Jersey on the west and the Cherbourg peninsula on the east which then turned eastward across the base of the peninsula to our drop zones. As we came abreast of the Channel Islands, from my post in the door I could see a great gray wall to the southeast where the Cherbourg peninsula should be. It was unexpected fog, the enemy of the airman, which was to be the first disrupting factor in our well-laid plans.

The air column, still flying in orderly formation at low altitude, made its final turn eastward and headed into the fog bank. It was very thick at first, so thick that I could not see the planes flying on our wingtips. Almost immediately, the formation began to break up as the flank planes, fearing collisions, veered to the right and left and some increased their altitudes. But there was little time for worry about the fog in our plane. The hookup signal came on quickly and Legere had us in the aisle attaching the static lines of our parachutes to the overhead wire which would trip the opening device on our chutes as we jumped. We checked our equipment and stood in file, each crowding against the man in front to insure a rapid exit when the time came. I was almost riding on the back of Legere who was to lead the stick out the door. Soon the fog became broken, and we could see patches of ground from time to time as we flashed over the Merderet River; by the time we entered the landing area, it was almost completely clear of fog. It was a thrilling sight to see; the sky ablaze with rockets, burning aircraft on the ground, and antiaircraft fire rising on all sides. The green light flashed—the signal to jump—and out we went shouting, "Bill Lee," in honor of our former division commander instead of "Geronimo," the traditional war cry of the parachutists.

As the plane roared away, I was left floating to earth in a comparative quiet, broken only by occasional bursts of small arms fire on the ground. Since we had jumped at about 500 feet, to shorten the time during which we would be floating ducks for enemy marksmen, there was a little time to

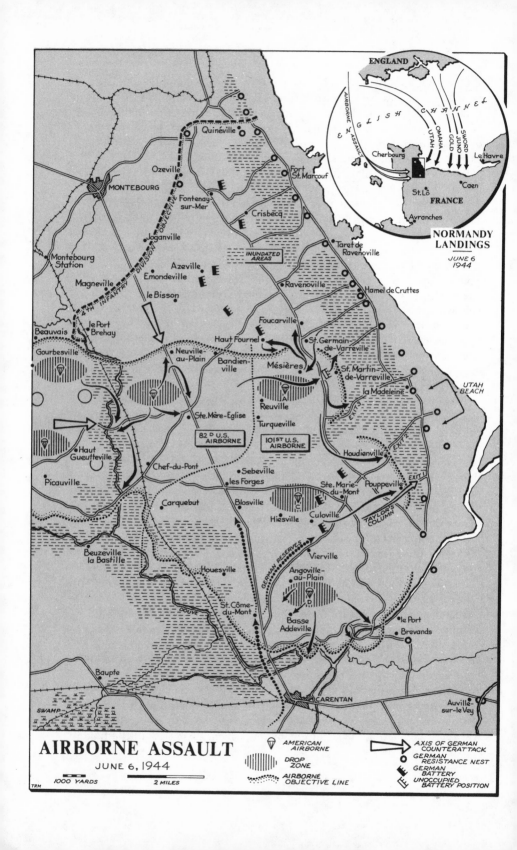

AIRBORNE ASSAULT

JUNE 6, 1944

1000 YARDS

2 MILES

AMERICAN AIRBORNE

DROP ZONE

AIRBORNE OBJECTIVE LINE

AXIS OF GERMAN COUNTERATTACK

GERMAN RESISTANCE NEST

GERMAN BATTERY

UNOCCUPIED BATTERY POSITION

NORMANDY LANDINGS

JUNE 6 1944

ENGLAND

ENGLISH CHANNEL

AIRBORNE ASSAULT

UTAH OMAHA GOLD JUNO SWORD

Cherbourg

Le Havre

Caen

St. Lô

FRANCE

Avranches

UTAH BEACH

Quinéville

Ozeville

MONTEBOURG

Fontenay-sur-Mer

Fort St. Marcouf

Crisbecq

Joganville

Montebourg Station

Azeville

Emondeville

Magneville

le Bisson

Taret de Ravenoville

Ravenoville

Hamel de Cruttes

Beauvais

le Port Brehay

Gourbesville

Haut Fournel

Foucarville

St. Germain-de-Varreville

Neuville-au-Plain

Bandien-ville

Mésières

St. Martin-de-Varreville

la Madeleine

Reuville

Ste. Mère-Eglise

Turqueville

Houdienville

Haut Gueutteville

82D U.S. AIRBORNE

101ST U.S. AIRBORNE

Chef-du-Pont

Sebeville

les Forges

Picauville

Carquebut

Blosville

Ste. Marie-du-Mont

Pouppeville

Hiesville

Culoville

TAYLOR'S COLUMN

Beuzeville la Bastille

Houesville

Vierville

GERMAN RESERVES

Angoville-au-Plain

St. Côme-du-Mont

Basse Addeville

le Port Brevands

Baupte

CARENTAN

Auville-sur-le-Vey

SWAMP

4TH INFANTRY DIVISION OBJECTIVE

INUNDATED AREAS

DOUVE

EXIT 1

EXIT 2

EXIT 3

TRM

try to select a point of landing. At the last moment, a gust of air caused me to drift away from my comrades of the stick and only by a mighty tug on the shroud lines did I manage to escape becoming entangled in the top of a tall tree. Then I came down with a bang in a small Norman field enclosed by one of the famous hedgerows which compartmented the countryside. In most places these hedges consisted of rows of trees planted on earthen banks which, in combination with the trees, presented formidable obstacles to military operations of all sorts. Many a parachutist that morning found himself suspended from one of those tall trees, from which he could only hope to lower himself by a rope before a German rifleman found him.

At last on the soil of Normandy, I began to struggle out of my parachute, expecting that some of my men would appear to help me. But looking around I saw not a single soldier, only a circle of curious Norman cows who eyed me, disapprovingly I thought, as if resenting this intrusion into their pasture. I was still attempting to extricate myself from my chute when a German machine pistol opened up in the next field with the telltale sound of a ripping seat of pants which energized me to frantic struggles to free myself. In the wet morning grass it was a terrible job to unbuckle the many snaps, and I finally gave up and used my parachute knife to cut my way out. Then reluctantly abandoning my leg bag and its contents, I started out, pistol in one hand and identification cricket in the other, to find my troops—a lonely division commander who had lost or at least mislaid his division.

Moving in the shadow of the hedgerow, I became aware of the smell of freshly turned earth and soon came upon some newly dug trenches, a warning that the Germans were probably nearby and to proceed with caution. This I did, creeping in the shadows along the hedgerow to the end of the field. There I heard someone just around the corner of the hedge and veered toward the sound ready to shoot. But then there was the welcome sound of a cricket to which I quickly responded in kind and jumped around the corner. There in the dim moonlight was the first American soldier to greet me, a sight of martial beauty as he stood bareheaded, rifle in hand, bayonet fixed, and apparently ready for anything. We embraced in silence and took off together to round up others of our comrades who were beginning to appear.

As the night was only about five hours long in that latitude, there was just about one hour left in which to assemble the troops who had landed in the vicinity. Three battalions of parachute infantry should have arrived in the area before me, but it was apparent that the drop had been badly scattered and that only a few members of these battalions had reached their destinations. However, I soon ran into Tony McAuliffe, Gerry Higgins, and Julian Ewell, the commander of a battalion of the 501st Parachute Infantry which had been scheduled for this drop zone. Together we beat the nearby fields until daylight by which time we had assembled about ninety soldiers, the odd remnants of various units and services. They ranged in rank from general to private and in skills from radio operators, cooks, clerks, and military police to riflemen, engineers, artillerymen, and Reuben, the war correspondent. We were long on officers but short on combat troops, particularly infantry, a fact that has led me to comment later that "never were so few led by so many."

Despite the long hours spent in England poring over the maps of this part of Normandy, I was not sure exactly where we were until the first morning light. Then I recognized to the northeast the church steeple of Ste. Marie-du-Mont which indicated that we were approximately on the intended drop zone of the Division Headquarters. However, we had only a sprinkling of the troops assigned to the critical mission of securing the southern causeways of Utah Beach.

Now beginning to appreciate the wide dispersion of the troops—about 80 percent of our parachutists had landed in a rectangle twenty-seven by fifteen miles—I decided to send Colonel Thomas Sherbourne of the Division Artillery with a small detachment westward to Hiesville where we had planned to set up the Division Command Post while I moved with the remainder of the troops to take over the mission of seizing the exit of the southernmost of the causeways. I put Ewell in command of the column with orders to move on Pouppeville, occupy, and hold it until the leading troops of the 4th Division could pass over the causeway. Then McAuliffe, Higgins, and I attached ourselves to the column to supervise the job.

As we turned eastward, we came on the first farmhouse in our path. The members of the family were battened down inside as the war swept over and around them but responded when we pounded on the front door. I spoke to the farmer and asked him the location of the nearest German troops which he identified as Ste. Marie-du-Mont. Then I inquired about the poles which he had set up in one of his fields to serve as an obstacle to airborne landings. In England before our departure, we had been very much intrigued by this poling of fields which had taken place throughout Normandy, thinking that from the pattern of the poles we could deduce something of the German plan of defense. But to the hour of our take-off we had perceived no plan or method in the poling operations. Now I had a farmer who could explain it.

So I asked him why he had poled one of his fields and not the other of his small farm. His reply showed the folly of assuming rationality in human behavior. "The Germans told us farmers to pole all our fields by June 15. My cow never liked that west field so I poled it first." In this case, the whim of a French cow was the controlling factor, not the plans of the German General Staff. As I was about to go, the farmer asked me to wait a moment, went back into the house and returned with a clip of World War

I rifle ammunition. He gave it to me with the injunction *"Allez me tuer un Boche."* ("Go kill me a German.")

It was now after daylight as we pushed eastward. The landing on Utah Beach had begun, and we were the privileged spectators of the greatest military show of history. The sea was filled with landing craft, the air with fighters and bombers. Bombs were falling on both the Utah and Omaha Beach defenses and our Navy had opened up on shore targets with heavy guns. Fired with high velocity on a flat trajectory, their shells would hit the beach and then ricochet inland emitting bloodcurdling screams as they passed overhead. Resisting a temptation to stand and watch the show, we continued across country toward the beach in a column of two's with patrols out to the front and flank, picking up a few more men as we went.

We made our first contact with the Germans as we neared Pouppeville where our column halted on the outskirts while Ewell organized his attack on the town. The resistance was light, but it was a time-consuming task to clear out each house and eliminate the snipers. While we senior officers observing the operation controlled with difficulty our impatience to get into the act, Ewell went about his business with professional thoroughness and mopped up the village by about noon. In so doing we captured some forty prisoners and suffered about twenty casualties. One of these was Larry Legere who received a severe hip wound which resulted in his evacuation for long hospitalization in the United States.

Shortly after the occupation of Pouppeville, we could hear the firing of the troops of the 4th Division approaching from the beach. To avoid the possibility of a collision of the two forces, I sent a patrol to meet them and inform them of the situation around Pouppeville. Very soon the advance guard of the 8th Infantry appeared to the cheers of our parachutists. It was an historic moment, the long-planned junction of the air and seaborne assaults on Hitler's Fortress Europe. Utilizing the communications of the 4th Division I conveyed the welcome news to General Bradley's headquarters afloat offshore.

Our mission finished in this part of the field, I turned our little column around and started inland for the division command post at Hiesville. It was hard going not because of the enemy but because of the condition of my legs as the result of the pre-D-day squash game. Just east of Hiesville, we ran into Colonel Robert Sink, commanding the 506th Parachute Infantry, who during the morning had had a hot fight in the vicinity and had captured a German field artillery battery of which he was very proud, explaining that henceforth he would have his own regimental artillery. He warned us, however, that there were lots of "hostiles" nearby and that we should be prepared for anything.

Hiesville was merely a group of farmhouses which we had chosen as our command post from a map in England because of its central location in relation to our division missions. When we reached it in the late afternoon, Colonel Sherburne had the command post in operation, radio contact established with a few subordinate units, and its defense organized against a surprise German attack. He had quartered most of the elements of the command post in a farmhouse which was surrounded by a high stone wall constructed so solidly as to constitute a formidable redoubt. Once arrived and divested of impedimenta, I set to work with Higgins to evaluate the situation of the Division as we approached the end of the "Longest Day."

The situation was far from clear in most parts of the division sector. The causeways were secured and the 4th Division was having no difficulty in landing; that was the most encouraging news. However, unit reports received at Hiesville accounted for only about 2,000 of the 6,600 parachutists who had jumped that morning and these were intermingled in groups of various sizes, many including men from the neighboring 82d. In the course of the day, the men had shown remarkable initiative in forming small task forces under the officers or noncommissioned officers who happened to be present and then heading for the nearest division objective, as we had done at Pouppeville. Much equipment had been lost in the drop, including virtually all of our parachute artillery. Two small glider detachments had landed, one in the morning with the parachutists, the other at the end of the day. They had brought in important heavy equipment including a long-range radio capable of communicating with England, antiaircraft and antitank weapons, and medical equipment. But we had paid a heavy price in the loss of Don Pratt, the Assistant Division Commander, who was killed in the crash of his glider in the morning landing.

If the news was good from the beach, there was little known about the situation to the north or to the south. The 82d was heavily engaged to our west where it had encountered considerable German strength. I had immediately available at the end of D day only about 1,000 troops under Colonel Sink. So there was little to do as night fell other than to direct Sink to move south at daylight with all the men he could collect, establish contact with our units along the Douve, and take over our second mission, that of covering the south flank of the VIIth Corps and its divisions moving north toward Cherbourg.

It took us three days to assemble our scattered parachutists, bring the 327th Glider Infantry from the beach where it had arrived by ship to a position on our left flank, and clear out patches of resistance north of the Douve. During these days, my principal concern was a German counterattack, which I expected nightly after D day, but except for sporadic small-scale bombings there was no enemy reaction to disturb us.

We launched a pincers attack against Carentan on the night of June 9–10, the 327th Glider Regiment under Colonel Joseph H. Harper making an unopposed crossing of the Douve near its mouth while the 502d attacked southward astride the Cherbourg-Carentan highway. The advance here was severely constricted by the causeway formed by the road which created a defile covered by fire from German trenches to the south. Here occurred the only authentic bayonet charge to which I can testify in the course of a war in which the bayonet was used far more frequently against ration cans than against the enemy. The charge was led by Lieutenant Colonel Robert G. Cole against the German position blocking the exit from the Douve River causeway. Cole, who received the Medal of Honor for his gallantry, was later killed in action in Holland.

The 502d by this time was under Lieutenant Colonel John H. Michaelis who assumed command of the regiment when its colonel, George Moseley, broke his leg in the D-day jump. Moseley was a veteran parachutist who had worked without stint to prepare his regiment for Normandy. It was an odd quirk of fortune that this experienced jumper should have been a casualty while Millener, my assistant chief of staff for operations, made the first jump of his career on D day without injury. It was hard to tell Moseley that he must give up his regiment and return to England. I found him on D + 1 being pushed about the battlefront in a commandeered wheelbarrow while he directed his troops with a cane. It took my personal order to get him to the aid station on the beach.

The battle for Carentan lasted for three days during which I was constantly scuttling in my jeep from one flank of the Division to the other. The pincers formed by our two flanks came together on June 12 in Carentan, which I entered from the east with Bud Harper's glider troops. On June 13, we received the delayed counterattack which I had been expecting; it was mounted by the 17th S.S. Panzer Grenadier Division and the 6th Parachute Infantry against our troops on the southwest outskirts of Carentan. As an airborne division was very weak in antitank weapons, we might have had considerable difficulty in beating off the attack had not General Bradley, unsolicited, sent us the reinforcement of a combat command of the 2d Armored Division commanded by Colonel John H. Collier. Our hard-pressed infantry welcomed the tanks with cheers, patted their steel hulls, then plunged after them down the hedgerows in pursuit of the Germans flushed from their shelters by the tanks. By the end of the day, the German threat was completely dissipated, and the Division organized a defensive position covering Carentan which it held during the ensuing weeks while the American divisions from Utah Beach occupied the peninsula and port of Cherbourg to the north.

The battle for Carentan ended our part of the serious fighting in Normandy as we were withdrawn to England following the capture of Cherbourg and before the Allied breakout from the beachhead. In the campaign, our casualties totaled some 3,800 men, approximately one-third of the men who reached Normandy. It was a heavy price to pay but far below what had been estimated in the planning phase in England. If the 101st withdrew a smaller division than it had arrived, the battle had welded it into a confident, veteran outfit ready to undertake any task which the future might hold.

For the senior airborne commanders, the campaign held many lessons. The feasibility of large-scale airborne operations had been verified although the scattered drop of the parachutists was renewed evidence of the need for greater accuracy of Air Force navigation in darkness. Until such accuracy was clearly demonstrated I was convinced that parachute commanders would have to expect dispersion and should make provision for it in their planning. If a mission required the strength of one battalion on the spot to carry it out at night, planners should assign it about three times that number to compensate for the probable dispersion.

Overshadowing the airborne lessons of the Normandy landings was the revalidation of the wonder-working effects of concentrated power used with surprise, mass, and mobility in accomplishing great military purposes. The Allies achieved these effects through a willingness to put it all "to the touch" and in so doing won it all. The fate of Hitler's Reich was sealed in the course of just one week's fighting, in which time fortress Europe was breached and the Allied armies were firmly established on the continent.

CHAPTER 6

The Arnhem Operation

Upon the return of the Division in mid-July to its old billets in southwest England, it resumed training, and we at headquarters set to work planning a series of possible airborne operations to support the Allied ground forces which, in the meantime, had broken out of the Normandy beachhead. By early August they were streaming eastward across northern France in hot pursuit of the retreating Germans. In England, we came under a new command structure, the First Allied Airborne Army, created as the result of the airborne experience of Normandy. To give unified direction to the future operations of airborne and troop carrier units, General Eisenhower had established this Army under the command of Lieutenant General Lewis Brereton, a highly regarded American Air Force officer and had assigned to it all the American and British troop carrier units and airborne divisions. The American divisions, now including the 17th, were incorporated in the XVIII Airborne Corps under General Ridgway, while General Gavin took over the command of the 82d Airborne Division. There were changes also within the 101st. Gerry Higgins succeeded to the vacancy of Assistant Division Commander created by the death of General Pratt, and Bud Millener became my Chief of Staff.

In the course of the next three months, we developed successive plans to mount airborne operations at three places, Rambouillet near Paris, and Tournai and Liège in Belgium. None of these plans was carried out because the rapidity of the ground advance of the Allied forces which overran the German resistance made the airborne operations unnecessary. As viewed by General Bradley, by then commander of the Fifteenth Army Group, these operations would have been positively disadvantageous as they would have required the diversion of troop carrier aircraft from their mission of transporting supplies by air to the rapidly advancing ground columns and of fighter aircraft to protect the airborne landings. Thus, it

85

was not until September 10 that we received a mission which was finally executed; the operation received the code designation of Market-Garden but has become popularly known as the Arnhem operation after the name of the Dutch city which was its farthest objective.

Before launching into an account of Market-Garden, I should mention a few episodes of this second sojourn in England. It was the period of the attacks of the German V-1 bombs, those slow-flying, unmanned aircraft, whose chugging motor provided a warning of approaching danger and made them harder on the nerves than the later V-2's which, having a velocity greater than sound, gave no warning. I had to make several trips to London during this period and got a quick fill of V-1's. One of my purposes was to get a uniform made by one of those Saville Row tailors who have specialists for each part of a gentleman's suit. One of my fitters was a dignified, gray-haired gentleman who was meticulously slow and accurate with every move of a pin. Occasionally when we would hear a V-1 approaching, he would excuse himself and say, "Could we sit down for a moment? I really don't do my best work when one of those chaps is overhead." Personally I would have welcomed a dugout to jump into, but unfortunately Saville Row was lacking in the conveniences of the battlefield.

On August 10, General Eisenhower visited the Division to review it and to present the Distinguished Service Cross to several members of the Division for gallantry in Normandy. When in the course of the review the recipients came forward to receive their decorations, they ranged in rank from colonel to private. After the reading of each citation, Ike would step forward, pin on the medal, and congratulate the soldier. As the last man, a Private Rogers approached, the General turned to me and asked me why a man who had earned such a high award was only a private. Caught unprepared, I could only speculate, looking at the soldier's uniform, that he probably didn't show up well at inspections and parades but was at his best in battle. Then Ike asked, "Would you mind if I made him a corporal today?" Naturally I didn't mind. So after pinning on his medal, General Eisenhower greeted him: "Congratulations, Corporal Rogers," and the review broke up.

After the departure of our distinguished guest, I called Bob Sink, Rogers' regimental commander, and told him about his new corporal. Sink, always on the alert for favorable publicity for his regiment, immediately assembled the visiting press and had a picture taken of him pinning on Rogers' corporal chevrons which eventually appeared in American and European press with the caption, "Ike makes Rogers Corporal."

The story ought to end here, but alas, no. Sudden fame went to Rogers' head, inducing an irresistible need to celebrate in a glorious spree followed by a period of absence without leave. Sink having gone to London for the weekend, the delinquent hero was brought before the second in command, Lieutenant Colonel Charles Chase who promptly busted him back to the grade of private for his derelictions. Sink, upon his return to camp, was dismayed to learn this news and mildly admonished Chase for his summary justice explaining, "Charley, you can't 'bust' Ike's own corporal." Chase replied with dignity, "Sir, I did not know that he intended the title to be hereditary." General Eisenhower was delighted with this story when I later related it to him, saying, "Golly, that will be a lesson to me to leave the making of corporals where it belongs—with the colonels."

It was a tribute to the skill of the airborne staffs, now adept from past experience in planning many canceled operations, that the Army and Air Force units could mount the complex Market-Garden operation with only one week's advance notice. It called for landing the 82d and 101st Airborne Divisions and the British 1st Airborne Division (with a Polish Brigade attached) to assist the British Second Army to advance rapidly into Holland along the highway from the Albert Canal and to secure a bridgehead on the Rhine at Arnhem. It was a bold, risky undertaking which sought to turn the flank of the Siegfried Line and cross the barrier of the Rhine in an area which was believed lightly defended. In compensation, it was interspersed with many natural obstacles—rivers, canals, narrow bridges, and roads converted into defiles by the adjacent marshy fields.

The plan was to put down the 101st in the Eindhoven-Veghel area, the 82d around Nijmegen and its important bridges over the Waal, and the British 1st Airborne at Arnhem to seize the last and most critical bridge in the long series extending northward from the Albert Canal some sixty miles to the south. The airborne commanders, remembering their experience in Normandy, were unanimously in favor of running the risk of a daylight landing rather than those incidental to a landing in darkness. Our views were accepted, and D day was set for September 17.

Market-Garden was the biggest airborne operation of World War II, which is to say of all time. The D-day assault included 20,000 parachutists, some 1,500 transport planes, and about 500 gliders, and was protected by over 1,000 Allied fighters. In this D-day landing the 101st had over 400 C-47 transport aircraft and 70 gliders carrying nearly 7,000 officers and men. The remainder of the division arrived progressively by air and ship over the next six days. Our initial mission was to secure fifteen miles of highway extending from Eindhoven to Veghel and to seize and hold the bridges in the area for the use of the spearhead units of the British Second Army advancing from the south. Although our objectives on the ground were scattered, I insisted on putting all the troops arriving the first day into a compact area between Zon and Veghel in order to have them within supporting distance of each other at the outset.

My plane took off from Welford airdrome with Colonel Frank McNeese again the pilot and Lieutenant Colonel Patrick C. Cassidy, one of my best battalion commanders, as jumpmaster. We were airborne about 10:00 A.M., flew down the Thames through the antiaircraft balloon barriers and then headed eastward across the Low Countries. Once over land, I could follow with ease our route from the map and noted the accuracy with which we passed the various check points. Fortunately, our fighter escort had cleared all German aircraft from the sky and it was not until we were approaching our drop zone that we stirred up the first German antiaircraft fire.

Standing in the door ready to jump behind Cassidy, I saw the plane on our wing hit by ground fire and flames start licking back from the engine under the fuselage. Cassidy was so fascinated by the sight that I had to nudge him to remind him that the jump signal was on. Later I learned that the Air Force pilots of the burning plane never wavered in their steady course to the drop zone where their parachutists jumped to safety while the pilots crashed to their deaths.

As we jumped from our plane, as far as one could see were parachutes of many colors floating gently to earth in the warm afternoon sunshine. In contrast to the scattered drop in Normandy, there were no lonely officers roaming about looking for their units—the fields were alive with American soldiers assembling their equipment and hurrying to the rendezvous points of their companies.

With the members of my immediate party, I hurried through the fields verifying the presence of our battalions in their appointed locations, then joined the 1st Battalion of the 506th Parachute Infantry under the command of Major James L. La Prade. This battalion was to assemble with maximum speed, move south to the Wilhelmina Canal, then east to the Zon bridge which was the nearest division objective. La Prade got his men going in less than an hour but ran into considerable fire on his way to the canal. Meanwhile the rest of his regiment, assigned the capture of Eindhoven after passing through Zon, moved toward the bridge from the north. Both columns converged on the town, silenced a German 88 mm. gun firing from its center, and then rushed for the bridge. Unfortunately, the Germans blew it up just as we were about a hundred yards from it, and the explosion showered us with debris. This was a disappointment since it slowed Sink in getting his men across the Wilhelmina Canal and prevented him from moving on Eindhoven until the following morning.

By the end of D day, we had set up Division Headquarters in Zon and were in communication with the 502d and 506th Regiments but not with the 501st, which had been dropped to the north in the vicinity of their objective, the town of Veghel and the bridges nearby. Nor had we heard from the leading corps of the Second British Army which had hoped to reach Eindhoven by that time. Actually, the 501st was on its objectives at Veghel, but the British had moved only about half the distance to Eindhoven from their original line of departure at the Dutch frontier. The only setback in the plans of the 101st had been the blown bridge at Zon which required heavier bridging equipment to repair than we carried in

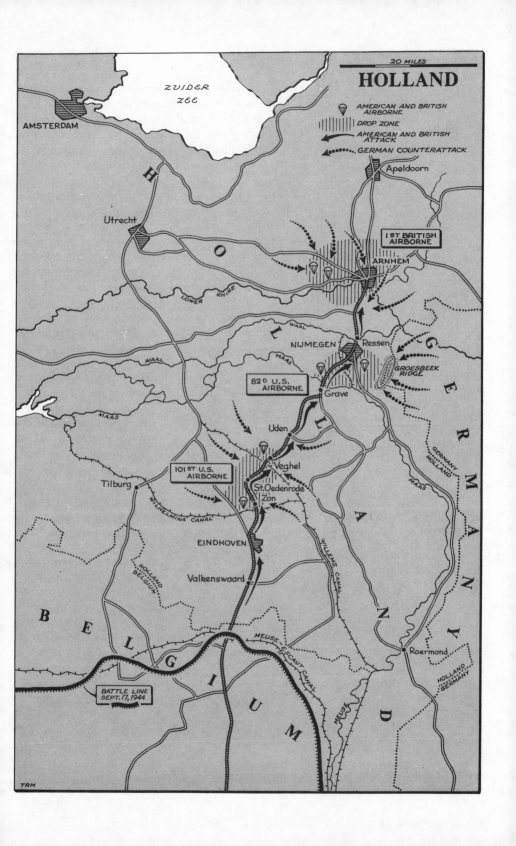

our Division. So I went to bed reasonably content, accepting the offer of a local priest to use his room in an annex to the village church.

By the next morning, the British had expected to reach Zon, but all that I knew about them was they they had not got to Eindhoven. So I paid a hasty visit to the nearby town of St. Oedenrode which Colonel Cassidy had occupied the previous day with his battalion and then hurried toward Eindhoven to join Sink's regiment.

Eindhoven was and is an important city of well over 100,000 and is the home of the Phillips Electric Company. Because of its size and the solid construction of its buildings, Eindhoven would have been hard to take if the Germans had put up a serious defense. Instead, Lieutenant Colonel Strayer's 506th Battalion penetrated the heart of the city against little resistance and received its capitulation about 2:00 P.M. I drove into town in my open jeep shortly thereafter, ducking apples tossed at the Americans by the cheering Dutch population.

Here I must pay tribute to the Dutch civilians for their invaluable assistance throughout the Holland campaign. The members of the underground, identified on D day by orange armbands, were everywhere, bringing us information on the Germans and on the local situation. They served as a secondary intelligence service throughout the campaign, and, thanks to their diligence and cooperation, we were never surprised by the Germans in the course of the combats of the following weeks. There were also unorganized civilians, not members of the underground, who were just as anxious to help, forcing food on us which we did not need and offering us all their available beer which we did need and quickly consumed.

Learning in Eindhoven that the British were drawing near from the south and having assured myself that they had been informed of the condition of the bridge at Zon and of the need for bridging equipment, I returned to the glider landing zone near Zon and watched over 400 gliders bring in two battalions of the 327th Infantry and miscellaneous small units. General McAuliffe, who had been in command of the glider formation, gave me a hair-raising account of his ride in a glider towed by a plane that had been badly shot up enroute and he made it quite clear that henceforth I could count on him as a parachutist but not as a gliderman. To feel really conspicuous, there is no better way than to ride a glider over enemy-held territory in daylight.

Later in the day, British engineers preceding the main column arrived at Zon and repaired the bridge during the night. At daylight on September 19, D+2, the first tanks of the British Guards Armored Division crossed the canal just twenty-four hours behind schedule. They reached Nijmegen later in the day but could not cross the Waal bridge, still defended on the north bank until September 23. By that time the gallant British parachutists at Arnhem had been badly cut up by German panzer units which, undiscovered by Allied intelligence, had been resting and refitting in the area. After a bloody fight, they obliged the British to withdraw from the vicinity of the Arnhem bridge and to abandon the effort to hold a bridgehead there. Thus, in the end, Market-Garden accomplished everything except victory at the critical point.

The operations of the 101st Airborne Division in defending its sector of the Eindhoven-Arnhem highway resembled nothing so much as the operations of the U.S. Cavalry in defending the railroads as they pushed westward through Indian country. Our task was to keep the Germans from cutting this road which was the lifeline of the Second Army. The fulfillment of the mission called for highly mobile operations by task forces put together quickly to counter the recurrent German thrusts from the flanks of the highway. Such attacks were frequent and came with little warning in spite of the intelligence work of the Dutch underground. Successively Zon, Best, Veghel, and Uden became the scene of heavy fighting, but the road was cut only twice in this period and then only for a few hours.

In such fighting there were no safe rear areas; everyone was in the front line. The second day in Zon, a group of German tanks appeared outside the Division Command Post and knocked down the steeple of the church, which collapsed on my empty bedding roll in the room which the hospitable priest had lent me on D day. Lieutenant Colonel Roger Parkinson, the Division Ordnance Officer, was killed at close range in the Division rear Command Post at St. Oedenrode. It was a rough school of warfare which taught even the small units that they must expect the enemy at any time from any direction. It also gave an opportunity to young commanders to display and develop their tactical skill in virtually independent operations. Lieutenant Colonels Julian Ewell and Harry Kinnard of the 501st, both to become lieutenant generals in the Vietnam war, gave particularly brilliant demonstrations of tactical versatility in leading their battalions in the combats around Veghel.

By the end of September the Germans had moved away from the flanks of the highway in our initial sector so that early in October we leapfrogged up the road to the island between the Waal and the Rhine north of Nijmegen. This was the so-called polder country, marshy fields with the water level only a few inches below the surface, incapable of bearing heavy vehicles and impossible for the digging of entrenchments which filled immediately with ground water. All vehicular traffic had to stay on the roads where they were exposed targets to the many artillery batteries which the Germans had deployed on the north bank of the Rhine.

The campaign on the island was a muddy, inglorious defensive conducted under the constant observation and guns of the enemy. Losses were high for the results obtained. One particularly sad loss was that of Colonel Howard Johnson, commanding the 501st Parachute Infantry. "Skeets" as everyone called him, was a military anomaly, an Annapolis graduate in the parachute infantry. His courage in battle was legendary, but it was this virtue carried to excess that contributed to his untimely death. He always refused to take cover when the German shells began to fall and eventually, on October 7, one came over which, in soldier language, had his number on it.

In a unit such as the 101st, it was a constant task to impress on the officers the folly, indeed the unfairness, of unnecessarily exposing themselves to enemy fire. The strength of a fighting outfit is the mutual respect of all its members of whatever rank. Shared danger breeds admiration for the hardy, utter intolerance for the weak, and a fierce loyalty to comrades. Students of military history have often tried to determine why some men fight well and others run away. It never seemed to me that ideological motives or political or moral concepts had much to do with it. If I could get any of my men to discuss a matter so personal as their honest reaction to combat, they would tell me that they fought, though admittedly scared, because "I couldn't let the other boys down" or "I couldn't look chicken before 'Dog Company'." These are simple reasons for simple virtues in simple men whom it is an ennobling privilege to command. For their officers, that privilege carries with it the responsibility to stay alive and look after them. This was a sound precept but one hard to impress on the officers of the 101st who, like their men, didn't want to "look chicken." By ducking shamelessly for shelter at the warning whine of any incoming round, I tried to convince them that taking cover was not "chicken." But I never converted Skeets.

Upon making contact with the British ground forces on D day, the Division became part of Lieutenant General Sir Miles Dempsey's Second Army but, by the nature of the combat along the highway, we pursued a fairly independent existence, unbothered by superior commanders as long as the highway stayed open. In the Nijmegen area, we were in the heart of the British Army, a division of Lieutenant General Horrock's XXX Corps. The British treated us with the utmost consideration and soon we were enjoying the best of both worlds, American rations and British rum. The experience gave me the opportunity to compare differing national ways of exercising command. In planning operations, for example, I was struck by the contrast between the relations of the commanding general of a British division with his corps commander and analogous relations in our army. At the usual morning conference of division commanders, the British corps commander would ask what each of us would suggest for his division to do on the following day. If an offer of some activity was forthcoming, it was accepted with little discussion but apparently there were no hard feelings the next day if some obstacle had arisen and nothing had taken place. After working for such driving U.S. Corps commanders as "Lightening" Joe Collins and Matt Ridgway, I was not accustomed to such gentleness and really didn't care for it.

Throughout October we had some very sharp defensive actions on the island but, by the end of the month, the attacks died down and left us only the rain to contend with. In this period I saw my first jet fighter, a German plane which flew over our positions so rapidly that its bombs exploded before we heard the roar of its motors. Also, our night observers reported one of the first V-2 firings on England, apparently launched from a site just north of the Rhine. The first report made me suspect the sobriety of the observer, but about the same time higher headquarters informed us that these new terror weapons were falling in the London area.

The war in the shadow of the dikes allowed us ample opportunity to apply our skills at patrolling in unusual terrain. I have always felt that the patrol record of a division is one of the best indices of its fighting edge because patrolling, particularly at night, is a stern test of small unit leadership and performance. The information obtained by patrols is usually the most valuable that a commander can get on the immediate tactical situation and hence is worth the price which bold patrolling often entails.

In Normandy we had stressed deep patrols south of the beachhead and often gave rewards for notable performance in such currencies as liberated cognac and future recreation passes to stir up interregimental competition. We continued this practice in Holland where some of the patrolling feats were truly spectacular, none more so than one conducted in late October by Lieutenant Hugo Sims of the 501st. It was a carefully planned six-man patrol with the mission of crossing the Rhine in rubber boats under cover of darkness, working its way about six miles inland to the Arnhem-Utrecht highway and there calling down artillery fire on targets in the vicinity during the hours of daylight of the following day. At darkness Sims and his men were to seize a passing German truck, pick up a prisoner or two, and drive boldly back to the river where his rescue boats would be waiting. After the event Sims' story was related in detail by an American magazine under the title, "The Incredible Patrol." It was indeed incredible because when Sims and his men arrived safely back at their boats, they had with them thirty-two prisoners, all of whom were then ferried safely into our lines on the south bank.

A somewhat similar episode in October was the rescue of 138 British parachutists, survivors of the Arnhem battle, along with four American pilots. From the Dutch underground we had learned of the presence of these men in hiding since the Arnhem battle among the farms and villages on the north bank. With the Dutch we worked out a plan to get boats across the Rhine to rendezvous with the survivors at a prearranged point. The operation was carried out without a hitch on the night of October 22–23, to the great credit of all concerned.

Few decorations are worn with greater pride than the Purple Heart, awarded to men who have been wounded in action against an enemy. I suppose that most soldiers would like to earn one but fervently hope that the price won't be too high. I got mine with shameful ease on November 9 under somewhat embarrassing circumstances.

During the Arnhem operation, General Ridgway was in the unhappy position of a corps commander with no divisions to command since his 82d and 101st had been lent to the British. Early in November he paid a visit to both divisions and inspected their positions. In my sector one stop was at a mortar observation post in the belfry of a church which just peered over the dike of the Rhine downstream from Arnhem.

Ridgway and I climbed a ladder inside the tower to the belfry, spoke to the sergeant observer there, and looked over the landscape on the German side of the river. Then Ridgway turned to the sergeant and at length asked him to put a mortar concentration on a point of woods a few hundred yards away on the German side. The sergeant, unperturbed, cranked his field telephone and spoke to someone at the mortar position in the fields behind the church. "Joe," he said, "remember the dead horse we used as an aiming point yesterday? This target is about fifty over and 100 left. Ten rounds when you're ready." The rounds were in the air almost at once, and their accuracy was impeccable; but I was far from happy about the way my sergeant had shortcut the standard methods of adjusting fire as prescribed in the mortar manual. Although an artilleryman and not the expert on infantry weapons which Ridgway was, I was sure the "dead-horse" method of adjustment was not in the book.

A couple of days later, I returned alone to the church tower and chided the sergeant a bit for not abiding by standard techniques of fire in the presence of the Corps Commander. Then I picked a new target across the river and told him to adjust on it by strictly orthodox methods. The sergeant protested feebly that the Germans had several roving guns on the other side that day and that we were likely to stir them up, but I brushed the objection aside and told him to get on with the adjustment. This time there was no quick flight of projectiles to target but a long tedious shifting of individual rounds right and left, over and short. In the midst of the adjustment, a self-propelled gun began firing at our tower, but the rounds bounced off the heavy masonry without causing damage.

When the sergeant had finally got his rounds on target and I had commended to him a thorough review of the mortar manual, I climbed down the ladder and into the courtyard just in time to rendezvous with a small German shell which exploded a few yards away, raising a cloud of dust and sending me rolling with a small fragment lodged in the *sitzplatz*. When I opened my eyes, there was my bug-eyed sergeant hanging out the window of the belfry calling to his telephone operator, "Joe, I think the Krauts got the old man in the tail." That is how I got my Purple Heart.

After dusting off my dignity, I drove first to a nearby aid station, then to Division Headquarters to make sure that no exaggerated report of my injury got out over the communications net. Then, after lunch, I went to our evacuation hospital by way of the Nijmegen Bridge with the warning sign put up by the British, "Bridge under fire. Get mobile." There Lieutenant Colonel Wallace Graham, after the war President Truman's White House physician, extracted an embarrassingly small shell fragment from a hip. Regardless of its size, the medicos insisted on assigning me as an outpatient to a large hospital in Reims which was conveniently near to Camp Mourmelon to which the Division was about to withdraw.

At Mourmelon, advance parties from the Division were already at work when I arrived preparing for the arrival of the units from Holland. After a short convalescence, I moved to camp where I was received most courteously by the French commandant whom I was replacing. He was an elderly, retired brigadier general who went to great pains in showing me the training facilities and explaining the administrative operation of the camp. When he was about to take his leave, he explained that he had a single request of the incoming American commander. He was quite proud of the *maison de tolérance* which he had established just outside the camp for the solace of his French soldiers. The girls had been carefully chosen, and their behavior had always been above reproach. He sincerely hoped that I would view their activities with a benevolent eye and see that no harm befell them.

I was obliged to explain that what he asked was not in accord with American military practice and could not be granted. I might have added that General Eisenhower had recently been under fire back home for allegedly being soft on prostitution and that this was hardly the time for a division commander to sponsor a *maison de tolérance* whatever the quality of the inmates. So I was obliged to turn down my French colleague who departed sorrowing at this uncivilized reaction to a thoroughly humane request.

The airborne divisions were wonderful in combat but hard to handle when the fighting stopped. The 82d had also returned from Holland and was billeted on the opposite side of Reims from the 101st. Off duty, the men of the two divisions met on the streets of the city and resumed their former arguments at varying levels of intensity as to which division was the better. They also showed a similar, if competitive, appreciation for French girls and wine.

As the only senior French-speaking officer in the two divisions, it fell frequently to me to go into Reims and placate the mayor and his officials after some particularly flagrant act of troop unruliness. I remember one occasion when, in response to instructions from General Ridgway, I went to see the major about excesses of attention displayed by some of our soldiers for the ladies of Reims. I found the Hotel de Ville in an uproar and the mayor really upset. The situation had become so intolerable that, in his words, the virgins of Reims were no longer safe on the streets because the persistent parachutists would not take "no" for an answer—they even struck reluctant ones on the nose.

I expressed my sense of humiliation if indeed American soldiers had been guilty of such conduct and asked if there were any of the victims to whom I might make formal apology. "Oh yes," he said, "they are in a ward in the city hospital." So off we went to the hospital and down the corridors to the door of a small room which the mayor threw open the door with a dramatic flourish exclaiming, "*Voilà les vierges de Reims!*" There were only three to be sure, but they all had bloody noses. So I apologized profoundly and slipped away, hoping without much confidence that the culprits had been from the 82d, not the 101st.

An important task in Mourmelon was to prepare after-action reports on the operations in Holland and identify the lessons which we had learned. In general I had been quite satisfied with the performance of the Division, indeed, of the entire airborne operation. I felt that the failure to achieve the Rhine bridgehead was due to causes largely beyond the control of the airborne forces. The critical fault had been in the concept of an army attack on a front measured by the width of one road. Even if the British ground commanders had driven northward with the ardor of a Patton, that single road would have presented most serious logistical difficulties to sustained operations. As it turned out, it was the slowness of the ground advance and the bad luck of the British Airborne Division in landing among unreported German armored units that were the immediate causes of the failure at Arnhem. However, Market-Garden, in driving a deep salient into the German front which liberated much of Holland, gave evidence of the effectiveness of airborne troops in surprise attacks of strategic dimensions.

CHAPTER 7

From the Bulge to Berchtesgaden

Early in December I was ordered back to Washington to represent the XVIII Airborne Corps in discussions taking place regarding changes in the organization and equipment of the airborne divisions. Ever since the employment of the 82d in Sicily, it had been apparent that many changes were necessary in the structure of the airborne division to take into account battle experience which now included that of the Holland campaign. On December 5 I took off with my aide, Captain Thomas White, flying by way of Scotland to Washington where I arrived the following day. There I paid calls on Secretary of War Stimson and General Marshall and then plunged into a round of conferences. I had little difficulty with the General Staff in getting the desired changes in the airborne organization, primarily because General Marshall had passed the word that the division commanders in combat should get what they wanted.

With this matter out of the way, at General Marshall's direction I made a tour of inspection of a number of airborne installations and looked at some of the new airborne equipment under development. The latter included the first of the recoilless 75 mm. guns, new types of winter clothing, and the new airborne transport plane which the Fairchild Company was building in Hagerstown. I also paid a visit to the 13th Airborne Division in North Carolina which was just finishing its training prior to going to Europe.

In the midst of my travels, the local press began to carry reports of a new German offensive in the region of the Ardennes in Belgium, but, as they seemed exaggerated, I paid little attention. I had returned from Holland impressed by the comparatively low quality of most of the German units we had encountered and the evidence of poor morale and loss of fighting edge in the Wehrmacht. But on the morning of December 21, an official announcement from Washington that a heavy attack was in full swing brought me hurrying back to the Pentagon. There on the situation map in the Operations Division was the blue symbol of the 101st Airborne Division in the center of the Belgian town of Bastogne, surrounded by a sea of hostile red symbols. Everyone in the Pentagon seemed to know all about its plight except its division commander who knew nothing.

I was rapidly brought up to date by the staff, who described the breakthrough into the Ardennes and the critical situation created for General Middleton's VIII Corps. This crisis had led to the decision to commit to action the two airborne divisions resting in Mourmelon a hundred miles away, their hurried movement by truck into Belgium on December 18, and their entry into combat on December 19, just in time to check the advancing German columns.

The mission of the 101st was to hold the key road junction of Bastogne without which the German advance to the west would be critically restricted. Arriving in darkness, Brigadier General Tony McAuliffe, in command in my absence, had deployed the infantry regiments to cover the principal routes of approach and ordered Colonel Ewell, now commanding the 501st Parachute Infantry, to advance to contact with the Germans and, in the language of the staff manual, to "develop the situation."

The situation, as it shortly unfolded, became very critical but by December 21, when I was being briefed, the Division now reinforced with numerous units of artillery and armor seemed solidly established on its defensive positions. However, during the previous evening, it had become completely encircled as the Germans surged westward on both sides of Bastogne. At this critical juncture I found myself much like General Sheridan at the start of the battle of Winchester, except that I was more than a hundred times farther from the battlefield where I belonged.

I went at once to General Marshall, gave him a quick oral report of my recent travels, and asked his permission to return to Europe at once. He agreed, but the weather decreed otherwise. The same foul weather which had controlled the timing of the German attack in Belgium now blanketed the entire northern Atlantic, causing all planes to be grounded for four miserable days during which I could do nothing but watch the Battle of the Bulge from the Pentagon. On the morning of December 24 I was told that the first plane since the advent of bad weather was leaving that evening—it was a cargo plane but did I want a ride? There was nothing I wanted more, so I called my aide, Tom White, who was visiting his family in Boston, told him the plan of departure, and returned home to pack and help my wife prepare for Christmas. After the Christmas tree was decorated and the presents laid around it, I took leave of the bravest soldier in the Taylor family, to whom this book is dedicated, and drove to Andrews Air

Force Base outside of Washington where the cargo plane awaited. White and I climbed in among the crates and boxes and we were finally off.

It was undoubtedly the longest flight across the Atlantic since Lindbergh's. Clock time was against us as we flew east so that Christmas Day was passed in the air and we did not reach Orly airport outside Paris until December 26. Once on the ground, I jumped into a waiting sedan and drove to General Eisenhower's headquarters on the edge of Versailles. At the entrance, although wearing the uniform of an American major general, I was obliged to show my identification tags before being admitted. This was my first intimation of the extent of the parachutist scare which by then extended from the Bulge to Paris.

This scare was the doing of my old adversary, Lieutenant Colonel von der Heydte, who as commander of the 6th Parachute Infantry had faced our Division in Normandy. It was to him that Hitler had given the task of organizing on short notice a parachute drop ahead of the German forces driving into the Bulge. Since their costly victory on Crete, the Germans had attempted no further parachute operations and had allowed their parachute units to become ordinary infantry which merely preserved the names of former airborne units. So von der Heydte had few veterans to call upon for his mission and was reduced to using troops with little or no parachute training. The Luftwaffe was equally unprepared to provide pilots with troop carrier experience. Nevertheless von der Heydte put together a ramshackle task force which, after many tribulations, executed its jump mission in the darkness and snow of the early morning of December 17.

The drop was widely scattered and von der Heydte never assembled more than a few hundred men. He accomplished very little in a direct military sense but rumor, inflated by the extensive use of dummy parachutists, magnified their strength, stimulated fruitless diversions of American units to round up nonexistent parachutists, and caused soldiers and civilians deep in France to look under their beds at night for concealed parachutists.

As von der Heydte was reaching the end of his rope, he sent his American prisoners into the Allied lines on the north face of the Bulge along with several of his own wounded. Thinking he was facing the 101st, (actually he faced the 82d), he addressed me the following message written in pencil on a German army field message blank:

> North of Mont Rigi
> December 17, 16:00 hours

General Taylor
Commander of the 101st Airborne Division

General:
    Herewith I send you six American soldiers whom we have taken prisoner and several of my regiment wounded in the jump. You will remember me; at

Carentan and in Holland I fought against you. At Carentan you demanded my surrender. I now beg you to take as good care of my wounded as you know my regiment did of the wounded of your division.

With highest respect,

Baron von der Heydte
Lieutenant Colonel commanding
a parachute regiment

I never met von der Heydte until after the war when I ran into him by chance at an industrial conference in Chicago. By that time, he had become a professor in one of the great German universities and looked far more the scholar than the ubiquitous parachute leader who upset the sleep of so many that cold December.

Once inside the Headquarters, I went to see my old friend Bedell Smith, Ike's Chief of Staff. He quickly vetoed my request for an airplane to parachute into Bastogne, assuring me that a detachment of the 4th Armored Division had broken through the German lines and had made contact with the 101st that day. He added that the American armor was evacuating the many wounded in Bastogne whose care had been a primary concern of General McAuliffe from the start of the battle. Smith had nothing but highest praise for the Division whose gallantry at Bastogne was by now public knowledge world-wide as was Tony McAuliffe's monosyllabic reply, "Nuts," to the German commander who had asked for the surrender of the town.

After calling on General Smith, I left the headquarters at once and drove to Mourmelon to pick up my battle gear and see my new Chief of Staff, Mike Michaelis. Mike, who had been commanding the 502d Parachute Infantry until seriously wounded in Holland, had just returned to duty after a period of hospitalization in England. Rather than send him back to the physically strenuous life of a troop commander, I made him Chief of Staff, a position made vacant by the death of Bud Millener during my absence.

Intending to leave the next morning for the front, I reached Mourmelon at about 7:00 P.M., was briefed on the local situation, and went to bed. But, unable to sleep, I woke up Tom White and my driver, Charles Kartas, and took off by sedan in the middle of the night for Belgium. It was a long drive, enlivened during the hours of darkness by occasional shots from trigger-happy rear area soldiers still watching for German parachutists. In Luxemburg I called on Generals Bradley and Patton both of whom were confident that the German drive was stalling and described plans for a counterattack against the flanks of the Bulge.

Leaving Luxemburg by jeep, I drove north through Arlon to the sector of the 4th Armored Division which had broken through to Bastogne the

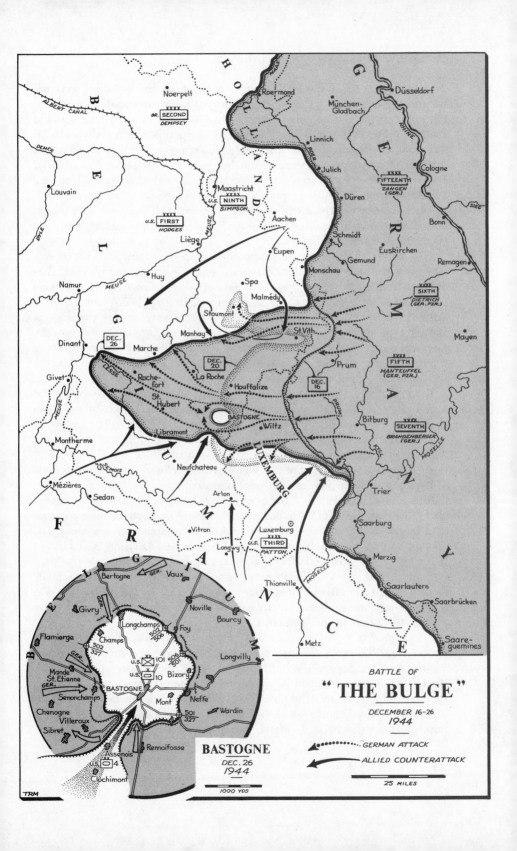

BATTLE OF

"THE BULGE"

DECEMBER 16-26
1944

••••••► GERMAN ATTACK

━━━► ALLIED COUNTERATTACK

25 MILES

BASTOGNE

DEC. 26
1944

1000 YDS

previous day, and at the headquarters of the lead unit obtained information on the current situation and the state of the road ahead. I found that the tanks of the 4th Armored Division had withdrawn from Bastogne but that the road via Assenois was believed to be open. My armored friends offered me a tank to ride into town but, preferring mobility to protection, I decided to stay with my jeep. At our last stop before making the dash for Bastogne, there were three war correspondents warming themselves at a stove in a front line billet. I pointed to the vacant seat in my jeep and offered to take one of them with me into Bastogne. All declined with thanks and thereby lost a headline story on what was, for the moment, the most spectacular episode of the war.

The run up the Assenois road was little more than a mile. While it was littered with the debris of yesterday's combat, the burned-out hulls of tanks and charred truck bodies, there was now only light firing in the woods on either side but still enough to discourage loitering. We knew we were safely home when we ran into a group of 101st engineers at the edge of Bastogne picking up supplies which had been parachuted that day into the Division sector. They gave us directions to the Division Command Post in the center of town which we reached at 4:10 P.M., December 27, just as the winter darkness fell on the snow-covered Ardennes.

In the command post, McAuliffe and the division staff had assembled for a predinner drink. In the course of a hilarious reunion, I described to them the reaction of the outside world to the defense of Bastogne. They were incredulous when I told them they were heroes and indignant when they learned that they had been "rescued." The attitude of the Division had been expressed the first day the German lines closed around the town—"They've got us surrounded, the poor bastards!"

After dinner, McAuliffe went over the situation of the Division, emphasizing the confidence of all hands and the lack of concern for their conspicuous isolation. The strength of the Division less attachments was about 700 officers and 9,500 men. Thanks to the 4th Armored Division, ammunition had been replenished and all the wounded evacuated. While only one road was open, that was a lot better than none. I radioed III Corps Headquarters, to which the Division was then assigned, that the 101st Airborne was ready to join the offensive operations which I expected to begin shortly against the flanks of the German salient.

It was good to be home again. The two great disappointments of the war for me were the cancelled airborne assault on Rome and my absence during the first ten days of the battle of Bastogne. But my disappointment in the latter case was softened by deep pride in the performance of the Division and happiness over the belated recognition of an outstanding soldier, Tony McAuliffe. Unfortunately, because of his new fame, we were soon to lose him from the 101st. In Paris, Bedell Smith had promised me to give him the next division command available and it was forthcoming a few days later. He left us in early January, following a dinner at which we solemnly presented him with a pair of leggings to replace the parachute boots which symbolized the Airborne he was leaving.

I spent the next three days going over the defenses and talking to commanders. The positions of the frontline units were generally strong with good fields of fire and favorable observation. The town itself was a hub of the principal roads traversing the southern Ardennes, one which the Germans badly needed as they drove west and again as they began to withdraw. But now it was too late for them to take it. With four infantry regiments solidly installed on the access routes, supported by elements of the 9th and 10th Armored Divisions, and several extra battalions of artillery, Bastogne was not for taking. Instead it had become a counterbulge into the German south flank and a potential base of departure for attacks against it.

Weather was in many ways more formidable than the enemy. The skies were heavily overcast most of the time, making friendly air support uncertain. But this did not prevent the German bombers from operating freely at night, and because of its prominence as a road junction, they found Bastogne with little difficulty. The shortness of daylight and the haze, which hovered over the fields of snow, limited visibility favorable to combat from about eight in the morning to four in the afternoon. About one hour of this daylight at the end of the afternoon had to be set aside to allow our soldiers to dig in and button up for the night. The ground was frozen so hard that the infantry often had to get help from the engineers to dynamite cavities to serve as foxholes.

I soon found that the battle had not ended with the opening of the Assenois road; in fact, the heaviest fighting at Bastogne took place just after the turn of the New Year. It began on January 3, following a warning order from VIII Corps to prepare to attack to the northeast in conjunction with a general offensive by Patton's Third Army to cut off the base of the Bulge. This order led us to initiate a number of local attacks along our front to improve our readiness to participate in this offensive. Simultaneously, the German high command ordered new attacks on Bastogne from the northeast, north, and northwest. The result was a series of sharp contacts as opposing columns encountered each other at close range in the snow and fog. Fortunately, our troops were usually operating on known terrain and they inflicted heavy casualties on the Germans, whose frozen dead soon littered the fields like snow-covered logs.

On the northern face of our defenses, the Germans were strong in tanks whereas our airborne troops were weak in antitank weapons. Nevertheless, the infantry of the 502d manning that sector stood their ground and proved their ability to pass the sternest test demanded of a soldier in combat—to stay in a foxhole while an enemy tank runs over it and then attack it from

103

the rear. Bazookas and grenades disposed of some of the tanks; most of the others fell to the heavy guns of our tanks and tank-destroyers which were rushed to the scene of action.

On the following day, January 4, it was the sector of the 327th Glider Infantry which was the focal point of action as the enemy, beaten off elsewhere, attacked the northwestern face of our perimeter. Here again the enemy was thrown back to end two days of fighting in which, for the first time since the beginning of the battle of Bastogne, the Germans had displayed an ability to mount simultaneous attacks in different places. Had they done so in the early days before we were solidly dug in, the outcome might have been different.

Elsewhere, the American counteroffensive had bogged down and the order for us to pass to the offensive never came. I took advantage of the lull to move the Division Command Post from the barracks in the middle of town, where it had been located since the arrival of the Division. I had never liked this location as tanks moving through town tore up our wire lines and the German bomber pilots had visited it so often that they could find it in their sleep. Early in the month, I had set up a tactical command post in the small chateau belonging to the Baroness Greindl, a little over a mile to the southwest of Bastogne. Up to that time it had been the command post of a front line company of the 327th. Although only a few hundred yards from the enemy and therefore often under mortar fire, it was far more quiet at night and its communications less susceptible to interruption than the bull's eye in the center of Bastogne. So I decided to move all the remaining elements to Isle-le-Pré at the extreme southwest of the Division sector. This decision was accelerated after German long range artillery had greeted a visit of the VIII Corps Commander, Lieutenant General Troy Middleton, with a surprise concentration which killed several men and wounded others.

On January 9 and 10, the Division prepared again to support a counteroffensive against the south face of the Bulge. However, after two days of bitter fighting in the ever-present cold and snow, the attack was again called off, by Army headquarters this time because of a German threat developing to the south in the Saarbrücken area. The offensive finally got off on January 13, with the Division attacking to the northeast, and continued unbroken until successfully completed on January 17. By this time, U.S. armored forces on the north and south flanks had joined hands north of Bastogne and the Bulge was eliminated. On the same day, the 101st took its final objective, Bourcy, the dominant terrain feature to the northeast of Bastogne, an operation which for us ended the Battle of the Bulge.

After Bastogne, the rest of the war was anticlimactic for the 101st. Hitler had lost his last good divisions in the Bulge and never put up another real fight on the western front. As a result, our final contributions were limited to two periods on the defensive west of the Rhine followed by a drive across southern Germany to the purported National Redoubt area in the vicinity of Berchtesgaden. The first defensive sector was in Alsace near Hochfelden which we held from January 26 to February 25. Here military action was limited largely to aggressive patrolling across the Moder River while we were absorbing recruits who were arriving in large numbers to fill the losses suffered at Bastogne and retraining the infantry units which by this time comprised almost one-third new men with no battle experience.

In contrast to the infantry divisions which rarely got out of action and which therefore had little opportunity to refit and retrain, the 101st as an airborne division was more fortunate throughout the war. In each of our major campaigns, Normandy, Holland, and Bastogne, we lost about a third of our combat strength in the course of very intensive fighting. After each campaign, however, we had an opportunity for retraining, twice in England and now in Alsace. As a result, in spite of the many magnificent soldiers whom we lost in action, I never felt that the Division ever lost its sharpness. Much of this sustained combat readiness resulted from the careful attention we paid to the new men who joined us.

A recruit arriving in a new unit feels lonely, homesick, and insecure. Someone has to welcome him when he arrives and make him understand that he is truly wanted. That responsibility is shared by every officer in the channel of command, beginning with the division commander. I made it a point to try to meet every new soldier joining the Division, usually assembling them in small groups for a handshake and an informal talk. A standard question for a new man was why he had volunteered for parachuting and whether he enjoyed it. On one occasion, a bright-eyed recruit startled me by replying to the latter question with a resounding "No, sir." "Why then, if you don't like jumping did you volunteer to be a parachutist?" I asked. "Sir, I like to be with people who *do* like to jump," was the reply. I shook his hand vigorously and assured him that there were at least two of us of the same mind in the Division.

At the end of February, the Division moved back to Mourmelon to prepare for further combat and to receive the first Presidential Distinguished Unit Citation ever awarded to an entire division for gallantry in action. This was our reward for the defense of Bastogne, presented on March 15, by General Eisenhower in the presence of high U.S. and British officers on the review field at Mourmelon. It was a proud day.

Earlier in the month, I had been a bystander to an incident which controlled the course of the last months of the war. On the evening of March 7, General Eisenhower had invited Ridgway, Gavin, and me to dinner at his advanced headquarters in Reims. In the course of the dinner, an aide came in and whispered to our host that he was wanted on the telephone in the next room. I could hear his voice rise as the conversation progressed but could not get the drift.

When he returned, I had never seen him so radiant. "That was Brad [Bradley] and you know what, he's got a bridge across the Rhine. And he apologized for it, said it was badly located at Remagen and asked what should he do about it? I told him to throw across as many divisions as he could lay his hands on." So the Rhine, the last barrier protecting Hitler's Reich which we had fought so hard in vain to breach in Holland was in our hands, the gift of an unwary German engineer detachment which failed to blow the bridge in time.

On April 1 we received another defensive mission, this time along the Rhine opposite Düsseldorf, to assist in sealing off the Ruhr to the west while friendly forces east of the river encircled and occupied it. It called for little military activity beyond patrolling across the Rhine but did give us our first introduction to the problems of military government and the care of displaced persons.

We had scarcely got well settled into our new sector of responsibility when I learned of a plan to move the Division southward to the Seventh Army to join in its advance across Bavaria to the so-called National Redoubt. Whether Hitler ever really intended to make a final stand in the Alps around Berchtesgaden, I have never known; but the Allies took the possibility very seriously in April and May 1945. As a result a force of three divisions was directed to the area. The honor to lead the advance on Berchtesgaden was conceded to General Le Clerc's French Armored Division with General O'Daniel's 3d Infantry Division and the 101st following in second echelon behind Le Clerc. To get into position for the advance, we had to make a long motor march on a mongrel collection of borrowed vehicles and amphibious trucks (DUKW's) from Düsseldorf via Manheim, Ulm and Landsberg to the vicinity of Miesbach southeast of Munich. All along the way east of the Rhine, the roads were jammed by American columns moving east and endless streams of German prisoners shuffling west, tired but most happy to be in American, not Russian hands. Progressively, the Division stretched out from the Rhine into southeastern Bavaria in the column elongated by the effects of inadequate transport and highway bottlenecks.

In the vicinity of Landsberg outside Munich, we saw our first example of a concentration camp and smelled the stench of the prisoner dead, many burned by the guards only a few hours before the arrival of the American troops. In Landsberg was the prison in which Hitler had written *Mein Kampf* in 1924, proclaiming the coming struggle which had just ended for him in the Führer bunker in Berlin.

On May 4 the Division received an order to move on Berchtesgaden behind Le Clerc's tanks sharing the Salzburg autobahn with the 3d Infantry Division. Unfortunately, a bridge was destroyed on our side of the autobahn, so that 3d Division units got into Berchtesgaden ahead of us on the afternoon of May 4, followed by two battalions of the 506th Parachute Infantry. A third battalion of that regiment, contending with broken bridges and light German resistance in the mountains south of the autobahn, pushed its way into town from the west. I heard my last hostile shot of the war with this battalion in a pass a few miles outside of town.

In Berchtesgaden, we found many fires in progress, some the result of a recent Allied bombing of Hitler's headquarters above the town, some set by members of the S.S. garrison as they fled into the mountains, and some caused by the French soldiers, who celebrated their entry into this holy city of the Nazis by emptying their guns into the buildings with the abandon of Hollywood bandits raiding Dodge City. On all sides the Berchtesgaden area was swarming with German fugitives, military and civilian, trying to escape the Russians and now blocked to the west by the advancing American troops. We soon had our hands full, sorting out and disposing of the bigwigs among our prisoners, of whom the most important was Field Marshal Kesselring, the German defender of Italy and Hitler's last Commander in Chief in the West.

Kesselring was captured aboard his command train at Saalfelden south of Berchtesgaden where he surrendered to me on May 10. From there, I took him to Berchtesgaden for safekeeping until instructions could be obtained from Army headquarters in Munich. We put him up in a hotel, the Berchtesgadenerhof, which was promptly besieged by reporters of the American and European press demanding an interview.

After receiving authority from Army headquarters, I arranged a meeting between Kesselring and the press in the lounge of the hotel, putting the Field Marshal at the head of a long table and the press in a cluster at the opposite end. Some refreshments including tea and wine were placed in front of the reporters, and then I explained that Kesselring was ready for questions but that no photographs were to be taken. Thereupon, I sat down with General Higgins behind Kesselring to watch the show.

Kesselring, a disarmingly mild-appearing Luftwaffe officer, somewhat beyond middle age, with a ruddy face and graying hair, was clearly on the spot and knew it. Already the Western press was accusing him of war crimes committed in Italy and what he was about to say in this press conference was sure to be used against him. The very first question asked was: "What did you think of Hitler?" He took a deep breath and replied, "Hitler was the most remarkable historical character I ever knew." I thought that Kesselring, without the protection of the Fifth Amendment, had given about as innocuous a reply as possible, and throughout the interview, he continued to demonstrate deftness in defending himself without antagonizing his questioners.

After the meeting had broken up and the reporters departed, I sent Kesselring in custody back to Army Headquarters in Munich. But the episode did not end there. A few days later a friend in England sent me a clipping from a London daily. It was a picture of Kesselring, apparently flanked by

Generals Higgins and Taylor, with a pile of glasses and bottles in front of the three with the caption "Another back-slapping party with the Nazis." Some unknown reporter had taken an unauthorized photograph from his end of the table which projected the bottles of the reporters to make them appear in front of the Field Marshal and the two American generals. Almost at once inspectors from Army Headquarters descended upon Higgins and me, and I nearly lost my job before I could tell the full story. It was a period in both the United States and the United Kingdom for excoriating senior Allied officers for overconsideration of captured German leaders. Only a few days before a neighboring division commander had allowed himself to be photographed shaking hands with Goering, an imprudence which set off a tremendous outcry at home, where outraged patriots demonstrated the continuing verity of the saying "War hath no fury like a noncombatant." Under the circumstances, I was fortunate in having strong proof of innocence of any Nazi-coddling.

Other prisoners who caused less trouble included General Guderian, the great Panzer leader, short, dark, and full of anecdotes about the war on the Russian front. Like the other German officers with whom I talked, he was unwilling to concede any military virtues to his Soviet opponents beyond their willingness to take enormous losses in mass attacks and to keep coming. Another interesting captive was Lieutenant General Tolsdorf commanding the LXXXII Corps. Noticing that he walked with a limp I asked him how he had acquired it. "From a mortar round of your division at Bastogne" was his reply.

Civilians of note included: Robert Ley, the leader of the Nazi Labor Front; Julius Streicher, the notorious Jew-baiter; and Franz Schwarz, treasurer of the Nazi party. Important in a different way was Eric Kempke, Hitler's chauffeur, who gave the first authentic account of Hitler's last hours in the bunker in Berlin, which, I understand, remains today the best evidence of Hitler's end.

We rounded up not only important people but valuable treasure as well. Shortly after our arrival we found a freight train of about eight box cars on a siding just outside of Berchtesgaden which, when opened, were found to contain paintings and statuary obviously of great value. While we were unloading and storing these art objects, many damaged by bullets fired into the cars by the French, a German informer told us that, a few days prior to our arrival, a similar train had come into town and that he had seen objects carried from it into a nearby air shelter.

The shelter, when examined, appeared completely empty, but engineers tapping on the walls detected hollow sounds in several places which caused them to tear out the concrete. Underneath they found two vaults dripping with moisture which, filled with rich art objects, suggested the caves of Ali Baba and the Forty Thieves. Although some of the paintings and tapestries were already damaged by water, we rescued everything and

108

put our new discoveries with the earlier ones in a Luftwaffe barracks nearby where we could inventory what we had and provide for their security against fire, weather, and theft.

Our cache turned out to be all or most of Goering's Berlin art collection which he had shipped to safety just ahead of the arrival of the Russians. Along with the two trains, he sent his curator and purchasing agent, Walther Andreas Hofer, who with his wife soon made their presence known to us in Berchtesgaden. I put Hofer in charge of cataloging the collection, and he proved most useful since he knew all the pictures and sculptures and where they came from. Most of the famous art galleries of Europe were represented. I supposed that most of the objects were the loot of German conquest, but Hofer insisted that Goering had paid for all of them. If true, one can be reasonably sure that he fixed the price and paid with Nazi marks. In any case, the collection was of enormous value, and I never slept easily until it was evacuated to Munich for disposition by the Allied authorities there.

Very soon a new problem presented itself—the American military tourists who descended on Berchtesgaden like Pharoah's locusts. With the fighting ended, passes to travel about Europe were given freely, and most of the soldiers wanted to see Berchtesgaden. The center of interest was the Ober Salzburg where Hitler had had his famous chalet with the picture window looking up the valley toward Salzburg. It was now a burned-out shell, as were all the other structures in the vicinity, but there were enough interesting remnants in the ruins—Bavarian tile stoves, fragments of glass and furniture—to provide mementos for the early hordes of souvenir hunters. The later ones found only scorched earth.

Above the Ober Salzburg was the Eagle's Nest which most people who had seen it in the movies pictured as Hitler's place for meditating evil. When the Division first arrived, the peak of the Eagle's Nest was covered with snow and the elevator at the bottom of the 500-foot shaft had been put out of action by the departing S.S. troopers. We noted, however, that its switch panel indicated several stops suggesting a number of floors in the shaft above. To get to the top, we had to climb most of the way over the snow but the view of the mountains from the peak was worth the exertion. The Eagle's Nest itself was something of a disappointment for those looking for the ultimate command post of Nazidom. There was really nothing there but a magnificent oval living room covered with a Chinese rug woven to its shape together with limited dining and cooking facilities— apparently a place built for pleasure, not for plotting. We were told that Hitler rarely came here and had not visited it at all in the last six months of the war. There were no lower floors, as one of my officers verified by lowering himself with a flashlight down the elevator cables to the bottom of the shaft.

We never had enough troops to guard all the things that needed protection. We had an area of responsibility about fifty miles square and every-where things of great value were being found daily. One day, driving in my jeep deep in the mountains southwest of town, I noticed the tower of a small *schloss* far up in the hills, half concealed by the trees. I drove up to the door and in my poor German demanded the caretaker to show me inside. To my amazement the place was filled with musical instruments of all types, sizes, and descriptions. It was not surprising that one was Mozart's piano since this turned out to be the Salzburg musical museum, housed in the mountains during the war to escape the Allied bombers.

From May 23 to June 22 I was on leave in the United States. A benevolent War Department had decided that many of its combat generals needed what the soldiers call "R and R," rest and rehabilitation, and while not feeling tired, I welcomed the opportunity to visit my family whom I had seen so little during the past three years. When we got to New York and we were filing into the Waldorf to meet our wives, one of my happy companions observed: "Heroes today. Bums tomorrow." I was often reminded of this bit of philosophy during the "hate-the-brass" period following the war when the senior officers were charged with everything that had happened in the war except the final victory.

At home I learned what I had suspected—that the 101st was earmarked to go to the Pacific at some unspecified time and that we should plan and train accordingly. So upon my return to Europe at the end of June, I made the rounds of all the units telling them all that I could about our probable future. Anticipating their probable lack of enthusiasm for going around the world to another war, I pulled out all the stops in appealing to their pride of unit and trying to stir up enthusiasm for new worlds to conquer. Speaking before one regiment, I ended with the peroration, "We've licked the best that Hitler had in France and Holland and Germany. Now where do we want to go?" Instead of "Japan," as I hoped, they bellowed back as one man, "Home," and then laughed at their discomfited commander who should have known better than to ask such a question.

On July 28 I received a memorable visit from General Marshall who had been attending the Potsdam Conference. In the course of the afternoon he spent with us, he told General Patton and me about the recent explosion of the experimental atom bomb at Alamogordo and the plan for its use against the Japanese "on the first moonlight night in August." He added his estimate that about two bombs would end the war. However, this estimate of future events was apparently not shared by the War Department because a few days later, the Division was ordered to withdraw to the Auxerre region in France as the first leg of its movement to the Far East. We had hardly reached this destination before the Hiroshima bomb exploded, and we were soon celebrating V-J day with our Allies.

My days in Europe with the 101st were nearly at an end. I suddenly received orders relieving me from the Division and assigning me as Superintendent of West Point. On August 22 I took an emotion-laden leave of my troops in a division review at Auxerre. For all their hard-boiled reputation, generals can be terribly sentimental about their units and their men. Standing bareheaded at the foot of the reviewing stand, I received the last salute of these gallant soldiers, their ribbons and streamers recalling our battles together. They had put stars on my shoulders and medals on my chest. I owed my future to them, and I was grateful.

CHAPTER 8

═══

Superintendent of West Point

On September 4, 1945, I became the fortieth Superintendent of West Point, in succession to Major General Francis B. Wilby and the thirty-eight others who had held this position since the Academy was founded in 1802. From their photographs lining the frieze of the Superintendent's office, they seemed to eye the new incumbent in questioning appraisal as I took my seat at their desk. They symbolized the Long Gray Line to whom I was now responsible and by whom I would be held accountable for the stewardship of the Academy. Based upon their record, my tenure of office might last as long as sixteen years as was the case of Colonel Sylvanus Thayer, a distinguished educator, whose enduring contributions earned him the title "Father of the Military Academy." Or it might be as brief as five days as was the case of Major P. G. T. Beauregard, appointed Superintendent by a Southern Secretary of War at the outbreak of the Civil War and quickly relieved upon the latter's departure for the South. In my case, I lasted until January, 1949, a few months more than three years, about an average tour.

Upon assuming command, I received no special instructions or guidance from my military superiors in Washington other than an expression of strong interest on the part of General Eisenhower in the maintenance of the Honor System and in the improvement of the teaching of military leadership. Throughout my tour, I was allowed to conduct the affairs of the Academy with minimum official interference so that, if things went wrong, I had only myself to blame.

During my first year as Superintendent, I set as my primary task a thorough study of the Academy as it was in relation to what it should become in the postwar period. I was particularly interested in ascertaining whether the curriculum was consistent with the principles of a general education or whether a tendency to premature specialization had crept in during the

112

war years. On the military side, I wanted to be sure that we were concentrating our attention on the requirements of leading the civilian soldier rather than the professional enlistee of prewar days.

The statement of the mission of the Academy approved by the War Department was, I thought, an eminently satisfactory expression of what we should try to accomplish. It was to give the cadets a four-year course of undergraduate study designed to develop the qualities and attributes essential to the progressive development of a graduate throughout a lifetime career as an Army officer. The courses of instruction and training were to stress the development of character and integrity, give a balanced and liberal education in the arts and sciences, and provide a broad, basic education rather than develop individual proficiency in the technical duties of junior officers of the various branches of the Army. These professional skills were recognized to be essential, but they should be left to postgraduate schooling following West Point. In other words, the Academy was not to be a trade school producing second lieutenants but a liberal educational institution for developing future military leaders and inculcating in them a dedication to the values proclaimed by its motto, "Duty, Honor, Country." This latter task required that the cadets be reared from a comparatively early age in a military environment where their training could be closely supervised by carefully selected officers who, in their persons, exemplified the values pursued by the Academy.

This statement of mission was our starting point in 1945 as we undertook to extract guidance from the lessons of World War II for the development of the Academy in the postwar years. Fortunately, my predecessor and his associates had anticipated much of the requirement and had already designed a new four-year curriculum to replace the curtailed three-year course of the war years. This curriculum had been approved just as I took command, but I preferred to reopen consideration of it to the extent necessary to assure myself personally of its adequacy. At my recommendation, the Secretary of War invited a board of consultants, headed by Dr. Karl Compton, president of the Massachusetts Institute of Technology (MIT), to visit West Point and assess the new curriculum. Their report, filed in November 1945, commented favorably on the methods of instruction, the equipment of the academic departments, and the composition of the proposed curriculum. It was somewhat critical of the inadequate leisure afforded the cadets and of the weight of the curriculum which should be lightened, the report suggested, by a reduction in the military instruction. Dr. Compton concluded: "Because of the variety of duties which fall to the lot of an Army officer, to provide a foundation of liberal education in the general fundamentals, an enlargement of social vision and a development of cultural appreciation become increasingly the essential mission of the Academy."

I received the recommendations and comments of the board gratefully

113

and drew heavily upon them during the next few years. The academic re-orientation effected in that period was significant but far from revolutionary as it was sometimes described. There was a slight but perceptible shift of emphasis toward the social sciences and humanities at the expense of the mathematical-scientific components of the curriculum. West Point had long since ceased to be essentially an engineering school as it had been in the early nineteenth century, but at engineering flavor still clung to the curriculum until World War II. Now in the postwar period, my colleagues and I took the position that mathematics and science should be taught not to make engineers and technicians but to provide a rigorous mental training for all cadets and to serve as a basis for understanding the applications of technology to the needs of the military profession. We applied a similar test to all other disciplines taught in order to verify their relevance to the whole officer corps rather than to any part.

On the side of the social sciences and humanities, the Academy had made great strides since my cadet and instructor days, largely because of the influence of Colonel Herman Beukema and several other brilliant professors. Shortly after I arrived, Beukema was reinforced in the Social Science Department by a professor of similar stature, Colonel George A. Lincoln, who, like several other new professors appointed following the war, had given up the star of a brigadier general to become a permanent professor with the rank of colonel. Another example was Colonel A. D. Stamps who had built up a dynamic Department of Military History stressing the study of military leadership. To reinforce this field in which General Eisenhower had expressed a personal interest, I directed the establishment of a new course called the Psychology of Military Leadership and staffed it with officers who had been notably successful as leaders in World War II. The decorations on their coats were impressive evidence of their right to teach leadership and induced in the cadets a respectful attention.

Based on my own past experience, I felt that the English Department had always been the weakest in the academic structure. I suspected that the trenchant views of Jefferson Davis on the subject expressed on leaving the post of Secretary of War were still valid: "It has long been the subject of remark that the graduates of the Military Academy whilst occupying first rank as scholars in the exact sciences, were barely mediocre in polite literature. Their official reports frequently exhibit poverty of style." With the pick of our graduates available for assignment as instructors, there had never been a dearth of highly qualified teachers for the undergraduate courses of the Academy, except in English. An inspired English teacher is hard to find in most civilian schools and seemed particularly rare among the graduates of the Military Academy. So I was determined to pay personal attention to the teaching of the subject, first by scrutinizing the selection of the professors of the department and second, by supervising the quality of instruction in the classroom. Moreover, I put the support of my office behind the encouragement of public speaking and debating, knowing from experience the vital importance of easy oral expression for Army officers who spend so much of their career in explaining their profession and justifying its needs to civilian superiors.

As for the task of explaining West Point itself, in my role as spokesman, I devoted much time to developing a lucid answer to the question "Why West Point?" For a national institution then approaching its sesquicentennial year, the Academy was remarkably little known by the nation it served. Or, better said, it was known for wrong or inconsequential things. Its parades of gray-coated cadets resplendent in sword and plume were brilliant spectacles, but they were not West Point. We were proud of our athletes too, and in 1945 boasted the leading college football team of the nation. But athletic prowess also was but one aspect of West Point. What needed better understanding, I thought, was its role as a national institution for training future leaders responsible for our national security.

For this purpose I set about organizing a quiet campaign to answer "Why West Point?" primarily for the benefit of groups with a particular interest in West Point and secondarily for the general public. Without going into its ramifications, I will only say that this activity accounted for much of my time: many banquet speeches, visits to West Point Societies, letters to alumni and parents, appearances before Congressional Committees, and calls on colleges and universities. Feeling that the best justification for West Point was the cadet himself, we encouraged cadets on furlough to accept speaking engagements in their home towns and sent cadet debating teams around the country to participate in intercollegiate tournaments.

Our postwar pre-eminence in athletics was an asset for making West Point better known but it also entailed many headaches for the Superintendent. In the first place, it exposed West Point to the charge of building its football team from draft-dodgers who were protected from the war for three years by their status as cadets. The charge was grossly unfair to most of the cadets and, where true, probably should have been directed less at the cadets than at parents who sought a safe haven for their sons. The lesson to me was that, in time of war, no cadet should be admitted to the Academy without first having served at least a year in the Armed Forces.

Big-time college football as it developed after World War II did not fit readily into the West Point pattern of education. Previously, the team had belonged to the Corps and every cadet was proud of it. Schedules were of reasonable difficulty and length, and gate receipts were a secondary consideration. When I was a cadet, the Army-Notre Dame game was played on the Plain with the spectators seated in temporary stands with no admission charged.

As Superintendent, I found this simplicity long since departed. Schedules were made several years in advance after extensive negotiations. As Superintendent I never saw a game played which had been scheduled during my tenure. The players were heavily burdened by the load of the academic schedule to which was added the need to prepare themselves to face the best teams in the country each Saturday. To utilize every minute of a working day, they followed a schedule quite different from that of other cadets. They practiced as a group, ate as a group, and often studied in groups under cadet tutors who volunteered to help them. This distorted pattern of life isolated the football squad from the rest of the Corps and eventually led to a spiritual alienation which, I am sure, contributed to the tragedy of the cheating scandal a few years later, resulting in the dismissal of virtually the entire football squad. It has always been a cause of deep regret that as Superintendent I did not perceive clearly or soon enough the potentially baneful influence of big-time football on West Point.

For the moment, I was feeling the more immediate consequences of success on the gridiron; the pressure to schedule more teams, to play in postseason bowl games, and to permit our players to travel the football banquet circuit. Our outstanding stars, Blanchard, Davis, and Tucker, were household words across the country and were the idols of the younger generation. I received a sobering reminder of the shadow to which they relegated the Superintendent on the occasion of the visit to West Point of a delegation of prominent New York civic leaders. Upon departure, the head of the delegation called at my office to thank me for the courtesies of the Academy and then, as a final accolade, turned to his young son, aged about twelve, and asked, "Bill don't you want this distinguished General's autograph?" Bill looked me over coldly from head to foot and then replied, "Naw, I want Blanchard's."

I told this story to General Eisenhower when he was about to become President of Columbia University, pointing out the danger of an all-victorious football team if he expected to be number one on the Columbia campus. He had carried on some of his negotiations regarding that position with Columbia trustees including Thomas Watson, Sr., at my house during a June Week visit to West Point in 1947. On the way to graduation parade, he turned to me and said, "Do you know what Tom Watson and those fellows want me to do? Become President of Columbia University! Why I barely got through this place!" I always felt that he took over that position with sincere enthusiasm, expecting to have the opportunity to exercise his remarkable qualities of leadership on the student body of Columbia. I am afraid that he was largely unaware of the nature of the primary duties of a university president with the emphasis on money-raising and administration, or perhaps he hoped to change their nature into something more congenial. In any case, my warning about big-time football may have deterred him from making Columbia a gridiron power.

Although I had had four years as a cadet and five years as an instructor before returning as Superintendent, I had never appreciated the many ad-

116

vantages which West Point enjoyed as an undergraduate college. The most obvious one was that Congress paid the bills both for the Academy and the students. The Superintendent had no fund-raising chores, and no cadet was ever forced out of school for inability to pay tuition and board. Another advantage derived from this financial independence was the ability to afford the small classes of ten to fifteen cadets which had been the instructional unit of the educational system installed by Sylvanus Thayer more than a hundred years before. He had insisted not only on the small unit of instruction but on the importance of close supervision of the daily work of every cadet. This was a luxury requiring many junior instructors which few civilian colleges could afford.

To fill these junior positions, West Point had access to all its young graduates throughout the Army. Professors watched each class closely as it passed through the Academy and earmarked those showing an aptitude for teaching. These they later recalled to the faculty, usually after they had received a year of postgraduate preparation. This reliance on West Point graduates for instructors gave rise to some concern over excessive inbreeding and homogeneity in the faculty and caused me to seek earnestly for qualified teachers from civilian life. While I was fortunate in getting scholars such as Dr. George Stephens and Dr. Russell Alspaugh as professors to lead the English Department, it proved very hard to attract able young teachers for the classrooms. The thought of teaching undergraduate subjects indefinitely at a military school was not appealing to most members of the teaching profession, oriented in general toward postgraduate instruction and research. So in spite of efforts to recruit civilians, we were obliged to continue to depend on young officers for most of our instructors who, I must say, compared very favorably with those whom I observed on my trips through the academic world.

There were many attacks on West Point in the "hate-the-brass" period after the war. Some were directed at the old school tie advantages which allegedly accrued to its graduates and which presumably accounted for the large number of generals drawn from a group constituting only about one percent of the officer corps. This criticism overlooked the fact that most of these generals had been selected by a non-West Pointer, the Chief of Staff, George Marshall. Another charge related to the narrowness of the military mind and its presumed West Point origin. I hoped that our graduates, as military men, had military minds, just as I hoped and expected my lawyer to have a legal mind. As to the quality of their military minds, the record of our graduates in World War II was an adequate testimonial.

A more insidious attack was one which received some support from misguided friends: West Point should be made into a postgraduate school of military specialization. Such a change of the West Point mission would, I felt, be fatal to its historic role as the fountainhead of Army leadership. The quality of that leadership depended upon the preservation of the stan-

117

dards of honor and integrity of the officer corps, which in turn were the values which provided the unifying purpose of a West Point education. Such intangibles can be inculcated only in young men in the formative period of their lives which Thomas Jefferson described as the time of "aptness, docility and emulation of the practices of manhood in which such things [ethical principles] are soonest learned and longest remembered." If the Academy became postgraduate, the students would arrive with their habits and character formed for better or for worse and West Point could do little about changing them.

Fortunately, we were able to stave off the movement to make West Point postgraduate or to make any fundamental changes in its educational objectives. At one time, I was startled to find that General Eisenhower was apparently giving serious attention to one such proposal—to divide the residence of the cadets at West Point and the midshipmen at Annapolis so that a student would spend two years at one school and two at the other. Fortunately, there were so many practical objections to this proposal that it was short-lived. As an example, the facetious question was raised as to what would happen if West Point dismissed the Annapolis star fullback while he was serving his tour in a gray coat? More serious were the possible detrimental effects on undergraduates of changing environmental forces and standards. It was hard for me to believe that a young man would be better prepared for postgraduate civil life by spending two years at Harvard and two at Yale than by four years spent at either one. The argument for unity in undergraduate education was even stronger in the case of the Academies with their intense dedication to implanting a vocation for a single profession, the Army or the Navy.

This matter of inculcating a lasting vocation for the military service was one of my primary interests. The Academy had many assets supporting this purpose: the majestic beauty of its setting on the highlands of the Hudson, the record of accomplishment of its graduates, and the inspiration of the Long Gray Line which one felt everywhere. A Superintendent could do certain things to reinforce these influences; the selection of the officers who serve as living models to the cadets was one. In this period following the war, I must say that West Point had never before had such an assemblage of impressive battle-proved veterans on its faculty, and their influence on the Corps was proportionate to their quality.

The cadets needed to know the officers intimately if the latter were to make their influence felt. I remembered the first visit my mother paid to West Point when I was a cadet. I was to meet her at the visitors' benches following a parade, but as I approached, I saw that she was talking to an officer of the faculty. In fact, she was seated by none other than the Professor of Mathematics, Colonel Charles P. Echols, a horrendous ogre in cadet eyes. So I hid quietly behind a tree until the colonel had departed and then hurried to Mother to reveal his identity. She was totally unimpressed with her narrow escape. "Why, I found him a charming gentleman," she responded. I often told this story to my colleagues in this period and urged them to display their charm with less diffidence to cadets and their families than had Colonel Echols and his contemporaries on the faculty.

To do my part, I concentrated on getting to know the senior cadet officers and the members of the Honor Committee who supervised the working of the Honor System. I felt strongly as did the Commandant of Cadets —first Gerry Higgins of 101st fame, then Colonel Paul Harkins, a former Deputy Chief of Staff to General Patton—that we should give the senior cadet officers as much responsibility as possible for the training and discipline of the Corps. We did so to the full extent possible within the limitations of the time available to the cadet officers. After all, they too had to study and pass examinations. But it was particularly important, I thought, that they have responsibility for the training of the plebes if excesses of upperclass zeal were to be avoided in carrying out this important function.

Over the years the harsh treatment of the entering class had often been an issue of controversy, one difficult to justify to Congressmen, parents, and critics in general. The summer training period immediately following entrance known as "beast barracks" was and is a particularly difficult time for young men suddenly thrown into a strange and seemingly unfriendly environment. The training was intentionally tough to shock the new cadets out of the easy ways of civilian life, to get them quickly on their mental toes, and to harden them physically for the strenuous life of a cadet. It was also designed to instill instant obedience to authority, on the sound principle that no one is entitled to command who has not first learned to obey. This plebe training was largely in the hands of the cadets of the First Class (seniors) under the general supervision of Army officers of the Tactical Department.

It was very easy for hard training to deteriorate into hazing, although for years hazing had been an offense punishable by dismissal. Apart from the effect on the plebes, it would be inexcusable if the authorities at West Point allowed its graduates to acquire methods of command unsuited to the training of the citizen soldiers whom they would lead. For these reasons, I insisted on a complete review of the plebe system, appealing to the senior cadet officers, as MacArthur had to my class twenty-five years before, to root out any practice which could not be directly related to making a better cadet out of the plebes undergoing training. I was fond of quoting the definition of discipline enunciated by a former Superintendent, Major General John M. Schofield of Civil War fame. He said:

> The discipline which makes the soldiers of a free country reliable in battle is not to be gained by harsh or tyrannical treatment. On the contrary, such treatment is far more likely to destroy than to make an Army. It is possible to impart instruction and to give commands in such manner and such a tone of

119

voice to inspire in the soldier no feeling but an intense desire to obey, while the opposite manner and tone of voice cannot fail to excite strong resentment and a desire to disobey.

To reinforce this theme, I brought many leading military figures to the lecture platform to present to the cadets some of the men whose deeds exemplified the right kind of leadership—men like Eisenhower, Arnold, Spatz, Collins, Gruenther, "Wild Bill" Donovan, and many others.

Along with the need to develop the latent qualities of the cadets, particularly the attributes of leadership, there was a concurrent requirement to eliminate the cadets who demonstrated an inability to meet the standards of the Academy. But all such standards must be reasonable and be fairly applied. To verify their continuing validity was another duty of the Superintendent.

Academic failure in any course at the end of a semester had always been cause for dismissal or reversion to the following class. This standard was rarely challenged since failure to pass was a verifiable fact established by the grades a cadet received during the semester or in final examinations. What concerned me was not the academic standards for dismissal but the tendency to increase the academic work load of the cadets and to raise the academic standards for their admission. West Point was having the same difficulty as most other colleges in finding time for all the instruction required for an undergraduate degree within the bounds of a four-year program. Our professors, all perfectionists striving to improve their contribution to cadet education, were always adding something new to their courses, and demanding more instruction time at the expense of the two and a half hours of daily leisure available to a cadet in his seventy-two-hour work week. One of my jobs was to protect the cadets from this well-intentioned overburdening and to adjudicate the competition for their time among the academic and military departments.

Another aspect of this same problem was a growing desire to require candidates for admission to have completed college level courses, particularly in mathematics and the sciences, so that the West Point departments could omit certain elementary courses. Higher entrance requirements of this sort would gain some of the added time the professors were seeking but would violate the long-standing principle that any well-grounded graduate of a good American high school should be able to enter West Point. I felt that this principle was still important both for military and social reasons. And I felt that we should continue to keep West Point within reach of young men without the means to attend a special preparatory school or college. With General Eisenhower in mind, it seemed a reasonable slogan to adopt: "Don't make West Point impossible for a young man with only the background of Abilene High School."

The attrition rate of a West Point class had always been high, 20 to 25

120

percent in four years, the result of academic failures, resignations, and occasional discharges for bad conduct. Yet in spite of this vigorous elimination process, most West Pointers would concede that every graduating class contained a few men who should have not received the diploma of the Academy and the commission of a second lieutenant. Although meeting all the usual standards, they, were known to their classmates and to many of the faculty as lacking in leadership and as poor prospects for the officer corps.

But how could we identify such cases in time to give corrective training or in extreme cases to eliminate them before graduation? In an effort to find an acceptable answer, we set to work devising a system which would carry out an existing War Department regulation permitting the discharge of a cadet for demonstrated inaptitude for the military service. I recognized full well the difficulty of evaluating the potentialities of young men still in the course of development and resolved to move cautiously in this uncertain field. The aptitude system, as eventually approved, emphasized a corrective effort and reserved recourse to dismissal for extremely rare cases of obvious maladjustment. In determining a means for rating a cadet in aptitude, we depended upon his evaluation by the officers nearest him, the judgment of professional psychologists on the faculty, and the appraisal of the cadets in his company. The latter process may suggest a popularity contest, but it is surprisingly simple to answer a question such as: "Out of the twenty members of your class in A Company, whom would you want most to have at your side in battle? Whom the least?"

On the whole, I felt that we made a promising beginning in the research of aptitude for the service, its sources and indicators. The military service is something like the Church; it is not for everyone, only for those with a true vocation. Some may be born with the vocation; others may acquire it through association and training. Some never sense the vision, and if they remain in the service they do so to earn a living and not to realize an aspiration. The Academy has an obligation to protect the government from expending time and money on inferior officer material and to protect the individual from entering a profession in which he is unlikely to be successful or happy. The aptitude system was a beginning in meeting this obligation.

In trying to improve the quality of the West Point product, there is one vital area over which the Superintendent can exercise no control—the selection of candidates for admission. Most of the cadets are nominated by Congressmen, some of whom view this privilege as a patriotic duty, others as a political perquisite. Actually, most Congressmen are very conscientious in checking the quality of the young men whom they nominate and many follow their subsequent careers in the Academy and in the Army with interest and pride. But while the appointment system assures a broad national representation within the Corps—a very important consideration —it surely does not assure that the Corps of Cadets comprises the best qualified young men in the nation who, at any particular moment, wish to make the Army their career. Reform of the selection system offers the most promising avenue I know toward the goal of getting the best heads of young America into the cadet hats of West Point.

I do not suppose any of my predecessors as Superintendent ever left that post with the happy feeling that they had accomplished all that they wanted. Certainly I did not. I had hoped at least to present diplomas to the class of 1949, the class which entered with me in 1945. But General Bradley, now Chief of Staff, thought otherwise. So on January 28, 1949, I turned the Academy over to my successor, Major General Bryant E. Moore, took leave of the Corps, and drove to New York to board an Army transport for my new assignment in Germany.

CHAPTER 9

U.S. Commander, Berlin

My first assignment in Germany was that of Deputy Chief of Staff at the U.S. Army Headquarters in Heidelberg under Lieutenant General Clarence R. Huebner. It was a very desirable post which carried with it a beautiful house overlooking the valley of the Neckar. Shortly before departing for Europe I had received a letter from Lieutenant General Walton H. Walker commanding the Eighth Army in Japan, asking if I would like to become his Chief of Staff. As I had already received my orders to Germany, there could be only one reply; but I was struck by the fact that again either luck or fate appeared to guide me to Europe rather than to Asia. Thus I did not get in on the ground floor of the Korean War but, as in the case of Bastogne, I found subsequently that there was more than enough war to go around for a late comer.

I had only begun to get the grasp of my job in Heidelberg when a series of events occurred which eventually caused the Taylors to move from the Neckar to Berlin. The end of the Berlin blockade on May 12 was followed by a series of administrative changes which ended the postwar military government of West Germany and substituted a civilian High Commission representing the United States, the United Kingdom, and France. General Clay, who had been the American Commander and Military Governor with headquarters in Berlin, retired from the Army covered with honors and John J. McCloy became High Commissioner with his office in Frankfurt.

These changes posed the question of how the Allies would henceforth exert their authority in West Berlin. Although the termination of the blockade had raised high hopes that better days were ahead for the city, the Soviets soon demonstrated that the Cold War was by no means at an end. They began with a series of new harassments directed at the communications between the city and the West which, though less spectacular than the blockade, were nevertheless serious in their effects. They were evidence to the Berliners that the Soviets had not swerved from their long-range goal of extending their control over the entire city and making it the capital of the so-called German Democratic Republic to be set up in the East. In the face of this renewed threat, the question was how best to organize the Allied representation in Berlin to frustrate the Soviet political offensive.

It was in the context of these developments that McCloy asked for my assignment as the senior U.S. representative in the city. I had known McCloy since prewar days, when he was Assistant Secretary of War under Henry L. Stimson, and I welcomed the opportunity to work with him again. In due course, I was relieved from my post in Heidelberg and proceeded to Berlin to set up my new establishment.

Having arrived in Berlin, I drew up a plan for the organization of my office which was eventually called the Headquarters of the U.S. Commander, Berlin, quickly shortened to USCOB. Despite Biblical warnings against serving two masters, USCOB worked concurrently for the High Commissioner and the U.S. Army Commander, Europe. In the first capacity, he was the personal representative of the High Commissioner and exercised general supervision over the State Department contingent in Berlin. In the second, he was a deputy to General Handy, now commanding in Heidelberg, and responsible to him for all American military activities in the city.

In this assignment I was most fortunate both in my American chiefs and in my Allied counterparts as well. The British Commandant in Berlin was Major General Geoffrey Bourne and the French, Major General Jean Ganeval. Both were able and cooperative colleagues who were just as devoted to Free World objectives in Berlin as I. While Washington, London, and Paris were sometimes at odds over Berlin policy, we three rarely differed on matters of substance affecting the city. Our Russian counterpart, a major general who lived in Karlshorst never took his seat in the Kommandatura, the four-power agency established at the end of the war to administer the city. Since 1948 when the Russians withdrew from the Allied Control Authority, the Kommandatura had become in fact a tripartite body dealing only with the government of West Berlin.

The mayor of West Berlin was the doughty Ernst Reuter, a one-time Communist turned Social Democrat and a formidable foe of his erstwhile comrades. In addition to being an able administrator, he was an accomplished orator who could fire his people to heights of enthusiasm or steel them to dogged, sustained resistance at a time when much depended on maintaining the morale of the city. He was an invaluable leader to have at the head of the municipal government at such a time.

During my service as USCOB, I received useful training in the tactics of the Cold War which in Berlin contained all the elements of the global struggle plus a few local variants. In effect, West Berlin was a fortress of the West under constant siege, over a hundred miles within the enemy lines, hopelessly outgunned and outnumbered by the forces which invested it. From a military point of view, it was completely untenable, but no one residing in it, either Allied or German, ever suggested its surrender. Personally, I was completely confident that the Soviets would never risk the consequences of a direct military attack upon the city, but at the same time, I was very conscious of the political, economic, and psychological threats constantly hanging over it.

In the months immediately following my arrival in September 1949, the most pressing problem was the city's economic situation. It had always been bad since the war but had worsened as a result of the Soviet blockade. Unemployment had reached 160,000 at the end of the blockade and rose to nearly 300,000 by the turn of the year. This latter figure represented about 25 percent of the labor force and 15 percent of the total population of the western sectors.

There was no quick or easy remedy for this depression. At the end of the war, the Russians had carried away the best industrial machinery for use in the East. The limited output obtained from what remained was difficult to sell to the West where, since the blockade, businessmen had lost confidence in the ability of the Berliners to deliver under their contracts. The possibility of reversing this downward trend depended upon the Marshall Plan and the ability of Berlin industrialists to use its assistance to good effect. Marshall Plan funds were just beginning to become available in quantity when I arrived, and I was lucky in having an outstanding economist, Howard Jones, on my staff to guide their use. Jones got along well with the Berlin industrialists who were some of the ablest in Europe, representing such former giants as Siemens, Telefunken, and AEG. They knew what needed to be done, and working with Jones, they proceeded to put American funds to work in rebuilding the city's war-ravaged industrial plant.

I derived great pleasure from supervising the economic program and watching the city rise from the rubble of its bombed-out buildings. In my two years as USCOB, I got to know far more about the factories, utilities, transportation system, schools, churches, and labor unions of Berlin than I ever knew about any American city. There was always some new construction project to open or some newly finished one to dedicate and either event called for the presence of the American Commandant as the representative of the Marshall Plan program. Also there were public works projects to help relieve the unemployment, financed in part by the West German government, which provided, rather reluctantly, a considerable annual subsidy to the city.

In Berlin, the Social Democrats were the majority party with the Christian Democrats a close second and the Free German Party a poor third. I got to know the leaders of all three, but because of Mayor Reuter's affiliation, I probably knew more Social Democrats. These I found to be of a different breed from those I had known in the Rhineland and elsewhere in Europe. In Berlin their party supported a strong, militant resistance to Communist encroachments and showed no repugnance for the use of force as required to fend them off.

When the Korean War broke out in the summer of 1950, I was interested in gauging the reaction of my Berlin colleagues to the American response, particularly to President Truman's decision to commit U.S. Army forces to the defense of South Korea. I asked a leader of the Social Democrats what he thought about Truman's action, expecting him, as a member of a traditionally pacifist party, to be somewhat critical of it. To my surprise, he supported it enthusiastically, and when I asked why, he replied, "We Berliners have seen how generous you Americans have been in helping us with your money to rebuild our city. But it is something else when you support your principles not with pancakes (*Pfannkuchen*) but with the lives of your men."

The continuing Cold War brought us Americans very close to the Berliners in the comradeship of the frontline. There was hardly a day when the Soviets or their East German puppets did not perpetrate some unfriendly act designed to harass the West Berliners, undermine their morale, or discredit their western allies. There was an incessant anti-American propaganda campaign, waged largely by the Soviet-controlled Radio Berlin, which sought to convince the West Berliners that their hope of survival was in the East and that the best thing for them was to get the Americans out of their city. The Communists had many ways to bedevil the two million Germans of the western sectors, the most common one being the harassment of rail, truck, and water traffic in and out of the city. In addition, they could stop the elevated railway, which served the entire city, or withhold the electric power produced in East Berlin upon which our side of the city was largely dependent. They could harass the thousands of workers who daily crossed the boundaries between East and West Berlin on their way to work, exacting payments from them in the West Berlin mark which was five times as valuable as the East mark.

The peak of the postblockade harassment was a giant rally by the so-called Free German Youth at Whitsuntide in 1950. It was announced that the rally was to be followed by mass invasion of West Berlin by the 300,-000 youths expected to attend. Although such a reckless provocation seemed highly unlikely, neither the Allied Commandants nor Reuter could fail to take all precautions against it. During the spring we held a series of exercises involving the West Berlin police, two militia battalions organized from among the Berlin unemployed, and the troops of the Allied garrisons. Together we sought to develop techniques for the control of hostile crowds with minimum violence and without resort to firearms. Finding standard military equipment generally ill-suited for the purpose, we developed var-

Maxwell D. Taylor, age 6.

Milton T. Davenport, grandfather of General Taylor, in Confederate uniform.

West Point Yearbook Photo, 1922.

Captain Taylor with Colonel Stilwell and foreign military attachés, Peking, 1937.

Taylor after his first parachute jump at Fort Benning, Georgia, 1943.

Churchill and Taylor visit the 101st Airborne before D day.

General Bradley awards the Distinguished Service Cross to General Taylor, Normandy, June 1944.

Distinguished Service Order from General Montgomery, Normandy, 1944.

Off for Holland, September 17, 1944.

Discussing the Holland campaign with the troops.

Taylor and General McAuliffe at Bastogne, December 1944.

Town Square of Bastogne during the battle.

Generals of the VII Corps review the Division in Bastogne, January 1945. (U.S. Army Signal Corps)

Eisenhower reviews the 101st Airborne following the defense of Bastogne, March 1945. (U.S. Army Signal Corps)

The Eagle's Nest, Hitler's favorite hideout, Berchtesgaden, May 1945. (U.S. Army Signal Corps)

Major General Maxwell Taylor and Brigadier General Gerald J. Higgins with their prisoner, Field Marshal Albert Kesselring, May 1945. (U.S. Army Signal Corps)

Eisenhower reviews Graduation Parade at West Point, 1947.   (U.S. Army
Signal Corps)

The character on the right was the creation of film producer John Farrow as a
practical joke on the Superintendent while making a film at West Point.

General Taylor with his family at West Point: Jack, the General, family
cocker Po, Diddy, Tom.

General Clay dedicates the Freedom Bell in Berlin, October 24, 1950. (U.S. Army)

The Allied Commandants (Tayor, Ganeval, Bourne) and Mayor Reuter, Berlin, 1949. (U.S. Army)

Secretary of State John Dulles receiving a briefing at the 1st ROK Division, August 5, 1953. Present: Army Secretary Stevens, Senator Henry Cabot Lodge, General Taylor. (U.S. Army)

Adlai Stevenson and Taylor ready to fly from Seoul to a U.S. carrier in Sea of Japan, May 19, 1953. (*Look* Magazine)

General Taylor with parents after being sworn in as Army Chief of Staff, June 30, 1955.

General and Mrs. Taylor with Cadet Tom Taylor, 1958. (U.S. Army)

Above: A toast with Sihanouk in Phnom Penh, 1955. (USIS) *Right:* Army Chief of Staff returns to Korea and meets Syngman Rhee, 1957. *Below:* Chiang Kai-shek presents the order of the Cloud and Banner, October 1958.

A tennis game at Fort Myer, Virginia.   (U.S. Army)

ious expedients, such as the use of water cannon, improvised tear gas dispensers, and electrical shortcircuits on our trucks to shock anyone trying to overturn them. But in spite of all our preparations, I was far from relaxed as the day of the rally, May 28, approached. What I feared most was a *levée en masse* on the part of the West Berliners who were quite capable of tearing limb from limb any young Communists rash enough to invade their city.

As is often the case when one is well prepared for trouble, the day of the rally was an anticlimax. At the last minute, the Communist leaders modified their plans to exclude any incursion into the Western sectors and the day passed quietly. In a U.S. Army helicopter, the first ever used in the city, I flew along the boundary between East and West Berlin and watched the youths marching along the East Berlin streets. I must say that they were impressive, not so much by their numbers as by their disciplined goose-stepping to Communist music in much the same way that their fathers had marched for Hitler.

In this period I learned a lot about Cold War planning and the need for the integration of resources of many origins. Our assets in Berlin were not insignificant but, to be effective, they had to be blended together by a single authority for a common purpose. These assets included spiritual elements, such as the unity of purpose of the West Berliners and the Allies and the quality of their joint leadership. There was the growing productivity of the Berlin industry reinforced by Marshall Plan financing. There were military assets represented by the Allied garrisons, limited in size but high in quality, and propaganda resources represented by ten West Berlin newspapers and the powerful radio station RIAS (Radio in the American Sector). The problem of Reuter and the Allied Commandants was to combine these resources in effective, timely programs of action and reaction.

To meet this requirement for integration, we developed the practice of meeting at noon each day usually at the Schoeneberg Rathaus which served as the city hall. Always present were the three Commandants and Mayor Reuter, each of whom usually brought his press officer. As the situation required, we would include the troop commanders, the Chief of Police, the head of RIAS, or selected newspaper editors. The dominant subject of discussion was usually the question of how to respond to the Soviet molestations and propaganda of the past twenty-four hours. These matters were dealt with on the spot. Occasionally, there were longer term projects for which promptness of action was not so important or which required reference to our High Commissioners.

As an example of the latter category, we conceived a project to carry the propaganda war to the enemy by exploiting his sensitivity to the penetration of free thought into Communist territory. Remembering the attraction to the New York public of the Times Square news in lights, I enlisted McCloy's assistance to obtain funds for a somewhat similar news screen overlooking East Berlin at Potsdamer Platz. As we began its construction, the Communist authorities were outraged and made it the target of their bitterest invective, even threatening to shoot down this invasion of their privacy. But it was completed without incident and set in operation under the caption *"Die Freie Presse Meldet"* (The free press reports). The news presented in running lights did nothing more than just that—it reported world events factually and without comment, using the power of the simple truth as a telling anti-Communist weapon.

I would not suggest that the defense of Berlin was a private affair conducted only by us who lived within its walls. We had the powerful backing of the three Western powers, particularly of the United States, and were thus able to do many things for Berlin which were far beyond the capabilities of our local resources. One such project was the installation of the Freedom Bell in the tower of the Schoeneberg Rathaus.

The bell, cast in Croydon, England, by a world-famous bell maker, is a beautiful work of art which has become a symbol of West Berlin, proclaiming in brazen notes the hope of freedom to the captive peoples of the East. But its installation was a chore for the American Commandant who had the responsibility for putting it into its present position at the top of the Rathaus tower. In the first place, there was the problem of moving the bell, which weighed several tons, through Communist territory to West Berlin. It could be transported only on an open flat car of the Reichsbahn so concealment of movement was impossible. The best we could do was to disseminate deceptive routing instructions which we hoped would confuse any Communist ill-doers and then hope for the best. The bell came through safely but certainly not unnoticed, as it was covered with anti-American "Ban the Bomb" inscriptions.

The next matter of concern was to get it suspended in the Rathaus tower, a formidable engineering task, but one well within the capabilities of our Army engineers. The final hurdle was to be sure that it rang at the right time at the dedication rally in the Rathaus square. General Clay, an idol of the West Berlin population, was to make a dedicatory address which was to reach its climax with the first ringing of the Freedom Bell. My job was to be sure it rang when General Clay pressed the button on the podium.

The rest of this tale could probably be used as an example of the military mind preparing for the worst possible case. We first installed and tested an electric circuit which actuated the striking mechanism from General Clay's push button on the podium. But that circuit might fail on D day. So we placed two brawny soldiers equipped with sledge hammers in the tower alongside the bell and connected them with a field telephone located at my seat beside Clay's. If I directed them by telephone, they would beat the bell with their hammers. But what if the telephone circuit failed? For that contingency, we placed a soldier with a red undershirt in a high building across the square. If I waved my handkerchief to him, he would wave his shirt to the tower and the soldiers would then beat the bell.

On the appointed day, the Rathaus square and its environs was a solid mass of cheering humanity. The speaker's stand on the Rathaus steps was filled with leaders of the Western world. Clay made an eloquent address, pressed the button and the voice of the bell rang out to the people behind the Iron Curtain. Thinking of what would have happened if it hadn't rung, I did not regret the excessive precautions.

The importance of Berlin has been described in many figurative terms: as a hot spring preventing the freezing of the Communist lake around it, as a show-window of the West exposing by contrast the bareness of the East or as an escape hatch for the inmates of the concentration camp of East Germany. It was all of these things, but I was also impressed by its role as a peep-hole into the Communist world. Its geographical location gave it enormous value as an intelligence base which the Allies exploited for all it was worth. I never knew exactly how many intelligence services operated in and out of West Berlin, but it would be safe to guess that there were more agents per acre in the town than any other place in the world.

The Soviets and East Germans were, of course, thoroughly aware of these clandestine activities and did what they could to circumvent them. Their counterespionage people engaged in frequent kidnappings in the Western sectors, whisking their victims off into East Berlin where they usually disappeared forever. But despite their great sensitivity to being spied on, the Soviets never interfered seriously with the Potsdam Mission. This mission was a group of American officers living in Potsdam who were accredited to the Soviet Commander in Chief as a liaison mission representing the American Army Commander in Heidelberg. There was a counterpart Soviet Mission stationed in Frankfurt which performed a similar liaison function for the Soviet Commander, and each had the right of free circulation throughout the zone of Germany to which it was accredited.

The American Mission was of great value to us, not so much for the positive as for the negative information which it collected. The greatest military threat to Western Europe was a Soviet surprise attack from East Germany, and such an attack could hardly be mounted without some indication being detected by the Potsdam Mission as it cruised through East Germany. The Russians occasionally barred it from areas being used for maneuvers, but that fact itself was a useful warning of a military concentration which needed watching. I never understood why the Soviets allowed this arrangement to continue, because the intelligence collected by their mission could not have had the same relative value to them as the product of our mission had for us. It may have been that they were not averse to permitting a peek into their rear area which allowed us to see for ourselves that nothing really sinister was taking place and thus to avoid a possible misunderstanding on our part which could have serious consequences.

In February 1951 I was ordered back to Washington for my first tour of duty in the Pentagon. I left Berlin with regret, but it was clear that the defense of the city was a long-term struggle which would never end in my time there. The city, I felt, was making definite progress, but its viability over the long pull would always be dependent on factors which could change with little warning. The first was the morale of the West Berliners themselves, amazingly good during my tour but highly sensitive to signs of wavering on the part of their friends in the West. These friends included their fellow countrymen of West Germany who subsidized the city but could do little to defend them against the threat of military attack. For defense, West Berlin remained dependent on the guarantees of the United States, the United Kingdom, and France, and only the United States had the power in being to give the Communists pause. Here, as in so many other places about the Communist periphery, the survival of a staunch ally depended on the continuing credibility of the American commitment.

CHAPTER 10

With the Eighth Army in Korea

Although I was not aware of its significance at the time, the period in the Pentagon following my return to Washington in February 1951 was in effect preparation for participation in the Korean War as Commander of the Eighth Army. In Washington, I became briefly Assistant Chief of Staff G-3 (operations and training) to General J. Lawton Collins, my former corps commander in Normandy and now Chief of Staff of the Army. This assignment was of short duration as, in August, I was promoted to Deputy Chief of Staff for Operations and Administration with the rank of lieutenant general. In both positions I worked closely with the dynamic Secretary of the Army, Frank Pace, who had been appointed to that position at the age of thirty-eight after serving as Director of the Budget. Teamed with "Lightning Joe" Collins, he provided much of the impetus behind the activities of the Army during the early years of the Korean War.

As was the case for most of the Army staff, Korea at once became my main preoccupation. But it was not until May 1951, nearly a year after the war began, that I could escape from my Pentagon desk long enough to visit that country for the first time since my rapid transit through it in 1937 en route to Peking. This time, my primary purpose was to evaluate the capabilities of the Korean Army about which Washington had many doubts. It had been a dismal disappointment at the outset of the war and had done little to reestablish its reputation among American commanders during the subsequent campaigns from Pusan to the Yalu and back to Seoul. President Rhee was constantly demanding more divisions for his Army, but MacArthur had not been convinced of the feasibility of a major expansion, largely because of the dearth of leadership material. In Wash-

131

ington, the Army staff was unenthusiastic about providing the Koreans with additional quantities of scarce equipment which, judged by past behavior, they might quickly lose to the enemy. American troops in Korea were tired of taking casualties from American weapons captured by the enemy from Korean (ROK) units.

During my visit I found the American commanders confident and in generally good spirits though still a bit shaken by the dismissal of MacArthur in the previous month. But by the time I arrived, the dust had pretty well settled, MacArthur was gone, Ridgway had taken over the United Nations Command, and Lieutenant General James Van Fleet had been put in command of the Eighth Army. When my hosts got away from the subject of these changes and around to talking about my primary interest, the ROK Army, I found that few of the senior officers favored any major increase in its size until it had proved its reliability at its current strength.

It took very little investigation to find out what was wrong with the ROK's. They had been asked to do too difficult things with inadequate training under conditions which would have tested the best troops in the world. Recruits who only a few weeks earlier had been working in the rice paddies and had never seen a gun were being thrown into intense combat with results that could be expected. The unrelenting pressure of combat with one crisis following another had prevented the institution of a methodical training program up to this point, although the American commanders were thoroughly aware of the need of one.

I returned to the Pentagon convinced that we had to work harder at building up the Korean Army if we were ever to extricate ourselves militarily from Korea. We had to stop reproaching the "gooks," the disparaging *nom de guerre* given our allies by many Americans, for misbehavior in battle until we had given them a preparation for the ordeal which at least approximated that of their American comrades. We had to learn to utilize this Korean manpower to defend Korea. To say that it could not be done was simply not acceptable.

When I made my report to Secretary Pace and General Collins I found that I was preaching to men long since convinced of the need for a boldly conceived expansion of the Korean forces. It was hard to set a goal in numbers for their ultimate strength until we had more experience with the training problem, but as an initial goal a balanced ten division force seemed quite ambitious for an army which, at the start of the war, had consisted of eight weak divisions totaling fewer than 100,000 men. So that figure was taken with the understanding that it would be raised as progress warranted and, as a matter of fact, by 1953 it reached twenty divisions.

Frank Pace, having identified me as an officer who in the past had participated in the operational activities of the Army without having to concern himself with such grubby matters as the budget, personnel, procurement, and logistics, made a point of putting my nose to the administrative

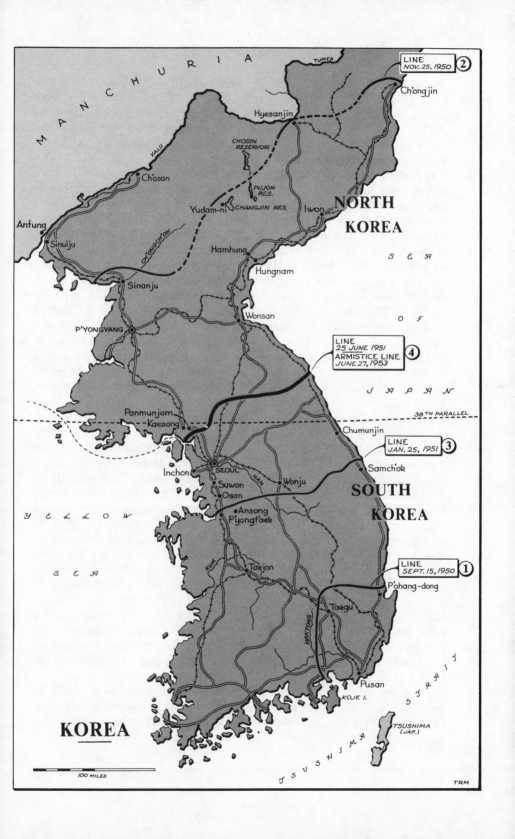

KOREA

grindstone and keeping it there. Although I would not have picked the job, I was grateful for this experience when I became Chief of Staff a few years later. I am convinced that no officer should rise to senior command without having acquired on the way an understanding of the problems at the seat of government related to raising, training, and equipping the forces which he commands.

In seeking background on some of the events of the war which had occurred prior to my return to Washington, I was particularly curious to learn more about two matters. The first was why we had not used atomic weapons in the early days when we were in real danger of being run out of Korea. From my vantage point in Berlin I had expected a mushroom cloud to rise from the battlefield at any moment after the landing of our forces on the peninsula. But I found in Washington that there had been cogent military reasons, apart from political, for having withheld atomic weapons. In the first place, we had too few of them at that time to risk their expenditure so far from the major threat to our security which, the Joint Chiefs of Staff (JCS) agreed, was in Europe and not on the mainland of Asia. A secondary reason was that the mountainous terrain of Korea would have limited the effectiveness of these weapons which were not designed for such a battlefield. Finally, it was feared that their employment here might reveal shortcomings which would have diminished their deterrent effect elsewhere.

The second question which troubled me was why our forces had crossed the thirty-eighth parallel after the victory at Inchon and marched to defeat on the Yalu. Here the answers I received were less satisfactory. It was clear that the dramatic reversal of our fortunes at Inchon after the dismal retreat to the Pusan perimeter had had an intoxicating effect, not only on American leaders but on our U.N. allies as well. After the Inchon victory MacArthur could do no wrong, and nobody in Washington was prepared to challenge his judgment on matters of strategy. Certainly the JCS, all younger men with far less prestige than the great proconsul, were not inclined to take him on; indeed, as their theater commander they felt it one of their duties to protect him from bureaucratic restraints on his military freedom of action. In such an atmosphere, apparently no one was overly concerned about jettisoning the original war objective of repulsing the North Korean invasion and substituting for it a new and far more ambitious one, the unification of all Korea by force of arms. Washington was certainly not blind to the danger of Chinese intervention, but MacArthur's assurances to President Truman at the Guam meeting on October 15 appear to have quieted most of the audible apprehensions.

There are many controversial aspects about this campaign to the Yalu, some of which may never be completely resolved. The question which intrigues me in particular has been rarely discussed either during the war or after. What would we have done if the march to the Yalu had been successful? MacArthur crossed the thirty-eighth parallel with a directive from the JCS to take as his first objective the destruction of the North Korean forces and, thereafter, the unification of all Korea through democratic elections under the auspices of the United Nations. Let us suppose that he had succeeded in destroying the combat capability of the North Korean forces and the Chinese had not intervened. What would we have done then?

MacArthur at Wake, looking forward to a quick victory, had told President Truman that he hoped to have the Eighth Army back in Japan by Christmas. In this case, he planned to leave in Korea an American corps of two divisions, a force of about the same size as the one which we have maintained in South Korea since the armistice. But the tasks devolving on the half-trained ROK Army and this American contingent would have been enormous. They would have had to defend a hostile frontier of over 400 miles facing superior Chinese, Russian, and North Korean forces and exposed to attacks ranging from harassing raids to a major counteroffensive. In their rear would have been a hostile population containing thousands of Communists and fellow sympathizers capable of providing the manpower for a dangerous guerrilla movement. The setting would have been somewhat analogous to the situation in Vietnam with the Yalu replacing the seventeenth parallel and the problems of Saigon transferred to Seoul on an enlarged scale. One pales to think of what the consequences of such a victory might have been in terms of the duration and cost of American support for its aftermath and I, for one, have always felt appropriately grateful for having been saved from such problems by the Chinese sensitivity, hardly surprising, to the approach of a large hostile force to its borders.

Among other things which I discovered about the war on my return to Washington was that, for the American public, the bloom was undoubtedly off the war. Popular support for Truman's courageous response to the aggression of 1950 had initially been high and had held up surprisingly well during the dark days of the Pusan perimeter. It soared with the Inchon victory but plunged downward following the retreat from the Yalu. When I arrived for duty in the Pentagon, the polls were showing that about half of the citizens interviewed felt that the United States had made a mistake in getting into the Korean War. Concurrently, the President's popularity had dropped to a point where only about a quarter of those polled thought Truman was doing a good job.

By the end of the year, Truman was involved in acrimonious bickering with the Congress over his undeclared war. Senator Robert Taft led the Senate critics of the war, and fellow Republicans gave a sympathetic hearing to disgruntled generals such as MacArthur and Van Fleet, who criticized publicly the constraints placed on the military conduct of the war. The national behavior showed a tendency to premature war-weariness and precipitate disenchantment with a policy which had led to a stalemated war. This experience, if remembered, could have given some warning of dangers ahead to the makers of the subsequent Vietnam policy. Unfortunately, there was no thoroughgoing analysis ever made of the lessons to be learned from Korea, and later policy makers proceeded to repeat many of the same mistakes.

The last serious military activity before the opening of the armistice negotiations occurred in April and May 1951, when the enemy launched a new offensive. The Eighth Army, after halting it, initiated a counteroffensive which slowly pushed the enemy back beyond the thirty-eighth parallel along most of the front. This success caused, or at least contributed to, the timing of the Communist acceptance of armistice negotiations which opened at Kaesong in North Korea on July 10 and later moved to Panmunjom.

The opening of negotiations was hailed in the West as a dramatic step toward peace and created the impression that hostilities would soon end. Military operations gradually died down, although General Van Fleet cried loudly for authority to improve his front line in anticipation of an early cease-fire. But Washington and the general public felt that it was folly to expend lives with peace "just around the corner," so in November, Van Fleet was directed to limit his operations to an active defense of the existing front. This was the beginning of the military stalemate which lasted until the last months of the war in 1953.

In this period I continued to be concerned largely with staff activities related to the expansion of the Korean Army which we could now accelerate because of reduced fighting. Also, I monitored the logistic problems which were arising, particularly the very sensitive matter of the ammunition supply. As the war became the defense of a fortified front, ammunition consumption rates began to rise very sharply, and emergency measures had to be invoked to increase the production rates in our American factories. Orders were placed in Japan to supplement home production. The long pipeline from factory to battery required large stockpiles of each caliber of ammunition on the front, and the flow was never uniform or perfectly adjusted to day-to-day needs. But, although General Van Fleet was never entirely happy with the ammunition situation, I never knew of a case where the supply available was insufficient to support the essential needs of the tactical situation.

The fact was that the efficiency of our artillery techniques, which permitted the rapid massing of dozens of batteries on a single target, encouraged infantry commanders to make exorbitant requests for fire support. It was not uncommon to have all the artillery of a division, about seventy-two guns, available to fire in support of a twelve-man patrol. Eighth Army outposts were constructed with sufficient overhead cover to permit our artillery to fire directly upon them without danger to the defenders inside. Naturally, the latter preferred to button up and to call for the defensive concentrations of the artillery rather than to expose themselves in using their own light weapons. Such tactics undoubtedly saved lives but put an enormous burden on the supply system and, to some unmeasurable extent, adversely affected the self-reliance of the infantry.

As 1952 drew to a close, General Van Fleet indicated a desire to retire. He had chafed under the restrictions placed on offensive operations and insisted that he had been held back from achieving a decisive victory. His chronic unhappiness affected relations with his superior, General Mark Clark, who had succeeded General Ridgway when the latter had moved to Paris to become the commander of the forces of the North Atlantic Treaty Organization in Europe. Hence, his request to retire occasioned no surprise.

I was surprised, however, when I was selected to succeed him as I had had no prior indication that I was next in line for the assignment. Naturally, I was delighted to get this field command even though the defensive strategy to which the Eighth Army was condemned was no more appealing to me than it had been to Van Fleet.

At the same time, I was not inclined to dispute the correctness of this defensive strategy at the stage of the war at which I took command. Our unwillingness to keep military pressure on the enemy during negotiations had been a mistake, I was sure, but by 1953 it was an established policy, and it was too late to try to change. The cost of attempting a breakthrough of the heavily fortified front facing the Eighth Army was clearly beyond anything the new Eisenhower Administration would or should pay simply to move the line somewhat farther north into Korea. At one time, I estimated that to breach that front would require about eight additional U.S. divisions and a readiness to use tactical nuclear weapons. Beyond that cost, to march to the Yalu again as President Rhee demanded would raise all the former questions of being able to afford this kind of success: the need to garrison heavily the long Manchurian frontier; the troop requirements for occupying North Korea; and the time-consuming difficulties involved in establishing a stable government based on U.N.-supervised elections. Hence, I had no hesitancy in assuring President Eisenhower, Secretary of Defense Wilson, and the other senior officials in Washington, who probed my views before my departure, that I was quite prepared to live with a defensive strategy and not kick against the pricks.

Considering the Administration's passive attitude toward the war in Korea, I was rather taken aback by the aggressiveness of Secretary Dulles' views on the containment of Red China. He described to me a strategy which he viewed as a three-pronged seizure of the dragon, one prong emerging from Korea, another from Taiwan, and the third, I was surprised to learn, from India. The Secretary was not quite clear as to the timing and circumstances of these holding operations, but it was evident that he had activist notions beyond anything I had expected from a senior official of the new Administration.

Having apparently passed the tests in Washington, I departed for the Far East and arrived in Tokyo on January 29, where I was met by my new boss, General Mark Clark. After a few days spent in visiting military installations in Japan I flew to Seoul with General Clark on February 3. En route, I took advantage of a long talk about Korean problems to show him a draft of the mission of the Eighth Army as I understood it. The key paragraphs read as follows:

a. Defend the present line of contact with minimum losses consistent with maintaining the integrity of the position, with obtaining the information necessary for the security of U.N. forces, and with retaining effectiveness for offensive combat.

b. Employ all means at the disposal of the Eighth Army to create a capability for general offensive action by a date to be indicated by the Commander-in-Chief, Far East [Clark]. This action will include the continued development of Korean forces within the limits of approved ceilings, available equipment, and ROK leadership with the ultimate goal of creating a force of approximately twenty divisions. This force should include Korean combat and service support type units, in order to develop a balanced force capable of defending South Korea in the case of U.N. withdrawal.

c. Emphasize troop-leading techniques for the development of an offensive spirit consistent with the requirements of b. above.

General Clark approved this draft which thereafter served as my strategic guidance throughout the time that I commanded the Eighth Army. The date of readiness for a general offensive action was never set, neither by General Clark nor his successor, General Hull.

General Van Fleet met us at the airport in Seoul and installed me in a room in Army Headquarters, which then was occupying buildings of Seoul University. General Clark returned to Tokyo the next day and in preparation for my assumption of command, I began a tour of the front and of the installations in the communication zone reaching down to Pusan. In the course of touring the front, I was impressed with the number of exposed outposts of questionable usefulness and resolved to study at once the possibility of eliminating all or most of them. My tour also reminded me of the size of the Army—almost a million men, if one counted the Korean Service Corps, which provided porter service for the movement of supplies in mountainous areas. This army was deployed over a varied terrain, ranging from rice paddies in the west to mountains in the east and extending about 125 miles from the China Sea to the Sea of Japan. As I looked over its fortifications and dug-in weapons representing countless months of work to construct, and behind this front the farms, cultivated by the Korean divisions to supplement the inadequate Korean Army ration, I wondered if such a vast, entrenched force could ever pull up stakes and pass to mobile, offensive warfare if it had the opportunity. By 1953 position warfare was all the Army knew, and I resolved to shake it up as best I could by repeated training exercises involving changes in the position of units.

The communication zone was a tribute to the logisticians who had laid out and developed the vast complex of depots, supply and communication facilities which supported the life and activities of the fighting front. However, these facilities had been located without concern for possible air attack to which they were most vulnerable, particularly the ports of Pusan and Inchon. A surprise attack upon these ports by a few bombers could have brought the war to a standstill for weeks. This vulnerability put another damper on any enthusiasm for a general ground offensive, or indeed, for the air attack on Chinese targets north of the Yalu. For the moment, there seemed to be a tacit agreement on both sides which permitted our air activities to extend over all North Korea, including the renowned MIG Alley in the northwest corner of the country. So long as our air force stayed within these bounds, the enemy appeared disinclined to undertake air operations in South Korea beyond an occasional nuisance raid into the Seoul-Inchon area by slow propeller aircraft. This arrangement always seemed like a good deal to me, one which should not be disturbed without a truly compelling reason.

My tour of the front gave me my first opportunity to get a good look at the enemy positions facing us. They formed a continuous scar across the landscape from coast to coast, a zone pockmarked with shell and bomb craters testifying to the weight of the firepower on our side. Whereas we put our trenches and observation posts boldly on the tops and forward slopes of the hills, the enemy were obliged to keep most of their positions on reverse slopes on the backside of the hills, through which they dug tunnels to afford apertures looking out on our lines. Through them they observed our activities and fired many of their weapons, including roving artillery pieces. Where the terrain obliged them to live in positions which we could observe, they built many alternate shelters and trenches and moved about frequently to avoid our artillery fire and bombing.

In terms of numbers, the enemy had facing us well over a million men, mostly Chinese veterans except for one North Korean corps, the remnant of the Army defeated at Inchon. Behind the front, they were obliged to commit many more thousands of their men to the service of supply and to the defense of the coasts. They had not forgotten Inchon and had to by ready for another amphibious landing. While they had almost endless reserves of unused manpower in China, I eventually developed a feeling, never substantiated, that their forward deployments represented about the largest force that could be maintained logistically under the difficulties of supply created by our air and artillery interdiction. At the time when I

139

took command, however, there were intelligence reports of a further enemy buildup, and counterpreparations were in progress to meet a renewal of Communist offensive actions.

After a week of touring South Korea from front to rear, on February 11, I relieved General Van Fleet, who promptly retired from active service. A vigorous field commander with a broad experience in training foreign troops, he left his mark on the combat readiness of the Eighth Army, particularly the Korean units. In carrying out the expanded training program begun in 1951, Van Fleet had built up the ROK Army to a strength of about half a million men. In addition to their tactical units, the Koreans provided a valuable contribution in the form of three to four Korean riflemen attached to each American infantry squad. Known as the Korean Augmentation to the U.S. Army (KATUSA), they had got off to a bad start in the beginning because of their lack of basic training, but by 1953 they had established their worth in the eyes of most American commanders. American soldiers rotated so rapidly that by the time I took command the only real veterans in the Eighth Army were the KATUSA's who came and stayed for indefinite tours in American units.

In 1951 rotation had been introduced in the American forces to alleviate the inherent unfairness of a limited war which required the participation of only a small part of the national military manpower. From that time on the Eighth Army was never a completely trained fighting force; it was always retraining on the job in the presence of the enemy. Officers and men alike came individually rather than in units and so departed after about one year's service. The Army Commander did not rotate, but everyone around him did. In my twenty-two months in Korea, I had four chiefs of staff, either as the result of rotation or of the need to reward incumbents of that taxing position with the command of a division in the course of their short tour of duty.

Van Fleet had blazed a trail for me in coping with the training problems which I now inherited. I felt no particular concern about being able to deal with such professional matters, but he left me a far more delicate problem in picking up his close relations with President Rhee. Van Fleet had sympathized with Rhee's passionate desire to reunify his country and had shared his low opinion of U.S. and U.N. policy following the retreat from the Yalu. I knew that Rhee regretted Van Fleet's departure and that he suspected me of being a partisan of the Washington policy which he distrusted.

I soon verified his suspicions in the course of the public controversy over the alleged ammunition shortage which Van Fleet stirred up following his retirement. As I was thoroughly familiar with the ammunition situation because of my involvement with it at the Pentagon, I saw no cause for alarm about ammunition and so stated when queried by the press in Seoul. My views did not deter the Congressional critics of the war from siding with

Van Fleet, and as a result, one of my first visitors was Pace's successor, Secretary of the Army Robert T. Stevens. Together with General Clark, we toured the Army front, visiting ammunition depots and discussing the supply situation with commanders. In the end, Stevens was able to return to Washington and state from personal knowledge that there was no ammunition crisis in the Eighth Army.

In the early months of 1953, activity on the front was much the same as it had been since the start of the armistice negotiations, a series of patrol and outpost actions. Even on the defensive, an army must patrol vigorously in order to keep its fingertips on the enemy and avoid being surprised. I found that the Army had been patrolling with a vengeance, sending out several thousand patrols a week along the 125-mile front. But upon examining the product in terms of information obtained and prisoners captured, I found the results very meager. As I looked into how unit commanders prepared patrols for their dangerous missions, I found the reason for the lack of success.

As I had learned in World War II, night patrolling is a stern ordeal which demands picked men and meticulous preparation including rehearsals on terrain resembling that to be traversed by the patrol. Also, if the patrol leader can fly over the area in daylight, his task at night becomes much easier. Few, if any, of these things were being done in the Eighth Army, and too many patrols were allowed to follow repeatedly the same route, thereby inviting ambush by the patient Chinese who would lie concealed for days waiting for an unwary patrol. To improve quality at the expense of quantity, I directed all units of the Army to take greater pains in preparing patrols and to hold a careful post-mortem after each one to discover what had gone well or badly.

To emphasize the Army Commander's personal interest in patrolling, I established the practice of bringing the leaders of important patrols to Army Headquarters to describe their actions to me and my staff after the event. Although I was told that some of them found the appearance at headquarters a greater ordeal than the patrol itself, this evidence of interest in patrolling soon raised the quality of the product and at the same time the after-action reports of the leaders reminded us at headquarters of the hazards we were asking our men to run to obtain information for us.

I have mentioned the apparently excessive number of outposts in front of the main battle position outposts which invited and often received enemy attacks. An outpost in front of a position may serve one of several purposes: to give warning of an enemy approach, to slow down an enemy who approaches, or to defend a terrain feature which is important to the defense of the main battle position. I initiated a study of all our outposts to verify their importance in serving any or all of these purposes and to oblige local commanders to decide in cold blood in advance of an attack which outposts were in the third category and thus presumably warranted

141

a counterattack if taken. I wanted to have very few of the latter because of the heavy cost of retaking a lost position.

Toward the end of March, before we could complete the survey of the outposts, the issue involved was brought home vividly by a heavy attack on outposts Old Baldy and Pork Chop on the front of the U.S. 7th Division. The action raged for five days on and around these two relatively unimportant positions. But the battle itself soon made them important, and every soldier lost added to that importance and made their successful defense a matter of unit pride. Learning that the 7th Division Commander, Major General Trudeau, and the Corps Commander, Lieutenant General Kendall, were preparing a counterattack after Baldy had been partially overrun, I went forward to the site, discussed all aspects of the proposed counterattack with the commanders, decided it was not worth the likely cost, and called it off. The 7th Division had already lost about 300 men although it had imposed many more casualties on the enemy. I was glad to take the responsibility for the decision and relieve the unit commanders from seeming to accept defeat, a bitter pill for proud soldiers like these.

These engagements proved to be only the first of a number of attacks on outposts on the front manned by American and Commonwealth troops, most of which were beaten off but usually only after very intensive fighting. It was a characteristic of this period that whereas the rest of the front might remain completely peaceful a local action of the highest intensity could flare up for a few days at almost any exposed outpost. The enemy seemed to be probing to find a soft spot along the front against which to mount a major attack.

Meanwhile some progress was being made in the negotiations at Panmunjom. Agreement was finally reached on the exchange of sick and wounded prisoners which began on April 20 under the name of "Little Switch." When it came to an end on May 3, the United Nations Command had turned over to the enemy 6,670 patients and had received 684 sick and wounded in return. The success of the operation justified some optimism with regard to overcoming the last major obstacle in the armistice negotiations, the disposal of the remaining prisoners of war. For the time being, negotiations were deadlocked by our insistence on no forced repatriation of prisoners, an issue which had resulted in an interruption of the talks from October 1952 until they were resumed during "Little Switch."

If this indication of progress was welcome to the United Nations Command, it was just the opposite to President Rhee. From the outset of the armistice talks, Rhee had bitterly opposed any compromise settlement which would leave his country divided. He knew that he had only few years to live and that he would never again have such military power in his country to impose its unification and was determined not to let the opportunity escape. He agitated vigorously and publicly against the negotiations, hinted broadly that his government would not be bound by the terms of any armistice, and floated rumors that he might withdraw ROK forces from the operational control of the United Nations Command if the latter persisted in negotiating away the integrity of his country.

Rhee was known to be a major political problem long before I got to Korea, and upon my arrival I found that one of my major tasks was to keep him reasonably tractable. I cultivated his acquaintance in every way I could and made it a practice to invite him to all the important events affecting the training and expansion of the Korean Army. He appreciated this consideration and never seemed more happy than when presenting the Korean colors to a new unit of his Army.

I found him a very appealing old man and became genuinely fond of him. He was a curious mixture of an Old Testament prophet defying the devil and all his works, and a shrewd Oriental politician, wise in the ways of the West where he had received much of his education. He knew how to play on the heartstrings of the American officials who visited him, often posing as a confused old man, devoted to his country but needing help to lead his people out of the wilderness. To win sympathy, he could pretend to have trouble with the English language (which he spoke almost perfectly) and to suffer from physical infirmities which vanished when he took off with me on a strenuous tour of the front. He could quote passages of the Bible meekly to his purpose and then turn with a snarl to damn his enemies with unrestrained passion.

During operations, he was a great help to me in dealing with Korean commanders. When we visited a unit in action, he always wanted to know who of the senior officers had done well, who had done badly, and then praised or chided them accordingly. He was deeply respected by his young generals, but many were afraid that he would do something rash which would cause the withdrawal of American support from the Korean Army. They knew well the limitations of their own forces without American help and worried that Rhee might carry out his threats to go it alone in a march north.

I enjoyed traveling about the country with Rhee and watching the popular reaction to his presence. In the villages, the elders in their white robes would welcome him, and he would chat benevolently with them, asking about local problems just as any American politician might do on a visit to his constituents. At some point, one of the elders would usually bring out a white scroll and the brush and ink of the Oriental calligrapher. Rhee was famous throughout the world of the Chinese character for the quality of his calligraphy, which even to my foreign eye had a vigor and balance with a sensible aesthetic appeal. Placing the scroll on the table and taking brush in hand, Rhee would hesitate a moment, choose a Confucian text to inscribe, and then paint the complex Chinese characters in a vertical column without the slightest guideline to assist in spacing and aligning them. He gave me such a scroll upon my departure from Korea, the characters of which translate roughly to: "Wisdom, courage, virtue—100 battles, 100 victories." What better motto for a soldier?

For all his charm, Rhee was not above using me for his political purposes. On our trips together, whenever the opportunity presented itself to harangue his fellow citizens on the wickedness of an armistice, he would guide me to a seat on the platform alongside the podium while he took off violently against the folly of my bosses in the United Nations Command, to the warm applause of the audience. To avoid being photographed absentmindedly applauding an assault on the policy of my country and its allies, I took a Korean aide along to nudge me whenever Rhee said something which it was impolitic to applaud.

After the resumption of armistice talks on April 26, Rhee's apprehensions rose, leading him to inform General Clark that he positively would not turn over North Korean prisoners to the enemy if they did not wish repatriation. Nor would he allow a member of the proposed Indian Custodial Force, which was to supervise the prisoner-of-war exchange, to set foot on Korean soil. Indians, he insisted, were Communists in disguise. Both Clark and I were quite sympathetic on the first point but dead against his obvious desire to upset the negotiations and to nullify the long, exhausting efforts to get an armistice which would end the fighting on terms which would protect the prisoners who refused repatriation.

Every device conceivable was tried to placate the old warrior, including a personal letter from President Eisenhower which General Clark and Ambassador Ellis Briggs presented on May 25. But while it offered assurances of continued U.S. support for South Korea, it did not propose a bilateral treaty and hence completely failed to satisfy Rhee. In early June President Eisenhower tried once more to soften him by another personal letter, but still to no avail. Thereafter his campaign against the armistice reached a new level of intensity, with many shrill threats to march north (*Puk chin*), to release the non-Communist prisoners of war threatened with involuntary repatriation, and to use force to deny entry to the Indian Custodial Forces.

Throughout this troubled period I worked closely with Clark and Briggs in trying to bring Rhee around. On June 9 I had a session with him in which I found an argument which seemed to impress him. I urged that an armistice and the proposed political conference to follow it had the advantage of gaining time for the training of his army and its expansion to the ultimate goal of twenty divisions. I emphasized the unreadiness for combat of many of his divisions and the impossibility of accomplishing anything like *Puk chin* through their unaided efforts. He seemed to yield to the argument and moderated his demands to four points which appeared within the range of compromise: the limitation of the postarmistice political talks to sixty days, a bilateral security treaty with the United States, the expansion of the Army to twenty divisions, and the barring of the Indians from

South Korea. I felt that the United Nations Command could probably meet these points but Rhee was careful to say that he was not ready to take a final position.

While the assurance of Rhee's cooperation in carrying out an armistice was the most immediate problem, the Eighth Army still had an enemy to fight who did not allow himself to be forgotten. Probably because they considered an armistice to be near, the Communists began a new series of attacks directed mostly against Korean units in the II ROK Corps sector east of Kumhwa. On June 10 three Korean divisions, the 5th, 8th, and 9th, came under heavy attack and in the course of a week fell back slowly to prepared positions some 3,000 meters to the rear. Casualties were high, over 7,000 on our side and probably at least as many for the enemy. This action turned out to be the first phase of one of the biggest battles of the entire war, the Kumsong salient.

The II ROK Corps commander was Lieutenant General Chung Il Kwon, later to become Chief of Staff of the ROK Army and in 1970 Prime Minister. When the battle started he was suffering from a heavy cold, but he quickly threw off his aches and pains when the magnitude of the enemy attack became apparent. To give him every assistance, I lent him for use as a deputy corps commander Major General Samuel T. Williams, known throughout the Army under the sinister sobriquet of "Hangin' Sam," then commanding the U.S. 25th Infantry Division. He was an old friend from Leavenworth days for whose professional judgment and experience I had the highest regard. He and Chung turned out to be a most effective team in fighting the battle of the Kumsong salient.

I took another step to bolster the high command of the corps. At that time, the highest reward for a ROK general was to be sent to Leavenworth to attend a special course for foreign officers. It happened that when the Kumsong battle began three former ROK division commanders were in Seoul about to leave for the States to attend the course. I called them to my office, told them an attack was on and that Leavenworth was off until the situation at the front was restored. Then I sent them back to General Chung for combat assignments, feeling sure that at least three of his divisions would do their best to end the threat in the shortest possible time.

The situation stabilized on June 18, but just as the enemy became quiet President Rhee opened a second front. On that very day, at his order, some 25,000 Korean prisoners of war who had refused repatriation to the north were released from their stockades, and the fat was in the fire. Washington was aghast at Rhee's perfidy, our allies were reproachful of the American leadership which had permitted the thing to happen, and the Communists at Panmunjom enjoyed a field day in castigating the United Nations representatives as collaborators with Rhee in the jailbreak. Privately, they showed genuine anxiety over our ability to carry out the terms of an armistice in the face of Rhee's intransigence.

While Clark, Briggs, and our negotiators tried to pick up the broken crockery and arrive at some kind of understanding with Rhee, the enemy resumed his offensive. This time he chose the mountains east of Kumwha and selected outposts farther to the west. The pressure built up rather gradually, reaching high points in attacks against outposts Arrowhead and Pork Chop in late June and early July. Arrowhead was held, but the cost of continuing to defend Pork Chop became so prohibitive under the massed Chinese attacks that I authorized its evacuation.

The center of gravity of operations then swung back to the Kumsong area which, we now know, had always been the sector where the enemy planned to stage his final prearmistice show. We had ample warning, not in the specifics of time and place, but we had sufficient intelligence that a major blow was impending to be fully on the alert. It fell on July 13, a well-coordinated attack by elements of five Chinese armies against the front of five Korean divisions, most of which had been engaged in the earlier phase of the Kumsong battle. By the morning of July 14, the position of the Capitol and 3d Divisions was so deeply penetrated that I ordered all five divisions to fall back behind the Kumsong River which I had planned to hold in case of a major attack on the salient.

It was a difficult operation to carry out—a daylight withdrawal under heavy pressure by troops unaccustomed to mobile operations. Fortunately, we had the 3d U.S. Division and the 11th ROK Division available in reserve to backstop the withdrawal in case it should get out of hand. It turned out that they were needed, because some of the retreating units passed beyond the Kumsong River line and had to be stopped and reformed on a new line south of the position along the river.

On July 15 enemy pressure slackened as the result of heavy casualties and lack of transport so that, on the following day, I ordered the II Corps to counterattack and restore the position along the Kumsong. It took four days to do so, but on July 20 the corps again reached the line of the river; the front was stabilized, and the battle of Kumsong salient was over.

In a sense the battle had been a graduation exercise for the ROK Army which had demonstrated its ability to recover from a heavy blow and come back fighting. At the same time it reminded Rhee of the formidable strength which the enemy had built up during the long haggling over the armistice, and it certainly convinced his commanders of their inability to break through to the north on their own. Although I had had many anxious moments while maneuvering the Army reserves to support the II Korean Corps, I never had any doubt about defeating this last hurrah of the enemy. It was, however, a sobering experience to observe the willingness of the Chinese to expend their lives in great numbers right up to the last day of this bloody war.

While the Army was struggling with the enemy on the battlefield, General Clark was still laboring mightily to regain control of our cantankerous ally, President Rhee. In this task he received a reinforcement in the Assistant Secretary of State for Far Eastern Affairs, Walter S. Robertson, whom President Eisenhower sent to help persuade Rhee. While Robertson worked on Rhee, Clark, armed with authority to wind up the armistice in spite of Rhee, undertook to convey to senior Korean commanders the thought that America's patience with Rhee was nearly exhausted. To show we were in earnest we reduced the flow of supplies to Korean forces, particularly ammunition and petroleum products, to a trickle and held back deliveries of equipment for the expansion of the ROK Army. I went about reminding Korean generals of the dependence of their country and their Army on the Americans and the uncertainty of that support if Rhee continued his resistance to the armistice. To reinforce the point further, I held a press conference to express in public my confidence that the United Nations forces could extricate themselves from the conflict without too much trouble if the ROK's should decide to continue the war alone. I must say that I was glad never to have been required to make good on that statement; it would have been a tricky operation.

In the end Rhee compromised, and on July 12 he gave Robertson written assurance that he would not obstruct the implementation of the terms of the armistice, although he still had grave concern over its consequences. In exchange, he received a number of important concessions from us: the promise of a bilateral security pact, of long-term economic aid, and of continued support for the twenty division program; also, an understanding that the United States and South Korea would withdraw from the postarmistice political conference after ninety days if no substantial progress had been made by that time.

With Rhee quieted and the Kumsong battle terminated, there were no further important obstacles to concluding the armistice. A final arrangement for the exchange of prisoners was worked out on the principle of no involuntary repatriation. In Panmunjom, at 10:00 A.M. on July 27, Generals William K. Harrison and Nam Il, the chief negotiators of two sides, signed the armistice which was countersigned by General Clark that afternoon at Munsan-ni in a ceremony which I attended with other senior officers of the United Nations Command. At ten o'clock that night the artillery fire of the Eighth Army, which had risen in a crescendo as the hour approached, abruptly ceased and the shooting war was over.

The next morning at daylight I set out in my helicopter from the western end of the front and flew down the center of the no-man's-land which separated the two armies. The Communist troops were already out in force, standing on their battered hilltops, waving flags and banners bearing Communist slogans and shouting songs of defiance and victory. They had prepared for this day for months, intent upon impressing the world that they

147

were the victors and we the vanquished—a reminder that for them the conflict had not ended with the shooting. Our men watched this propaganda display in silence, merely glad that the ordeal of battle was over.

CHAPTER 11

Postarmistice Korea

The termination of hostilities presented me with a whole new set of problems which could be summarized by one question: what to do with an army of almost a million men with no enemy to fight? I knew the dangers of idleness and boredom and in anticipation had drawn up a long list of useful activities to occupy the troops. Now was the time to set about them.

In the first place, there was work to be done arising from the implementation of the armistice. There were camps to be built for the returning prisoners and arrangements to make for transporting to Taiwan the Chinese prisoners who refused repatriation. The exchange of prisoners took place between August 5 and September 6 during which time the United Nations Command returned about 75,000 to the enemy and received back some 12,000. My old friend General William Dean, who had commanded the U.S. 24th Division in 1950 and had been captured in the first days of the war, was one of the last to return. I met him at Munsan-ni and took him to Army Headquarters for dinner, hoping to effect some decompression of the emotions of a man who had been in virtually solitary confinement for two years. Throughout the evening Bill, normally a relatively taciturn man, never stopped talking in his enjoyment of conversing with friends in the English tongue.

Another consequence of the armistice was a need to resite our defensive positions in compliance with the requirement to establish a 4,000-meter demilitarized zone between the opposing forces. This was a Herculean task, requiring endless thousands of man-hours of work in surveying and constructing new fortifications often in very mountainous terrain. Fortunately, we had helicopters to assist us in getting the heavy timbers for the bunkers from the valley roads to the crests where they were needed. For the senior

149

officers, it was a useful professional exercise in field engineering and in the tactics of organizing a defensive zone which, in the end, resulted in a much stronger position than the one upon which we had ended the war.

In this postarmistice period, we worked hard not only at improving our military position but our environment and ourselves. Throughout the countryside in which our troops lived were the débris of war—destroyed villages, damaged public works, homeless farmers, jobless wounded. With time on their hands, American soldiers began to look about and take an interest in the unhappy lot of their Korean neighbors. On their own initiative, prompted only by a desire to help the unfortunate, they banded together in joint enterprises with local communities to do simple things like repairing a culvert or cleaning out an irrigation ditch. This spontaneous help-your-neighbor movement suggested to me the possibility of a large-scale project, country-wide in scope, which could give effective expression to this humanitarian impulse.

I found an ally for this project in Dr. John A. Hannah, the Assistant Secretary of Defense for Manpower who, before entering government, had been President of Michigan State University. He visited Korea in late August, and I had the opportunity to show him some of the troop activities in community aid. He was quick to sense the possibilities of this kind of thing and offered to help in Washington in obtaining support for an army-wide program. I countered by asking authority to divert up to $15 million in military supplies and materials and to use Army engineering equipment for constructing approved projects to assist the people of Korea. My thought was that the Army would provide the heavy construction equipment, the materials which were not locally available, the skilled labor, and the supervisory personnel. The community receiving the benefit of a project would provide the land, the local materials, and the unskilled labor. Thanks to Dr. Hannah's assistance, I received approval of this program in November at which time it was formally launched under the title Armed Forces Assistance to Korea (AFAK).

The AFAK program was initially an American project, but soon the ROK and U.N. forces became anxious to take part. My staff set up a procedure for allocating resources to troop units anywhere in South Korea. Soon most of the country was covered with AFAK areas which proceeded to sprout new schools, churches, orphanages, dispensaries, and irrigation systems. Villages were restored and often were named after the troop unit responsible for them. It was a revelation to see the effect on troop-civilian relations when the men in uniform began to regard the neighboring village as their village to be protected against all comers.

In looking for other useful activities to keep the Army busy, I decided at an early date to take as a goal the elimination of illiteracy from the American troops and to make at least a start on the problem with the Korean soldiers. In examining the educational record of the Americans, I was shocked to find that about 10 percent of the Eighth Army could not produce evidence of having completed four years of grammar school, the bureaucratic minimum criterion for literacy. While the illiteracy average for the American Army world-wide was about 5 percent, the Eighth Army, its cutting edge in contact with the enemy, was forged from men who often could barely read or write. I knew what had happened; the relatively well-educated men had been drained off along the personnel pipeline leading from the training centers in the United States to Korea to provide headquarters personnel, specialists, and technicians at the expense of the quality of the combat units on the front. The armistice lull afforded an opportunity for the Army to attack this problem of illiteracy, using its own resources in its own way.

First, we sorted out and tested our presumed illiterates and were pleased to find that many who had not had four years of schooling could pass the practical literacy tests which we gave them. Self-instruction and the contagious quality of education which rubs off on the unschooled members of a literate society probably accounted for this reduction of numbers. Simultaneously, we inventoried the Army for soldiers qualified to teach, and, thanks to the wide variety of talents found in a citizen army, we never had difficulty in staffing the dozens of literacy schools which we set up throughout the Army. The goal of the instruction was to give all soldiers at least a fourth-grade education and noncommissioned officers an eighth-grade level. I was surprised how many career noncommissioned officers of senior rank needed this instruction. By November 1954 nearly 18,000 soldiers had received schooling and had raised their education level to minimum standards.

Throughout these months, the ROK Army continued to expand in accordance with our agreement with President Rhee. It reached an authorized strength of eighteen divisions at the end of 1953 and twenty in the following year. There was still some uneasiness in Washington about this growth in Korean military strength because of Rhee's continuing threats to march north alone. On a visit to Korea shortly after the armistice, Secretary of State Dulles had asked me what I thought of this threat. I told him that, in my judgment, Rhee's commanders were thoroughly aware of the folly of such an action and, if ordered north, they would merely lean against the northern edge of their foxholes. But I warned that there could be embarrassing incidents; for example, any Korean artilleryman intoxicated with march-north propaganda could pull the lanyard on his artillery piece and cause a serious breach of the armistice. Dulles, impressed by this thought, urged me to keep the ROK Army on a tight leash through control of its ammunition and gasoline, but I was obliged to remind him that there would always be some slack in that leash, represented by the supplies which must always be in the hands of the troops.

I nearly became an embarrassing incident myself and a victim of the excesses of the march-north madness. On a visit to the Korean Second Army Headquarters at Taegu in January 1954 I was receiving a briefing from a senior Korean commander, Lieutenant General Kang Moon Bong, in the presence of a large number of Korean and U.S. officers. In the course of the briefing a side door opened and a young Korean officer slipped into the hall and walked toward the front-row seat which I occupied close to General Kang, the speaker. The intruder had a paper in his hand, and as he headed toward my seat below the podium I remember thinking that he probably had a message for me. Suddenly he stopped a few yards away and whipped out a pistol which he waved menacingly in my direction. For a moment everyone was paralyzed except General Kang, who dropped the pointer which he had been using and leaped on the back of the would-be assailant. Then everyone came to life in a confused mêlée directed at disarming the culprit, who when subdued turned out to be Major Kim Ki Ok, a march-north fanatic. It was with difficulty that I kept him from being beaten to death but I succeeded and exacted a promise from my Korean friends to protect him from summary punishment and to give him due trial. Then we resumed the briefing, General Kang breathless but unruffled.

Although I made every effort to keep this incident quiet, on my return to Seoul, I called on President Rhee and gave him a full account of the abortive assassination. I told him that, in my judgment, Major Kim should not be punished but rather the march-north agitators who had planted the thought in his mind that the Eighth Army commander was a prime obstacle to the unification of his country. Rhee seemed genuinely upset by the incident but while conceding that Major Kim might have wanted to scare me a bit, he refused to believe that any Korean officer would do me harm. I was not amused and told him so.

In the course of building the Korean Army, I had many occasions to reflect on matters of military organization in the light of the lessons drawn from the Korean War. I was convinced that our American triangular division, based on three large infantry regiments, was outmoded and regretted that it was being perpetuated in the new ROK Army. Hoping to interest their senior officers in possible innovations and wishing to experiment for my own purposes, I set aside one of the last Korean divisions to be organized as an experimental division.

During most of 1954, aided by Lieutenant General Bruce Clarke and a number of other senior American officers, I studied several possible organizations, testing each as thoroughly as possible by realistic training exercises. From these experiments we reached certain conclusions with regard to the principles which should guide the restructuring of the infantry division. In the first place, it should be adaptable either to a nonnuclear limited war on the Korean model or to war in a European theater of operations where the use of nuclear weapons might be expected. To have this dual capability, it must be able to disperse into small units capable of independent action and to reassemble swiftly when it was safe to concentrate without danger of attack by nuclear weapons.

Fortunately, this kind of organization had become possible by the improvement in signal communications which now permitted a division commander to control more units than the traditional three regiments. Our Korean tests indicated that the optimum number of subordinate units was about five, a fact which led us to consider a pentagonal rather than a triangular structure for our new division.

In the Korean War, our American divisions had been too heavy in terms of the equipment carried for the kind of fighting which developed. After the stalemate, they were weighted down with tanks, heavy trucks, and amphibious equipment which diverted manpower from combat to their maintenance and repair. I felt that the basic division should be stripped down to the equipment normally required for operations anytime, anywhere. The special needs of specific theaters could be met by the attachment of equipment drawn from central pools for the duration of the requirement.

Finally, we felt that the current American division was short of riflemen, the men who win the battles and pay for victory with their lives. There were too many crew-served weapons of intermittent utility which absorbed manpower needlessly. So I proposed that we get more men out of division rear areas and into the foxholes of the combat infantry.

In dealing with these questions of divisional organization, I was fortunate to have Bruce Clarke as the Deputy Army Commander. In World War II, Clarke had been the very successful commander of an armored division and was known throughout the Army as a profound student of military organization and training. He shared my views, or most of them, as to the needs of a new division, and he reinforced my urging of Korean commanders that they adopt a light division of the kind which we were studying.

In the end we had little success in convincing our Korean friends of the need for changes as radical as the ones which we were contemplating. There seemed to be two causes for their resistance. In the first place, they saw that a light division would have less organic armor and artillery and feared that they would receive fewer of these highly valued weapons from the American military aid program if their division tables of organization did not call for them. In the second place, although the Korean commanders were generals in their thirties who should have been receptive to innovation, they were reluctant to put aside what they had learned about the old triangular division and readjust their tactical thinking to new formations and combinations. I warned them that what I was advocating would probably influence the structure of the new American division, which was sure to be adopted after the Korean War, and that they would be left behind with an outmoded organization. But they stood pat to the end, and politely declined to engage in a program of division modernization.

Meanwhile, as the end of 1954 approached, there were changes for me in the offing. I had received my fourth star in the midst of the Kumsong battle and would have been quite content to remain the Eighth Army Commander indefinitely if I could have brought my family to the Far East. However, I realized that a reunion in Korea would be impossible until the country quieted internally and the armistice had proved viable. But, I did put in a strong plea to General John E. Hull, Mark Clark's successor, to be allowed a home leave as soon as the postarmistice roll-up of surplus forces and supplies was well underway.

The haste with which Washington had begun to reduce the American forces following the armistice was very worrisome. It suggested the stampeded dismantling of our Armed Forces following World War II, which had contributed to the advent of the Cold War and to the necessity to fight in Korea. The first divisions to be sent home were the two federalized National Guard Divisions, the 45th which left in March and the 40th in May. Concurrently, we began to remove excess supplies to the United States and to transfer to the Koreans those stocks necessary for the completion of the twenty-division program. This transfer had to be done cautiously as long as there remained any chance that Rhee might again kick over the traces.

The stocks and reserves of equipment to be removed were enormous and required nearly a year to sort, pack, and evacuate. I was always being surprised by what I found in the supply system and impressed by the thoroughness of the logistical planners who had anticipated our every need. But sometimes their thoroughness startled me. I recall one rainy day dropping in at the big quartermaster depot in Seoul and, with the depot commander, rummaging through the warehouses, marveling at the extent of the inventory. In the corner of one room, I saw a pile of sacks which seemed to smell of tobacco and asked the commander what they contained. "Tobacco stems for our homing pigeons," he replied. "What, do our pigeons smoke?" I inquired. "No," he replied, "but the Quartermaster Department has found that in the mating season homing pigeons like to line their nests with tobacco stems, and, you know, the season opens next week."

I don't know whether I was impressed or frightened by this evidence of long-range logistical planning. I could see somebody's reminder file in a Washington quartermaster office with a note, "Three months to mating season of homing pigeons in Korea." Such a note had set in motion the bags of tobacco stems causing them to arrive just at the right time to bring domestic happiness to our homing pigeons. Never having seen a pigeon in use in the Eighth Army, I wondered what the cost effectiveness analysts would have said about this effort expended on the tobacco stems.

It was not until June 1954 that I felt justified in going on home leave, but when I did, I indulged myself in one lasting over a month. Upon my arrival in Washington, there was the usual round of official calls followed by several days of hard work with the Pentagon staff. The principal subjects for discussion were the ROK Army build up, the roll up of supplies, and the disposition of the residual American forces and installations which were to remain in Korea. By this time, most of the decisions bearing on these matters had been made. One was to assign me to Japan to command all the Army forces in General Hull's Far Eastern Command, which included the corps of two divisions left in Korea.

With most of my official work accomplished, I slipped out of town with Diddy and our son Tom for complete quiet in Castine, Maine, where several West Point professors, old friends of ours, had summer homes. After ten wonderful days of tramping in the woods, tending lobster pots, and dining on their catch, we returned to Washington in time for my departure at the end of the month. Back in Korea, the plans approved in Washington were in full swing, and programs were on schedule. As my task became largely one of supervising their execution, I found that I had more leisure than before and could indulge more in such pastimes as handball, tennis, and Korean lessons. When I first arrived, I had started to work on this difficult language but had had little leisure for it during the shooting war and the turbulent days following the armistice. But I had made some progress, aided by the fact that Korean and Japanese belong to the same family of languages and both had had a similar problem of adapting the Chinese character to a language completely different from Chinese.

Eventually I got to the point of being able to read a speech in Korean and, at the dedication of a new Korean Army headquarters, gave a public performance in the presence of President Rhee. I never did a thing in Korea that pleased the old man more; there is an irresistible flattery on the part of a foreigner who tries hard to speak the local language, whether well or badly does not matter. My Korean aide, Captain Paik, who had been one of my patient tutors, reported proudly that when I began to speak Korean one old woman in the audience burst into tears. My conclusion was that she couldn't stand the slaughter of her native tongue.

When I moved to Japan, I gave up my last field command after nearly two years on the job. While I still commanded from Japan what was left of the Eighth Army, that once great fighting machine—the handiwork of Walker, Ridgway, and Van Fleet before me—was no more. It is true that the command of that great Army had not been the same to me as the command of the 101st Airborne Division in World War II. A division is the largest force in which the commander can get close to his troops and have a feeling of kinship with them. An army is too big for that, particularly the Eighth Army with all of its attachments including the twenty-division Korean Army. In Korea, I dealt primarily with corps and division commanders and only occasionally got down as far as regiments and battalions. My primary concern in the shooting war was with keeping the Army supplied and maneuvering its reserve divisions to forestall and repel enemy attacks. After the shooting stopped, my primary responsibilities involved the implementation of the armistice, the phase-out of the U.S. forces and supplies, the expansion of the Korean Army, and our relations with Rhee. All of these were important and interesting, but they produced none of the emotional involvement which characterized my command of the 101st.

My service in Japan proved to be a rather short postscript to my service in Korea. Shortly after the turn of the year I learned that General Hull was retiring and when I was summoned to Washington without warning in February, I surmised that it was to discuss my succession to the Far East Command. In Washington, I found it was that and more. President Eisenhower had me under consideration to succeed General Ridgway as Chief of Staff, and he and Secretary Wilson wished to explore my state of mind before making a decision.

During his two years as Chief of Staff, General Ridgway had had a very difficult time in the atmosphere of the new Administration with its commitment to a strategy of Massive Retaliation. Although I admired his staunch opposition to this strategic fallacy and doubted that my attitude would be significantly different from his, I had no difficulty with the questions addressed to me by the President and Wilson. Oddly, they were not interested in my views on world strategy but wished to be assured of my willingness to accept and carry out the orders of civilian superiors—something about which I would not have expected to be questioned. In the end I apparently satisfied my interrogators and left Washington with the understanding that I would succeed General Hull very briefly as Commander in Chief, Far East Command, and return to Washington in June to become Chief of Staff of the Army.

As I prepared to embark on this next episode in my career, quite naturally my thoughts turned to what I had learned from the Korean experience, particularly as it might apply to my new assignment. There was much to be drawn from it, but, like most participants in the making of history, I had had little time to meditate upon the significance of passing events. While awaiting return to Washington, I took time to review many aspects of the Korean War hoping to obtain the full illumination of this experience for future decisions bearing on our actions in Asia. Though the popular cry "No more Koreas" was ringing in the halls of Congress, I was sure that there was much of importance for the future to be derived from the first limited war waged by the United States since the advent of nuclear weapons.

For one thing, the war illustrated the difficulty of convincing the American people and keeping them convinced for the long pull of the necessity and justification of exposing the lives of a small segment of our manhood for a stake far from home with little visible relation to the national security. It provided renewed evidence of our need for a crusading motivation or an inspiring slogan to offset the national urge to get an unpleasant job over quickly and to return to normalcy. Unfortunately, Truman had been short both of slogans and of military resources to speed up the war. The demobilization following World War II had so depleted our strategic reserves that the skeleton divisions scattered over Japan were all we had to meet the sudden invasion of Korea. The narrowness of our escape from defeat should have conveyed a message to the Eisenhower Administration to increase its limited war forces. Instead, the reaction was to rely more heavily on the deterrent effect of our growing nuclear stockpile.

The Truman-MacArthur conflict might have served as a useful postwar case study of civilian-military relationships and of political restraints imposed on military operations. Much could have been gained from a frank discussion of errors made both on the civilian and on the military side. But the Eisenhower Administration allowed the opportunity to pass. Indeed, at the start of his administration, President Eisenhower took a surprising action adverse to cordial civilian-military relations which could have had a seriously adverse effect on the reputation of the Joint Chiefs of Staff as a completely nonpolitical body. Under Truman the Chiefs had loyally supported the President and the principle of civilian control in his conflict with General MacArthur but had come under fire from Senator Robert Taft and other Republican leaders for their conduct of the Korean War. Senior military officers were shocked when President Eisenhower upon assuming office replaced all the old Chiefs in apparent deference to this Republican criticism. Although unintended, I am sure, there was a strong suggestion that a team of Democratic Chiefs of Staff had been replaced by a team of Republicans.

I might interject that I have often been asked how senior military officers viewed President Truman's relief of MacArthur. While generalization is always dangerous, I would say that most officers sympathized with MacArthur's complaints over political restraints on military operations and agreed with his view of the essentiality of military victory once the sword is unsheathed. Yet, I do not recall ever hearing a senior officer criticize the action of President Truman in relieving him, although the clumsy way it was done was often deplored. The General's political maneuvers in opposition to the President, while serving as his field commander, were thoroughly obnoxious to most officers reared in the service tradition of complete abstention from partisan politics.

I have already indicated my view of the Panmunjom negotiations and their value as an illustration of the difficulties in dealing with the Communists at the conference table. Their ability to combine diplomacy, propaganda, bluff, and military pressure into an integrated force behind their over-all objectives was a lesson which should have stimulated us to emulation.

Apart from these broader questions, most of my reflections as I left Japan necessarily bore on military aspects of the struggle in which I had been involved. A central theme was the importance of learning to use our military resources more effectively in limited war. One could not helicopter over the front as I had done hundreds of times and see the valleys filled with heavy equipment, rarely if ever used, without being impressed with the inapplicability of many of our modern weapons to a Korean-type war. In combination the enemy, the terrain, and the weather tended to nullify the usefulness of much of the costly equipment procured during and after World War II in preparation for another world war one, presumably to be fought primarily in Western Europe.

The enemy was very clever in reducing the effectiveness of our fire power by his tactic of closing rapidly on our positions in the darkness and gripping us so tightly that it was dangerous to call down artillery fire or air strikes. Having gotten to close grips, he then dug in like a mole, turning up so much earth in so many places that we never knew where to find him. With his boundless patience and industry, he learned to move supplies at night in rear areas using so many roads, trails, and diversified means of transport that our completely dominant air arm was unable to interdict the battlefield and prevent his resupply. He used the weather skillfully for protection from our superior fire power. A notable example just before the armistice was the Kumsong offensive, which was timed to coincide with very bad flying weather limiting effective air support to about one day in ten.

The mountainous terrain limited the freedom of use of our weapons on many parts of the front. It restricted the movement of armor and trucks to the narrow valleys which could be blocked by mines, obstacles, or flooded rice paddies. Thus our tanks were often reduced to the role of stationary pillboxes supplementing the fire of other ground weapons. Much of our transport stood idle in the motor parks while still requiring men for its maintenance.

The absence of an enemy air force or navy limited the useful employment of much of our air and naval strength. Except for the MIGs in the northwest corner of the Korean peninsula, there was no enemy to fight in the air. In the absence of a naval adversary, the mightiest warships of the world were obliged to content themselves with bombarding unimportant shore targets hardly worthy of their shells. Finally, there were no targets in Korea which, in the view of the JCS, justified the use of nuclear weapons; and, had their use been requested by the military, there would have been powerful political objections—our own and those of our allies—which could not have been overcome. I commented to General Ridgway that this self-imposed abstention from the use of nuclear weapons in Korea was a strong reminder that we could never be sure of their use elsewhere, particularly as the Soviet atomic arsenal increased. It was another cogent argument against the emerging doctrine of Massive Retaliation.

Whatever the reasons for the limited effectiveness of many of our weapons, the fact remained that much of our vast military expenditures had gone to provide weapons and equipment which did not meet the conditions presented by the Korean War. That conflict ended with our forces checkmated by an Oriental army strong in numbers and courage, well-trained in tactics appropriate to the terrain, but primitively armed with equipment much of which we would have consigned to military museums. With the limitations placed on many of our heavy weapons, the burden of combat fell upon the infantrymen, and there were never enough of them. Their movement forward or backward, up and down the peninsula, was the measure of victory or defeat. All the vast panoply of our fighting services—the bombers, the warships, the artillery, and the tanks—had as their direct or indirect purpose the protection and progress of the infantry soldier. It was with him that the ultimate decision rested, supported at close grips with the enemy only by his light weapons, his personal courage, and his comrades on the right and left. And often the rich republic for which these men exposed their lives had not taught them to read or write.

The quality of the enemy soldiers—tough, disciplined, and enduring—raised uncomfortable thoughts about the future of the West in Asia. It had been a sobering experience to observe in the hard fighting just before the armistice the willingness of hundreds of thousands of Chinese to return repeatedly to the attack of our lines in the face of devastating artillery and infantry fire at a time when most of them knew that a truce was only hours away. It showed the ruthless character of their leaders, and the total discipline which they were able to impose. It also raised serious questions as to how the soft, humanitarian West could compete with such people. It emphasized the great importance of our learning to train and utilize friendly Asian manpower for Asian battlefields instead of sending our own troops into such an environment. In the end we had done quite well in developing the ROK Army, I thought, but we still had much to learn about the Oriental soldier. Inevitably, he would be a key factor in the balance of power in the Far East, and we must know him well if we were to continue to play an important political and military role in that part of the world.

Korea also taught the great cost of projecting modern military power into an undeveloped Asian country. To develop and support our forces and those of our allies called for the construction of ports, airfields, roads, pipelines, and depots, requiring tens of thousands of workmen and hundreds of millions of dollars. The end product was a logistic system which was a tribute to its artisans but which represented an enormous outlay of national resources. While it permitted our forces to maneuver in rear of and along the front, it would not have supported a major advance to the north without a further slow and costly extension. It always had an Achilles heel, the extreme vulnerability of the ports to air attack. One wonders how

159

much attention was paid to the logistic lessons of Korea before we embarked on the construction of a similarly vast logistic system in another underdeveloped Asian country, South Vietnam.

Most military men would say that soldiers should only have to worry about winning wars and not about their costs. Up to a point that attitude is justified, but not if it signifies indifference to waste or misuse of national assets which are the ultimate source of national power and security. No one is likely to deny that our men in battle are entitled to everything they need for their survival and for the success of their mission, but it is the duty of senior military officers and civilian officials to make a determination of what those true needs are and to eliminate the pseudoneeds which do not pass the test.

No thoughtful officer could serve in Korea without concluding that not even our rich country could afford to wage a major war on the plush scale of the Korean operations. I have already mentioned the limited utility of many of our heavy weapons and the inordinately heavy consumption of ammunition which was fired at a rate no other army had ever approached up to that time. Perhaps we could afford such extravagance in a static limited war, but we would break the national resource bank if we tried it on a large scale.

Added to these strictly military costs were those associated with transplanting the American way of life to the Korean battle zone. To make our men as comfortable and contented as possible in a distant war for which many had not volunteered called for post exchanges, snack bars, ice cream factories, and other excrescences which certainly did not meet the criterion of "putting blood on the enemy's shirt." Yet there was considerable justification for them in this limited war where the sacrifices fell so unevenly and with so little equity. But the standards of comfort set were too high to be supportable in a major war.

Before closing the Korean chapter, it may be timely to anticipate our later discussion of the Vietnam conflict and draw some comparison of these two episodes of recent history. I find interesting analogies but also many dissimilarities.

From the point of view of the United States, both were limited wars in the sense that our national survival was in no danger and that we employed only a limited amount of the power at our disposal to overcome an adversary whom we wished to defeat but not destroy. Not only did we allocate only a part of our total power to these conflicts but in both instances we applied drastic restraints on the use of that power. These took the form of limitations placed on the weapons used, on the targets attacked, and on the area in which ground operations could be conducted. The restraints were not all symmetrical. In Korea, after the retreat from the Yalu, offensive ground operations were more restricted than in Vietnam, where there were virtually no limitations on offensive actions within the confines of

South Vietnam. On the other hand, even when the bombing of North Vietnam was permitted on a large scale, the sorties were controlled rigidly from Washington in a way unknown in the air war over North Korea. At the root of the restrictive measures in both cases was a fear of expanded conflict and a desire to reduce American casualties, particularly after the opening of negotiations. Public opinion, especially that of our allies, provided a damper in both wars on any bold use of military power.

Our initial goal in Korea was the repulse of the North Korean attack but, in the euphoria following Inchon, we changed goals in midstream and undertook, with the U.N.'s blessing, to unify all Korea by force of arms. The defeat at the Yalu, however, forced us back to the original objective of restoring the status quo more or less at the thirty-eighth parallel. In Vietnam, the goal has always been double-barreled but always the same: the repulse of the aggression of North Vietnam and the right of self-determination for the South Vietnamese in the choice of their government. This goal was first set by President Eisenhower and has been retained essentially unaltered by his successors.

In both wars the enemy were aggressive Asian Communist states, but the form taken by their aggression was different. In Korea, it was an overt invasion across the thirty-eighth parallel supported by the Big Lie that the aggression came from the South. In Vietnam, the initial enemy were the elusive Vietcong guerrillas, clandestinely supported from North Vietnam, who utilized subversion and terror as prime forms of attack. From 1965, the composition of the enemy changed as tactical units of the North Vietnamese Army infiltrated and took over the burden of the main conflict which progressively assumed a more conventional form.

In both wars we were supporting a local Asian government with limited resources in leadership, governmental organization, and administrative skills. In Korea, however, we had the patriarchal figure of President Rhee to serve as a popular symbol of the national resistance whereas in South Vietnam no such outstanding leader came forth to lead the country. President Diem came closest to Rhee, but his task of providing national leadership for a people divided for centuries along ethnic, religious, and regional lines was far more difficult than that of Rhee who led a relatively united country. Neither Diem nor his long line of successors ever displayed the popular appeal needed to rouse and unite a people who had never had the opportunity to achieve a sense of nationhood.

The United States had similar problems in developing indigenous military forces in both countries and experienced similar disappointments in the early years of both efforts. In each case, the local forces had to receive much of their training on the battlefield under the guns of the enemy, but after Inchon, there was always a relatively secure rear area in Korea in which to recruit and train the troops. No such safe haven ever existed in South Vietnam because of the ubiquitous guerrillas and the fluid nature of

161

the conflict. In the end, the American advisory effort succeeded in welding together very sizable and effective indigenous forces in both countries, about 600,000 in Korea and over a million in South Vietnam which should henceforth be sufficient to defend their homelands against their neighbors without American troop support.

The command structure in the two wars was notably different. In Korea, the war was conducted under the aegis of the United Nations with the American Commander in Tokyo concurrently acting as U.N. Commander with the Korean forces under his operational command. As a subordinate U.N. Commander, I exercised all aspects of Command over the U.S. Eighth Army and its communication zone but had only operational control—that is, the authority to direct military operations—over the Korean Army and the U.N. contingents.

It was possible to conduct the Korean War in the context of the U.N. charter only because the Russians had made the mistake of boycotting the Security Council following the invasion of South Korea, which in their absence voted U.N. participation. In the case of Vietnam, the Soviets made no such mistake and had a representative always present in the Security Council, ready to veto any U.N. participation in the conflict. Hence, the nations assisting South Vietnam with troops did so under bilateral agreements or the provisions of the Southeast Asia Treaty Organization (SEATO). This arrangement was not as satisfactory politically as that in Korea, but oddly it produced more troops. Excluding Americans, there were only about 39,000 foreign combat troops in Korea, but some 68,000 in Vietnam. In both cases, the United States made important financial contributions to the support of the Allied contingents.

Toward the end of both conflicts, the United States became bogged down in frustrating negotiations. It took two years and seventeen days to negotiate an armistice at Panmunjom, and there is still no final peace settlement. The Vietnam negotiations opened in Paris on May 10, 1968, and at this writing, three and one-half years later, they remain stagnated without either an armistice or a peace settlement in sight. In neither negotiation has the record of American diplomatic achievement been very impressive, although the record of Panmunjom is somewhat better than that of Paris. In Korea we did not pay in advance for the privilege of sitting down at the negotiation table; we got there primarily because the enemy field commanders were happy to escape heavy military pressure by opening negotiations. Our principal fault in Korea was the removal of the military pressure on the enemy during the negotiations and our failure to react aggressively as soon as negotiations became stalemated. While our negotiators necessarily made some concessions along the way to the ultimate armistice agreement, they won the big issue, that of the voluntary repatriation of the prisoners of war.

In our efforts to find a peaceful termination of the war in Vietnam, we made several critical concessions: the cessation of the bombing of North Vietnam, the placing of a ceiling on the strength of our forces in Vietnam, and later the unilateral reduction of our forces below that ceiling. Thus we removed any inducement to reasonableness on the part of our adversaries even before we got to the negotiating table. The final outcome is at present unclear, but the prospect of an acceptable negotiated settlement is not bright.

In both negotiations, the Communists demonstrated their skill in combining talking with fighting and in turning the negotiation table into a sounding board for propaganda and invective. In both cases, we seemed to have learned very little from the past, particularly in Paris where our over-readiness to make unrequited concessions and our failure to insist on reciprocity as a governing principle largely nullified the successes won by our fighting men.

Both wars were fought far from home, and popular support for both soon declined. However, in coping with this weakening of the home front, President Truman had the advantage of the visibility of the aggression on the part of North Korea. Also, it was never difficult to know how the Korean War was progressing. The movement north and south of the clearly delineated battlefront was a visible measure of victory or defeat.

In Vietnam, by the nature of the fighting, there was never a front line, only a confused ebb and flow of separate and seemingly unrelated small actions. There were no defensive positions or terrain features to be stormed or crossed like the Siegfried Line or the Rhine; there was nothing worth capturing in the country side, only jungle and rice paddies. So our Saigon headquarters was driven to the body count as the only device to measure progress, a method which soon became odious to a large segment of the American people. Thus President Johnson had a much more difficult time in explaining his war than did President Truman.

Finally, both wars raised an unanswered question: Can a democracy such as the United States carry a prolonged limited war to a successful conclusion?

CHAPTER 12

Army Chief of Staff

When Diddy and I departed from Tokyo *en route* for Washington, I carried a heavy dispatch case of "think pieces" bearing upon my new assignment as Army Chief of Staff. They included an evaluation of the Eisenhower New Look and its supporting strategy of Massive Retaliation; an analysis of the 1955 text of the "Basic National Security Policy"; a draft "National Military Program," which set forth my own ideas of a defense program consistent with the needs of the national security; and a long list of Army objectives and programs which I hoped to carry out upon my return. As I reread these documents today, they convey an impression of innocent optimism which the next four years were to temper although, I am glad to say, not completely dispel. But at least no one could say that the new Chief of Staff did not know where he thought he wanted to go.

After two years of the Eisenhower Administration, the main elements of its national security policy were fairly clear. They included placing main reliance on nuclear weapons to deter or defeat Communist aggression of all varieties and avoiding involvement in limited wars such as that in Korea. While conceding the need to deal with so-called brush fires, the Administration operated on the highly dubious assumption that if the Armed Forces were prepared to cope with nuclear war, they could take care of all lesser contingencies. If minor aggressors were not deterred by our nuclear forces, we would be prepared, in the words of Secretary Dulles, to use our nuclear weapons vigorously and at places of our own choosing.

Even at a time when the United States had preponderant nuclear power in relation to the Soviet Union, such a doctrine offended the common sense of many thoughtful people and aroused their skepticism as to its practicality. To eradicate such doubts, particularly among the military skeptics, President Eisenhower approved in October 1953 a National Security Coun-

164

cil paper which authorized the JCS to plan on using nuclear weapons, tactical as well as strategic, whenever their use was desirable from a military standpoint.

In my judgment, this authorization was even more misleading than previous statements of nuclear weapons policy because it encouraged our military leaders to think that they would be allowed to use these weapons pretty much as they saw fit without political constraints—something hard to believe and frightening in its implications. While this policy statement proved useful to the Administration as a basis for justifying the reduction of conventional forces and stifling debate within the JCS, it also led the Air Force to build bombers which could be readily used only to drop nuclear bombs and the Navy to construct carriers with insufficient storage space for munitions other than nuclear. Much of our military hardware began to reflect the effect of this fallacious guidance.

Although I returned to Washington with no illusions as to the difficulties I would encounter, I was encouraged by some of the language which I found in the latest version of the Basic National Security Policy. This was the annual publication of the NSC which purported to provide policy guidance for all components of the government involved in national security. This year, 1955, it acknowledged for the first time the possibility that, as the Soviet nuclear weapons stockpile grew, our Communist enemies might be expected to step up local aggressions with reduced concern for provoking the United States. This possibility would require us to maintain mobile ground forces, suitably deployed with tactical nuclear weapons, able to deter local aggressions or to punish them swiftly as directed by the President if they occurred.

These thoughts were quite compatible with my own views as to the need to recognize and make provision for waging limited wars determined to be in the national interest. They seemed to back away from the original Administration position that we could not afford to prepare for every kind of war and hence must depend primarily on a great capacity for nuclear retaliation. Working from this new text, I prepared the draft paper entitled "A National Military Program" previously mentioned that set forth the kind of national security doctrine which I thought necessary for the coming period, when the nuclear armament of the two opposing camps would in effect cancel out each other. It stressed that national security was supported by many components of strength other than military—political, economic, psychological and intellectual—all of which contributed to the aggregate of power applicable to the needs of our security. Hence, the "National Military Program" should be linked with all other related programs to obtain maximum effect in deterring general war, in deterring or defeating local aggression, or in surviving in general war if deterrence failed. This draft, after some refinements, eventually became the Army's position paper on national security policy for the next four years and served as the point of departure for the new strategy of Flexible Response. While it was never concurred in by the JCS or the Department of Defense, I believe that it had some influence in bringing the Eisenhower Administration in its late years to introduce some flexibility into the national strategy.

In addition to these documents, my dispatch case also contained a list of objectives and supporting outline plans which I hoped to pursue in the Army. They primarily concerned ways and means to improve the combat readiness of the Army in support of a strategy of Flexible Response and to improve its morale depressed as it was by the precedence given to the needs of the Navy and Air Force by the ex-Army man in the White House. Specific measures included the refinement of "A National Military Program" and its presentation to the JCS, the reorganization and re-equipping of Army divisions in the light of the Korean experience, and an improvement of relations with Congress where the budgetary savings claimed for "more bang for a buck" had generated considerable support for the strategy of Massive Retaliation. I hoped also to remove the chill which affected the attitude of the President to his old service and to work out some way of seeing him regularly. This would have required a modification of the current practice whereby the Chairman alone reported on business of the JCS at a weekly meeting with the President.

With this satchelful of homework, the Taylors departed from Japan on June 5. Our routing through Europe allowed me on the way to pay my first visit to three countries of South Asia (Burma, India, Pakistan) and to spend several useful days in Europe to obtain an updating on the problems of the NATO area. In Europe, I had useful discussions with many old friends and associates of former years. In Heidelberg, Tony McAuliffe of Bastogne fame was in command of the Army forces in Europe; in Paris, General Alfred Gruenther was Supreme Allied Commander, Europe, with Lieutenant General Cortlandt Schuyler as his Chief of Staff. Cort Schuyler had been a roommate of mine as a cadet and later a fellow instructor on the faculty of West Point. In this same period of teaching, Gruenther had been an instructor of chemistry, a fact which made him a valuable collaborator in manufacturing a powerful, but potable, home brew in flagrant violation of the prohibition laws of the period. Gruenther contributed his scientific knowledge whereas all I could give to the illicit operation was unskilled labor and the shelter of my apartment.

The briefings which I received at the European headquarters were an excellent review of the problems, military and political, which bore on the security of the NATO area. After the Korean experience, I was particularly impressed with the fragility of the logistic base which supported the U.S. and allied forces in Europe and set limits to their capability for sustained combat. It was clear to me that we had too many forces in Europe if we were going to depend on the "trip-wire" strategy supported by the Massive-Retaliation school and not enough balanced strength for a sustained nonnuclear defense. I hoped that perhaps the low yield tactical nuclear weapons which our advancing technology now made possible might provide a partial answer to this dilemma.

We arrived in Washington on the morning of June 23, where we were met by Secretary of the Army Bob Stevens and General Matt Ridgway. While circling the Andrews airfield to land, I received a message from Stevens waiting on the ground below which said, "Welcome back. I have just resigned." This was sad news to me, for I had formed a warm friendship with the Secretary during his several visits to Korea and from that distance had followed sympathetically his struggle, virtually unassisted by his superiors, to protect the Army from the savage attacks of Senator Joe McCarthy. Since I had felt sure of being able to work easily with him, it was a disappointment not to have him as Secretary during my tenure as Chief of Staff.

His announced successor was a man whom I did not know, Wilber Brucker, a former Governor of Michigan and, at the time of his selection, the General Counsel of the Department of Defense. My first reaction to this appointment was negative, as it appeared that Secretary of Defense Wilson had reached into the ranks of his official family to get a safe man to run the Army in accordance with Wilson's predilections. Experience soon proved, however, that whatever the motive behind the appointment the consequences feared did not ensue. Brucker was too honorable a man to yield to unjustified pressure and developed into a stalwart defender of the Army's role in national security. If he had a fault it was that in arguing the Army case before the Secretary of Defense he became "more royalist than the King," sometimes to the detriment of his effectiveness.

At 11:30 A.M., June 30, I was sworn in as the twentieth Chief of Staff of the Army. After the tumult which attends such occasions had subsided, I settled down behind my new desk wondering what claim I had to it and what assets I brought to the job.

For one thing, I could be grateful to the Army for having given me a sound preparatory training, first in its school system from West Point to the Army War College, and later in command and staff assignments of ascending importance, well distributed among Washington, Europe, and Asia. It had afforded me the privilege of working closely with such personalities as Marshall, Eisenhower, Clark, Collins, Ridgway, and many others. Now it had given me the Vice Chief of Staff of my choice, General Williston B. Palmer, who had many of the qualities and much of the experience of which I felt a lack. In combination, these were not inconsiderable assets to bolster a new Chief of Staff.

What does a Chief of Staff do? Having often been asked the question by my civilian friends, I might digress for a moment to answer it in my own

167

words, not in the text of law and regulations. The Chief of Staff—I speak here only of the Army Chief although my comments usually apply to his Navy and Air Force counterparts—is the senior military officer of the Army during his appointment. He does not command the Army; indeed, he has direct command authority only over the immediate staff around him. His direct boss is the Secretary of the Army and all orders and instructions which the Chief of Staff may send to components of the Army are in the name of the Secretary. Because of the Secretary's paramount role, the Chief of Staff spends much of his time in keeping his Secretary informed, in providing him with advice and recommendations, in supporting him in his conferences with the Secretary of Defense and before Congress, and in promulgating and carrying out his orders and decisions after they have been formulated. Implicit in this latter function is the follow-up on secretarial decisions to see that they are, in fact, carried out as intended.

From this brief description of the relations between the Chief of Staff and the Secretary, the need for these two men to work together congenially in perfect confidence is self-evident. Fortunately, there has been a long tradition of harmonious civilian-military relations at the top of the Army, symbolized by the open door between the adjoining offices of these two officials. In recent history, probably the Stimson-Marshall team during World War II is the best example of fruitful civilian-military collaboration. At any rate, it was the model which I had constantly in mind as I set about establishing an effective rapport with Mr. Brucker.

Thus far I have accounted for only about one-half of the duties of the Chief of Staff, those strictly Army-related functions which he performs under the direction of his Secretary. He has another role as the Army representative on the JCS. In this capacity, he is independent of the control of the Secretary of the Army and serves as a member of a committee inserted between the Secretary of Defense and the Unified and Specified Commanders, that is, the generals and admirals who command the field forces which fight our wars overseas and defend our shores and continental airspace. He attends regular meetings of the JCS three times weekly and is subject to call at any other time since it is understood that he will give priority to his JCS duties over those of his service. In advance of such meetings he must prepare himself carefully to contribute all that he can to the deliberations of this body which by law constitutes the principal source of military advice for the Secretary of Defense, the National Security Council, and the President.

Over and above these functions which are based on statute and regulation, the Chief of Staff has an unspecified, but highly important, task of flying the Army flag at home and abroad wherever the Army is on duty. He must visit the men who do the Army's job, get information at first hand from them, and serve as the Army spokesman in uniform wherever needed. Since he has limited time for absences from his Pentagon desk, he has to schedule these field activities carefully in the interstices between the tasks which are his by law and regulation.

Broadly, this was the job upon which I embarked in June 1955 and held for four years. I have written elsewhere in *The Uncertain Trumpet* about the rewards and tribulations of this assignment, and shall not repeat here more than is necessary to the themes of this book. A subject of obvious relevance is the evolution of the strategy of Massive Retaliation from its early purity to a hybrid which, by the time of my departure from the Pentagon in 1959, bore some resemblance to the strategy of Flexible Response soon to be adopted by the Kennedy Administration.

The information which I had received in Tokyo regarding the New-Look strategy proved to be quite accurate. Secretary of Defense Wilson, strongly supported by the Chairman of the JCS, Admiral Arthur Radford, was earnestly engaged in carrying out a national security policy based upon reliance on strategic nuclear weapons and the maintenance of a stable military budget within the means of an unstrained national economy. The New Look stressed the importance of organizing the national defense for the long haul with annual military expenditures stabilized in the $33 to $34 billion range, a figure which was expected to maintain forces of roughly 2.8 million men of whom about a million would be in the Army. If the budget, the force levels, and the industrial input into defense could be stabilized, it was believed that results would be a more efficient defense, a national economy protected against excessive and fluctuating defense spending, and a tolerable burden for the taxpayers—all impeccable objectives.

I had been on the job only a short time when it became apparent that forces of such a size could not be supported under any such budget and that something would have to give. As the pressure mounted, it was national defense which gave way before the requirements of the budget and the economy; and within the shrinking defense budget it was the needs of limited war which bore the brunt. To prevent, or at least to limit, the attrition of the limited war capability became a primary task for me as Chief of Staff.

There were numerous reasons why the New-Look military program could not be carried out at the price which the Administration was willing to pay. First, there was the inevitable inflation which reduced the purchasing power of the military dollar and made a fixed budget, in effect, a declining one. Then there was the unexpectedly high cost of the new strategic programs—missiles, bombers, and submarines—which, being for the most part innovations with no background of cost experience, quickly overran the figures forecast in Mr. Wilson's budget. Another factor was the mounting concern for the air defense of the United States, something which we had never worried about in the past but which now demanded big money. From 1957 there was the disquieting evidence that we had underestimated Soviet progress in the strategic field while at the same time crises involving Lebanon, Suez, Hungary, and Taiwan reminded the Administration that the threat of brush-fire wars had not been neutralized by our strategic superiority.

All of these factors pressed against the dollar ceiling on military expenditures and only President Eisenhower's personal devotion to the cause of a balanced budget and a stable economy kept the lid from blowing off sooner than it did. As I had feared, the only way to relieve the pressure acceptable to the New Look was to cut military manpower, particularly that of the Army. Despite Mr. Brucker's and my efforts, the Army declined over the years from roughly a million men and eighteen divisions in 1954 to 870,000 men and sixteen divisions in 1959. Meanwhile there was no adequate compensation for this loss in numbers through the modernization of Army equipment, most of which dated from World War II.

In spite of these enforced economies, the defense budget slowly rose year by year until it passed $41 billion in 1959. Meanwhile, the percentage of the budget allocated to each service remained remarkably stable, roughly 23 percent to the Army, 28 percent to the Navy-Marine Corps and 46 percent to the Air Force. This figure attested to the continued emphasis on preparing for general nuclear war, although there was some lip service paid to the need to cope with limited aggression. The only substantive change in strategic doctrine which I could detect was a growing willingness to concede the possibility of mutual deterrence in the use of strategic nuclear weapons, an impious thought which a few years earlier would have enraged the advocates of Massive Retaliation who insisted upon unchallenged nuclear superiority as the objective of our defense policy. Then, as now, no one undertook to define precisely what was meant by such terms as superiority, parity, or adequacy in measuring the strength of nuclear stockpiles, but the polemicists were ready to fight over them at the drop of a hat.

Today I can look back with comparative detachment on those turbulent years fraught with well-nigh continuous conflict with my colleagues of the JCS and Defense Secretaries Wilson and McElroy. They were wearing times, quite different from anything I had known in my previous service. While I never particularly minded the conflicts with my Pentagon peers, I felt keenly the increasing coolness of my relations with the President and regretted being a disappointment to him as I was sure I was.

There was no question about the sincerity of the President's fear of weakening the economy through excessive military spending and of exceeding the limits of the willingness of our people to pay for their security. But he had no way of determining the needs of a sound economy other than through the acceptance of the personal, unsubstantiated views of advisers such as the Secretary of the Treasury, George Humphrey, a conservative banker with an overpowering manner in Cabinet debate. Whereas the generals and admirals had to prove their needs to the satisfaction of both the executive and the legislative branches of the government, there was no such procedure for examining the spokesmen for the requirements of the economy. When we Chiefs showed lack of appreciation of their arguments, we were often castigated as being parochial and ended in the Administration doghouse. I often had occasion to remember the words of Admiral Robert B. Carney, the retiring Chief of Naval Operations at the time I arrived as Chief of Staff: "You're one of the good new Chiefs now but you'll be surprised how soon you will become one of the bad old Chiefs." By the end of 1955, I had achieved this changeover and remained a "bad Chief" until my retirement in 1959.

In the climate of the Eisenhower Administration, it was hard to make the case for limited war to the satisfaction of the decision-makers. Limited war suggested Korea, a thought which was repulsive to officials and public alike. While one could always cite the possible need to assist some of the many countries to whom we had made commitments since World War II, in spite of the Korean experience, the Administration insisted that troubles affecting these countries would be kept small by the deterrent effect of our nuclear power. The resources needed for limited war were largely ground forces using unglamorous weapons and equipment—rifles, machineguns, trucks and unsophisticated aircraft—items with little appeal to the Congress or the public. Secretary Wilson once sent back an Army budget to get us to substitute requests for newfangled items with public appeal instead of the prosaic accoutrements of the foot soldier. It was partly a misguided response to this urging which drew the Army into a costly and losing competition with the Air Force in producing an Intermediate Range Ballistic Missile (IRBM) at a time when the ammunition reserves for basic Army weapons were far too low for comfort. It also led me to conjure up the Madison Avenue adjective, "pentomic," to describe the new Army division which was designed on a pentagonal rather than triangular pattern with atomic-capable weapons in its standard equipment. While it was true that at the time the Army had only the cumbersome Honest John rocket and the heavy eight-inch howitzer capable of firing nuclear munitions, nuclear weapons were the going thing and, by including some in the division armament, the Army staked out its claim to a share in the nuclear arsenal.

It is hard to be sure just where the strategic issue stood by the close of the Eisenhower Administration. To the end, there was never a clear indication of priorities among the functions to be performed by the Armed Forces, no yardsticks of sufficiency to serve as standards for performance by functional forces, little guidance as to the resources to expect for the tasks assigned, and no intimation of the possible constraints and limitations which might be imposed on the use of these resources in time of war. In particular, the question "How much is enough?" never received an answer with regard to the needs of any strategic function except as it was answered by the money finally allocated to it in the annual budget.

Deterrence was a term which often entered into the debates; everybody was for it, but few could agree as to its requirements. In determining how much was enough to deter general nuclear war I tried in vain to obtain a differentiation between the needs of deterrent forces themselves and those for hedging against the failure of deterrence. The former required, I thought, a missile-bomber force of limited size but enjoying maximum protection for its weapons and for the communications which linked these weapons to the President who must give the order to fire them. The nearer this force approached invulnerability to surprise attack, the more effective would be its deterrent effect. To develop such a force I supported the Air Force program for an Intercontinental Ballistic Missile (ICBM) in hardened silos, the Navy Polaris program, and the early initiatives of the Army in developing an antiballistic missile which might add significantly to the invulnerability of this deterrent force. But I favored only a few hundred strategic weapons in it and an antiballistic defense only for its weapons and communications and not for the entire country.

Having concentrated all necessary resources to maximize the deterrent effectiveness of such a force, I favored giving a much lower priority to those requirements of strategic warfare which might arise if and after deterrence failed. These requirements to hedge against the failure of deterrence included: missiles and bombers beyond the needs of the deterrent force; expensive early warning systems which were unlikely to produce warning in time to be acted upon; country-wide civil defense measures to protect population; and large reserves of supplies accumulated in the hope that some would escape bomb damage and be available to meet postattack needs. The aggregate of these items represented billions of dollars and should be funded, I thought, only if resources remained after meeting the higher priority needs of limited war.

This approach to maximize the deterrent effect of strategic forces, if adopted by the Department of Defense, would have provided useful guidance to the military planners. But such a proposal was never acceptable to the partisans of the overriding importance of strategic weapons who would recognize no differentiation in priority between deterrent and hedge forces. So the problem of rationalizing the requirements of strategic forces had to await the computer analysts of Secretary McNamara's day, who eventually achieved a pseudoscientific approach which represented some progress although there were areas in which this new methodology was open to challenge.

The absence of clear guidelines for determining the military force structure had many adverse consequences and, among other things, contributed to the seemingly endless wrangling among the services. It also increased the stresses in civilian-military relationships at the top of government. When the Chiefs could not agree among themselves on strategic matters, the issues had to be referred to their civilian superiors for adjudication, an unpleasant responsibility which brought them into the inter-service line of fire. The resulting audible static in the Pentagon often aroused demands from Congress and the press for the Secretary of Defense to knock military heads together, the assumption being that parochial generals and admirals were responsible and should be brought to heel by the hand of civilian control. The atmosphere thus created was hardly favorable to the conduct of the important business of national defense.

During these years I often had occasion to reflect on this matter of civilian-military relations and the meaning of civilian control. The normal officer in the Armed Forces, sworn to defend the Constitution, never challenges the right, indeed the essentiality of civilian control, but there is always a wide range of views as to what it is and how it should be exercised.

The purpose of civilian control, as I understand it, is to assure the responsiveness of the Armed Forces to the lawful orders and directives of the President and of his civilian subordinates in the chain of command. It is exercised at several focal points in the structure of the government. The President exercises it both as Chief Executive and Commander in Chief in the course of conducting foreign and domestic policy. He sets the ultimate goals of policy, approves the broad programs in support of these goals, and authorizes the resources allocated to the Armed Forces. He decides where, when, and how to use military forces. He has sole authority to permit them to use nuclear weapons. He promotes their senior officers with the advice and consent of the Senate and approves the assignment of their senior commanders. With the advice and consent of the Senate he picks the Chiefs of Staff and their Chairman.

Second only to the President in the control of the military is the Secretary of Defense who administers the Department of Defense and acts as principal assistant to the President in national security matters. He is the immediate subordinate of the President in the military chain of command and issues all orders to the combatant forces in his own name, using for this purpose the Joint Chiefs of Staff as his military staff. At the direction or with the approval of the President, he assigns military missions and, with the assistance of the JCS, supervises military operations. He prepares and defends the defense budget, controls the use of the funds made available for military purposes, and issues the regulations which govern the Armed Forces. A resident of the Pentagon, he is the strongest civilian force in the day-to-day control of the Armed Forces.

The service secretaries under the Secretary of Defense have an analogous authority over their respective departments and forces. They do not have authority over military operations against a foreign enemy, but may have responsibility for operations directed at maintaining internal security. In September 1957, when President Eisenhower decided to send Army troops to Little Rock to enforce school desegregation, the channel of responsibility was from the President to the Attorney General, to the Secretary of the Army, then through the Army Chief of Staff to the troop commander in Little Rock. Neither the Secretary of Defense nor the Joint Chiefs of Staff were involved, nor, I might add, did they want to be.

Outside the executive branch, the Congress plays an important role in controlling the military. Its primary control is by the purse strings, but Congress also approves the size, composition, organization, and major equipment of the Armed Forces. It holds hearings and investigations and passes laws, bills, and authorizations bearing on the activities of the Armed Forces and its individual members. The Senate concurs in the promotion of all generals and admirals.

In spite of this long list of checks on the military, the question recurrently arises as to the adequacy of civilian control. Certainly there are enough controls built into the governmental machinery—policy guidance, command authority, budgetary constraints, control of the assignment and promotion of officers—to permit the President and his civilian chiefs in the Pentagon to do what they like with the military, restrained only by Congressional and popular reactions. Mr. Truman showed that a President limited in popularity but long on courage could deal with a national military hero who had stepped out of line. In canceling an important air strike in the Bay of Pigs affair, President Kennedy demonstrated that a President can intervene personally in the conduct of a military operation, but can also live to regret it. President Johnson was charged by one wing of his critics with exerting excessive restraints on the use of our military power in Vietnam and by another with being unduly under the influence of the generals. In part because these conflicting criticisms seemed about even in quantity and quality, and thus to counterbalance, I have concluded that the presidential control exerted in Vietnam was probably about right. My over-all feeling is that there is no challenge to civilian control with which an official of proper character and training cannot deal. A greater danger is that untrained or self-important officials may use their power arbitrarily to override the professional military judgment in military matters to the detriment of the national security.

As the end of my fourth year as Chief of Staff approached, I decided to request retirement. Secretary of Defense McElroy very considerately offered me a further extension of my term, but·I honestly felt that I had exhausted my usefulness in that position and that it would be well for the Army to get a new leader. At the age of fifty-eight, I was loath to leave the military service which had treated me well beyond my deserts for over forty years but there were only two positions in which I might have been interested, Chairman JCS and Supreme Allied Commander, Europe. However, both of these posts were filled by highly qualified officers who had no apparent intention of retiring. Indeed, with my dissenting views on the strategy of Massive Retaliation, I would have been a most unhappy choice for the Chairmanship which should always be occupied by an officer generally sympathetic to the military policy of the Administration.

In my final months I was busy putting into order the papers bearing on my years as Chief of Staff since I had long since decided to carry to the public the important issues which I had supported in the privacy of government. The principal matters affecting the national defense which in my opinion required action could be summarized in a few brief paragraphs which later became the theme of *The Uncertain Trumpet*.

There was a crying need, as I have repeatedly mentioned, for the civilian leadership to provide the Joint Chiefs of Staff with more explicit guidance if they were to structure the Armed Forces in consistence with the threats to our security as anticipated by the President and his political advisers. For the sword to be an effective instrument of foreign policy, its forgers must have some understanding of the purposes to which it may be put and, hence, know something of the future goals of national policy and the obstacles to them which may have to be resolved by military force.

Based upon the guidance received, the Armed Forces would then need a restatement of their functions which would take into account what they had become since 1947 when their roles and missions had been last defined. Such a restatement would not be easy to compose to the satisfaction of all parties, but it would be worth the effort if it would diminish the waste of resources and the friction in service relations which arose from overlapping functions and the gray areas in service responsibilities.

I was convinced that the budget process added to our difficulties in making a rational allocation of resources, and I intended after retirement to renew the arguments I had made over the years for budgeting by military function (strategic forces, tactical forces, continental air defense, antisubmarine warfare, etc.) rather than by service (Army, Navy, Air Force). Under the latter method, deeply imbedded in tradition and custom, it was literally impossible to know what a budget contributed to the aggregated combat capability of the Armed Forces.

Finally, I was soured by my experience in the JCS area: the insistence of the civilian leadership on trying to wring a consensus from the JCS; the difficulty of getting a hearing on matters in dispute from the Secretary of Defense or the President, both of whom preferred to deal only with the JCS Chairman; the slowness and cumbersomeness of doing business by committee, particularly when operational matters requiring prompt action were involved. I felt that there must be a better way to organize the top echelon of the military hierarchy. The solution which I eventually advocated would have separated the advisory and the operational staff functions of the JCS, assigning the first to a Supreme Military Council consisting of three four-star officers of the Army, Navy, and Air Force who were either retired or were on their last tour of active service. The operational staff functions would have been given to a single Chief of Staff serving the Secretary of Defense, supported by a Joint Staff appropriately organized to deal with these staff functions. The service Chiefs of Staff would then have had no duties other than those in support of their service secretary. The Supreme Military Council, I thought, would offer advice less colored by service bias than that emanating from active Chiefs of Staff, while the latter would be relieved of the excessive burden resulting from their dual obligations to their service and to the JCS. The Chief of Staff of the Secretary of Defense would assure operational efficiency and dispatch in carrying out approved policy unattainable by a committee of generals and admirals.

Although this proposal had considerable merit, there was always a serious question in my mind about one feature of it, namely, the ability of three senior officers other than the service Chiefs of Staff to provide the kind of advice needed by the civilian leadership—especially, the President. The latter needs to know at any moment whether the capabilities of his Armed Forces, present or future, are sufficient to meet his purposes; if insufficient, he needs responsible advice as to what should be done to attain the necessary level of military effectiveness. Such matters involve the military budget, and a competent presidential adviser on such matters must have an intimate knowledge of the individual service budgets. Would it be possible to find such knowledge among the members of a Supreme Military Council who operated on the sidelines without direct contact with service problems? Most of my military colleagues of the period would have answered in the negative.

In the years after I reached the foregoing conclusions and committed them to writing, I have often been asked whether I still believed that they were valid or whether I had had afterthoughts. Several of my proposals have been justified by subsequent events. Since 1960, no one in authority has sought to defend Massive Retaliation as a surefire, all-weather strategy guaranteeing a cheap but adequate national defense. Successive administrations have tried to improve the quality of the policy guidance available to the Armed Forces, although in my view much still remains to be done, particularly in the establishment of yardsticks of sufficiency for the functional forces. Why do we need 1000 ICBM's and not 800 or 1200? Why must the Navy always have fifteen carriers and not thirteen or seventeen? What is the magic of forty-one Polaris submarines? Why does the Army need seventeen divisions rather than fifteen or nineteen? We are still about as far from rational answers to such questions as we were in 1959.

The functional budget which I favored is now an established procedure, thanks to Secretary McNamara and his first Comptroller, Charles Hitch. We spend our defense money now in terms of functions, in recognition of the truth of President Eisenhower's statement that the Army, Navy, and

Air Force will no longer wage war as separate services—war will be waged by task forces drawn from all three services operating under a unified command.

The updating of the statement of service roles and missions which I proposed has never been undertaken. It is a hot issue which no Secretary of Defense would like to take on, not even Robert McNamara who rarely missed a chance to chivvy the Pentagon's sacred cows. In the interest of intramural harmony in the Department of Defense, it would probably be wise to continue to avoid the discord which would arise in seeking formal changes in roles and missions and instead to adjust them as the Secretary of Defense sees fit by means of budget decisions.

It is about the reorganization proposal for the JCS that my views have changed most over the years. My service as JCS Chairman from 1962 to 1964 allowed me to appreciate the effect of different personalities in key positions upon the functioning of the JCS system, an experience which demonstrated to me that the existing system could be made to work far differently without formal changes from what I had known as Army Chief of Staff. An aggressive, incisive Secretary of Defense like McNamara could and did speed the decision-making process which had dragged so interminably from 1955 to 1959. He could and did delegate to the Chairman authority to take many of the operational actions required to carry out approved policy decisions and thus circumvented many of the inherent delays of the committee system. The service Chiefs of Staff learned to turn over more of their service duties to their deputies and thus freed themselves for greater attention to their JCS duties. Although these improvements left unresolved many of the defects in cumbersome Joint Staff procedures which are designed primarily to protect service interests, I am unaware at this moment of any major change in the JCS organization which would offer advantages to compensate for the disruption of existing procedures now well established by long usage. Progress in the Pentagon will depend less on organizational changes than on the personal qualities of the Secretary and of the Chiefs and their ability to work harmoniously together in mutual forbearance.

CHAPTER 13

The Bay of Pigs

Upon retiring from the Army, I set to work writing the book which I had long been contemplating, *The Uncertain Trumpet*, which was eventually published in 1960. At the same time, I accepted an offer to serve as Chairman of the Board of the Mexican Light and Power Company and, in September 1959, moved to Mexico City to take over the job.

The stability of our future apparently assured, Diddy and I settled contentedly into the very pleasant life of the Mexican capital. The company was the largest power company in Mexico, serving the rapidly growing capital and its environs. MexLight was about as international as a business enterprise could be, having its headquarters in Toronto, its principal stockholders in Belgium, the source of most of its capital in Wall Street, and the market for its product in Mexico. Its staff was made up largely of Mexicans but with a considerable sprinkling of Americans and Europeans among the officers and technicians.

Like most utilities its growth was fettered by the power rates which in our case were set by the Mexican government; the latter was not inclined toward generosity to a corporation which was popularly regarded as a symbol of Yankee industrial penetration. Because of the low rate schedule, the company was having great difficulty in expanding its capacity to meet the population and industrial growth in its area of responsibility, and consequently it often incurred the ire of its customers for inadequate service. The situation might have reached critical proportions had not the Mexican government received a financial windfall in the form of a $100 million loan from an American insurance company which enabled it to buy enough stock to obtain operating control and to change the management. So by the end of 1960 the Taylors were on the move again, this time to New York where I accepted the position of president of the Lincoln Center for the Performing Arts, then in the course of construction.

The early months of 1961 were spent in learning another new job and acquiring some experience in the ways of architects, construction engineers, and opera buffs. About mid-April, as a casual reader of the press, I became aware that something out of the ordinary was going on in Cuba. My general impression was that Castro was encountering serious internal difficulties and faced a situation which might blow up at any moment. I assumed, as most readers probably did, that the expected explosion had occurred when press and radio on April 15 carried reports of air strikes against targets in the vicinity of Havana and Santiago, apparently the work of rebel Cuban pilots. The events of the subsequent days were too confused to be followed intelligently by a businessman preoccupied with problems far removed from Cuba, but it was reasonably clear that things were going badly for the rebels and that the U.S. Government was involved to some undetermined but important degree. By April 19, when a force of Cuban insurgents capitulated on the south coast of the island, it was all too evident that the new Kennedy Administration had suffered a major defeat, although its causes and dimensions were still unclear.

On April 21, two days after the collapse of the beachhead in the ill-starred Bay of Pigs, I was attending a business luncheon in New York when I received word that the White House switchboard was trying to reach me. As I knew that many government officials and agencies communicate through that switchboard, this was not particularly arresting news. So I finished luncheon leisurely and then returned the call from an adjacent office. The White House operator, without pausing to explain the origin of the call, switched on a male voice, that of John F. Kennedy. This did startle me as I had had very limited contact with the new President. I had met him briefly in 1948 when, as Superintendent of West Point, I had accepted the invitation of Congressman Kennedy to address a meeting of the Joseph P. Kennedy, Jr. Post of the Veterans of Foreign Wars in Boston. I had seen virtually nothing of him during my years as Army Chief of Staff, although as Senator he was a member of the Senate Armed Services Committee, before which I appeared many times. As a matter of fact, I do not recall that he was in attendance at any of my appearances.

During the recent presidential campaign, I had been a resident of Mexico and had been obliged to follow the election from a distance. In all honesty, I must admit that had I voted in the Democratic primary that year, I would probably have cast my ballot for Senator Johnson, whom I knew much better than Kennedy. As Chief of Staff, I had had ample opportunity to see Senator Johnson in action and had formed a high opinion of his effectiveness on the Armed Services Committee and his understanding of the needs of national defense.

Once Kennedy became the Democratic candidate and began speaking out on national and international issues, I found much to like in the candidate. I was particularly interested in early indications that he had recognized the deficiencies of a military strategy based upon Massive Retaliation and would do something to change it. In a campaign speech, he indicated an intention to seek military advice from senior retired officers, mentioning Generals Ridgway, Gavin, and Taylor along with Admiral Robert B. Carney as the kind of people he had in mind. About the same time, he sent me a friendly note regarding the strategic views presented in *The Uncertain Trumpet*, which he described as "most persuasive" and helpful "to shape my own thinking." All of this was good news to a scarred veteran of the Pentagon wars who had fought in opposition to Massive Retaliation and in support of Flexible Response.

I had no other communication with the Kennedy team until a couple of days after the inauguration when, to my great surprise, the new Secretary of State, Dean Rusk, telephoned to ask if I would consider accepting the ambassadorship to France. Although flattered by the offer, I had no hesitancy in declining as I had just signed a five-year contract to serve as president of Lincoln Center and could not consider asking relief from it except for the most urgent reasons. Furthermore, I knew that my wife was worn out with moves about the world and wanted to settle down in the New York apartment we had just bought—the first home of our own in thirty-six years of married life. So I declined the honor with appropriate expressions of thanks.

Now, three months later, President Kennedy was on the phone with a new and entirely different request. After identifying himself he said that, as I must realize from the press, he was in deep trouble as a result of the Bay of Pigs. Would I come to Washington at once and discuss the matter with him? Without hesitation I agreed to be at the White House the following day at 10:00 A.M.

When I arrived the next morning, I was ushered into the Oval Room and there met President Kennedy, Vice-President Johnson, and McGeorge Bundy along with a few other officials who drifted in and out. I sensed an air which I had known in my military past—that of a command post that had been overrun by the enemy. There were the same glazed eyes, subdued voices, and slow speech that I remembered observing in commanders routed at the Battle of the Bulge or recovering from the shock of their first action. In this instance, the latter was a more accurate analogy because this new administration had, indeed, engaged in its first bloody action and was learning the sting of defeat.

Seated for the first time alongside the famous presidential rocking chair, I heard from the unhappy Commander in Chief his own account of what had occurred. He explained in broad outline the origin and purpose of the Bay of Pigs operation, what it had intended to do and how it had ingloriously failed. All of his advisers had assured him that it was the right thing to do and that it had a good chance of success. Why had they all been wrong? What was the cause of failure? He assured me that he was not looking for a scapegoat, that he was taking all the blame himself, but he must learn why he had failed. He showed deep remorse over the fate of the Cuban prisoners captured in the beachhead, knowing that Castro was quite capable of summarily executing them.

After going over these matters in considerable detail, President Kennedy then explained that he wanted me to conduct an investigation to answer that nagging question: Why did the venture fail? At first, it appeared that he wanted me to do this alone; later, apparently having second thoughts, he designated me as chairman of a committee consisting of his brother Robert, Allen Dulles, and Admiral Arleigh Burke. I agreed to serve in this capacity but reminded him of my obligations to John D. Rockefeller III, the Chairman of the Board of Lincoln Center. Immediately he placed a call to Rockefeller, explained the situation to him, and asked for the loan of my time. Although I whispered that I thought one month would be enough, he indicated to Rockefeller that the job might take two or three months. But knowing the danger of loitering long in Washington, I mentally resolved to try to complete my work in accordance with the shorter estimate and to get back to the safe haven of Lincoln Center before becoming further entangled in the official fly-paper.

I shall not undertake here a detailed history of the Bay of Pigs affair beyond that needed to illustrate the blundering use of national power in support of a questionable national interest. Its origin was in a policy paper of the Eisenhower Administration promulgated in March 1960, which set forth in general terms a program of covert action to bring down the Castro government. I do not recall that the paper undertook to argue the need to overthrow Castro; it was judged self-evident that he was a dangerous influence and a potential disturber of the peace in the hemisphere. The program contained in the paper called for the use of selected Cubans to constitute a refugee political opposition to Castro, the organization of covert intelligence and political action teams within Cuba, and the creation of a paramilitary force outside of Cuba capable of conducting covert military operations on the island. This program gradually took form under the direction of the CIA and, by the time of the advent of the Kennedy Administration, it had accumulated considerable assets. The military component consisted of a reportedly well-trained Cuban Brigade of about 1,200 men, a minuscule air force of seventeen B-26's and a few transport planes, and a dozen amphibious landing craft. This force had been trained at secret bases in Central America and by spring was deemed by the CIA ready to undertake an amphibious landing on Cuba.

Whether or not to use the brigade soon became a major matter of debate within the new Administration. The military officers lent to the CIA, who had trained the Brigade, were proud of their handiwork and predicted an excellent performance if the force were committed to action. However, they also emphasized that it was a waning asset that had to be used soon or their men would drift away. The resulting feeling that it was urgent to get something out of this force before it was too late became a potent influence in convincing Kennedy to proceed with an operation about which he was instinctively dubious. After all, it was argued, if the Castro threat could not be curbed by Cubans, it might be necessary some day to use American forces for the purpose.

From the start, the plan for the expedition was constantly plagued by changes made necessary by new factors coming to the fore. One such factor was the deep concern of President Kennedy to keep the operation covert, a code word of the CIA which describes an activity in which American involvement is concealed or, at least, is plausibly disclaimable. This fixation on covertness exercised a baneful influence on the operational plan from the start to finish, often causing changes detrimental to the success of the military operation. It was the factor which caused the CIA to be placed and kept in charge of the operation, since the CIA was regarded as having some kind of special claim to the direction of any covert action of the government. Actually the Cuba operation in its principal aspect was almost purely military, an amphibious landing on a hostile shore, an operation which war colleges throughout the world have always recognized as one of the most complex and difficult in the military repertoire.

Since the United States would be the obvious source of any jet aircraft which might be employed, to preserve covertness the insurgent air force was limited to propeller B-26's of the World War II period which were available in many secondhand markets. Every effort was made to give the impression that they operated out of fields within Cuba, although in fact they were based in Nicaragua with a turn-around time of nine hours for second missions to Cuba.

All Americans were banned from the combat zone, even American civilian contract pilots who were badly needed to reinforce the limited number of Cuban pilots. The remote Bay of Pigs was chosen as the site of the landing, and the debarkation itself was to be made at night to avoid observation of the landing craft whose presence might suggest American participation. For the same reason, the plan called for the withdrawal of the troop transports over the horizon before daylight but, as we shall see, this feature of the plan could not be carried out.

Up until the last moment, President Kennedy had grave misgivings about the operation, and he sought to preserve his freedom of decision as long as possible. D day was successively delayed from April 5 to April 10 to April 17. Throughout this period, the President reserved to himself the right to cancel the landing on twenty-four hours' notice.

The operation, now known by the code word Zapata, began on April 15 with dawn air strikes by eight B-26's against the airfields occupied by Castro's air force. Although launched from Nicaragua, the planes flew a pattern to suggest defector pilots from Cuban fields, even though the time consumed in so doing risked alerting Castro to the imminence of the seaborne attack. As might have been expected, the strikes were only partially successful in destroying aircraft on the ground, but our military leaders were not too concerned at the time since heavier strikes had been planned for the morning of D day, April 17. Unfortunately, these were canceled by President Kennedy on the evening of April 16 because of the hubbub caused in the United Nations by the April 15 strikes. As a result, the Cuban Brigade landed in the face of an unneutralized air force which included a few T-33 jet trainers which were surprisingly effective and more than a match for the obsolete B-26's supporting the landing.

The Cuban Brigade got ashore pretty much as planned but soon came under nearly continuous air attack which destroyed two supply ships which carried much of the expedition's reserve ammunition. As a consequence, there was a shortage of ammunition on the beaches almost from the start, a shortage which was aggravated by the heavy firing of trigger-happy troops in their first combat. Castro's ground forces reacted promptly, rushing infantry, tanks, and artillery to counter the landings. Except for a small airdrop, efforts to bring in additional ammunition failed and the Cuban Brigade, thereby made incapable of further resistance, surrendered at the end of the third day. While the immediate cause of its failure was lack of ammunition, the basic causes were far deeper. It was to probe these causes that the Cuba Study Group, as our foursome was now called, set to work on April 24 in improvised offices provided in the Joint Staff area of the Pentagon.

CHAPTER 14

The Cuba Report

The charter of the Cuba Study Group was set forth in a letter to me signed by President Kennedy on April 22, which contained the following language:

> It is apparent that we need to take a close look at all our practices and programs in the areas of military and paramilitary, guerrilla and anti-guerrilla activities which fall short of outright war. I believe we need to strengthen our work in this area. In the course of your study, I hope that you will give special attention to the lessons which can be learned from recent events in Cuba.
>
> Since advice of the kind I am seeking relates to many parts of the Executive Branch, I hope that you will associate with yourself, as appropriate, senior officials from different areas. I have asked the following to be available to you in this fashion: Attorney General Robert Kennedy from the Cabinet, Admiral Arleigh Burke from the Joint Chiefs of Staff and Director Allen Dulles from the Central Intelligence Agency. I hope that each of them will have an opportunity to review and comment on your conclusions. But in the end what I want is your own report, drawing from past experience, to chart a path towards the future.

There were several interesting points in this letter. One was the almost passing mention of the Bay of Pigs, which was to be the primary subject of our investigation. Another was the broad invitation to make excursions into any aspect of limited and guerrilla warfare, the first intimation I had received of the President's deep interest in those activities later lumped together for convenience under the heading of counterinsurgency. A third point was the choice of my collaborators in this enterprise. It was quite clear that I was being given associates each of whom had a special interest in the outcome of the investigation. Robert Kennedy could be counted on to look after the interests of the President while Burke and Dulles, repre-

184

senting two organizations deeply involved in the operation, would see that no injustice was done to the Chiefs of Staff or the CIA. As the sole disinterested member and chairman of the group, I could foresee possible difficulty in reconciling the views of my colleagues as the investigation progressed.

We went to work under a full head of steam, resolved to finish our task in about a month and to give to it all of the time necessary to stay on schedule. As I had no other duty, this concentration of effort caused me no difficulty, but it was a great burden for my colleagues who were not relieved of the responsibilities of their regular assignments during this period. But they accepted the heavy schedule of work which I prepared without complaint.

Our first action was to record the testimony of some fifty witnesses who were interviewed in the course of twenty-one meetings. They were the principal participants in the operation, beginning with the American trainers in the camps in Central America and ranging upward through the ascending echelons of responsibility to the Secretary of State, the Secretary of Defense, the Joint Chiefs of Staff, and the senior officials of CIA. We also interviewed a few Cuban participants but the ones we needed most were in Castro's jails in Cuba.

We found it an engrossing but complicated task to assemble and analyze the testimony of so many witnesses and reduce the product to a coherent account of events, causes, and effects. Our witnesses were generally most cooperative and gave the impression of holding nothing back. I doubt that dissimulation would have been possible, as they were faced by four friendly but probing interrogators with considerable experience in the matters under investigation. In our personal relations, the four of us turned out to be a congenial team who worked harmoniously together in resolving the many contentious issues.

Burke and Dulles I had known and respected for many years, but Bobby Kennedy was a complete stranger whom I was getting to know for the first time. I was impressed by his ability as a thorough and incisive interrogator of witnesses, always on the lookout for a snow-job, impatient at any suggestion of evasion or imprecision, and relentless in his determination to get at the truth, particularly if it bore on a matter affecting John F. Kennedy. His attitude toward the President was unusual, quite the reverse of the usual fraternal relationship in which a big brother looks after a junior. It was Bobby, the younger, who took a protective view of the President, whose burdens he always sought to share or lighten. In watching Bobby at work on the Cuba Study Group, I liked his performance, and our work together was the start of a warm friendship which, in spite of later differences on Vietnam policy, lasted until his tragic death seven years later.

Our team made a preliminary report to President Kennedy on May 15 at a luncheon at the White House. It was merely a progress report to tell him how we were conducting our work and the trends which were developing in our thinking. I do not recall that he indicated any particular reaction other than satisfaction that we were on schedule and would produce a final report in mid-June. In compliance with that undertaking, on June 13, we delivered to him a single copy of our report, held to one at his direction, which set forth what had taken place at the Bay of Pigs, our conclusions, and recommendations.

In drafting the report, we directed a very large part of our effort to sorting out the facts relating to the four principal issues which emerged from the testimony we received: (1) the inadequacy of the air support of the landing; (2) the failure of the Brigade, when defeated on the beaches, to break out into the interior in guerrilla bands; (3) the responsibility of the Joint Chiefs of Staff for the military deficiencies; and (4) the contradictions in the understandings and attitudes of senior officials involved in the operation.

The evidence left no doubt about the inadequacy of the air support of the beachhead and the disastrous consequences to the ammunition supply. Failure to control the air was a result of the inadequacy in numbers and quality of the B-26's and the lack of sufficient Cuban pilots to keep the planes over the beachhead. Furthermore, this tiny air force was not allowed to use its full strength against the Castro airfields in the surprise attack on April 15, and had no fighters capable of dealing with Castro's planes, particularly the three T-33 jet trainers. Finally, as mentioned previously, on the evening of April 16, President Kennedy canceled the dawn strike scheduled to precede the landing of the Brigade.

As this last point was an important one, we examined closely the circumstances surrounding this cancellation to find out how and why the President had made it. We learned that, upon hearing of the cancellation order, two senior CIA officials went to Secretary Rusk and tried to persuade him to permit the dawn strikes. Rusk explained that, for reasons relating to Ambassador Stevenson's presentation of the American case before the United Nations, the President had ruled against any further air strikes until the planes could operate from a beachhead airstrip. Rusk testified to us that while the CIA officials had insisted that the D-day strikes were important, they did not appear to view them as vital. When offered the opportunity of telephoning President Kennedy directly, they did not accept the offer so that the President went to bed without knowing the full implications of his decision. Meanwhile, the Joint Chiefs of Staff were not informed of the cancellation and hence did not have an opportunity to intervene.

How effective a D-day strike would have been had it taken place is, of course, a matter of conjecture. Castro, in a press interview the following June, stated that he had dispersed his planes in anticipation of such a strike, but this statement has been disputed. My own opinion is that even if the April 17 attack had been carried out as planned, it would not have materially affected the outcome of the landing. There were too many other

186

things working against it. Nevertheless, the incident is an unfortunate example of ill-timed civilian intervention in a military operation without adequate consultation with those responsible for its success. In the wake of the Bay of Pigs affair, numerous reports appeared in the American press, usually from Cuban exile sources, to the effect that the United States had promised air support to the Brigade in case of dire need and had failed to deliver. Our group found absolutely nothing to support this allegation. The operation from beginning to end was dominated by an obsession to conceal the American hand, and all participants thoroughly understood this point. This was to be a Cuban liberation expedition mounted from non-U.S. bases, executed by Cubans with no visible American help and with no Americans in the combat area. The only relaxation of this ground rule was a reluctant authorization to use American naval ships and planes in support of rescue operations after the collapse of the beachhead.

We found that the failure of the Cuban Brigade to resort to the so-called guerrilla option was one of the matters which preyed most on President Kennedy's mind after the defeat. He told me that he had been repeatedly assured that, if worse came to worse, the Brigade could dissolve as guerrillas into the Cuban swamps and mountains. His associates had the same impression, although McNamara believed that there was a sea evacuation option as well. The Cuban Brigade, however, had been told before departure that if the landing ran into difficulty because of heavy surf or enemy opposition they were to disperse for evacuation by boat. Only as a last resort were they to take to the swamps for guerrilla operations. Hence, when disaster struck, the remnants of the Brigade fell back to the beaches where they were rounded up and taken prisoner by Castro's forces.

One of the most controversial issues which we examined was the responsibility of the Joint Chiefs of Staff for the military failures of the operation. Had they fulfilled their statutory responsibility to the President as his principal military advisers?

To this question the Chiefs gave a stout affirmative reply, pointing out that they were not in charge of the operation but merely in a supporting role to the CIA with a responsibility only for appraising and commenting on the CIA plan and for providing assistance in training and logistics. They felt that they had been obliged to work under circumstances which made it very difficult to carry out even these duties. In the interest of secrecy, there was no advance agenda circulated before the meetings and no written record of decisions kept during them. Furthermore the plan prepared by the CIA was always in process of revision so that the Chiefs never saw it in final form until April 15, the day of the first air strikes.

In developing the plan, there had been much debate over the choice of the landing site. The Chiefs preferred Trinidad since the area was farther from Castro's known troop locations and was near the Escambray mountains, historically a guerrilla hideout. But President Kennedy and his advisers from the Department of State did not like Trinidad because of its visibility and the absence of an airfield there suitable to support combat air operations. For these reasons it was decided about mid-March to shift the landing area to the Zapata (Bay of Pigs) area even though its remoteness made it less likely to attract local recruits once the beachhead was established. On the other hand, Zapata had the advantage of an airstrip long enough to allow combat operations to originate from it. This advantage appealed to State officials who were most anxious to discontinue strikes out of Nicaragua as soon as possible and who wished to give the impression that they originated from within Cuba.

In due course the Chiefs were asked to appraise both the Trinidad and Zapata plans, which they did in writing. In commenting on the military feasibility of the Trinidad plan in early February, they expressed the view that the Trinidad beachhead area was the best in Cuba for the purpose. They were of the opinion that it could be held by the Cuban Brigade against initial attacks, but would be eventually overrun if there were no popular uprising or substantial reinforcements. While they considered initial success likely provided certain personnel and logistic deficiencies in the plan were corrected, they stressed that ultimate success depended on the popular reaction within Cuba. In any case, even if only partial success were achieved, they thought that the operation could contribute to the eventual overthrow of Castro and, hence, was worth the risk and cost.

By mid-March, the President's growing dissatisfaction with the Trinidad plan caused the CIA authorities to propose three alternatives to the Trinidad site, one of which was the Zapata area. Asked to comment on these alternatives, the Chiefs in a memorandum to the Secretary of Defense expressed a preference for Zapata from among the three but added that none of the alternatives was considered as feasible or as likely to accomplish the objective as Trinidad. Our investigation revealed the fact, never accounted for, that neither the Secretary of Defense nor any other senior official appeared to have been aware of this clearly stated preference and hence the views of the Chiefs never influenced the decision on this point.

Piecing all the evidence together, we concluded that whatever reservations the Chiefs had about the Zapata plan, about the propriety of having the CIA continue to conduct a military operation of growing complexity, or about the erosion of military requirements by political considerations, they never expressed their concern to the President in such a way as to lead him to consider seriously a cancellation of the enterprise or the alternative of backing it up with U.S. forces. Generally speaking, the civilian officials with whom we discussed this matter felt that the Chiefs had been insufficiently forthright in expressing their reservations. Robert Kennedy quoted the President as saying on D day that he would rather be called "an aggressor in victory than a bum in defeat" and stated his belief that the President would have gone as far as necessary for success had he known in time what had to be done.

Our group concluded that whatever their handicaps—and they were many—the Chiefs had certainly given the impression to their colleagues of having approved the Zapata plan and of having confidence in its feasibility. They gave no clear warning to the President of possible failure. Regardless of their own opinion as to the adequacy of their performance, there was no doubt that John F. Kennedy felt that they had let him down.

This unhappiness with the Chiefs hung like a cloud over their relations with the President after the Bay of Pigs episode. On May 27, I ran into him by chance outside his office in the White House. He said that he had decided to go over to the Pentagon and talk things out with the Chiefs and asked whether I had any suggestions as to what he should say. By pure luck, I had a working paper of my own in my pocket which bore precisely on the subject on his mind—the responsibilities of the Chiefs to the President in all aspects of the Cold War. I gave it to him and suggested that he might want to use it to draw upon. I think that he was a little shaken and perhaps made a little suspicious by the readiness with which I produced my paper, but in any case he took it, rushed off to the Pentagon, and, as I learned later, used it extensively in his discussion with the Chiefs.

In talking to them the President reminded the Chiefs of their basic responsibility to him as his principal military advisers and expressed the hope that their advice would always come to him directly and unfiltered. He stated explicitly his view that this advice from the Chiefs could not and should not be purely military, since most of the problems which concerned him were shot through with political, economic, and psychological factors as well as military and he, as President, had to take all into account. While he expected the Chiefs to present the military arguments for or against any course of action without fear or hesitation, he wanted them to know that he regarded them as more than military specialists and looked to them for help in fitting military requirements into the over-all context of any situation. He recognized that perhaps the most difficult problem of government is to combine the available assets of many departments in an integrated, effective pattern. This was an historic statement of one President's view of the role of the military in the formulation of national security policy, one which later became the text of a National Security Memorandum issued in June of that year.

In the testimony which we assembled, there were many contradictory views expressed by senior officials with regard to important aspects of the Bay of Pigs operation. It was difficult to be sure what many of the principal participants regarded as the immediate objective of the exercise and what they had in mind when they spoke of the success or feasibility of the operation. While all were agreed that the primary purpose was to strike a blow at Castro before he could be further reinforced with Soviet weapons and technicians, and while the Cuban Brigade remained an asset in being, there was a considerable difference of views as to what was expected to take place in the beachhead. The military generally felt that a landing could be effected and the invasion force could hang on for some days if it landed with surprise and achieved control of the air. This was a big "if" when one considered the feebleness of the "political" air strike on D-2 which was sure to tip off the imminence of the landing and to offer Castro the opportunity to scatter his air force.

There were rather vague hopes among a few officials of a popular uprising without which, everyone agreed, there could be no complete success. One Chief thought that the CIA had painted an unduly optimistic picture of this possibility whereas another Chief viewed the landing as being primarily for the purpose of distributing arms to civilians who were expected to swarm to the beachhead. In support of this view, the reserve supplies for the beaches included arms and equipment for 30,000 such recruits, although Allen Dulles stated to us that he had never believed that such an uprising was in the cards and that CIA had no definite plan for instigating an uprising. But, in seeming conflict with this statement, the CIA had 15 million leaflets calling for an immediate uprising which awaited delivery at an airbase in Nicaragua.

Most of the other civilian leaders interviewed appeared hopeful of an uprising but not overly optimistic. Rusk, McNamara, and Bundy were united in describing the whole operation as marginal. Rusk seemed to give it the highest rating for probable success, about fifty-fifty, but he said that everyone involved had recognized it as risky business and that failure would be costly. He concluded wryly that he and his associates had erred in overestimating the international effects of failure and in underestimating the effect on Washington. No one was inclined to assign the principal blame to anyone else. They all seemed to agree that it was not the failure of any one department, agency, or individual—it was a governmental failure in which all had participated.

Against this background of sometimes conflicting testimony, we reached our conclusions and made our recommendations. We were unanimous in both categories. We concluded that the Zapata operation was of such magnitude that it could never have been conducted in such a way as to permit concealing or disclaiming U.S. involvement. For this reason, and because of its predominantly military character, we thought that about November 1960 the responsibility for the operation should have been taken from the CIA and given to the Department of Defense. But at the same time, and before proceeding further, the entire project should have been reviewed to determine whether it was in the national interest to go ahead. Such a review would have forced a reconsideration of the probability of success and the cost of failure. If it passed this test, all necessary resources should have been dedicated to assure its success—with that word clearly defined—and all tangential considerations detrimental to success should have been rejected. Thereafter, if any such considerations arose to endanger the operation, it was the duty of the President's advisers to warn him against them. This conclusion resulted from our feeling that neither CIA nor the military participants had presented to the President in sufficiently forceful terms the probable effect of some of the decisions prompted by nonmilitary factors.

While the immediate cause of failure on the beaches was a shortage of ammunition, there was a dangerously marginal character about the entire project resulting from the numerical weakness of the Brigade, the paucity of air support, the lack of replacements for battle losses, and the dependence on local volunteers in Cuba for even short-term survival. These fundamental weaknesses made for a fragility which invited disaster with the first adverse turn of luck. This adverse turn occurred in the form of destructive enemy strikes on the shipping of the expedition, though one had the feeling that if this misfortune had not occurred another would have, with similarly disastrous results.

A final defect was the jerry-built organization improvised to run this complex operation extending from Washington to the beachhead. There was no permanent machinery in Washington designed to deal with such an undertaking so one had to be improvised. When the action heated up communications quickly broke down, and the Washington leaders were soon without the information necessary to guide their decisions. The Cuba Study Group concluded that, if our government was to use its power effectively and flexibly in a Cold War environment, it was essential to have a permanent governmental mechanism capable of bringing into play the resources of many departments and agencies in support of presidential decisions.

In the light of these conclusions, we suggested the formation of a Strategic Resources Group (SRG) reporting to the President to be a sort of Cold War operations center. Its membership, as proposed, would consist of a presidentially-appointed chairman, the Under Secretary of State, the Deputy Secretary of Defense, the Director of the CIA, the Chairman of the JCS, and other senior officials on invitation as needed. We proposed to give the SRG a small staff and a Cold War Indications Group to keep tab on the sensitive areas of the world and to maintain an inventory of government assets for Cold War purposes. It would serve as a staff to the President in planning and conducting any Cold War operation involving more than one department.

We were convinced that the recent Cuban experience indicated the need for the Joint Chiefs of Staff to feel the same sense of responsibility for contributing to the success of the Cold War as to declared war, and we recommended that the President so instruct them formally along the lines of his oral statement on May 27. We further recommended that a formal after-action critique be held by the President with the principal actors to review the recent events and to decide how to do better in the future. Such an occasion would afford the President an opportunity to pull his shaken forces together, to give them new guidance, and to restore confidence and good feeling in the ranks. It would also allow him to set in motion a reappraisal of Cuban policy for the post-Bay of Pigs period. Should new and positive action be initiated against Castro or should we sit back and hope that time and internal discontent would eventually bring him down? As a group, we four were inclined to positive action, but we recognized the need to appraise the Castro threat in the broad context of the world political situation and American commitments elsewhere.

After discussing our recommendations with his senior advisers, the President eventually approved all except the one relating to the establishment of the Strategic Resources Group. Dean Rusk was less than enthusiastic about an interdepartmental committee reporting to the President with a potentially important role in foreign affairs which might impinge on the traditional responsibilities of the Department of State. As a result, the concept of the SRG was progressively modified in discussion and finally in January took the form of the Special Group Counterinsurgency (CI), which I shall describe later.

The after-action critique which we had urged took place in the President's sitting room in the White House with an attendance which included the President, Secretary of State Rusk, Secretary of Defense McNamara, the Joint Chiefs of Staff, McGeorge Bundy, senior CIA officials, and the members of the Cuba Study Group. I made the presentation for the Group, outlining the entire Bay of Pigs operation as we had reconstructed it, the mistakes as we saw them, our conclusions and recommendations. Since up to that moment no one present, except the President, had had the entire operation laid out before him, the audience followed the presentation with intense interest. At the end there was animated discussion but with no indication of resentment or ill feeling among the officials whose conduct was under review. When it was over and the visitors had filed out, the President turned to me with a wry grin and said, "Well, at least nobody got mad."

I think that our critique was useful insofar as it went and, indeed, set some kind of record as a conscious effort on the part of an administration to derive the lessons from an important episode in time to apply them to problems of the future. To be complete, however, we might profitably have reviewed the alternatives open to the President in the spring of 1961 and tried to decide what would have been the best course of action to have undertaken then. As I saw his alternatives in retrospect, they were: (1) to cancel the operation and disband the Brigade; (2) to infiltrate groups of the Brigade progressively into Cuba for purposes of intelligence and sabotage; (3) to use the Brigade as an amphibious landing force without direct U.S. participation but avoiding the most glaring mistakes made in operation Zapata; and (4) to put the Brigade ashore and be prepared to support it with as much U.S. military power as needed for the successful execution of a clearly defined mission.

Cancellation would have been the cautious course of action, but it would have wasted the asset represented by the Brigade, comforted Castro, and vastly discouraged the thousands of Cuban exiles dedicated to restoring the freedom of their country. The President's political opponents at home would have accused him of timidity in abandoning a course of action which his Republican predecessor would presumably have carried out.

As to the second alternative, the President himself had at one time suggested giving up the landing in force and infiltrating into Cuba the members of the Brigade in commando detachments of 200 or 300 at a time. He was talked out of the idea on the ground that these groups could never survive in the face of Castro's very efficient state police. An added objection might have been that most of the men in the Brigade would probably have refused such dangerous and relatively inglorious employment.

If the Brigade were to be used as an amphibious landing force, it could have been much more effective if some of the mistakes uncovered by the Cuba Study Group had been avoided. If the obvious fact had been recognized at the outset that no one would ever believe that an amphibious landing force had crossed the Caribbean from Central America to Cuba without the knowledge and acquiescence of the U.S. government, many of the defects in the operation could have been corrected. Without concern for covertness, sufficient jet aircraft could have been provided the Cubans to neutralize Castro's air force; air strikes would not have been limited by political considerations; sea evacuations by the U.S. Navy could have been provided for emergency use; and Washington could have decentralized control of the tactical operations to U.S. military authorities in the battle area. All ambiguity could have been removed from the availability of the guerrilla option. But even with these improvements, I can see little reason to believe that much more could have been accomplished than getting the Brigade ashore, keeping it in action for a limited time, and then dispersing the survivors into the bush or withdrawing them by sea.

The fourth alternative would have been the preference of most military men, namely, to use the Brigade as a spearhead supported by U.S. naval and air forces with U.S. ground reinforcements afloat over the horizon ready if needed to land and expand the beachhead. This course of action would certainly have presented a more honorable posture for a great power than one which suggested cringing from open responsibility for action which could never be plausibly denied. But there is a question as to what would have been the objective of an operation in this form. If the Cuban populace did not rise and the Brigade bogged down, would we have invaded the island with U.S. forces to finish off Castro? At some point, we would have had to make this decision or choose between withdrawing or dispersing the Brigade since it could not have been sustained indefinitely in a shallow beachhead even with U.S. support from the sea. In short, if we were not prepared to invade the island, this course of action would offer little more than the preceding alternative while committing U.S. prestige to a much greater degree. In 1961, with our troubles in Berlin and Southeast Asia, it would have been most unwise, in my judgment, to have committed the necessary military resources to carry out an invasion and occupation of Cuba. If that view is right, the fourth alternative becomes merely a variant of the third, more straightforward perhaps but no less unpromising in ultimate outcome. Such an analysis appears to me to tilt the scales in favor of alternative one, cancellation.

CHAPTER 15

Military Representative
of the President

In the course of our work together on the Cuban study, Bob Kennedy asked me on several occasions whether I would be interested in returning to public life in Washington. I shrugged off his early inquiries saying that I had a most engrossing job at Lincoln Center and was not looking for another assignment in Foggy Bottom. However, as our report neared completion Bob came to me with a very specific proposal: the President wanted me to succeed Allen Dulles, who was retiring from the directorship of CIA. I meditated long over the matter and consulted with my wife who, after over thirty changes of residence, well deserved the relative quiet of our new life in New York. But now the circumstances were different from those when I declined the ambassadorship to France. We had a new President, badly shaken by his recent experience in Cuba, who needed someone with military experience in his immediate entourage whom he could consult readily with regard to the military matters reaching his office. If I were offered such a job, Diddy and I agreed that I had an obligation to take it.

This conclusion having been reached, I returned to the President and told him that I definitely did not wish to become the Director of the CIA, much as I respected the importance of the assignment. On the other hand, I had given my life to the military profession and, if there was any way in which that experience might assist him, I would be happy to put it at his disposal. There followed several periods of discussion as to what might be arranged. At one time, the President considered reestablishing the position of Chief of Staff to the President, the title held by Admiral William Leahy during World War II. However, the major justification for that position had been the absence of a chairman to preside over the meetings of the Joint Chiefs of Staff, where General Marshall, the Army Chief of Staff, and his opposite number, Admiral King, Chief of Naval Operations, did not always get along well. In 1961 there was a Chairman of the Joint Chiefs of Staff with statutory authority to perform the analogous task of presiding over the Chiefs of Staff and keeping the peace between them.

While this matter was under consideration, President Kennedy asked me to go to Gettysburg to brief General Eisenhower on the findings of the Cuba Study Group. The timing of the visit was occasioned by the appearance of an article in the *Saturday Evening Post* which alleged that President Eisenhower had had a plan for using the Cuban Brigade in a landing which envisaged American military intervention if needed for success. It stated specifically that under this plan American aircraft would intervene if necessary to maintain air superiority and to prevent the destruction of the anti-Castro forces.

I undertook the mission with some trepidation, as I suspected that I was still in the bad graces of the General, whom I had not seen since my retirement in 1959. I was glad to have Allen Dulles as a companion, and I asked him to toss my hat into Ike's office ahead of us to see how he treated it. On June 23 we flew to Gettysburg by helicopter and called on General Eisenhower in his office in the center of town. The hat overture was not needed as the General was his warm, cordial self and expressed satisfaction that I was returning to active duty. He quietly dismissed the magazine allegations, saying that he had never seen an operational plan for an amphibious landing in Cuba and had no knowledge of anything resembling the Zapata plan.

I summarized the Cuba Study Group report, including the conclusions and recommendations. He took issue with none of the points raised and appeared to indicate general approval of the report. He observed that the over-all lesson seemed to be the danger of changing an operational plan at the last minute. This thought led him to reminisce about the pressure placed on him just prior to D day in Normandy to cancel the airborne landings.

He recognized the need for improving the governmental machinery for handling complex interdepartmental operations such as the Cuban affair and showed concern over the dismantling of the NSC machinery carried out by his successor. But if the NSC could not do this job of coordinating Cold War operations, he agreed that some new agency was probably necessary to fill the gap. He appeared to have no doubt that Castro would have to be removed in the interest of hemispheric tranquillity and hoped that some mistake by Castro might pave the way. When we departed, he expressed his appreciation to President Kennedy for our visit and his hope that further public debate of the Cuban operation could be avoided.

Shortly after this incident, President Kennedy decided to install me in the White House as an adviser with the somewhat stentorian title of Military Representative of the President. After reaching agreement on the details, the President wrote a letter on June 26, 1961, asking me to serve in this position, which he described as that of a staff officer to advise and assist him with the military matters which reached him as Commander in Chief. Additionally, I was to have an analogous advisory function in the fields of intelligence and of Cold War planning, with particular attention to Berlin and Southeast Asia. Finally, to allay the understandable concern of those officials and agencies with responsibilities in these same fields—namely, the Secretary of Defense, the JCS, the NSC, and the Director of the CIA—the presidential letter made it very clear that the Military Representative had no command authority and was not to be interposed between the President and any of these individuals or agencies. To be doubly sure of no misunderstandings, the President at my suggestion called Rusk, McNamara, and me to his office to allow a frank discussion of their attitude toward my new assignment and to satisfy me that I would be *persona grata* in his official family.

Fortified by the reassurances given by the Secretaries, I returned to active military duty on July 1, 1961, just two years after retiring from the Army. I set up an office in a suite of rooms on the third floor of the Executive Office Building alongside the White House, assembled a small but highly competent staff of seven members drawn from the armed services and CIA, and hung out my shingle as "Milrep," the form into which my title had been quickly corrupted.

From the outset I had to bear in mind the need to reassure by deeds the officials mentioned in the President's letter who could read the words setting the limits to my job but still would wonder how the newcomer was going to perform. Secretary McNamara seemed to have no misgivings about my assignment, but I knew that my old military colleagues, the Joint Chiefs, could not be happy over the appearance on the White House scene of a competitive source of military advice. They were also aware of my views of the inadequacies of the Joint Chiefs system, which I had openly expressed in *The Uncertain Trumpet,* and would have grounds to fear that I would try to advance some of my heretical concepts in the White House. Fortunately General Lemnitzer, the Chairman, was a friend since cadet days at West Point. I told him that I did not view my responsibilities as competitive with the Chiefs and did not intend to serve as a White House roadblock to their recommendations. I suggested an early exchange of views on important matters prior to sending final papers to the White House so that I could develop my views concurrently and inform the Chairman in advance of any possible conflict. In turn, Lemnitzer promised to do all he could to prevent anyone from driving a wedge between us, a trend already visible in some of the press comment on my appointment. After these initial understandings our relations proceeded with no friction

197

of which I was ever aware, although I am quite sure that the Chiefs, as a body, never cared for the "Milrep" as an institution.

The adjustment of my new job to that of the Special Assistant to the President for National Security Affairs proved to be a more sensitive matter. McGeorge Bundy, the incumbent, was able, aggressive, and highly self-confident. The duties of his office had never been accurately defined but depended largely on what Bundy felt needed to be done. My interests in the fields of intelligence, Berlin, and Southeast Asia cut sharply across many of the activities which Bundy had been directing, and his initial reaction to me was one of considerable unhappiness. In due course, however, by cut-and-try methods, we worked out a satisfactory adjustment of relations based upon a continuing interchange of information regarding activities of mutual interest and the frequent attendance of staff members of one office at the briefings and meetings of the other.

The heart of my new business was to learn to serve President Kennedy effectively. As an old military type, I was accustomed to the support of a highly professional staff trained to prepare careful analyses of issues in advance of decisions and to take meticulous care of classified information. I was shocked at the disorderly and careless ways of the new White House staff. I found that I could walk into almost any office, request and receive a sheaf of top secret papers, and depart without signing a receipt or making any record of the transaction. There was little perceptible method in the assignment of duties within the staff, although I had to admit that the work did get done, largely through the individual initiative of its members. When important new problems arose, they were usually assigned to ad hoc task forces with members drawn from the White House staff and other departments. These task forces did their work, filed their reports, and then dissolved into the bureaucratic limbo without leaving a trace or contributing to the permanent base of governmental experience.

This lack of order, which probably troubled me more than it should have, resulted from at least two causes. The first was the lack of acquaintance of most of Bundy's staff members with the practices and procedures of a well-trained staff. Also the substance of their business was new to most of them, a fact that made some diffident about asking questions and hesitant to communicate freely with one another. The other cause was the action taken by President Kennedy shortly after assuming office in abolishing the Planning Board and the Operations Coordinating Board of the NSC. The first was the staff element charged with preparing papers for the consideration of the Council; the second was responsible for reporting to the Council on the performance of the departments and agencies charged with carrying out presidential decisions. With the abolition of these two boards, their functions were performed spasmodically when a need was perceived by Bundy or a member of his staff. Bundy explained to me that he recognized the need for these functions but that he intended to perform them by simpler and less formal procedures than had been the case in the Eisenhower Administration.

In making these somewhat critical remarks of the new Kennedy team, I should point out that they would apply with slight modification to most newly assembled staffs in any administration. A new administration always brings in its own crowd and feels obliged to make changes in old patterns of performance, if only to prove its capacity for innovation and fresh thought. It is rare to find a sense for organization among the politicians, lawyers, academicians, and writers who are likely to make up most of the new team. Except for an occasional business executive, such men have usually made their reputations by individual performance—they are not likely to be accustomed to playing on a team. Hence it takes time for them to adjust their private ways to the needs of official life and to establish a framework of accepted relationships with one another which, in effect, is the definition of organization. By the end of its first year, Bundy's staff had survived a shakedown period which included the Bay of Pigs, and it had acquired a professionalism which carried it through the subsequent crises of the Kennedy and Johnson Administrations. But the inexperience of the officials of any new administration makes its first year a hazardous time for the Republic.

As I meditated on ways and means to serve President Kennedy I often sought the advice of Bob Kennedy as to what was feasible and what was incompatible with the President's natural way of doing business. My task seemed to be one of anticipating problems of the President in the areas of my responsibility and of being ready to help the President when they came before him. This requirement meant that I must be aware at all times of the important issues in my area as they were taking shape in State, Defense, and the intelligence community, and which would eventually reach the President—quite an order as I soon found out. The solution I adopted was to assign a member of my staff to cover a given sector of the executive community where he was given entree to the key planning groups and gradually acquired the ability to keep me well informed of coming events. As an issue approached the President, I was able to warn him of its imminence and call to his attention its significance and general nature. By the time it reached his agenda for formal consideration, I tried to have in his hands an analysis of the issue, the contending arguments, and the key points which he must eventually decide.

I should like to be able to say that these efforts were successful and that, as a result, the President always entered the Cabinet Room thoroughly briefed and ready to resolve the problems awaiting him. The fact is that it was almost impossible to get a paper into his hand in time for him to digest it before he plunged into an important discussion. Not only was he the busiest and hardest working man in the world but, like his subordinates, he had little regard for organization and method as such. I am sure that I often appeared to him a stiff military taskmaster who wanted to take all the zest and spontaneity out of life by overinsistence on form and routine. In any case, the President would have little of my feeble effort at regimentation as he found it far more stimulating to acquire information from the give-and-take of impromptu discussion.

In looking back on my activities in the period from July 1961 until October 1962, when I became Chairman of the Joint Chiefs of Staff, I would say that they consisted of three streams which flowed parallel in time but in separate courses. All three had their origin in President Kennedy's letter of June 26, 1961, which indicated that he wanted particular assistance in Cold War planning, Berlin and NATO matters, and Vietnam-Southeast Asia policy.

Cold War planning turned out to be primarily a matter of planning defenses against subversive insurgency of the kind encountered in the post-World War II period in various countries on the Sino-Soviet periphery. President Kennedy entered office deeply impressed with the significance of this form of Communist-inspired aggression, and in his first NSC meeting on February 1, 1961, he asked Secretary McNamara to consider means of placing additional emphasis on the development of counterinsurgency forces. He took very seriously Khrushchev's speech of January 6, 1961, which promised Soviet support on a global basis for Peoples' Wars or Wars of National Liberation on the model of the guerrilla war in South Vietnam. Moreover, the Bay of Pigs experience injected a new urgency into Kennedy's concern for counterinsurgency preparations and led him to direct a number of actions to assist underdeveloped countries, particularly in Latin America, in increasing their military and police protection against the internal Communist threat supported externally by Castro.

It took some time for most American officials in Washington, myself included, to sense the full significance of the threat of Wars of National Liberation as President Kennedy viewed it. It required an increase in Vietcong terrorism and guerrilla activity in South Vietnam during 1961 to make clear what Khrushchev was talking about in his January address. It was true that a War of National Liberation was but a new name for an old game which had been played previously in the Greek civil war, in the Huk insurrection in the Philippines, in the guerrilla warfare in Malaya, and in Castro's rebellion in Cuba. They all had the common identifying mark of subversive aggression for the overthrow of a non-Communist government using terrorism and guerrilla warfare supported when possible from an external Communist source. This was the new technique which Khrushchev in Russia, Mao in China, and Ho Chi Minh in North Vietnam united in proclaiming as the preferred means for the future expansion of militant Communism, not merely in Asia but in Latin America and Africa as well. This was the threat which President Kennedy perceived and against which he wished to erect defenses.

200

By the end of 1961, in spite of the rather large number of actions initiated in the field of counterinsurgency, it was apparent to me that we were not doing enough to satisfy the President. There was increasing evidence of the need for a steering mechanism for these piecemeal efforts in order to develop an integrated governmental effort behind the counterinsurgency program. In December, two separate reports, one from CIA and the other from the Joint Chiefs of Staff, urged that the President establish a single, high-level authority for this purpose. The outcome of these studies was a presidential directive in January, 1962, which I drafted, establishing the Special Group Counterinsurgency (CI) to assure the ability to use all available resources, when and as directed by the President, in preventing and resisting subversive insurgency and related forms of indirect aggression in friendly countries. I was named chairman. Other members included: Attorney General Kennedy; Deputy Under Secretary of State for Political Affairs Alex Johnson; Deputy Secretary of Defense Gilpatric; Chairman of the Joint Chiefs of Staff Lemnitzer; Director of the CIA McCone; Special Assistant to the President for National Security Affairs Bundy; the Director of the U.S. Information Agency (USIA), Murrow; and the Administrator of the Agency for International Development AID Hamilton. The Special Group was to perform several specific functions: assure recognition throughout the U.S. Government that subversive insurgency was a political-military conflict equal in importance to conventional warfare; verify that this recognition was reflected in the organization and training of the Armed Forces and in appropriate programs of State, Defense, AID, USIA, CIA, and other participating departments and agencies; keep under review the adequacy of our resources for dealing with subversive insurgency, particularly in specific countries to be assigned by the President to the cognizance of the Special Group. The countries initially assigned were Laos, South Vietnam, and Thailand; others were added and some subtracted as time went on.

As an irreverent bureaucrat with a low opinion of the committee system, I found the Special Group a refreshing exception to my past experience. It was unique in that the principals gave top priority to their duties on it and rarely missed a meeting. Furthermore, they could bring no staff with them; hence, they were obliged to do their homework before they came and to speak their own pieces after getting there. Being the heads or deputy heads of powerful agencies of government, they had vast resources immediately available to them when they returned to their offices. Finally, they knew that the eye of the President was constantly on them and that the chairman reported their day's work to him immediately after each meeting. The presence of Bob Kennedy on the committee, with his energy and interest in its work, was another force which vitalized the membership and guaranteed unusually candid testimony on the part of those called before the Group. Bob was a bit rough on evasive witnesses.

With these advantages the Special Group got off to a flying start, and in the course of 1962 set in motion many projects of considerable long-term value. At its instigation the State Department, in collaboration with other departments and agencies, produced a statement of national counterinsurgency doctrine which served as a basis for the development of departmental doctrine throughout the executive branch. It supervised, commented, and reported to the President on the various counterinsurgency training programs which by the end of 1962 involved approximately 50,000 officer grade officials, military and civilian. It watched over the development of counterinsurgency courses in the curricula of the military school system, particularly in the War Colleges, and encouraged the State Department to establish a series of seminars on the subject at the Foreign Service Institute.

The President repeatedly emphasized his desire to utilize the situation in Vietnam to study and test the techniques and equipment related to counterinsurgency, and hence, he insisted that we expose our most promising officers to the experience of service there. To this end he directed that Army colonels eligible for promotion to brigadier general be rotated through Vietnam on short orientation tours, and he was inclined to require evidence of specific training or experience in counterinsurgency as a prerequisite to promotion to general officer rank. He looked to the Special Group to verify compliance with his wishes in these matters, a duty which we fulfilled by means of recurrent spot checks on departmental performance.

Police training in vulnerable countries was another activity which received continuous Special Group attention. To standardize and improve its quality in Latin America, we recommended and obtained the establishment of a police academy for students from Latin America which became a useful meeting ground for the law enforcement agencies of various countries which otherwise had little contact with one another. We also undertook to disseminate in Latin America the concept of civic action by local military forces on the model of the accomplishments of our troops in Korea. Our objective was to stimulate civic consciousness in the armed forces of these countries and to develop unity of purpose between soldiers and civilians. In time, civic action programs were set in motion in a dozen different countries in fields such as health, education, public works, agriculture, and irrigation. The U.S. role was limited to training indigenous trainers, never to undertake the impossible task of direct instruction of the local people.

I gave up the chairmanship of the Special Group in October 1962 when I became Chairman of the Joint Chiefs of Staff, but I continued to serve as a member thereafter. The rather feverish activity of the Special Group during the early months of its existence tended to subside after 1962 as counterinsurgency programs got under way, and the work of the Special Group became largely one of supervising implementation. It remained in existence at steadily declining levels of activity until in 1966 it merged with the Senior Interdepartmental Group of the Johnson Administration as I shall later describe.

CHAPTER 16

NATO Problems

While striving to increase the U.S. readiness to cope with subversive insurgency, President Kennedy faced an immediate threat at the other end of the war spectrum in Khrushchev's proclaimed intention to end the Berlin problem once and for all on his own terms. In his meetings with Kennedy in Vienna in June 1961, Khrushchev had renewed his threat of 1958 to make a legal end to World War II by signing a peace treaty with East Germany which would terminate the special quadripartite rights of the victors in Berlin. West Berlin would be designated a free city outside the surrounding Communist state, but its communications with the West would be turned over to the East German government. In a deliberate attempt to heat up the crisis, Khrushchev announced his intention to put this plan into effect by the end of 1961, and thus remove once and for all the "bone in the throat of the Russian people" represented by Berlin. Shortly thereafter, in July, he indicated that the USSR would suspend a previously announced reduction of 1.2 million men in the armed forces and would increase the Soviet defense budget by 33 percent.

Faced with this ultimatum, Kennedy accepted the challenge as one which involved the national security and the sanctity of U.S. pledges to its allies. He embarked upon an intensive program to increase the military and political strength of the United States and of NATO available to meet this threat. In the course of the many discussions arising from these efforts during the following months, I often had an opportunity to observe and appraise President Kennedy's views and attitudes toward the use of military power in support of foreign policy.

In the first place, he was a sincere convert to the need for a strategy of Flexible Response to replace the dependence on Massive Retaliation of the Eisenhower-Dulles era. He often expressed his sense of needing multiple options in the power struggle in which he was inextricably involved with the Communist world, and he looked to his advisers to show him alternative ways for keeping his choices open as long as possible. This desire to suspend decision to the last moment could sometimes cause trouble, as it had when he withheld the decision to land the Cuban Brigade until twenty-four hours before the event; yet it was thoroughly understandable on the part of a chief of state with his enormous responsibilities.

An avid reader of history, Kennedy had been greatly impressed by Barbara Tuchman's *The Guns of August*, which he often quoted as evidence that the generals are inclined to have a single solution in a crisis and thus tie the hands of the political leaders by leaving them with the choice between doing nothing and accepting an inflexible war plan. As he read Tuchman's book, it was the rigidity of the mobilization plans both of the Triple Alliance and of the Triple Entente which made it impossible for the diplomats to avert a world war in 1914.

In rebuttal, I fought back feebly—one never feels at his best in an argument with a President—saying that the generals would never have had the opportunity to entrap the political leaders if the latter had used political means with sufficient skill to avoid the need for recourse to war. Furthermore, they should have paid sufficient attention in time of peace to the plans and capabilities of their Armed Forces so that they would not be surprised by what the generals could or could not do in a crisis. I added that American political leaders of recent times had not always had this kind of information about U.S. forces, and I hoped it would be different in his administration.

The President had a healthy suspicion of military requirements as expressed by military leaders who, as everybody knew, would like "to fortify the moon." Although in the 1960 campaign he had used the alleged missile gap as a stick with which to beat the Republicans, he liked to look around the Cabinet Room during a military discussion and ask whimsically, "Who ever believed in the missile gap?" Only I would raise my hand. But whatever his skepticism on other points, he was convinced of the need to increase conventional forces, particularly since the renewal of the Berlin confrontation by Khrushchev; indeed, in 1961 and 1962 he often wanted Secretary McNamara to go faster and farther in increasing these forces than the Secretary was personally inclined.

As for strategic nuclear weapons, he acknowledged the necessity for having enough for deterrence and left it to Secretary McNamara to decide what enough meant in terms of numbers and types. To my regret he saw little if any promise in the small, tactical nuclear weapons which seemed to me to offer another option between the loss of a conventional war and escalation to the use of strategic nuclear weapons. I argued that they could be used with discrimination as to targets, destructiveness, and hazard to civilian populations. In the NATO area, in particular, they offered a means to repulse an onslaught by superior conventional forces in a period when our allies were not able or not willing to pay the price of parity with the Warsaw Pact in nonnuclear forces.

Although my arguments left the President unconvinced, he did not oppose contingency planning which included the use of tactical nuclear weapons. But he doubted the feasibility of restraining the spread of nuclear war once nuclear weapons were used on the battlefield and shared the feeling of some of his advisers that there were already too many tactical nuclear weapons deployed in Europe. However, he recognized the political impossibility of withdrawing such weapons under the eyes of watchful allies always doubtful of the American will to defend them if necessary with nuclear weapons.

These were some of the attitudes and biases which Kennedy brought to the problem of rearming ourselves and our NATO allies to meet the threat to Berlin. While he did not wish to appear to panic or to overreact, he made it plain that he wanted tangible results in increased strength in a short period of time. Although he rejected Dean Acheson's proposal for the declaration of a national emergency, he endorsed Acheson's views urging a prompt buildup of our nonnuclear forces, not only to meet the needs of Berlin but also to strengthen our military posture world-wide. But all of this was to be done in a low key, with no shouting but with a quiet determination which might be expected to impress Khrushchev.

Secretary McNamara, as the President's spokesman, explained to a Congressional subcommittee on July 31, 1961, the reasoning behind the course of action upon which the President was embarking:

> This is the basic short-term objective of the measures we now propose—to attain a greater range of military options together with the related deterrent and political effects which would go with them. The purpose is twofold: to deter the Soviets from pressing a Berlin crisis to the point of conflict, and to become better able to deal with any conflict which might nevertheless occur. We expect that our European allies will wish to make corresponding increases in their strength, so that our united efforts can have full effect and so that the solidarity of the Alliance can be demonstrated. . . .
>
> Although Berlin is now the focus of attention, these measures are also directed at the larger problem of Communist threats and pressures all around the globe. We have not lost sight of the dangerous situation which confronts us in Southeast Asia or the possibility of a sudden outbreak of trouble in other areas of the world. What we are seeking to achieve, and achieve quickly, is a peak readiness of our military establishment to respond promptly with appropriate forces, and in adequate strength, to any kind of armed Communist aggression anywhere in the world; and to maintain that posture until we can see more clearly what lies ahead. Because we cannot foresee with certainty how events may develop over the coming months, we cannot say at this time whether the strength increases we now propose will necessarily be permanent.

This was strong language which sounded very much like a restatement of the Truman Doctrine of 1947 and a renewed resolve to resist Communist aggression anywhere any time. The broad concept of military security as viewed by the Kennedy Administration was further emphasized by Secretary McNamara in another Congressional hearing when he stated that limited warfare forces "should be properly trained, equipped and deployed to deal with the entire spectrum from guerrilla war to full-scale limited war."

To give form and substance to the President's decisions required months of unremitting work throughout the government, particularly in the Department of Defense. The President made it clear at the outset that the budget should not set a ceiling on the military effort—we should be willing to pay whatever was necessary for security. As a result, he was soon receiving annual military budgets in the range of $50 billion in contrast to those of his predecessor in the range of $38 billion and confronting the consequences of an increasing loss of gold. In this new atmosphere I could not fail to recall a warning from Secretary of the Treasury Humphrey at an NSC meeting during the Eisenhower regime to the effect that the American people would not stand another 38 billion dollar defense budget. Convinced by President Kennedy of the reality of the Berlin crisis, the American people took his increased budgets with scarcely a murmur.

McNamara was the driving force behind the military build-up, but he seemed strangely reluctant to increase the forces on a permanent basis, insisting instead on a temporary incremental expansion. It was not until November 1961 that he approved the expansion of the Army from fourteen to sixteen divisions and then only after receiving a clear intimation that President Kennedy himself insisted upon it. But at the same time he set a ceiling of 960,000 men on the strength of the Army despite clear evidence that about a million men would be needed to maintain sixteen combat-ready divisions.

Even before the expansion got well under way, Secretary McNamara began planning for their contraction. An extraneous factor which motivated him was the disturbing loss of gold resulting from our heavy dollar expenditures overseas. To help the President reduce the drain McNamara, as a principal spender of dollars abroad, took the lead with his usual aggressiveness. When the news of his plans to contract our strength began to circulate in Washington and in our missions abroad, it produced a sharply adverse reaction, particularly in Europe. There General Norstad, as well as our Ambassador in Bonn and our Mission Chief in Berlin, were particularly disturbed over this apparent reversal of U.S. policy and its effect on the NATO alliance and the morale of Berlin.

I discussed this matter with the President early in January 1962, pointing out the possible consequences of a premature contraction. I recommended that he provide new guidance directing the Department of Defense to maintain the strength of our forces in Europe at existing levels and the units of the strategic reserve at home in a state of readiness for prompt deployment overseas. While I felt that the President was inclined to accept this recommendation, at the same time he was loath to overrule his Secretary of Defense and limited his action to asking McNamara how he proposed to meet the personnel requirements of a sixteen-division Army. This query resulted in a running discussion during the spring which ended in a series of modifications of plans, but the decision to reduce the Army was retained, although the effective date was set back from July to September.

One episode occurred early in this period which carries a moral for all new administrations. While still working on the Bay of Pigs investigation, I read with something like consternation a passage in the President's special message to Congress in May 1961 which indicated that he was directing a reorganization of the Army's division structure to improve conventional firepower and tactical mobility. He also announced that the Army expected to make ten reserve divisions ready for deployment to combat on eight weeks' notice. When I inquired into the background to these statements, I found that they had been submitted by the Department of Defense quite casually for incorporation in his speech as examples of innovations sponsored by the new administration.

My initial reaction was that the President had been led to make statements which would cause him subsequent embarrassment. I could not understand the proposal to reorganize the Army divisions since a careful reorganization had been carried out only a few years before during my service as Chief of Staff. Since any important change in the division structure affects the tactics, training, equipment, and logistics of the entire Army and hence its combat readiness, one should tinker with it only for the soundest of reasons; and I did not know of anything which had occurred so soon after the last reorganization to justify this action. As for the heightened readiness of the reserve divisions, I simply did not believe it possible. There were too many built-in obstacles in the reserve system to permit readiness for combat within eight weeks.

I went to President Kennedy, explained my reservations, and urged him to embargo further action on these matters until he had time to look into them at his leisure. The result was a memorandum from the President to Secretary McNamara asking a series of probing questions which I had prepared regarding both the division reorganization and the plan for increasing the combat readiness of the reserve divisions. This memorandum was a bombshell in the Pentagon, where no one had an immediate answer to the President's questions. In searching for something bright and new to embellish the President's speech, the responsible officials had got far ahead of the orderly planning process. As a matter of fact ultimate approval of the proposed division reorganization was withheld until January 1963, and the eight-week readiness criterion for reserve forces was eventually discarded as infeasible.

While Kennedy was able to make progress in improving our own military posture in fairly short order, it was a far different matter to induce a similar sense of urgency and achieve similar results among his NATO allies. In Europe, there was a complete lack of enthusiasm for increased conventional forces which were, costly and unpopular with the voters. The economists begrudged the diversion of manpower in the tight labor market while the politicians shuddered at the thought of using conscription to raise foot soldiers. The exaggerated claims for the merits of atomic weapons made by a decade of American spokesmen had been accepted most happily by these same Europeans who were now being asked to subscribe to what was soon tagged the new American strategy.

In point of fact, as Kennedy intended it there was no new American strategy, merely a shifting of emphasis away from the NATO nuclear strategy of the past. The President accepted the need to push the defenses of Western Europe to the Iron Curtain to reassure West Germany, the nation which, in case of war, had the most to lose in the shortest time. But he was not willing to leave that defense to a trip wire of ground forces which, if broken by a hostile reconnaissance detachment, would leave capitulation or a nuclear response as the only options. To avoid this unattractive dilemma, the American proposal was to develop adequate ground strength to check the aggressor long enough to permit some kind of communication between the two sides or, at least, a period of reflection by the invader on the possible consequences.

Unfortunately, the new American strategy was launched in a way which assured maximum European resistance. In the early days of the Kennedy Administration, relatively junior officials of both State and Defense, fired with a missionary zeal to reverse or at least reform the nuclear-oriented strategy of NATO, took off for Europe on various pretexts. There, in the course of making the rounds of the NATO capitals, they undertook to explain the Kennedy strategy and in so doing succeeded in arousing to new levels the ever-latent European suspicion of American motives. At the same time, they infuriated responsible American officials in Europe, such as General Norstad, who had to live with the aftermath of these visitations.

Washington was hard put to ease the tensions in the alliance caused by the growing controversy over NATO military strategy. In the search for ways to alleviate them, a group of NATO specialists in State were very much attracted by the possibility of creating a NATO-owned-and-operated nuclear force as a means to reassure the doubters of American reliability and to give Germany, in particular, the feeling of participation in the nuclear defense of Europe. The latter point was deemed particularly important in order to dampen German longings for national nuclear weapons which, it was feared, might reach them by way of France.

The first proposal for a NATO Multilateral Nuclear Force (MLF) of which I became aware was that an undetermined number of U.S. Polaris submarines were to be sold to NATO, armed with nuclear missiles kept under U.S. custody, and manned by crews representing all or most of the nations of the alliance. The missiles could be released for use and fired only under the same ground rules as the other nuclear weapons in support of NATO, namely, with the concurrence of the American President.

The MLF in this form looked to me like a gimmick of dubious political value and a military monstrosity. It seemed hard to believe that the NATO countries would pay the very substantial bill implicit in buying and operating the submarines, particularly since the use of their weapons would still be under the U.S. veto. Experienced naval officers, American and British, were aghast at the thought of nuclear submarines manned by mixed nationalities. They stressed the high level of training and the precision of operation required for such a complex weapons system as a ballistic missile submarine, and insisted that it was folly to try to operate one with polyglot crews with widely differing backgrounds of education and training.

To meet this criticism directed at the submarine aspect of the MLF, its supporters in the United States eventually proposed a variation based upon using surface vessels instead of submarines. This change reduced the estimated cost and voided some of the naval objections to the submarines. Admiral Anderson, our Chief of Naval Operations, conceded that the new concept could work and Lord Mountbatten moderated the criticism he had expressed for the submarine configuration of the MLF. The storm over the issue subsided and comparative harmony was restored by an agreement between MLF proponents in State and their opponents in the Pentagon to send a State-Defense team on a round of NATO capitals to explain the surface vessel concept and to measure the allied reaction.

Throughout this debate President Kennedy tried to maintain a position of uncommitted detachment. He listened to the arguments for and against the MLF, sympathizing with its objectives but recognizing the validity of many of the objections. He insisted repeatedly that he did not want the MLF to be advanced as an American proposal. It was merely one possible way of coping with the NATO nuclear problem, one which the United States would support if, and only if, the European countries were strongly for it and first met the NATO goals in conventional force.

Unfortunately, this disavowal of American sponsorship was largely nullified by the zeal of its American supporters who undertook to sell the idea to the torpid Europeans. In this way they placed an inevitable made-in-America stamp on the MLF concept that was a fatal handicap. Only a few Germans—far from a consensus of the leaders—showed a serious interest in it. The result was that the project, though never rejected, tended to fade away, but it left behind the impression of a rejected American overture.

While these intramural issues were being debated within the fortress of the NATO alliance, the threat to Berlin forced NATO leaders to look over its walls to the enemy beyond. Although Berlin fell outside the geographical limits of the NATO alliance, the United States, France, and Great Britain as occupying powers were responsible for its defense, and anything of importance happening in Berlin could affect the entire alliance.

Throughout 1961 tripartite planning to prepare against possible attacks on Berlin and its communications went on at a furious pace. It was laborious work since it required concurrence on many points from three governments often with quite different attitudes toward Berlin. The British clearly did not intend to risk war to save the city whereas the French were surprisingly aggressive in rejecting Khrushchev's threats, not because of any greater willingness to run risks for Berlin but because of greater confidence that Khrushchev was bluffing. President Kennedy, meanwhile, believed sincerely in the importance of the Berlin issue to the security and world standing of the United States. With these differences of view among the three governments, no effort was made to obtain formal approval of the plans for the defense of Berlin in a way which might suggest an advance commitment by any government to execute any plan. After tripartite review, all plans were filed away as illustrative of possible military reactions to possible acts of aggression and nothing more.

On August 13, in the midst of these preparations to defend Berlin, preparations for the construction of the Berlin Wall began, taking the West by surprise. Although everyone had been aware of the serious drainage of East German manpower through Berlin to the West and the great concern of the Communist leaders over its continuation, I know of no one in a responsible position in the United States or in NATO who had predicted or even hinted at the possibility of the erection of the Berlin Wall. Indeed, I would have thought that the erection of that forbidding wall in the heart of Berlin, suggesting a concentration camp behind it, would have appeared a particularly unhappy solution from the Russian point of view. But we know, at least by now, that despite the importance the Communists attach to propaganda as a weapon of the Cold War, international opinion does not restrain them from the use of naked power when they feel it necessary for their purposes. The Berlin Wall, the bloody suppression of the Hungarian revolt, and the use of military force to crush the Czech heresy were all illustrations of this fact. This unabashed toughness on the part of the Soviets was in sharp contrast to the shame-faced air with which we had tried to hide behind the fig leaf of covertness, our role in the conduct of the Bay of Pigs operation.

Several months after the event President Kennedy asked whether any of his advisers had recommended knocking down the Wall at the start. The answer was necessarily negative, if only for the fact that for some days there was no wall to knock down. The Soviet action on August 13 was merely the announcement of crossing point restrictions between East and

West Berlin and the positioning of East German police to enforce them. This announcement was followed by a second on August 23, reducing the number of crossing points and limiting the Western allies to a single crossing at Friedrichstrasse. The most belligerent action possible at the outset would have been to disregard crossing regulations.

In researching the point for the President, I found nothing in the record to show that any of his advisers had urged the use of force to resist the restrictions of August 13. At first, these were regarded as merely additional steps to control the flow of refugees and, as such, not inherently objectionable. Personally, I found the action of August 23 much more difficult to accept because it was aimed specifically and publicly at the Allied occupying powers. It had nothing to do directly with the restraint of refugees but appeared a deliberate attempt by the East Germans to humiliate the Allies and further depress the morale of the West Berliners who were crying for Allied action against the Wall as it rose. If we did not respond to this provocation, it would be hard to resist further East German restrictions on Allied movements on the autobahn, on the railway, or in the air.

Impressed by these possibilities, I recommended to the President that he consider two possible courses of action. The first was for the Western powers to announce that they would disregard the restrictions and would cross into the Soviet sector wherever and whenever they saw fit. The second was for the Western Commandants to inform the Soviet Commandant in Karlhorst that they would call on him at a certain time to discuss the matter and that they would cross at a point other than Friedrichstrasse. After being sure that the message had been received, they would proceed to this point and cross unless turned back by superior force. While this second course of action offered some risk, it provided a possible way to break the rhythm of East German initiative and to deter later and more dangerous provocations.

The President asked for comments on these proposals and found all of his advisers cool to them. Even the U.S. Mission in Berlin, usually a proponent of active measures, was negative. Hence, the only measures actually taken as a result of the initiation of the Wall were the dispatch of another U.S. battle group about 1,600 men to reinforce the Berlin garrison, a visit to Berlin by Vice-President Johnson, and the return of General Clay to the city in temporary residence as a personal representative of the President.

To improve my usefulness to President Kennedy in dealing with these NATO matters I decided to make my first visit to the NATO area since returning to active duty. In the course of two weeks in March 1962, I visited the principal centers of NATO activities in France, Germany, England, and Italy. Upon my return I reported to the President those impressions which had particularly struck me after an absence of nearly three years from Europe. They fell under three headings: the depressed state of Franco-American relations, the German nuclear problem, and the NATO attitude toward

212

the new U.S. strategy. That these issues existed was hardly a surprising discovery since all had long been under consideration in Washington but somehow they looked differently on the ground.

As to our relations with the French, their senior officials were openly bitter over our refusal to aid the French nuclear program and the gratuitous extension of our noncooperation to nonnuclear aspects of their missile and nuclear submarine programs. Every official, American or European, with whom I talked was perfectly convinced that de Gaulle would carry out his plans to get nuclear weapons regardless of the cost or American opposition and that, if he encountered insuperable technological problems, he might turn to Germany for help. We had the choice, it seemed to me, of continuing to refuse to help the French or of trying to negotiate a trade of technical aid in atomic matters for French concessions in other areas. The latter might take the form of greater French cooperation in NATO; the commitment of some of their nuclear weapons, when available, to multilateral NATO nuclear forces; or an overall normalization of Franco-American relations. Although such a deal could hardly be expected to convert de Gaulle into a grateful, cooperative ally, nevertheless it might induce him to withhold some of the monkey wrenches which, from time to time, he liked to toss into the NATO machinery.

In Germany I found ample evidence of the need to reassure that country with regard to our intentions to support a forward NATO strategy which would really protect their exposed cities such as Hamburg and Munich. The Germans were hearing much talk about a forward strategy to defend such places but not seeing the forces to give it reality. To allay their fears and to strengthen their ties to NATO, several possibilities seemed worth considering. The first involved a modification of the concept of a NATO multilateral nuclear force to give it immediate feasibility. It seemed possible to me to organize such a force at once by the allocation of existing American and British nuclear weapons (and possibly French at some future time) and to modernize it subsequently by the introduction of the new mid-range missile which General Norstad had been advocating. As an important innovation I suggested that General Norstad be authorized to assign the targets to such a force although he would still be required to request presidential authority to fire these weapons in accordance with the agreed NATO procedures. This authority to plan and call for nuclear fire support would not give Norstad command authority over the national launching forces which could be at sea, in the United States, or elsewhere. That authority would remain with the present national commanders.

To give substance to a forward strategy capable of imposing a significant pause on an enemy advance without resort to nuclear weapons, there was obviously a need for more conventional forces. Was there any possible way of convincing our reluctant allies to join us in providing them? Without any illusion as to the likelihood of ultimate success, I suggested to the

213

President that we seek a way to influence our allies in the direction of our strategic thinking without resort to further direct argument or exhortation, of which they had already received a superabundance. This might be accomplished by means of a comprehensive NATO review of the military requirement of an adequate forward strategy provided the review was conducted by military professionals unimpeded by constraints of national guidance but planning on the basis of assumptions approved by the NATO military committee. If our allies could be persuaded to undertake such a review much good might come of it. It would educate them in the realities of nuclear warfare about which they knew far too little and would oblige the United States to convey to the NATO planners information too long withheld about weapons effects, targeting, and estimates of enemy ground strength. In the context of the review, it might be possible to release such information without creating the suspicion that we were doing so merely to provide arguments for the new strategy.

If, in the end, we could establish agreed NATO troop requirements for a forward strategy satisfactory to the Germans, that would be an accomplishment in itself and should have other beneficial side effects. Aside from the educational value of the review, it would assist General Norstad in justifying his requirement for a new NATO medium range ballistic missile, a requirement which was encountering opposition from McNamara. It should also produce some agreement within the alliance regarding the role of low yield tactical weapons in extending the capability of conventional forces. Such matters could not be considered without getting into questions of NATO organization, command and control—matters long overdue for revision. I believed that more progress could be made in dealing with these intricate matters in the relatively cool atmosphere of a military study than in the high temperature often generated in NATO political meetings. In the end, the decision in this matter would have to be taken by the political authorities of the alliance, but an agreed draft proposal from the military planners could serve a valuable point of departure.

The President referred my views on these NATO matters to Secretaries Rusk and McNamara. Their responses were generally sympathetic but definitely not ecstatic. State was in no mood to reopen the issue of nuclear aid to France which, it was thought, would encourage German pressures for similar treatment. Rusk supported the need to present U.S. strategic views without giving the impression of exhortation and thought that the comprehensive military review might be a useful technique at some future time. For the moment, he preferred to concentrate on educating the NATO Council in order to give the political authorities a fuller comprehension of factors involved in our strategic thinking. As for the MLF, he supported the need for such a force not as an answer to military requirements of the Supreme Allied Commander, Europe (SACEUR), but rather for its political effect. Such an MLF should be owned, controlled, and manned multilaterally by NATO; an improvised force using existing national weapons such as I suggested would not fill the bill.

Secretary McNamara's response devoted considerable space to repeating the Defense view of the MLF which depreciated both its military value and its effectiveness in reassuring the Germans but acknowledged that it had some political-psychological value. He thought a NATO military review would be useful but should be delayed until midsummer. However, he opposed my suggestion that the NATO commander be given, in effect, operational control of the fire of all the weapons necessary to strike Soviet forces threatening Europe.

Both Secretaries commented on the unfortunate effect of the disagreement over estimates of enemy ground strength which had broken out within the alliance, with the Germans and Norstad on one side and the Americans on the other. McNamara in particular was convinced that the NATO estimate of Soviet combat-ready divisions was greatly exaggerated and had initiated a study which tended to deflate the Soviet nonnuclear threat. This difference in views on intelligence became another divisive issue in the alliance and another obstacle to the acceptance of a forward strategy based on a nonnuclear pause.

In the end I concluded ruefully that while my trip to NATO had provided me with useful insights into the current problems of the alliance, it had produced nothing which, at the time, the decision-makers at home found attractive as a basis for action. The experience also reminded me of the impotence of a presidential adviser in tilting with policies originating in and supported by the bureaucratic power bases in State and Defense.

CHAPTER 17

Southeast Asia: 1961

The problems of a President never present themselves as a series of separable issues which can be dealt with one at a time. and then be put aside. Rather, they come to him as a turbulent flood of intermingled ingredients, some related, others unrelated, which must be sorted out and arranged in some kind of pattern to facilitate study and interpretation. Thus, as the Bay of Pigs episode faded into history and while President Kennedy was still deeply concerned with Berlin and NATO, he was obliged to attend at the same time to the situation evolving in Laos and Vietnam on the other side of the globe.

During the final half of 1961 it was Laos rather than Vietnam which received the closer attention of Washington officials because of the great fragility of the situation there. In Vietnam the Diem regime seemed comparatively stable after having survived the early attempts at subversion by Ho Chi Minh's stay-behind Communist cadres and the conflict with the sects—the Cao Dai, Hoa Hao, and Binh Xuyen—in 1955 and 1956. It was Diem's surprising success in establishing comparative order which led Hanoi in 1959 to declare a War of National Liberation against South Vietnam which meant, as we found later, the initiation of a clandestine guerrilla war to overthrow the Diem government. On the other hand, the threat in Laos from the Communist Pathet Lao, supported by North Vietnam and the USSR, was apparent to all and evoked the possibility of U.S. military intervention long before it was considered for Vietnam. Not only was the hand of the external enemy visible in Laos, but the threat of the well-organized Pathet Lao insurgency was augmented by the divided political leadership in the country, the ineffectiveness of its armed forces, and the apathy of much of its population.

The status of Laos, like that of Vietnam, was a product of the Geneva Accords of 1954. Even before its independence it contained strong Com-

216

munist (Pathet Lao) elements which controlled the two northern provinces that later served as the base for Pathet Lao military operations. In addition to the Communist faction, the country was divided into an anti-Communist right wing led by General Phoumi Nosavan and Prince Boun Oum and a neutralist center under Prince Souvanna Phouma.

Between 1954 and the accession of the Kennedy Administration, the situation in Laos was characterized by political intrigue and ineffective military maneuvering as these factions jockeyed for power and sought to attract foreign assistance. Souvanna Phouma, who became Prime Minister in 1956, enjoyed the support of France and Great Britain, but Washington was initially suspicious of him because of his acceptance of Pathet Lao in his government and his desire for diplomatic relations with the USSR. Because of this, the United States eventually withdrew support from his government and switched to the anti-Communist Boun Oum who, in December 1960, temporarily unseated Souvanna Phouma by a military coup.

It was this confused scene which greeted President Kennedy when he took office in 1961. There was a clear possibility that the USSR, which for some time had conducted an air lift out of North Vietnam to supply the Pathet Lao, might join with other members of the Communist bloc in an attempt to overturn Boun Oum. A late act of the Eisenhower Administration had been to warn the Communists against any such intervention and to direct certain military movements in the Pacific to signal increased readiness in that part of the world.

The Pathet Lao responded in the early months of 1961 with renewed military activities directed at the Plaine des Jarres, activities which revealed the incapacity of Boun Oum's forces to hold off the attackers and soon raised serious concern for the safety of Vientiane and key localities in the Mekong River valley. At the same time, the Pathet Lao were strengthening their hold on the Laotian panhandle which contained the so-called Ho Chi Minh trails, the military supply lines used by North Vietnam in supporting operations in South Vietnam.

President Kennedy had a limited number of unpromising options to choose from in dealing with the disintegrating situation in Laos. He could let matters continue their downward drift while hoping that some equilibrium of forces would eventually be reached without endangering Thailand and Vietnam, or he could follow the advice of most of his military leaders (I had not yet joined them) and offer the Laotians additional military assistance in the form of military trainers and equipment, supplemented, if necessary, by the introduction of SEATO or U.S. forces. In the latter case, it was certain to be the United States which would have to provide all or most of the forces. A final alternative was to support the British proposal of March 23, 1961, to negotiate a cease-fire, reconvene the International Control Commission and reassemble an international convention on Laos.

The President rejected the do-nothing option as irresponsible and the

217

military solution as dangerous and probably infeasible. His SEATO allies offered no troop support; the Lao armed forces showed no zest for fighting; and his military advisers were divided as to the requirements and the consequences of open U.S. intervention. When he explained the situation to the Congressional leadership at a White House meeting in May, he received no encouragement to send U.S. forces into Laos, a course to which Kennedy, himself, was instinctively opposed. Had not a great American soldier, General MacArthur, in April warned him against committing U.S. ground forces to the Asian mainland? Further, the bitter Cuban experience still rankled and caused him to reflect openly on the folly of expecting to achieve a military success in remote Laos when he had failed so spectacularly on his own doorstep.

In the end, by the process of elimination, he chose the third course of action without completely discarding the option of military intervention. He supported the holding of an international conference on Laos which eventually assembled in May 1961 in Geneva and lasted until July of the following year. However, throughout the prolonged and often acrimonious negotiations in Geneva, he repeatedly used his military forces as an instrument to advance his political purpose of obtaining international guarantees for a neutral coalition government in Laos. In support of this objective he initiated military maneuvers in Southeast Asia to remind his adversaries that he had not rejected military intervention as a possible course of action. His most dramatic use of the threat of military force was in May 1962, in response to the spring offensive of the Pathet Lao who, after gaining an important victory at Nam Tha, threatened the northeastern borders of Thailand. To reassure the Thai and to discourage further enemy advances, the President moved an American task force of some 5,000 men into Thailand and kept it there until the following December. In this move he received token support from three SEATO allies, Britain, Australia, and New Zealand, each of which deployed an air squadron to fields in Thailand. While this minuscule assistance was of some political value, it was also an indication of the lack of military substance in the SEATO alliance.

In due course, after many fluctuations in the situation in Laos and at the negotiating table in Geneva, a coalition government under the premiership of the neutralist Souvanna Phouma was put together in June 1962, and in July the Geneva Accord was signed by the United States and other countries. It provided that all foreign troops and military personnel be withdrawn from Laos and the use of Lao territory for "interference in the internal affairs of other countries" was prohibited. The coalition government under Souvanna Phouma which emerged was a flimsy, jerry-built contraption with little promise of longevity, and Souvanna's subsequent survival as Prime Minister was evidence not of strength but rather a reflection of disinterest on the part of any of the principal signatories to the Geneva agreement in upsetting him and his government. The Geneva Accord did not result in the withdrawal of the North Vietnamese troops supporting the Pathet Lao or the cessation of the use of the Ho Chi Minh trails to supply the war in South Vietnam. Fighting on the ground continued around the Plaine des Jarres, ebbing and flowing with the monsoon changes of the weather. However, the dividing line between Pathet Lao-held territory and that under government or neutralist control did not change in any important way from 1962 for the next seven years. There seemed to be a tacit understanding on both sides that the fate of Laos would be resolved in Vietnam. For that reason the Pathet Lao took as a primary objective the protection of the supply lines in the Laotian panhandle, and maintained a *de facto* partition of the country on a north-south line which prevented any effective military action from the Mekong valley against their communications.

In the running debate over the course of action to be followed in Laos, I supported the President's view that the introduction of U.S. forces should be avoided if at all possible. From a purely military point of view, if such a thing exists, the logistical problem of supporting troops in combat in Laos via Thailand and the Mekong valley would have been very difficult, and the construction of a line of communication slow and costly. If Laos were to be defended by external forces, the place to use them would have been against the source of strength of the Pathet Lao in North Vietnam which was readily accessible to our forces by sea and air from the east. However, I found nothing in the Laotian situation in 1961 and 1962 to justify such drastic action and heartily approved of Kennedy's efforts to obtain a negotiated solution, backed by an occasional show of military force. My attitude was reinforced by the increasing demands of the Vietnam situation.

This period of work on Laotian problems gave me my first occasion to reflect upon the SEATO Treaty and its value to our policy in Southeast Asia. This loose coalition of eight countries certainly did not meet the first criterion of an effective alliance—a grouping of powers united by a common interest, each with something of significant value to contribute. Pakistan and France had absolutely no interest in resisting armed aggression in Southeast Asia and made no pretense of supporting even the principles of the SEATO pact. The United Kingdom had an interest, but because of problems in Malaysia and Hong Kong professed a lack of means to do more than retain nominal membership. This attitude was shared by the Philippines, which had a far greater immediate stake in the peace and safety of the area. Australia and New Zealand paid some service to their SEATO obligations and, as I mentioned, provided token air contributions to shows of force in the area. Only Thailand, the country directly in the path of any major Communist eruption into Southeast Asia, was deeply committed to SEATO. Her main contribution was the use of Thai territory as a logistic base for possible military operations and participation in the considerable contingency planning which went on under the SEATO banner.

With all its weaknesses, the alliance permitted a great many useful preparations to be carried out, especially the positioning of U.S. forces in advantageous locations in relation to possible trouble spots. It also enabled the President to take action in the area in the name of the treaty without obtaining additional Congressional authorization. But this freedom to intervene could be a hazard in itself if used imprudently by an impetuous President. Fortunately, Kennedy was in no mood after Cuba for military ventures far from home and was not inclined to listen to occasional recommendations from some of his advisers to move in force into the Mekong valley.

If at the start of 1961 Vietnam lagged behind Laos in priority of presidential concern, that condition began to change as the result of a series of events which occurred in the following months. Among these was a report on the Vietnam situation filed by Brigadier General Edward G. Lansdale after a visit to Vietnam in January, followed by a gloomy evaluation later in the spring by Lieutenant General Lionel G. McGarr, the Chief of the U.S. Military Mission in Saigon. But it was a letter dated June 9 from President Diem requesting assistance to increase his army by 100,000 men, which really set the wheels of government into motion.

Lansdale's report attracted attention because of the reputation which he had acquired in the Philippines during the Huk insurgency and in Vietnam in the early days of the Diem regime. He returned to Washington from his 1961 visit deeply impressed by the growth of the Vietcong threat and the increasing dangers to the country which he foresaw for 1961. He found the U.S. Embassy deeply discouraged and Ambassador Durbrow alienated from President Diem, who had developed a deep distrust of the State Department and all its works. Diem had barely escaped an assassination attempt in November of the previous year, an experience that inflamed his suspicions of many of his associates, including some senior American officials. To improve the situation, Lansdale recommended changes in American methods and in Embassy personnel but concluded that we should continue to assist Diem and try to reassure him regarding American motives, at least until a more promising leader appeared upon the scene.

As to improvement in methods, he urged that our military people get out into the field and work more in the combat areas where their influence could be more effective on their Vietnamese counterparts. On the political side, he spoke in general terms of the need to develop an opposition party which would attract the anti-Diem elements and thus serve as a safety valve for the explosive anti-Diem sentiment building up in the urban population.

As Lansdale's report antedated my return to Washington by several

220

months, I have no direct knowledge of how it was received, but I often heard it mentioned during the many discussions of Vietnam which I attended from June onward. I talked with General McGarr several times during his visit to Washington and on April 26 invited him to discuss the Vietnam situation with my colleagues of the Cuba Study Group. His account of the effects of Hanoi's declaration of a War of National Liberation in 1959 revealed to me for the first time the full significance of this term of Communist jargon used to describe the use of guerrilla warfare clandestinely supported from without the boundaries of a non-Communist state to overthrow its government. He estimated that President Diem controlled little more than 40 percent of the territory of South Vietnam and that almost 85 percent of his military forces were immobilized by the insurgency. The great problem was the long, open frontier with Laos and Cambodia which made control of enemy infiltration almost impossible. For this reason, the defense of South Vietnam was much more difficult than that of Malaya although, even so, the suppression of the insurgency there required over thirteen years. But not withstanding the obvious retrogression in Vietnam, McGarr had confidence in Diem, whom he regarded as one of the most effective anit-Communist leaders in the world.

My active involvement in Vietnam matters began about mid-June while I was still working on the Cuba report. I would fix the specific moment as a chance encounter with the President outside the door of his White House office. He was holding in his hands President Diem's letter of June 9 which he passed to me and asked how he should answer it. My effort to provide him an answer was the beginning of an involvement in the Vietnam problem to which I was to commit a large part of my life during the next eight years.

President Diem's letter was well written and anticipated many of the objections which he knew his request would raise. He cited the points which he had mentioned to Vice-President Johnson during the latter's visit in early May, namely that the situation in his country was becoming more perilous daily by virtue of the events in Laos, the increasingly equivocal attitude of Cambodia and the intensification of Vietcong activities. To counter these threats, Diem and his principal generals felt that they must increase the Army in the next two years from 170,000 to 270,000 and its divisional structure from seven to fifteen or sixteen divisions. He assured the President that the expansion was entirely feasible in terms of manpower but that he would need additional American assistance in the form of money, equipment, and military advisory personnel.

In answer to possible criticism that he was placing excessive reliance on military means to cope with a highly complex situation involving many nonmilitary factors, Diem used arguments like those of many American officials of subsequent years when charged with seeking purely military solu-

221

tions. While acknowledging that for the time being he must of necessity give priority to the needs of security, he stressed the continuing importance which his government attached to economic, political, and social problems. He cited some of the undeniable achievements of his government in these fields since 1954: the economic development of the sparsely inhabited areas of the Darlac-Kontum Plateau; an expansion of the strategic road system; the encouragement of diversification in agriculture; the increase of exports; and a general rise in the standard of living. He expressed pride in the progress made in education and health despite chronic shortages of trained personnel. In the political field he mentioned reforms which he had instituted such as an elective system for village officials and the creation of provincial councils and other measures to increase popular participation in public affairs. He expressed the hope that he could continue these programs, but to do so he felt that he must first reestablish some minimum level of law and order in the provinces. For this purpose he needed more soldiers to create the protective shield behind which political and social progress could be sustained.

It was a persuasive appeal, but one not easy to answer quickly because it raised serious questions of military and fiscal feasibilities as well as political considerations regarding our objectives in Vietnam, Laos, and Cambodia. Our military people were dubious about training the necessary officers and noncommissioned officers for such a force on the proposed time schedule. The economic situation was being reviewed at the time by a group of American experts under Dr. Eugene Staley, and their report would have to be taken into account in evaluating the financial aspects of a major force increase. Finally, our estimate of the probable course of events in Laos would have a bearing on any decision of this importance. Hence, I recommended to President Kennedy that he give Diem only an interim reply for the moment, citing a recent agreement to raise the ceiling of the Vietnamese Army from 150,000 to 170,000 and noting that it would take several months to carry out this increase. In the meantime, the U.S. government would study in depth the implications of Diem's request to go beyond this latest ceiling.

After such an interim reply, I suggested that the President consider a pending JCS proposal for a further incremental increase of the army to 200,000 but withhold decision on any figure until he received the Staley report. Simultaneously, he should get opinions regarding the ultimate goal for the Vietnamese Army from our representatives in Saigon, from Admiral Felt in Honolulu, and from the Secretary of Defense.

The President acted generally in accordance with these suggestions, which were consistent with the views of most of his advisers. On August 4 he approved an increase of Diem's army to 200,000 and called for advice on the broader policy issues raised by Diem's letter. Walt Rostow, who was at the time the primary South Vietnam specialist on McGeorge Bundy's

White House staff, responded that we should defer committing more men and money to South Vietnam until we found out more about the situation and verified that we had a solid political and economic foundation in South Vietnam to support whatever additional aid we might give. He suggested that I be sent to Vietnam with a mission to get the information not available in Washington.

In mid-July, Ambassador Federick E. Nolting, Jr., who had taken over the Saigon Embassy in the spring of 1961, sent to Washington a relatively optimistic estimate of the situation which concluded that American policy was generally on the right track although the likely rate of future progress was not determinable. He had strong praise for Diem's objectives and philosophy of government. Far from being a dictator relishing power for its own sake, in Nolting's eyes he was a dedicated patriot of high principles who would have preferred to be a monk rather than a political leader. Diem's strong convictions were to some extent a source of weakness in that they caused him to reserve too much responsibility to himself to the detriment of governmental efficiency and to the increase of his personal vulnerability as a political target. All things considered, however, Nolting felt that the United States should have no hesitation in backing Diem to the hilt. What was most needed, Nolting added, was to continue to build up the confidence of the South Vietnamese and to assist the government in regaining the popular support which had waned with increasing Vietcong success. To accomplish this, Nolting felt that there must be sufficient security throughout the country to permit a free choice of political allegiance to the people of Vietnam, especially those in rural areas.

During the summer and early fall my own part in the Vietnam issue was largely one of evaluating the adequacy of governmental planning not only for Vietnam but also for Laos, Thailand, and Cambodia. It was clear to me that we were faced with a Southeast Asia problem rather than a collection of independent national issues. But integrated planning was made difficult by the compartmentation by country within the internal organization of the State Department, by the national orientation of our economic and military aid programs; and by the irrelevance to Vietnam of much of the military planning which had been carried out under SEATO auspices. This planning had been directed primarily at the threat of a Korea-style Communist offensive mounted by North Vietnam, China, or a combination of both to push into the Mekong valley and thence into Thailand and possibly to Burma. In such a case, South Vietnam was viewed as a secondary theater in which the campaign would probably take the form of a thrust by North Vietnamese divisions down the Vietnamese littoral toward Saigon.

Such strategic concepts had a logic of their own but little bearing on the situation which was arising from the salami tactics of the Pathet Lao in Laos and the clandestine infiltration of guerrilla reinforcements into South Vietnam by way of the Laos panhandle. If military action in Laos were to assist the situation in South Vietnam, it should include a mop-up of enemy forces protecting the so-called Ho Chi Minh trails. But this kind of operation would require the undivided efforts of at least three divisions which would have to be American since the operation would be of limited interest to our allies other than Diem and he needed all of his available forces at home. Considerations such as these led me to conclude that we must develop a strategic estimate for all Southeast Asia before deciding on the ultimate size of the South Vietnamese Army or making any piecemeal adjustment to our Southeast Asian policy.

With so much unfinished homework in Washington, I initially resisted the suggestions that I lead a mission to Vietnam. The most recent enunciation of U.S. policy of which I was aware was contained in a National Security Action Memorandum of May 11, 1961. It stated that the U.S. objective in Vietnam was "to prevent Communist domination of South Vietnam; to create in that country a viable and increasingly democratic society; and to initiate, on an accelerated basis, a series of mutually supporting actions to achieve this objective." This language was quite consistent with past statements of Asian policy since the promulgation of the Truman Doctrine, but it gave little specific guidance as to the nature of the supporting programs desired or the results expected from them. However, the memorandum did contain language which recognized the possibility of having to commit U.S. forces to Vietnam if the situation took a turn for the worse, a contingency for which the Defense Department was directed to initiate planning. I assumed that any mission I might lead to Saigon would be expected to flesh out the bare bones of this policy statement with specific programs consistent with its broad but vague purposes. To assure a reasonably hospitable reception for the report of such a mission, it seemed important to me to reach some general consensus on most of the things we wanted to accomplish and identify some of the alternatives which such a mission should consider on the ground.

The President accepted my arguments for delay but pressed for a prompt examination of those matters which needed to be clarified before a mission should depart. Under the impetus of his direction, the Joint Chiefs undertook to analyze the manpower requirements of South Vietnam in terms of three missions: internal security, defense against a conventional attack by North Vietnamese forces, and defense against further guerrilla infiltration across the frontiers of South Vietnam. The requirements of the first two missions were comparatively easy to estimate, but the third depended upon unpredictable decisions in Hanoi and upon the nature of the anti-infiltration defense adopted in South Vietnam. If the latter were based upon static posts along hundreds of miles of the Laotian-Cambodian frontier, one set of forces would be required; if based upon offensive action by forces moving along the frontier and, if necessary, into Laos, another set would be required.

But these missions and requirements would also depend on what was taking place in Laos and Thailand. They could be drastically reduced if, for example, friendly forces from the west secured the Laotian panhandle and part of the Mekong valley; if offensive air and guerrilla operations could be mounted against the Communist enemy in Laos; or if our side could apply military pressure to North Vietnam, the principal source of enemy strength. Thus the planning widened into many variants and the discussions growing out of this planning occupied a large part of the President's time throughout the summer and early fall.

Among the nonmilitary measures taken in this period was the drafting of a White Paper by William Jorden of State exposing Hanoi's violations of the Geneva Accords and the extent of the infiltration into South Vietnam, for use before the International Control Commission and the United Nations. Other papers were prepared dealing with economic and budgetary matters, with actions which the United States might require of South Vietnam in exchange for further aid, and with a variety of concepts for controlling infiltration. Possibly appalled by the flood of papers generated at his direction, the President eventually put a damper on the planning activity by a directive which approved the issuance of the Jorden White Paper and directed among other things that "General Taylor should undertake a mission to Saigon to explore ways in which assistance of all types might be more effective." On the same day, he gave me a letter which read as follows:

THE WHITE HOUSE

WASHINGTON

October 13, 1961

Dear General Taylor:

I should like you to proceed to Saigon for the purpose of appraising the situation in South Vietnam, particularly as it concerns the threat to the internal security and defense of that country and adjacent areas. After you have conferred with the appropriate United States and South Vietnamese authorities, including the Commander in Chief, Pacific, I would like your views on the courses of action which our Government might take at this juncture to avoid a further deterioration in the situation in South Vietnam and eventually to contain and eliminate the threat to its independence.

In your assessment you should bear in mind that the initial responsibility for the effective maintenance of the independence of South Vietnam rests with the people and government of that country. Our efforts must be evaluated, and your recommendations formulated, with this fact in mind.

225

While the military part of the problem is of great importance in South Vietnam, its political, social, and economic elements are equally significant, and I shall expect your appraisal and your recommendations to take full account of them.

Sincerely,

John F. Kennedy

This was an important letter because it summarized, I believe accurately, the state of mind of President Kennedy and most of his advisers at the end of 1961 after months of study and debate over the Southeast Asia situation. It was drawn in strict consistence with the statement of U.S. policy set forth in the May NSAM which it, in effect, reaffirmed. I was not asked to review the objectives of this policy but the means being pursued for their attainment. The question was how to change a losing game and begin to win, not how to call it off. It reemphasized one of the principles which had always loomed large in the President's mind, namely, that the conflict was primarily a Vietnamese matter and that first call should be placed on Vietnamese resources—our contribution should be limited to filling the deficits which had to be met if our objectives were to be achieved.

The President closed his letter on a note which always prevailed in the councils of his Administration and, I would add, in the Johnson Administration as well, to the effect that this conflict was not a conventional military confrontation. While military force must succeed in establishing some indispensable level of security to protect political, social, and economic measures, success would be measured in the end in terms of progress in non-military forms of nation-building rather than in numbers of enemy killed and battles won. The President made it abundantly clear in private discussion that he fervently hoped that the necessary military force could be provided by the Vietnamese without the need to introduce U.S. ground troops into combat. I assured him that I shared that hope as did probably all or most of his military advisers but a government had to be ready to do the unpalatable when necessary in the national interest. Certainly President Truman had derived no pleasure from sending American soldiers into Korea—only the satisfaction of doing what he conceived to be his duty.

CHAPTER 18

Mission to Saigon

Armed with President Kennedy's letter, I put together a small task force which included a representative from each of the departments and agencies primarily involved in the Vietnam programs (State, AID, Defense, JCS, and CIA) and Walt Rostow from the White House staff to act as a sort of deputy for the expedition. I explained to my colleagues that I felt I had a mandate from the President to give him my personal views and recommendations upon return, that I would invite their assistance in drafting the final report but, in the end, I would decide what went into it and would take personal responsibility for it. I rather expected that there would be dissenting views within the group regarding my recommendations and was surprised when the time came that there was concurrence on all the main points of the report without my having made any particular effort to obtain it.

Walt Rostow was of great help to our party because of his broad historical approach to the events taking place in Southeast Asia. He had meditated deeply on the significance of subversive insurgency as a device for Communist expansion and had early recognized the need for identifying and proscribing it in legal terms. Also, he contributed the pen of an experienced writer to the drafting of many of the documents eventually produced by our task force, as well as an agile tennis racket to support me in an occasional doubles match.

En route to Saigon, we stopped in Honolulu and received an exhaustive briefing on the situation in Southeast Asia from Admiral Harry D. Felt, Commander in Chief, Pacific. He was convinced of the criticality of the situation in Vietnam and of the need for prompt U.S. assistance. But at the same time he stressed the importance of getting Diem to keep his provincial governors from intervening in military matters and to overcome a propensity of his commanders to sit on static defensive positions. With regard to the need for U.S. forces in South Vietnam, he was inclined to favor the introduction of logistic units, including engineer and helicopter units for selective assistance to the Vietnamese, but to withhold combat forces for the time being. In the long run, he saw no answer to the problem of halting infiltration short of placing sizeable ground forces, preferably SEATO troops, in Laos across the Ho Chi Minh trails.

In outlining work assignments and planning our actions after arrival, I had first to analyze the elements of the problems which we must attack in South Vietnam. In the language of the President's letter we were to find ways and means "to avoid a further deterioration in the situation in Vietnam and eventually to contain and eliminate the threat to its independence." To comply with this directive we would have to evaluate the causes and extent of the deterioration, find ways of improving the use of the resources presently available to the South Vietnamese, and decide what additional measures they might take. Only after forming some estimate of their ability for self-help and matching that estimate against what would probably be required to "contain and eliminate the threat to their independence" could we determine what we might contribute to fill the deficit. I agreed completely with President Kennedy that we Americans should do nothing for Vietnam which the Vietnamese could do for themselves.

Over the years, I tried to apply this formula to all forms of U.S. aid for Vietnam but found it a singularly difficult guideline to follow literally because of the time factor. As American officials gained experience with the governmental weaknesses and administrative limitations of the South Vietnamese, they discovered that there were many things the Vietnamese could probably do for themselves eventually, if they were given time, but the crises of the conflict often would not wait. In practice, the formula had to be modified to the effect that the United States should do nothing which the Vietnamese could do for themselves *in time*—and then hope to be reasonably accurate in evaluating the time factor. Also, it was important to be sure that the constraint of time was imposed by the enemy or by some objective factor beyond American control and not the result of an unrealistic American-imposed deadline.

Our mission arrived in Saigon on October 18 at a time when the situation was the darkest since the early days of 1954. Vietcong strength had increased from an estimated 10,000 in January 1961 to 17,000 in October; they were clearly on the move in the delta, in the highlands, and along the plain on the north central coast. The South Vietnamese were watching with dismay the situation in Laos and the negotiations in Geneva, which convinced them that there would soon be a Communist-dominated government in Vientiane. The worst flood in decades was ravaging the Mekong delta, destroying crops and livestock and rendering hundreds of thousands homeless. In flying over the flooded area shortly after our arrival I could see nothing as far as the horizon but a vast expanse of muddy water, broken only by the occasional roofs of houses still standing along the submerged roads and canal banks. The people who had not fled in time lived on the roofs and in the eaves of their houses and prayed for a subsidence of the waters. As a final misfortune, just as we arrived in Saigon a well-known Vietnamese officer, Colonel Huang Thuy Lam, the governmental liaison officer with the International Control Commission (ICC), was kidnapped and brutally murdered by the Vietcong.

In the wake of this series of profoundly depressing events, it was no exaggeration to say that the entire country was suffering from a collapse of national morale—an obvious fact which made a strong impression on the members of our mission. In subsequent weeks as we meditated on what the United States could or should do in South Vietnam, the thought was always with us that we needed something visible which could be done quickly to offset the oppressive feeling of hopelessness which seemed to permeate all ranks of Vietnamese society.

Upon arriving in Saigon we were immediately thrown into a maelstrom of official calls, briefings, discussions, and visits to the field. As Saigon is almost exactly half way around the world from Washington and thirteen hours removed in clock time, a traveler who arrives by jet aircraft after almost continuous flight is hard put to stay awake and keep his wits for the first two or three days. In my case, the initial strain was augmented by having to conduct business in French with Vietnamese officials who had not reached the proficiency in English which became common in later years.

Our first official action was to call on President Ngo Dinh Diem. As Diem was the key personality in the situation, the individual upon whom the success of American policy had been staked up to that time, the accuracy of our evaluation of his character, motivation, and political prospects was sure to have a major bearing upon the outcome of our mission. Hence, my companions and I approached this first meeting with the President, in full awareness of its importance. At the palace, I was not in a completely unfamiliar setting as I had been there before and had had the experience of an interview with Diem. This was my third visit to Saigon, the first having been in March 1955, when I visited my old Army friend, General J. Lawton Collins, then the President's Special Representative to Vietnam. On that occasion I was merely an interested visitor from the Far East Command seeking on-the-spot impressions of the events taking place in Southeast Asia. I returned two years later as Army Chief of Staff and had my first interview with President Diem. Thus when I returned in 1961, I was somewhat prepared for the ritual which ensued.

Diem was a short, rather stocky Vietnamese, sixty years of age but with no sign of gray in his jet-black hair. He had a grave but pleasant face with the dreamy eyes of a mystic and the quiet dignity of a mandarin trained to rule. He moved and spoke deliberately and was highly skilled in steering a conversation in the direction he wished it to go and in avoiding questions which he was not ready to answer. Our interview that day was similar to the one I had had before and those which I was to have later. It was interminably long, about four hours, and consisted principally of a monologue by Diem in French, to which I made an occasional interjection. This sometimes moved us onto a new topic, but more often left us impaled on a point which Diem was not ready to leave. Meanwhile, Diem smoked cigarettes incessantly and talked in somnolent tones that sorely tested the powers of attention of his overseas visitors, drowsy from too frequent changes of time zones.

Settling into my chair, I explained that President Kennedy had sent this mission to Saigon because of his concern over the resurgence of Vietcong aggression and his need to relate his decisions and plans affecting Vietnam to those of Laos and the rest of Southeast Asia. Beyond this need for regional integration of action, the President had the global problem of establishing priorities between the needs of Europe and Asia. Since the U.S. press had speculated loudly that our mission was primarily to evaluate the requirement for U.S. troops in Vietnam, and as Diem had recently intimated to Ambassador Nolting his interest in obtaining troops, I stressed that President Kennedy was thinking in terms other than military intervention and called Diem's attention to the strong representation of nonmilitary agencies on our mission.

I outlined the way in which we hoped to operate, with each member making contact with counterpart officials in Diem's government for the purpose of discussing common problems and seeking joint conclusions as to alternatives. I asked Diem's cooperation in making our visit one of maximum mutual advantage and expressed the hope that he would see me again before we left in order to discuss our tentative conclusions.

At this point Diem launched forth into a long exposition of the situation as it had evolved since 1954, after nine previous years of war between the Viet Minh and the French. Of late it had become complicated by the Cambodian situation and affected by the deterioration in Laos. He described how the Vietcong had increased their efforts to undermine his government, and how they were indirectly supported by the resources of a formidable North Vietnamese Army of 300,000 regulars supplemented by another 300,000 regional troops. These North Vietnamese troops, in turn, drew their logistic strength from a pipeline of war materials provided by the USSR and China, which also served the Pathet Lao. Thus, the aggregate picture was of a vast Communist alliance, directed by Moscow and Peking, for the purpose of bringing all Southeast Asia under its domination.

The strength of the Vietcong in South Vietnam, he explained, resulted from the presence of trained Communist cadres and war supplies left be-

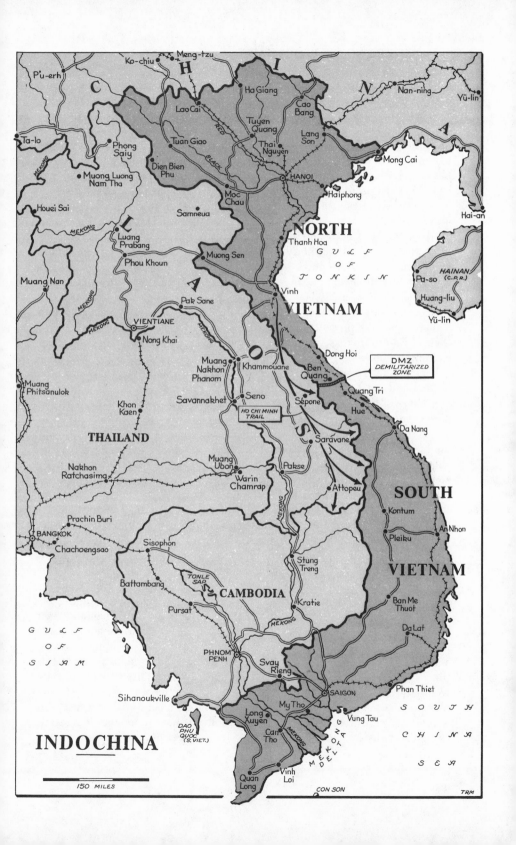

INDOCHINA

150 MILES

TRM

hind in the south in 1954 and from the subsequent infiltration of young South Vietnamese who had been taken north in 1954 for training. With his 150,000-man army, Diem found it impossible to contain the enemy forces in his country. They were particularly strong in the Mekong delta and in the high plateau (Kontum, Pleiku, and Darlac provinces), whence they were working their way down to the coast. He was deficient not only in troops but in paramilitary and police forces for use at the province and district level for local protection. He remarked that, in the past, the Americans had opposed the creation of such forces thinking that he was bent on creating a private army.

I replied that one of our primary purposes was to examine his need for more troops and paramilitary forces and that we intended to review the entire matter with General McGarr. I was doubtful, however, of Diem's ability to train officers and noncommissioned officers at a rate sufficient to meet the needs of a 250,000-man army. He readily conceded the existence of a leadership shortage, but he and Defense Minister Nguyen Dinh Thuan, who was present at the meeting, united in asserting confidence in their ability to increase the capacity of officer and noncommissioned officer training schools.

Diem underscored the importance of the road-building program which he had laid out for the high plateau area in order to gain access to the secret bases of the Vietcong in that rugged terrain. In response to my urging of more mobile offensive action by his forces to cover the frontiers, he indicated considerable doubt about the feasibility of such tactics. To combat infiltration he preferred the creation of depopulated zones between the Vietcong-dominated border areas and the principal population centers, zones in which artillery and aviation could be used without danger to civilians—a *cordon sanitaire,* as he described it.

We talked at length about the great flood in the delta, the most disastrous in this century. Diem was sure that the people would require much help after the water receded because they had lost nearly everything and almost a half million people were affected.

I offered Diem the opportunity on several occasions to raise the matter of American troops for Vietnam. I was aware that he had approached Nolting on the subject and needed to get his views without encouraging his hopes. He avoided the subject until near the end of the interview and then dealt with it with deliberate ambiguity. While he was definite about needing the help of our Seventh Fleet to control the seaward approaches to Vietnam, he indicated that he did not wish to ask for foreign troops at this time. However, he did want to have an agreed joint plan as to where they would be located and how used, if they had to be introduced. He explained that, up to now, he had hoped to be able to cope with the situation without foreign troops, but the situation in Laos and the increasing strength of the Vietcong were forcing him to reexamine his position. He considered it most important that, if U.S. troops ever came into the country, they should come with a commitment to stay and defend South Vietnam and not be subject to precipitate withdrawal by an act of the American Congress.

We moved on to a discussion of the need for a national plan which would pull together all resources in an integrated program to defeat the Vietcong. Washington had long pressed for such a plan but had never got one from Diem's government. The President spoke confidently about his ability to produce and implement such a plan as a part of the state of emergency which he had just declared. We ended our long session with his promise to provide us with this plan, if possible, in the course of my stay in Saigon.

There were many overtones of past U.S.-Vietnamese conflicts in our discussion, but these were muted as Diem preferred to make his points on this occasion by soft-voiced indirection. But we all knew that Diem was thinking about the years when the U.S. authorities had resisted his often expressed desire to increase his armed forces in preparation for a renewal of the struggle with the Communists which he was sure would come. In those days our officials thought of the defense of South Vietnam in terms of a conventional attack down the coast by North Vietnamese divisions to which the introduction of a SEATO force would be the appropriate countermeasure. In contrast, Diem had a strong feeling of the importance of securing the countryside and was more concerned with raising paramilitary forces to defend the villages and hamlets from a real and growing guerrilla threat. His desire for an American commitment to stay, if we introduced U.S. forces, was a reflection of his long-standing suspicion of American intentions, sharpened recently by the attitude of some American officials at the time of the attempt on his life the previous November.

One of our principal tasks was to evaluate Diem's political durability and to form some judgment as to the stability of his government. He already had many critics in Washington who were beginning to whisper their apprehension, "We can't win with Diem," a slogan which in later years was to become a rallying cry of the anti-Diem wing of our government and press. Could he win this politico-military horse race, or should we be looking around for another to back? How strong and deep was his domestic opposition, and what were its sources? These were some of the hard questions which my task force had to address and the time was short to get even tentative answers.

Diem obviously had many things going against him. A new spate of rumors about an anti-Diem coup preceded our arrival and followed our departure. The plotters were reportedly either disgruntled military officers who disliked Diem's intervention in military matters in support of the province chiefs or various Saigon intellectuals who inveighed against his authoritarian ways. Diem's brother, Ngo Dinh Nhu, and his wife had acquired a widespread unpopularity which affected the public attitude toward Diem. However, the real depth and breadth of the anti-Diem feeling were hard to gauge since all the Vietnamese press was concentrated in Saigon and did not reflect the outlook of the large rural population which was bearing the brunt of the war. Similarly, attitudes within the armed forces were hard to appraise. There was plenty of discontent among some of the senior officers, but how far down did it go?

Hoping to gain some insight into military attitudes, I paid an early visit on Major General Duong Van Minh, the Commanding General of the Field Command. "Big" Minh, as he was known, was an unusually burly Vietnamese officer who had gained a national reputation for his services in breaking the military power of the sects in 1966. He was equally famous for his missing front teeth, knocked out, it was said, by the butt of a Japanese rifle during the occupation of his country in World War II. I had met Minh on a previous visit and, like most Americans, I found him friendly and congenial, with the additional credit point of being a formidable tennis player.

It was public knowledge that Minh was unhappy with his lot under Diem, who had given him a position which appeared to confer the command of all Army Field Forces but which, in fact, had little real power. The channel of military command was supposed to run from Diem to Secretary of Defense Nguyen Dinh Thuan to Lieutenant General Le Van Ty, the Chief of the Joint General Staff, then to General Minh. But between Ty and Minh was a very ambitious and self-confident young officer, Brigadier General Nguyen Khanh, who, as Ty's Chief of Staff, actually issued orders to the Army and, thus, eroded Minh's authority. The resulting animosity between these two officers was to have serious consequences in later years.

Minh and I had scarcely exchanged greetings when Minh began to unburden himself of his grievances against Diem. He assured me that the situation in South Vietnam was very grave, largely because of the inadequacies of the President. Not only were the Vietcong getting stronger but the armed forces were losing the support of the civil population, who were becoming increasingly loath to provide information on the Vietcong. The government had to restore confidence among the people and stop favoring the Catholics if it was to restore peace and order.

Minh criticized, as did many American officials, Diem's practice of selecting province chiefs on political grounds and then giving them control over Army forces stationed in their provinces. Under this system, an Army commander in the field had to look to two masters, his superior in the tactical chain of command and his province chief. Minh viewed this dual system as a device for dividing and downgrading the military. These were about the only specific complaints which I could get from Minh, but I was somewhat startled by his willingness to criticize his President to a foreigner like me. I had not yet acquired experience with the Vietnamese bent for running down their closest associates to the casual passer-by.

After my call on Minh I went to see Lieutenant General Le Van Ty, the senior officer of the Vietnamese armed forces, whom I found much less interested in domestic politics and presidential behavior than in military matters of equipment and training. He pressed hard for reconnaissance vehicles to replace the worn-out French models in his current inventory and showed interest in the American M-113 personnel carrier which was undergoing tests. He argued the need for dual equipment to meet the differing requirements of conventional and guerrilla warfare. I expressed the view that the latter merited primary attention and mentioned the criticism in the United States that not enough attention was being paid to antiguerrilla training. Ty did not agree, saying that the Vietnamese had to maintain some degree of readiness for both kinds of warfare. We talked also about the need for greater mobility based on the use of helicopters and light aviation, and I took the opportunity to insist on the absolute necessity of a better intelligence organization. But there was not a word said about Diem and his misdeeds.

If this narrow sampling of opinions had not been particularly fruitful in developing a reliable impression of military attitudes toward Diem, my colleagues circulating among the intelligentsia of Saigon brought back a large bag of complaints. Most had been often reported to Washington, including the perennial one that Diem tried to do everything himself and trusted no one but the members of his own family. Our American political advisers had urged him for years to "widen the base of his government," as the phrase went, and he still had not done so. When I had called in 1957, at our Ambassador's suggestion, I had raised this point with Diem, who quickly replied by asking whom I would suggest for inclusion in his cabinet. Having anticipated the question and armed myself with two or three names provided by the Ambassador, I proposed them with more apparent confidence than I really felt. Diem ticked them off gravely: the first had been involved in the recent coup plot; the second had a French wife; and the third was too prosperous to be honest. So my list was quickly disposed of and, somewhat to my relief, we passed on to discuss other subjects on which I felt better qualified.

By 1961 these complaints against Diem were far more numerous and widely held, primarily because Diem was becoming increasingly introverted and suspicious, particularly since the recent attempt on his life. Meanwhile, American officials were losing patience with his stubborn resistance to political advice and criticism of him was strong at subambassadorial levels of the Embassy. In partial defense of Diem, I got the impression that he must have received a lot of rather naïve political advice over the years from young and inexperienced Embassy officers attempting to comply with State Department directives. He had considerable reason to doubt the superior judgment of transient Americans concerning the ability and reliability of men with whom he had spent most of his life. Also, he knew how limited was the untapped Vietnamese leadership available to reinforce his government. One of our background studies in Washington estimated that only 10 to 12 percent of the population had educational or technological skills useful in government and that over half of this number were either already in government or working in activities related to national security. That did not leave much talent in reserve, particularly since many educated Vietnamese would not have wanted to work for the government under any circumstances.

We consulted the principal American officials with regard to their views of Diem and what we could expect from him. Ambassador Nolting had apparently closed or at least narrowed the confidence gap which had separated Diem from his predecessor, Ambassador Durbrow, and was inclined to take a favorable view of Diem in spite of his well-publicized weaknesses. McGarr was for backing him to the hilt while continuing to work to improve his performance. In lower echelons of the U.S. Mission I got the impression of deeper misgivings about Diem's perfectibility; political officers, in particular, had known too long the frustrations of working with his unresponsive ministers to expect any sudden reversal of form. But the general feeling was that Diem had survived so many threats in past years—from the religious sects, the intellectuals, and the military malcontents—that we should not sell him short provided his principal military officers, with all their grumbling, remained loyal to him. Hence, after much discussion, my group concluded that, pending the appearance on the scene of a more promising replacement, we should stick with Diem, hoping to effect improvement by persuasion, by example, and by a larger advisory presence to assist his government and armed forces.

One item high on my agenda was to examine the quality of the intelligence which we had been receiving in Washington on conditions in South Vietnam and the activities of the Vietcong. There had been enough apparent contradictions in the reports to stir my suspicion that all was not well with the intelligence. While I could understand the difficulty of acquiring accurate information on an elusive, clandestine enemy operating in the forests and mountains, I could not see why we had so little hard information on such matters as rural attitudes toward the Saigon government, the loyalty of the armed forces to Diem, governmental activities in the provinces, South Vietnamese military casualties, and results of the interrogation of Vietcong prisoners and defectors. About such important activities of our South Vietnamese ally the data were usually lacking or suspect.

It did not require much effort to verify my suspicions of the intelligence which, for years, we had been collecting and plotting solemnly on graphs in Washington to use as the basis for our plans and programs. The fault lay on both the Vietnamese and American sides. The Diem government and its armed forces had seven intelligence agencies in operation, competing organizations which had been only recently placed under the coordinating authority of a newly organized Central Intelligence Organization (CIO), a faint simulacrum of the CIA. Because of rivalries between the intelligence services and lack of presidential support, the CIO was having great difficulty in getting started and thus far had exercised little real coordination.

As a result of diffused uncoordinated responsibility for the collection of information on the Vietcong, field commanders rarely received all the relevant intelligence on the enemy which existed some place in the compartmented system. Each province chief was in the collection business, using his police, the civil guard, or his own intelligence agent net; but the product amassed was rarely passed laterally to local military commanders in time for them to take action on it. There was no specialized telephone or radio net reserved for intelligence transmission. As a result, items of intelligence passed between units over the overloaded command radio and telephone net and often got lost. From such evidence it was clear that the Vietnamese armed forces had been fighting nearly blind for years without any possibility of reacting quickly against the fleeting enemy. Nothing resembling an integrated intelligence system existed in South Vietnam in 1961, and it required years of hard work before we ever obtained one. But an understanding of the magnitude of the intelligence problem was one of the most useful products of our mission.

The Vietcong was only one intelligence target about which we lacked reliable information. We needed to know many things about our ally in order to help him effectively. Cables from Washington poured daily into the Embassy and the American Military Mission asking for detailed information on the conduct of the war, the state of the economy, the progress of social programs, and on scores of other complex subjects. To obtain answers to the questions raised, our American officials had to repeat them to the appropriate element of the government or the armed forces and could do little more than forward to Washington whatever answer was eventually forthcoming. It took but little observation of the ways of the Vietnamese officialdom to realize that the answer provided was often not worth the cost of transmission. In many cases the government did not have the data requested and was faced with the dilemma of confessing its ignorance or making a quick "guesstimate." Usually the latter course was chosen. In other cases, the government did have the information requested but if furnished, it would reflect unfavorably on governmental performance. At such times the temptation was often great to doctor the information before releasing it into foreign hands. Under such circumstances it was not surprising that Washington plans and programs often did not correspond to the realities of the situation in Vietnam.

At the time I was inclined to blame our people in Saigon for not having warned Washington with sufficient bluntness of the dubious quality of the information which they had been transmitting. Why couldn't they have conducted spot checks from time to time? There were many reasons advanced to explain this lack of aggressiveness in delving into the true state of Vietnamese affairs. In the first place, there were too few Americans in Vietnam to provide anything like country-wide coverage of important governmental activities. The Military Mission had fewer than 800 personnel of all types and could provide military advisers no lower than the regimental level. Our civil agencies had nothing like these military resources. There were no civilian advisers within the governmental administration who could get an insight into the workings of the ministries, and, as for the provinces, Diem was very cold to American requests to poke about the countryside. Finally, I discovered that some military and economic officials felt that it exceeded the scope of their authority as set forth in Washington directives and violated the proprieties of their advisory relationship to "spy" on their allies and to report unfavorable things about them—even to protect their own government from being misled. I am afraid that I reacted brusquely to such nonsense and promised a prompt revision of any directive which justified such an attitude.

In our rounds of calls, the question of introducing American forces into South Vietnam generally came up for discussion in some form. There was a general consensus among Vietnamese and American officials that some U.S. forces were needed at once, but views differed as to their size and purpose. The military subcommittee of my task force was convinced that prompt military intervention was the best, if not the only way, of saving South Vietnam, and indeed all Southeast Asia. If any such action were to be taken, General McGarr stressed the importance of intervention in sufficient strength to tip the military balance decisively. On the other hand, some of our political officers felt that it was an open question whether the Vietnamese government could pull out of its slump even with increased U.S. military help and, hence, that we should go slow in our commitments to the Diem government.

Since the matter had to be discussed tentatively and very cautiously with the South Vietnamese, it was difficult to identify nuances of opinion among them but it was clear that a U.S. military presence of some kind was greatly desired. After our first interview Diem made no further mention of the condition that any American troops should come with a commitment to stay. Supported by Vice-President Tho, Secretary of Defense Thuan, and General Khanh, he began to press strongly for U.S. air, naval, and ground support. Diem's brother Nhu, who often seemed to me to talk in parables on most subjects, was explicit in specifying the need for U.S. technical and logistical troops, but he was opposed to the introduction of combat forces.

Personally, I had no enthusiasm for the thought of using U.S. Army forces in ground combat in this guerrilla war. I doubted the adaptability of our large units to the requirements of jungle warfare, particularly if they had to operate on the basis of the inadequate tactical intelligence then prevailing. There were the obvious risks of deeper military involvement following an initial commitment and of adverse psychological reaction among the Vietnamese people to the reappearance of armed white men in their midst in apparent replacement of the hated French. On the other hand, there was a pressing need to do something to restore Vietnamese morale and to shore up confidence in the United States, a confidence shaken by our seeming weakness in Laos. Nothing appeared so likely to be effective as the introduction of some U.S. troops to provide a visible symbol of the seriousness of American intentions. Such a force did not need to be large or have a combat mission. There was unlimited logistical work to be done to facilitate Vietnamese military operations, to prepare the way for the rapid introduction of SEATO or U.S. forces if that contingency should arise, and to assist in repairing flood damage in the south. This disaster gave the United States a humanitarian reason in addition to the military one for introducing engineer-type forces, and the termination of the flood could be used as a reason for withdrawing our forces if we wished to exercise that option. Taking all these factors into account, I gradually inclined to favor the introduction of a task force of several battalions of engineers, medical and signal troops accompanied by only enough infantry to provide local protection.

After two days in the field, one spent in the north along the DMZ and the second in an overflight of the flooded Mekong delta, I reassembled our task force for a series of final meetings in Saigon. On October 24, Nolting, Rostow, and I called on Diem to feel out his reaction to our tentative thinking on a number of points. I gave him a paper summarizing some of our views and then discussed them with him one by one.

At the head of the list was the proposal to unite in an effort to improve all phases of the intelligence needed to guide our joint action. As an example of what should be done, I mentioned the need for joint studies by U.S. and Vietnamese officials of the conditions in the provinces about which we Americans knew almost nothing. My people were convinced of the importance of on-the-spot verification of the situation, province by province, since it was clear that the conditions varied widely among them. Such studies should throw some light on the methods and extent of infiltration and the appropriate command relationships between provincial chiefs and field commanders. Although I knew that Diem was lukewarm to the idea of foreign inspectors in the provinces, he showed no reluctance in agreeing to this proposal and, in fact, praised it as a realistic way to arrive at a common view of rural problems.

We went over old ground about the importance of freeing the Army from static missions and giving it mobile tasks along the frontiers. I volunteered that we might be willing to bring in U.S. Army and Marine heli-

239

copter units to transport Vietnamese forces; I did not mention that I would keep such units under American control in the hope of influencing the conduct of ground operations along sound tactical lines.

With regard to the all-important matter of introducing American ground forces, I told him that his American visitors had given much thought to the possible role of such forces, if Washington were inclined to provide them. The plan which most appealed to us, I explained, would be to introduce U.S. helicopters at once for emergency use in the flooded areas and, as soon as possible thereafter, to bring in a flood relief task force to work with the government on the rehabilitation of the delta. After I had described my concept of its organization, Diem expressed enthusiastic support for the project and designated Vice-President Tho and Minister for Rural Affairs Quang to serve as points of contact to work with the Embassy in developing a plan to implement it.

We closed with a discussion of possible political-psychological actions to get a maximum effect from whatever additional aid Washington might decide to give. I stressed the need for developing a feeling among his people that something new and important was taking place, that a durable partnership had been established with the Americans, and that a turning point had been reached in the fight with the Vietcong. We discussed the desirability of an exchange of letters between him and President Kennedy, of an appeal by his government to the United Nations, and of an announcement by Diem of personnel changes in his government. Diem's response was affirmative on all points, but he interjected his usual caveat that qualified men were hard to find for the purposes of government As we broke up, I repeated that my ideas had no official sanction and represented only a broad outline of actions which, if approved, would have to be worked out in detail by his government and our Embassy. Diem said he understood and added that it would greatly help Vietnamese morale if, henceforth, our two governments were seen to act as partners in pursuit of common objectives.

On October 25 we flew to Bangkok where we met with Ambassador Young and his senior staff on the following day, then with Prime Minister Sarit Thanarat, Foreign Minister Thanat Khoman, and Air Chief Marshal Dawee. At the Embassy I summarized the results of our Vietnam visit and outlined some of our tentative conclusions. With Sarit and his people, we could talk only in guarded terms about our mission, evading the Field Marshal's obvious curiosity to know about any troop plans for South Vietnam. He volunteered that he thought U.S. troops were necessary there and that military action should be taken by unspecified parties to block the Ho Chi Minh trails in Laos. I mentioned the possibility that we might send logistic troops to help with the flood in the delta. Sarit replied that he thought that would be a good idea but growled *sotto voce* to his interpreter, "Dammit, I want to know if they will send fighters."

From Bangkok we flew by way of Hong Kong to Clark Field in the Philippines and thence to the Philippine summer capital in Baguio to work on our report. I had not returned to that beautiful resort since I had passed through with my family in 1939 on our way back to the United States after our tour of duty in Japan. I selected it on this occasion to take advantage of its quiet to put our report in final form. Former experience had demonstrated the importance of arriving in Washington from an overseas mission with a finished report in hand and prepared to give full time to defending one's case before the President and his associates.

Although the various members of the mission had had different sources of information and had developed their views separately, there was surprisingly little divergence of view among them on matters of substance. No one felt the situation was hopeless, but all agreed that the situation was serious and required urgent measures to reverse the downward trend. Fundamentally, we interpreted the events in Southeast Asia as a Communist attempt to extend power and influence by using a variant of Mao Tse-tung's classic three-stage offensive. In Laos and Vietnam, the Communists had succeeded in establishing a political base for subversion and in both countries had passed to the phase of guerrilla warfare in accordance with Mao's doctrine. Thus far, they had judged it too dangerous to move to the final phase of overt conventional warfare, but trained divisions existed in North Vietnam and Red China, available to support this transition should the time become ripe.

In Vietnam, the immediate purpose of the enemy was apparently to pin down the Vietnamese Army on defensive positions and to create a feeling of general insecurity by frequent ambushes, hit-and-run raids, and terrorist attacks. But the strength and resources of the enemy were shrouded in rumor, false information, and exaggeration so that the exact dimension of the threat was difficult to assess. For the moment, they seemed intent on producing a political crisis by a combination of military and nonmilitary means which might eventually lead to national unification on terms acceptable to Hanoi.

While the Communists had a tide running in their favor, we agreed that they were not without vulnerabilities. They were no longer fighting the French and could not carry the banner of national independence against colonial rule. Their guerrilla forces could not safely engage the South Vietnamese regulars and were forced to depend largely upon terrorism and intimidation. Hanoi felt compelled to conceal its involvement in South Vietnam and thus to limit its reinforcements to South Vietnamese trained in the north. Also, the Hanoi leaders could not forget the exposure of their homeland to destruction if the war spread beyond the borders of South Vietnam.

But these disabilities of the enemy provided slim encouragement as we considered the situation of our friends in the south. The military people on our mission estimated that the South Vietnamese army was obtaining not more than 60 to 70 percent combat effectiveness from the forces presently available to them. This lack of return on the military investment was the result of many of the factors already mentioned: lack of intelligence, a defensive outlook, a bad civil-military relationship in the provinces, and Diem's style of over-centralized government. Of course, there were also assets in the south: growing armed forces, a surprisingly resilient economy, and Diem, a man of stubborn courage and basic integrity. But time was pressing. To convert such assets into successful programs it was clear that American aid and guidance must be made available rapidly and in quantity to bridge the period of waiting for the development of new forms of indigenous strength.

Against the background of these considerations the time came for me to put aside other people's papers and with Rostow to write one for President Kennedy which would give him our best judgment of the courses he should follow. Except for the U.S. troop issue it was not very difficult to draw up the recommendations because most of the measures which needed to be taken were fairly obvious as long as our purpose was to "avoid a further deterioration in the situation in South Vietnam and eventually to contain and eliminate the threat to its independence." However, each recommendation had also to be measured against the criterion that the action required of the Americans did not represent something which the Vietnamese could do for themselves—in time.

My report made the broad recommendation that, upon receiving a suitable request from Diem, our government should respond with an offer to join in a massive joint effort to deal with the Vietcong aggression and to repair the ravages of the delta flood. In such an effort, U.S. representatives would participate actively, particularly in the fields of government administration, military planning, the conduct of operations, intelligence production, and flood relief. Their capabilities would be strengthened both by an increase in numbers and by a more aggressive performance of the advisory role than in the past.

In support of this expanded commitment, we made a series of specific recommendations to illustrate what we hoped would be included in this joint effort. We proposed that the U.S. government provide individual administrators for insertion into the machinery of the government to the full extent of their estimated utility and of Diem's willingness to accept and use them. We thought that this technique might be used to improve the intelligence system, beginning at the provincial level and extending upward to the Central Intelligence Organization. We also recommended that the U.S. government engage in a joint survey of the conditions in the provinces in order to arrive at a common understanding of the social, political, intelligence, and military problems in the villages and hamlets. We recognized that, even with full cooperation from Diem, it would take time to assemble qualified joint teams in numbers adequate for the scope of the survey, but we wanted the effort pursued without holding back the other elements of the program.

To free the Army for mobile offensive operations, we urged renewed efforts to improve the training and equipment of the Civil Guard and Self-Defense Corps (later called Regional Forces and Popular Forces) so that they could relieve the regular Army of static missions. To add to the mobility and effectiveness of the latter on the frontiers, we favored providing considerably more helicopters and light aviation and organizing a border ranger force for use against infiltration. The U.S. Government would have to provide the equipment and specialized units for such purposes as air reconnaissance and photography, certain kinds of airlift, special intelligence activities, and air-ground support techniques, since all of these functions exceeded the current capacity of the South Vietnamese forces and needed to be performed at once. For a similar reason, in response to a specific request from Diem we recommended that our government assist in effecting surveillance and control over coastal waters and inland waterways, furnishing advisers, operating personnel, and specially designed small craft. On the thorny issue of the introduction of American ground forces, I recommended that we offer to introduce a logistical task force of the sort I had described to Diem that would provide a U.S. military presence to raise the national morale and a capability for the support of military operations or flood relief. It would be able to defend itself and the immediate area which it operated with its own troops, would serve as an emergency reserve in a military crisis and could carry out logistic preparations to receive any subsequent U.S. or SEATO forces which might be ordered in. Our report closed with the proposal that the United States review its economic aid program to take into account the needs of flood relief and to reorient the emphasis to projects directly in support of the new joint program and away from long-term projects designed to produce results in the relatively distant future.

As a cover to our report, Walt and I drafted a letter to the President which expressed our overview of the problems which faced us in Southeast Asia. We stressed that we had no illusions as to the finality of our recommendations. We were merely sure that they represented actions that should be taken in the light of our current knowledge of the situation in Southeast Asia. Future needs beyond this program, we told President Kennedy, would depend on the kind of settlement eventually arrived at in Laos and the way in which Hanoi might adjust to such a settlement. If Hanoi's decision were to prolong and intensify the "War of National Liberation" declared against South Vietnam in 1959 with continued infiltration and covert support of guerrilla bands, then we would have to consider whether we could accept this kind of subversive aggression across an international boundary without allowing the victim of the aggression to react against its source. We stressed the fact that our government was facing a problem of major proportions in deciding how to cope with a new and dangerous technique for by-passing our traditional political and military defenses. While this broad subject was beyond the scope of our report, we expressed our deep conviction that the time might come in Southeast Asia when we would be obliged to attack the source of guerrilla aggression in North Vietnam and, in so doing, impose on Hanoi a price commensurate with the danger being inflicted on the south.

Our letter closed on the less somber note that our mission was leaving Southeast Asia feeling that the United States had a serious problem, but that the situation was by no means hopeless. Ultimate Communist success was far from inevitable if we could combine the many assets available to us into effective joint programs with our Vietnamese ally.

When the letter was signed, I felt that it marked the end of an important episode but also the beginning of a new one—a high point in our policy comparable in importance to the initiation of aid to Diem in 1954 by President Eisenhower. Knowing the President's eagerness to get his hands on our recommendations, I cabled him a summary from Baguio, hoping thereby to facilitate the consideration of the full report upon our return. Then we packed our bags, boarded our plane, and flew back across the Pacific to face the music in Washington.

CHAPTER 19

Return to Uniform

As I had expected, upon arrival in Washington we were immediately put on the witness seat before the President and his senior foreign policy advisers to testify to the results of our mission. I explained paragraph by paragraph the meaning and justification for my recommendations, arguing that, if implemented promptly and effectively, they should make a significant contribution to restoring national confidence in South Vietnam, improving the use of the resources presently available there, and bridging the time-gap required to increase the effectiveness of the Vietnamese forces. As an added advantage, the provision of this additional aid could and should be used as leverage to obtain concessions from Diem for the improvement of his government. But, I reminded my hearers, there was no guarantee that the recommended program was all that would be necessary to accomplish our ultimate purpose—self-determination for South Vietnam and its freedom from attack.

The recommendation of the introduction of a logistical task force naturally aroused the sharpest debate of any of the proposals. The Department of Defense estimated that it would require about 8,000 men to provide a unit capable of contributing significantly to the purposes which I had conceived for it. Would a force of that size be enough to raise the national morale and show U.S. determination, or would it serve only to stimulate requests for more troops? While the possible use of the flood as a justification for its introduction and the termination of the flood a reason for withdrawal offered certain advantages, I conceded that emphasis on the flood relief mission would weaken the psychological impact of our action. A forthright military justification for bringing in U.S. forces would make a stronger impression on South Vietnam as well as on the Communist world which was watching our actions.

On November 6 I met in private session with Secretaries Rusk and

245

McNamara and received the impression that both were in general accord with my report. On the following day, McNamara and the Joint Chiefs recorded their views in a carefully prepared memorandum for the President which supported my recommendations but with several important reservations. They felt that the chances were against, probably sharply against, preventing the fall of South Vietnam without the introduction of U.S. forces on a substantial scale and they believed that the modest force I recommended would be unconvincing and indecisive. In general, they viewed my proposals as a useful first step but only that. But, since this first step might lead to a much deeper military involvement, before taking it the U.S. government should deliberately and thoughtfully decide whether or not it committed itself without reservation to preventing the fall of South Vietnam to Communism and, if so, whether it was ready to pay whatever price that commitment might entail. They reminded the President that Hanoi and Peking might intervene and that as many as six American divisions might be required to resist these external forces—a very considerable American contingent but one which they thought could be fielded without serious impediment to the fulfillment of our obligations to Berlin and NATO.

McNamara and the Chiefs closed their paper with the recommendation that our government assume this broad commitment, affirm our willingness to support it by the necessary military actions, which by implication were likely to go beyond those proposed in my report, and then proceed to implement my recommendations. In taking this position, the Pentagon leaders expressed their awareness that many factors in the situation escaped U.S. control: the conduct of Diem and the other Vietnamese leaders, the course of events in Laos, the attitudes of Peking and Moscow, and the domestic reaction at home to strong measures in South Vietnam. With regard to the latter, they made the observation that the American people would probably respond better to a firm initial position than to courses of action which would lead the country in gradually. This, to my knowledge, was the first statement of the case against strategic gradualism which in later years was to become a major issue among President Johnson's senior civilian and military advisers; it constituted a prescient warning of the uncertainties involved in the course of action upon which we were about to embark.

After meeting with his people in State following his discussion with McNamara and me, Secretary Rusk apparently had second thoughts about the troop question and produced a paper for the President with which Secretary McNamara associated himself. It opened with an evaluation of the national interests involved in Vietnam, which was essentially a summary of the consensus arrived at in the long discussions of policy which had preceded and followed my mission to Saigon. It identified a number of national interests involved in the decisions we were facing: the regional conse-

246

quences to be apprehended from the loss of South Vietnam to Communism, in particular its effect on the rest of Southeast Asia and Indonesia; our obligations under the SEATO treaty; and the damage to the credibility of our commitments elsewhere if we were derelict to them here. Finally, it cited the likelihood of bitter domestic controversies in the United States if Vietnam were lost through American ineptitude or timidity.

Taking these matters into consideration, Rusk and McNamara joined in recommending to President Kennedy that the government commit itself to prevent the fall of South Vietnam to Communism and, in so doing, recognize that the introduction of American and other SEATO forces might become necessary. For this latter possibility, the Pentagon should prepare contingency plans for the use of American ground forces to assist in suppressing the Vietcong insurgency and for air strikes against targets in North Vietnam. An alternate situation to be covered by the planning was the case of large-scale external military intervention on the part of North Vietnam and, possibly, Communist China.

This recommendation for contingency planning carried with it a tacit rejection of the logistic task force proposal or, at least, its deferment. The paper argued against any such immediate action for the reason that, while it might improve South Vietnamese morale, it would increase the probability of Communist bloc escalation in some form and would risk stimulating a Communist resumption of hostilities in Laos and a breakdown in the Geneva negotiations. An added reason for wishing to defer the troop decision was a reluctance to take unilateral action if it were possible to obtain joint or concerted action on the part of our allies. However, the paper conceded that even if the Vietnamese greatly improved their own performance, they could probably not win the war if infiltration continued unchecked and the guerrillas continued to enjoy the safety of sanctuaries in neighboring territory. For this contingency, we should be prepared to introduce U.S. combat forces.

The paper supported the other recommendations of my report and expanded their general language into specifics to provide clearer guidance to the agencies that would have to carry them out. It also set forth a scenario of political actions to be synchronized with our announcement of increased aid, to include the release of the Jorden White Paper exposing the North Vietnamese violations of the 1954 Geneva Accords. The Jorden paper was intended to establish that Hanoi's recent acts amounted to a renewal of aggression in Vietnam, and hence justified a response in accordance with the warning issued by Under Secretary of State Smith in the final session of the 1954 Geneva Conference that the United States "would view any renewal of the aggression . . . with grave concern and as seriously threatening international peace and security."

The scenario also called for Ambassador Nolting to approach Diem to get certain prior concessions from him in exchange for our new undertakings. In general terms, we wanted assurance that he would carry out an effective and total mobilization of all resources available to him, move toward a decentralization and broadening of his government to embrace all non-Communist elements in the country, and overhaul the military command structure. Also, we wanted to be sure of Diem's cooperation in carrying out the joint measures of our new programs such as the provincial surveys, the improvements in intelligence and the participation of American advisers in civil administration. Once Nolting had obtained Diem's acquiescence in these points, we planned to have an exchange of letters between him and President Kennedy that would provide a public explanation and justification for the joint decisions and actions of the two governments.

After a discussion of this State-Defense paper on November 11, President Kennedy approved it at once essentially as written. All its points were incorporated in a National Security Action Memorandum (NSAM) approved on November 15 except for the formal affirmation of the broad policy commitment which his principal advisers had urged. Oddly, I do not recall that any particular importance was attached to the omission or that it aroused any particular discussion at the time. President Kennedy never indicated any opposition of which I was aware to the thesis that we must be prepared to go all the way if we took this first step—one of the prime lessons of the Bay of Pigs. Possibly he felt that the NSAM was an action memorandum which should not be cluttered with exhortations or statements of good intentions; possibly he felt that the statement of policy in NSAM-52 of the previous May was quite sufficient and needed no repetition. The decisions he was announcing could be quite properly regarded as merely implementing actions in support of this former statement.

His approval set in motion great activity in the Washington agencies—State, Defense, JSC, AID, CIA, and USIA—that had the primary responsibility for carrying out his decisions. But they were brought to a virtual standstill by unexpected resistance that Ambassador Nolting encountered when he sought Diem's agreement to the conditions which we were imposing for our increased assistance. Initially it was not clear whether Diem had substantive objections to any of the conditions or whether he was merely asserting his independence. In Washington we could make few overt moves before we were sure of the cooperation of our ally, and the press was clamoring for information from the White House. By November 27 we were considering recalling Nolting to expose him directly to Washington thinking on the situation and to put pressure on Diem by this indication of our unhappiness. On the chance that Diem might continue to be intransigent, the old search for a possible replacement for him was resumed in State. But again no one could suggest better possibilities than the unimpressive Vice-President Tho, the intelligent but mild-mannered Defense Minister Thuan, or a junta of unspecified generals. Fortunately, by dint of Nolting's skillful handling of Diem, the sensitive mandarin in Saigon who knew his arm was being twisted and did not enjoy it, the crisis passed and, to the enormous relief of Washington, on December 4 Nolting was able to cable Diem's agreement on all substantial points. A few days later the long-planned exchange of letters took place, one from Diem describing what he called "the gravest crisis in Vietnamese history" and promising full mobilization and cooperation with the Americans; the other, a reply from President Kennedy indicating that the United States was prepared to increase its contribution to the joint enterprise of freeing Vietnam from the Communist threat.

From the outset the inherent inertia in both Washington and Saigon proved truly formidable and it was the source of many of our administrative headaches during the next few years. In Washington there was a serious unevenness of performance among the executive departments arising primarily from the great concentration of power within the Pentagon. There, the leadership enjoyed the advantages of vast financial and personnel resources and of wide experience in planning and carrying out extensive programs analogous to those now needed in Vietnam. In charge was Robert McNamara, one of the ablest and most energetic administrators ever to come to Washington, who was off the starting blocks like a shot as soon as he received the go-ahead from President Kennedy.

In contrast, the nonmilitary agencies involved were not manned by operator types and knew little about this kind of planning and programing. State, which should have assumed a supervisory and coordinating role in the interrelated departmental activities in Washington, was staffed largely with Foreign Service officers trained to observe and report events abroad but not accustomed to taking action about them. AID and the USIA were new elements in the executive structure without a core of career experts to provide personnel stability and depth. The CIA, like the Pentagon, seemed to me to be well financed, well staffed, and generally capable of looking after the tasks assigned to it.

As a result, the Pentagon- and CIA-sponsored programs got off to a relatively fast start, whereas the political, economic, and information programs moved very slowly. Unequal progress among our programs plagued our efforts in South Vietnam for years and gave some ground for the charges of later years that the United States tended to neglect the political and social aspects of the situation and fatuously sought an impossible military victory. The critics could point to the fact that our military forces were often able to sweep away the Vietcong from areas long before the civil agencies were ready to exploit the security thus gained. I would vigorously deny any desire in the Kennedy or the Johnson Administrations to overemphasize the military programs, but the White House was naturally reluctant to hold them back to the pace of the slowest civil program. What was needed, I thought, was that interdepartmental steering mechanism serving the President which had been so badly lacking at the time of the Bay of

Pigs. Still averse to using the NSC for serious purposes, President Kennedy continued to depend on improvised task forces to integrate activities in support of Vietnam. These were generally committees of relatively junior officials who operated on the principle of consensus by compromise, a sure formula for flaccid leadership and faltering performance.

To give military direction to the new program, General Paul Harkins was designated the senior military commander in Vietnam, and in February he assumed command of the newly created U.S. Military Assistance Command—Vietnam, soon dubbed MAC/V. Harkins was a highly regarded officer with wide experience in World War II and Korea who had recently been deputy commander of the Army forces in the Pacific. His appointment raised the question of drafting a directive for him consistent with the desire of the President for unity of responsibility for all activities related to the counterinsurgency effort in Vietnam. The problem was how to write such a directive without infringing on Ambassador Nolting's responsibilities. After much discussion between State, Defense, and the Joint Chiefs in which I participated as the White House moderator, language was agreed upon which recognized the Ambassador as the senior U.S. representative in Vietnam but charged the Military Commander with direct responsibility for military policy, operations, and assistance to the Vietnamese armed forces. Harkins was to report to Washington through the military channels but would keep Nolting informed of his recommendations in ample time for the Ambassador to appeal to Washington if he did not agree. Although Nolting accepted the directive with obvious misgivings, it never became an issue during his association with Harkins. Both men demonstrated that mutual consideration which is the secret of successful civilian-military relationships.

I would like to be able to say that following these initial actions our plans and programs picked up momentum and rolled forward smoothly toward the goals set for them. Such was far from the case, and, even if the American performance had been perfect, the many deficiencies in leadership, organization, and intelligence in the Vietnamese government remained to impose delays on even limited progress. Diem did not change his ways overnight but remained what he had always been—a stubborn, suspicious Asian who was willing to make some paper concessions to get greater American aid but who did not intend to disregard his own judgment to appease foreign critics. He reluctantly allowed the joint provincial surveys a pilot run in three provinces but insisted that they concern themselves only with military and intelligence matters. He was still not willing to let American observers pry into political and economic matters in the rural areas.

I had no reason to doubt the sincerity of his intention to improve his government and to put the nation on a true war-footing. But a competent officialdom is the product of generations of experience and training, not something attainable by fiat or by the quick expenditure of American dollars. Failure to recognize this simple fact led us over the years to expect far too much far too soon from the Vietnamese government and to overload its fragile structure with more concurrent programs than it could ever have been expected to carry out. Diem knew pretty much what was administratively feasible in his country and what was not, but when this knowledge caused him to resist new American initiatives, he exposed himself to the charge of stubbornness and lack of cooperation.

In spite of obstacles, additional U.S. military and intelligence advisers arriving during the spring of 1962 began to produce measurable if undramatic results. CIA-conducted training of the Montagnards, the primitive non-Vietnamese people of the high Plateau provinces, offered some promise of creating border guards capable of relieving Army static posts and thus of effecting economies in military manpower. The new military equipment, particularly the helicopters and armored personnel carriers, began to arrive and had some effect in stirring Army units to mobile, offensive action. After a May visit to Saigon, Secretary McNamara reported publicly a feeling of great encouragement from what he saw but added privately that he felt that it would take years to defeat the Communists.

For me the first six months of 1962 were filled with diverse activities, some already mentioned. I gave top priority to implementation of the decisions resulting from my Vietnam mission but continued to work on counterinsurgency, the situation in Cuba, disarmament matters, and considerations of nuclear-testing limitations. The running debate on NATO strategy went on without interruption, particularly as it bore on the forward defense of Germany and the security of Berlin. Finally, there were discussions over the impending retirement of General Norstad.

By this time Norstad had been in Europe for twelve years, first as Commander of the NATO Air Forces, then for six years as SACEUR in succession to General Alfred M. Gruenther. Several times in the past he had expressed an interest in retiring but, in the spring of 1962, it became apparent that he meant business. My impression was that he had never felt completely at ease with President Kennedy and his entourage, possibly the result of his early collisions with the amateur strategists of the New Frontier who had invaded his premises. His work in NATO had undoubtedly been made difficult by the frictions arising over the new American strategy, by the derogation in Washington of NATO intelligence bearing on the Soviet ground strength, and by McNamara's refusal to support his recommendations for a NATO Medium Range Ballistic Missile. He never voiced his grievances in my hearing, but it was clear to me and probably to President Kennedy that they existed. Hence, it seemed timely to accept Norstad's request for retirement, and an announcement to that effect was made on July 20 with the understanding that the retirement would take place on November 1.

Before making the matter public, President Kennedy had to decide on Norstad's successor and the other changes in senior officers which any decision would entail. He considered both General Lemnitzer and me for the job, but I asked to be excluded from consideration for the same reason that had caused me to decline the Paris Embassy in 1961—I had lived too long abroad and wished to have the opportunity to discharge neglected responsibilities to my family at home. So in the end, the President nominated Lemnitzer to NATO and appointed me as his successor as Chairman, Joint Chiefs of Staff. At the same time, he selected General Earle G. Wheeler to succeed General George H. Decker as Army Chief of Staff. All of these changes were announced on July 19 with an effective date of October 1.

In retrospect, I think that these changes were probably in the interest of both NATO and the President. The NATO authorities were well acquainted with General Lemnitzer from his war service as Deputy Chief of Staff to Field Marshal Alexander, and, more recently, as Chairman of the Joint Chiefs; hence, his appointment to succeed Norstad was most welcome in Europe. At home, the President gained the opportunity to begin the reconstitution of the Joint Chiefs with men of his own choice.

Presidents have always wanted to pick their own Chiefs, a practice which has much to commend it. In saying this, I may appear to be contradicting the views which I have expressed elsewhere, deploring the action of President Eisenhower in replacing all the Chiefs at one time in apparent deference to the criticisms which Senator Taft and other Republican senators had leveled at their conduct of the Korean War. The way it was done at that time created the impression that an outgoing set of Democratic Chiefs was being replaced by an incoming Republican set. Any such suggestion of partisanship on party lines among the Chiefs was contrary to fact and repugnant to the professional military, who pride themselves on detachment from party politics at all times.

With the opportunity to observe the problems of a President at closer range, I have come to understand the importance of an intimate, easy relationship, born of friendship and mutual regard, between the President and the Chiefs. It is particularly important in the case of the Chairman, who works more closely with the President and Secretary of Defense than do the service chiefs. The Chairman should be a true believer in the foreign policy and military strategy of the administration which he serves or, at least, feel that he and his colleagues are assured an attentive hearing on those matters for which the Joint Chiefs have a responsibility. These considerations have led me to conclude that an incoming President is well advised to change the Chiefs, not with one sweep of the new broom, but progressively as he gets a chance to know the senior officers qualified for consideration and to evaluate their compatibility with his ways of thinking and acting.

When President Kennedy sounded me out about becoming Chairman, I was of course pleased to be considered but, at the same time, felt a certain depression at the thought of returning to the bear pit of the Pentagon where I spent four less-than-happy years as Army Chief of Staff. However, I recognized that the atmosphere had changed and that the strategic heresy of Flexible Response which I had advocated to little avail had become the orthodoxy of the Kennedy Administration. Also, I had gotten to know Secretary McNamara and, in spite of occasional differences of view, had a high regard for him as a man of decision who tackled fearlessly the tough problems of defense and refused to yield to the temptation to sweep them under the rug.

Before accepting the new assignment, I called on McNamara and asked him frankly about his attitude toward my proposed appointment. As he seemed genuinely pleased at the prospect, I proceeded to discuss specifics which worried me. I explained that during my year in the White House I had got the impression that the so-called Whiz Kids, the young and bright civilian assistants whom McNamara had brought in, had been allowed to swamp the Joint Chiefs with requests for studies to the point that their effectiveness had become seriously impaired. We readily agreed that the Chairman would have final say over the demands placed on the Joint Staff except when the request came over the signature of the Secretary or Deputy Secretary.

Another matter was the handling of situations when the Joint Chiefs held divided views on subjects requiring their advice or recommendation. I explained that, as a Chief, I had always resented efforts by the Chairman to impose uniformity or to obtain it by compromise. I told the Secretary that I respected the individual views of the Chiefs and felt that any dissent should be reported to the Secretary or even to the President without trying to circumvent the issue by noncommittal or ambiguous statements. McNamara said that he felt exactly the same way, that he would welcome split papers which outlined the pros and cons of the contending positions and that such a procedure was much more helpful to him in reaching a decision than the presentation of pallid compromises. He indicated a dissatisfaction with some of the past work of the Joint Staff and expressed the hope that I would do everything possible to improve its quality and timeliness. I promised to do my best and, taking advantage of the opportunity, enlisted his assistance in getting Major General Andrew Goodpaster, a much sought-after officer then commanding a division in Europe, assigned as my principal assistant.

As a final point, I mentioned the allegations which floated about Washington that his Whiz Kids had taken over much of the advisory role of the Joint Chiefs of Staff who were being regularly bypassed in the process. I told him that I recognized his right, indeed his duty, to seek advice from many quarters and that he could turn to whomever he liked—to his barber or chauffeur if he wished. The Joint Chiefs of Staff, however, had the statutory obligation to serve as the principal military advisers to him, the National Security Council, and the President, and I asked his help to assure that they were always given full opportunity to discharge this obligation. They could not and did not expect that their advice would always be accepted but it should always be heard. There seemed to be complete agreement between us on all of these points and I would say that we always operated in accordance with these understandings throughout my tenure as Chairman.

By chance, about this time President Kennedy made an unanticipated contribution to the theme of civilian-military relationships which was central to this discussion with Secretary McNamara. Early in June he went to West Point to deliver the commencement address to the graduating class. I had preceded him by two days to join my classmates in celebrating the fortieth anniversary of our graduation and so did not see the final text of his speech, although I had suggested earlier that he might include something about his feeling of the nature and importance of a military career.

A passage in his speech which caused considerable comment in West Point circles was one which was quite similar to a statement he had made the year before at Annapolis. In discussing the subsequent careers of the graduating cadets, he stated:

> The non-military problems which you will face will also be most demanding —diplomatic, political and economic. You will need to know and understand not only the foreign policy of the U.S. but the foreign policy of all countries scattered around the world. You will need to understand the importance of military power and also the limits of military power. You will have the obligation to deter war as well as fight it.

I was greatly pleased to find these words in his speech which sounded to me like the authentic thought of John F. Kennedy himself, not the contribution of some anonymous speechwriter. They are notably consistent with his appeal to the Joint Chiefs of Staff after the Bay of Pigs that they serve him as advisers on broad policy and not as purely military specialists. Stated by someone other than the President such views would have attracted criticism as being an overly broad interpretation of the role of military officers, and even as an invitation to them to trespass into fields which had been off limits in past tradition and practice.

The President's statement was all the more remarkable when contrasted with a passage from an address made by General Douglas MacArthur to the Corps of Cadets just a month before the Kennedy speech. MacArthur told the cadets:

> Your mission remains fixed, determined, inviolable—it is to win our wars. Everything else in your professional career is but corollary to this vital dedication.

General Taylor acting as military adviser to Secretary of State Dulles at Baghdad Pact Conference in Ankara, 1958.

With the President in the White House Garden.

With President Kennedy at Hyannis Port.

A meeting on the budget with President Kennedy at Hyannis Port, November 1961. Present: Lemnitzer, Taylor, McNamara, the President, Bell, Gilpatric, Wiesner, Sorensen. (Cecil W. Stoughton)

A meeting of the Special Group (counterinsurgency). In order, clockwise: Wilson (USIA), Lemnitzer (JCS), Johnson (State), Robert Kennedy (Justice), Taylor (White House), Gilpatric (Defense), McCone (CIA), Hamilton (AID). (Cecil W. Stoughton)

A budget meeting with the Joint Chiefs of Staff in Palm Beach in late 1962. Present: Shoup, Wheeler, Anderson, McNamara, the President, Taylor, Gilpatric, LeMay. (Cecil W. Stoughton)

Swearing-in ceremony in the White House Rose Garden as Chairman Joint Chiefs of Staff, October 1962.   (Cecil W. Stoughton)

Above: Taylor calls on President Diem in the course of his mission to South Vietnam, October 1961. *Left:* A visit to the Shah of Iran. *Below:* A dinner with Cambodia defense minister Lon Nol. (USIS) *Bottom:* A call on Sukarno in Djakarta.

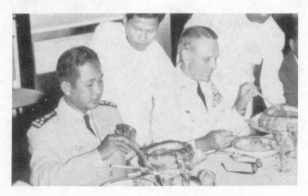

General Taylor, President Kennedy, and Secretary Robert McNamara in the Cabinet Room.   (U.S. Navy)

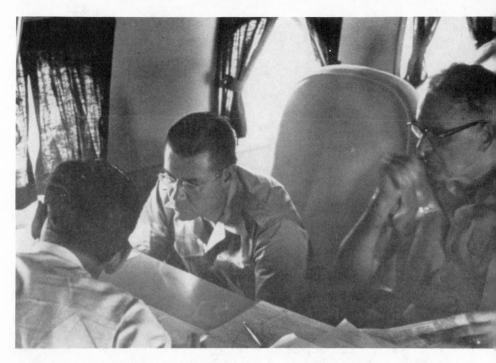

In flight to Vietnam, September 1963.

A visit to South Vietnam, September 1963. At table: Taylor, Ambassador Lodge, McNamara.

Swearing-in ceremony as Ambassador to South Vietnam in the Rose Garden, July 2, 1964.   (O. J. Rapp)

Taylor's first supersonic flight in an F-4.

Ambassador Taylor with General "Big" Minh and his family, Saigon.

A visit to a Vietnamese hamlet (top).

Ambassador Taylor and small friend.

Ambassador with Captain Tom Taylor greeting the arrival of troops of the 101st Airborne Division at Cam Ranh Bay. General Westmoreland in the background.

Tom Taylor in action with the Screaming Eagles. (U.S. Army Signal Corps)

Taylor reporting to the President in August 1965 after returning from his post as Ambassador.

Taylor reporting to the President and his advisers following his return from his post as Ambassador.

He elaborated on this thought, asserting in the most positive terms that the merits or demerits of our governmental process, such things as deficit financing, federal paternalism, power-group arrogance, rampant crime, low morals, high taxes, violent extremism, and personal liberties are great national problems but not for military participation or for military solution. If one took the General at his word, he would appear to have felt that officers were "not to reason why" in matters of foreign or domestic policy—theirs was but to win wars by military means and leave all other considerations to the civilians. This was in flat contrast with the views of the civilian President who was equally positive that officers do have responsibilities in the field of policy, particularly of foreign policy. To him, they were not merely men at arms, useful only for the dirty business of fighting wars—they had a duty also to deter wars and deterrence involves an appreciation of far more than purely military matters. They should know what military power can and cannot do and presumably recommend accordingly in invoking or withholding its use.

At West Point this conflict of views was noted at the time, and over the following years provided a topic for frequent discussion among the faculty and cadets. In 1969 I was asked to speak at West Point and was invited to reconcile the apparent contradictions between two great Americans, by that time both deceased. I tried rather lamely to do so, expressing the opinion that General MacArthur had probably wished to impress on his hearers the need for a deep military professionalism in the officers corps—it is no place for dilettantes, he seemed to say—and a dedication to the inexorable requirements of victory for which there is no substitute. But his own career had been studded with brilliant successes in the fields of the diplomat and statesman. He could not have intended to condemn his own record by suggesting that it is wrong for an officer to look beyond the battle field to apply his experience. As for President Kennedy, I felt that he was extolling the versatility of a MacArthur-type officer although I imagined he would have excluded from his praise certain episodes of MacArthur's career bearing on his relations with President Truman. I am not sure how successful I was in reconciling the apparently irreconcilable or whether the absent protagonists would have approved of my interpretation of their views.

Once the news was out that I was to succeed General Lemnitzer in October, it became very hard not to neglect my old job in preparing for the new one. There was much to be discussed with Lem and the key officers of the Joint Staff. It was important to quiet the inevitable rumors that the new Chairman would bring in his own team and evict present incumbents. There were long lists of proposed briefings to consider, some of which I had to take but most of which were deferred or rejected for lack of time. There were White House discussions over how to dispose of the jobs which I had been filling as Military Representative.

Meanwhile, there could be no forgetting the hot spots that had to be watched continuously—Cuba, Berlin, and Southeast Asia.

On August 9 I appeared at a confirmation hearing before the Senate Armed Services Committee. This was my first appearance before a congressional committee since my days as Army Chief of Staff, and I rather enjoyed seeing old friends and acquaintances. As I recall, there were only two matters of substance raised by the senators. Knowing my past record of opposition to Massive Retaliation and recalling the criticism of the Joint Chiefs of Staff system recorded in *The Uncertain Trumpet*, they directed most of their questions at these two points. Did my appointment indicate a change in the U.S. attitude toward the defense of Europe through nuclear weapons? Also, did I expect to initiate sweeping changes in the Joint Chiefs of Staff, perhaps even try to slip in that congressional *bête noire*, the single Defense Chief of Staff? I assured them that none of these apprehensions was justified, that I was returning to the Pentagon in no crusading spirit and, I hoped, uninfluenced by any bias derived from my past experience. The senators must have been satisfied, at least momentarily, as the vote for confirmation was unanimous.

In spite of some uneasiness over the evidence since July of increasing Soviet military aid arriving in Cuba, in preparation for my new assignment I felt it essential to devote the first three weeks of September to a badly needed refresher visit to the Far East. For this purpose I left on August 31 with a small party of staff assistants and returned on September 21, following an arc from Japan to Indonesia. Although the pace was fast and the pauses short, we had time to reflect seriously on the U.S. politico-military policy in this vast region, particularly as it related to Communist China. Since that country offered the principal strategic threat to this part of the world, it was essential to base our strategic thinking on the entire region from Japan to Burma which lay under the shadow of China. There was a need for aggregated planning which was particularly important for the use of the limited air power available to offset the growing Chinese Air Force. By this time, it was equipped with airplanes generally superior to those of our allies and deployed in depth on the continental land mass. The forces of our side, located in the relatively restricted areas of Japan, Korea, Okinawa, and Southeast Asia, offered exposed and highly vulnerable targets to this superior enemy.

While air defense seemed the most pressing military problem, it was clear that the ground force requirements, U.S. and allied, to meet a major attack originating on the Asian continent would always be astronomical as long as there was no authoritative guideline permitting us to plan on the use of tactical nuclear weapons. In NATO, we had undertaken an unqualified commitment to use these weapons if essential to the security of the alliance, and the NATO force structure was based upon that undertaking. If we would agree to treat a major Chinese attack in the same way, a much less risky business in view of the Chinese lack of a nuclear retaliatory force, we could greatly reduce military force requirements and add importantly to the deterrent effect of the forces we had. In short, we badly needed an integrated plan for the deterrence of China, one that would take into account all U.S. and allied assets to include our nuclear weapons. To obtain this integration became a prime objective after my return to Washington, but one toward which progress was always painfully slow.

My visit to Vietnam was of particular personal interest since it allowed me to form an impression of the progress of the many programs which stemmed from my previous visit almost a year before. To profit from this opportunity I first talked with Diem and the American officials in Saigon, then made a rapid tour of field activities. Along the way, I frequently had junior American officers assembled whom I interviewed without senior officers present in order to assure relatively uninhibited replies to my questions. It is always hard to convince the toilers in the field that senior visitors really want unpleasant as well as pleasant news and that they respect rather than resent the bearer of authentic bad tidings.

Many things were happening in South Vietnam as a result of the increased American presence. However, progress was uneven. We were doing well in such things as the training of South Vietnamese forces, the improvement of rural security, and the use of the Montagnards in frontier defense. Accomplishments in the political, administrative, and social fields were far less demonstrable. Although Diem seemed to be getting along well with Nolting and Harkins, he was still the difficult, suspicious introvert of the past and increasingly a target of criticism for the resident members of the American press who had never liked him. This sentiment was mutual for Diem had never trusted the press, indigenous or foreign, and never seemed to realize the disastrous effects for his government that a hostile press could create. Our officials in Saigon worked hard to little avail in trying to open channels of communications between him and the media. In the absence of even a moderately efficient Ministry of Information, the press turned more and more to the Embassy or our military headquarters for information that should have come from the government. But since American officials in 1962 were still dependent largely on Vietnamese sources for most of what they knew, the information which they passed to the press was tainted with the same inaccuracies as their official reports to Washington. But whereas Washington officialdom had some understanding by this time of the difficulty of getting the facts from an inefficient Asian dictatorship, the press showed no such tolerance and began a campaign to discredit official pronouncements, American and Vietnamese, a campaign which embittered relations between many of the press corps and the American officials in Vietnam. The hostility of the press toward Vietnam officials was even more intense. By the time of my visit in 1962, many newsmen were committed to a full-scale vendetta against Diem and his government which they pursued tirelessly until his overthrow a year later.

Finding some way to measure progress in our programs was another perplexing problem in Vietnam. Parts of the military program were measurable provided the performance data were accurate: the strength of forces, the intake of recruits, the output of the military school system, and the like. But the success of operations against the Vietcong was another matter to measure. Contacts with the elusive guerrillas were short, usually little more than a quick burst of fire followed by the disappearance of the enemy into the darkness or the jungles. The enemy was careful to carry away their killed and wounded so that it was difficult to identify the units and their losses. The seizure of terrain—hills, stream lines, villages—meant nothing in such a contest which resembled police actions against bandits more than military operations of a conventional pattern.

The measuring of success in nonmilitary programs presented even greater difficulties. While the government provided figures on the growth of the fortified hamlets, we Americans had limited means for verifying the accuracy of the figures or the degree of security existing within them. We soon found that there was a great difference between safety conditions before and after dark and in the wet and dry seasons. How should we present these fluctuations in security in our reports? Most officials agreed that an important measure of success was the restoration of the rural population to the control of the Saigon government but were at a loss to establish reliable criteria for governmental control. In spite of this problem of quantifying progress, my general conclusion was that we were achieving qualitative progress in the military and economic fields but that the socio-political programs continued to lag.

My last foreign stop on my way home was in Indonesia, my second visit to this vast, rich archipelago. I shared the Washington apprehension regarding the future of this emerging nation which Sukarno, with dubious motives, was steering alternatively to the right and to the left under the slogan of "guided democracy." I was warmly received by General Abdul Nasution, the Chief of Staff of the Armed Forces and Minister of Defense, who was clearly eager for some American military aid to offset the massive input of weapons from the USSR. Up to that time, our U.S. military contribution had been limited largely to the training of Indonesian officers in our military school system, a cheap but highly remunerative investment as later events were to prove. Apart from arms, Nasution hoped for help in the country-wide civic action program which the Army was conducting to neutralize the growing influence of the Communist Party (PKI) in the countryside. I left Indonesia pretty well convinced that we should support a modest military aid program, primarily for the purpose of maintaining and improving relations with the Indonesian Army which was the principal bulwark against Communism and a counterbalance to the formidable PKI.

My only contact with Sukarno, then the unchallenged Chief of State, was a call at his palace on a very hot evening. The open windows of the reception room offered unimpeded ingress to vast swarms of hungry mosquitoes. While trying not to wince under their attack, I listened to Sukarno discourse at length on the charms of his favorite stars of Hollywood but could arouse in him no similar interest in discussing the problems of his country.

Upon returning to Washington, there was the usual aftermath of discussions of my trip with the President, Secretary McNamara, and the Joint Chiefs, while, in my spare time, I prepared to move to the Pentagon. In the midst of this hubbub, President Ayub Khan of Pakistan came to town. One afternoon, President Kennedy asked me to take him by helicopter to Glen Ora, the Kennedy farm in Virginia, for a call on Mrs. Kennedy. I had known President Ayub quite well when he commanded the Pakistani Army before becoming President and so enjoyed undertaking this social assignment in order to chat with him.

En route to Glen Ora, I learned that the primary purpose of his trip to the farm was to permit Ayub to inspect the saddle horse which he had given Mrs. Kennedy on another occasion. Mrs. Kennedy met us graciously at an improvised helicopter landing pad and took us to a nearby stable where two saddled horses waited. I was greatly relieved that there was not a third for me as my last appearance on a horse had been in the San Antonio Parade of Flowers in 1941, and I doubted that I was prepared to cut a very dashing figure after a twenty-year layoff.

Ayub had his problem, too, one of a riding costume, as he had arrived at Glen Ora in a formal dark suit. But one of his aides had anticipated the need and appeared bearing a pair of white wool chaps, worthy of any cowboy star in Hollywood. Ayub pulled them on gravely over his striped trousers, mounted, and cantered off with Mrs. Kennedy without the slightest indication of self-consciousness, confident apparently that he was garbed in normal American equestrian style.

One of my last acts before departing the White House was to pay a farewell call on President Kennedy. I knew that of all the changes resulting from my move to the Pentagon the one which I would feel most was the loss of daily association with him. I told him that I hoped to retain as much as possible of this closeness in my new assignment and was pleased when he invited me to telephone him directly whenever it seemed necessary, a privilege I appreciated having but never used. No man has a right to impose himself on the President except for the most cogent reasons.

I mentioned to him some of the matters of unfinished business which I was leaving behind: the unresolved question of what to do about Castro

259

and many pending issues relating to NATO, particularly regarding the contingent use of tactical nuclear weapons. It seemed to me that we Americans were listening too much to Russian propaganda against these weapons and to our own fears of their premature or unauthorized use. As a result, we were creating inhibitions against their use in any case—even as a deterrent.

As a valedictory word, I mentioned my occasional concern over the absence of the military voice in the high councils of state. While the President had often indicated his understanding of the need for military advice in foreign policy formulation, that attitude was not universal at the top of the government. It was always tempting to exclude military representatives from the consideration of an issue if they were pretty certain to voice an unwelcome point of view. If this attitude resulted from any past dissatisfaction with the work of the Joint Chiefs, I promised to do all that I could to assure that the military voice would be clear, timely, and helpful. We shook hands, and I went home to dig out the uniforms which I had put away in 1959, presumably forever.

CHAPTER 20

Cuba—The Secret Crisis

On Monday morning, October 1, at eight o'clock, I arrived for work at the office of the Chairman Joint Chiefs of Staff just inside the river entrance of the Pentagon. It was largely a day of ceremony and protocol. First, General Wheeler was sworn in as Army Chief of Staff at the Pentagon. Then came a double ceremony in the Rose Garden of the White House where, in the presence of the President, General Lemnitzer was awarded the Distinguished Service Medal for his service as Chairman and I was sworn in by Robert Kennedy as his successor. Our families, friends, and colleagues made up the audience which listened to the usual speeches and responses which go with such occasions. It was a bright fall day and the world seemed full of promise as the Kennedy brothers surveyed the military chiefs of their Establishment.

Following the ceremonies, Bob McNamara took me to a luncheon in his office and afterwards to a meeting with the Pentagon press, most of whom I already knew from past associations. Like the senators whom I faced for confirmation, the reporters wanted to know if I was the man on horseback arriving to take over, but they also seemed to accept my disclaimer. From there, I went to my first meeting with the Joint Chiefs in the "Tank," Pentagon jargon for their conference room situated down the corridor from the Chairman's office. There I found assembled the principal military colleagues with whom I was going to work in this new phase of my career: General Wheeler; Admiral George Anderson, Chief of Naval Operations; General Curtis LeMay, Chief of the Air Staff; General David Shoup, Commandant of the Marine Corps; and Vice Admiral Herbert Riley, Director of the Joint Staff. We had all known each other before so that there was little to say except to express our hope and intention to work effectively together in the cause of national security.

The main issues awaiting me in my new office were essentially the ones which I had been following in the White House: Cuba, Berlin, NATO, Southeast Asia, arms control, a nuclear test ban treaty, the structure of the Armed Forces, and the defense budget. Duties in connection with counter-insurgency also remained with me as I had to represent the Joint Chiefs of Staff weekly on the old Special Group (CI) in the Executive Office Building. Among these matters, concern for Cuba was predominant during the early days of October just prior to the Cuban missile crisis.

A number of accounts of the Cuban missile crisis exist, the work either of direct participants or of observers on the sidelines with some view of parts of the action. As a matter of fact, no one except perhaps the President was aware of all that was taking place. Certainly I made no such pretense. Consequently, I shall not attempt to give a complete account of the complicated sequence of events from our acquisition of the photographic evidence of the presence of offensive missiles in Cuba on October 16 to the withdrawal of the last IL-28 bomber on December 6. Rather, I shall try to summarize the highlights of the crisis as I saw them and then use this summary as a basis for reflection on the significance of the events related.

In a way, the missile crisis was a sequel to the Bay of Pigs since Khrushchev justified his military build-up in Cuba in 1961 and 1962 as a defensive measure to discourage further U.S. "aggression" against his protégé, Castro. While American authorities were generally aware of the Soviet activities in arming Castro during the months after the Bay of Pigs, it was not until 1962 that we obtained reliable evidence of a very substantial increase in the volume and rate of arrival of military equipment in Cuba and directed the intelligence community to focus more attention on what was taking place. As a result, a regular schedule of U-2 flights was established to provide periodic photography of the island and our military aircraft began to make a practice of photographing Soviet vessels bound for Cuba. These rather modest efforts to learn more about what the Soviets were up to were further increased as the result of a growing number of rumors about missiles in Cuba, most of them generated by Cuban refugees. These reports made headlines in the American press and provided a theme for anti-Administration speeches in Congress where the members were warming up for the fall elections. Several senators began making bellicose noises, expressing acute discontent over the President's timid measures against Castro, limited at the time to efforts to isolate him politically from the rest of Latin America and to retard the Cuban economy through rather ineffective trade restrictions.

Years after these events it is difficult to reconstruct official attitudes toward the Soviet rearmament of Cuba in the fall of 1962. We knew that between July and September about seventy shiploads of war materiel had arrived in Cuban ports—tanks, artillery, MIG fighters, Komar short-range missile boats, and surface-to-air missile (SAM) equipment. At the same time it was estimated that the Soviet military technicians in Cuba had increased from a few hundred to some 4,000. We had no doubt that Khrushchev had placed a very formidable arsenal of modern weapons in Castro's hands and, in so doing, had provided him with the largest, best-equipped military force in the Western Hemisphere after our own. But it still looked like a defense-oriented program primarily for the purpose of providing Cuba with improved air and coastal protection.

The very profusion of rumors about offensive missiles in Cuba, most of them implausible and readily discredited, tended to dull the perceptivity of our intelligence agencies. It was easy to assume that even a well-documented report about missiles came from an observer who had confused the SAM's, which we knew were there, with surface-to-surface offensive missiles, which we did not believe were there. Indeed, there were some quite plausible reasons to believe that Khrushchev never would send offensive missiles to Cuba. The USSR had never let these weapons out of Soviet territory in the past, not even for installation in the European satellites. If in Cuba, they would create the problem of retaining Soviet command and control of them while on Cuban soil, as it was hard to imagine Khrushchev entrusting them to a wild man like Castro. Also, Khrushchev had no way of knowing what the U.S. reaction might be to such a provocative act on the part of the USSR. These factors, reinforced by solemn assurances by Soviet officials of the purely defensive character of their aid to Cuba, had led our intelligence community in mid-September to conclude that the establishment of offensive nuclear weapons on Cuban soil was unlikely. It is true that this conclusion was hedged by a warning that the advantages to the USSR of a nuclear weapons base on the Western Hemisphere as a cheap way to enhance the Soviet nuclear strength were so considerable that the contingency should not be completely ruled out. However, this caveat had little practical effect on our decision makers as it was the unqualified conclusion of the unlikelihood of the event which made the impression on the minds of U.S. officials.

September turned out to be the critical month for our intelligence collection efforts. We now know that in this month very important activities were taking place in Cuba which could have been photographed had we had a U-2 at the right place at the right time, but our limited flights were woefully unproductive for a variety of reasons. They were completely grounded from September 8 to 16 because of the loss of a U-2 over China and, when allowed to fly, they were hampered by bad weather and by operational restrictions. My impression is that the President was never made fully aware of these limitations on our primary source of information, mainly because the intelligence community did not bring the situation forcibly to his attention and urge approval of low-level reconnaissance when the U-2's could not fly.

When I returned to Washington from my trip to the Far East and settled into my new job as Chairman, I was immediately confronted with this lack of intelligence and joined with my military colleagues in urging accelerated U-2 photography of all areas of Cuba which were suspect as possible missile sites. By that time, raw intelligence from several untested sources was pointing to several such places which were made specific targets for U-2 photography as the overflights assumed an accelerated frequency. It was a flight on October 14 that produced the critical evidence which, when presented to President Kennedy on the morning of October 16, set in train the events of the now famous "Thirteen Days."

I think of the Thirteen Days as divided into two parts, the first being the secret crisis in the White House extending from October 16 to the President's speech on the evening of October 22. This speech initiated the second phase, the international crisis, which lasted until October 28, when Khrushchev capitulated by agreeing to withdraw all offensive nuclear weapons. Then after the Thirteen Days there was a final crisis over the verification of the withdrawal of offensive missiles and over the inclusion of IL-28 medium bombers among the weapons to be withdrawn. This final crisis ended on November 20 when Khrushchev again gave way.

The secret crisis began for me on the evening of October 15 at a dinner Mrs. Taylor and I were giving at our home at Fort McNair in southwest Washington. The guest of honor was to have been John McCone, the new Director of the CIA, but, unfortunately, an accident to his stepson obliged him to be absent. Our other guests were mostly officials, such as Deputy Secretary of Defense Gilpatric, Deputy Under Secretary of State Alex Johnson, and Lieutenant General Joseph Carroll, the Director of the Defense Intelligence Agency. Shortly after his arrival at the party, General Carroll led me into a corner and told me *sotto voce* that photographic evidence from an overflight of the previous day showed conclusively the presence of Soviet offensive missiles in Cuba. We whispered the news successively to those of my guests authorized to receive such information and agreed to meet in my office the first thing on the following morning to go over the photography.

As soon as we arrived in the Pentagon on October 16, Secretary McNamara, Deputy Secretary Gilpatric, and I studied the photographs with General Carroll and then adjourned to meet with all the Chiefs. There was no question about what we saw. We had observed the same equipment in photographs of the Soviet medium range missile sites in Europe too many times in the past not to recognize the eleven hundred-mile nuclear weapon which had been widely deployed along the western borders of the Soviet Union. I imagine that the emotions of the members of our little group varied widely, but my own reaction was primarily one of incredulous amazement. Why had Khrushchev committed such a foolhardy act as to challenge the United States on its own doorstep where he was at such a tremendous political and military disadvantage? The challenge was so blatant that he seemed to be asking for trouble. Could he really doubt the violence of the American response or was there something in the situation which escaped us? Surely such an astute fellow must have some trick up his sleeve which we did not perceive.

After this preliminary discussion, McNamara, Gilpatric, and I drove to the White House where the President had called a meeting for 11:45 with his principal advisers. Bundy had already shown him the photos, and the revelation had left him angry but composed. What seemed to affect him most was the perfidy of the Soviet officials who had gone to such pains to lie to him about the nature of the weapons being sent to Cuba. Later, in his speech of October 22, he was to recall the Soviet pledges regarding the defensive character of the Cuban armament, both the Soviet government's statement of September 11 and Gromyko's reiteration made in the President's own office on October 18, and to denounce with sledgehammer bluntness, "That statement was false." But now, faced with the hard facts, he was all business and opened the meeting with a review of the latest intelligence.

The ensuing discussion focused first upon the question of whether the missiles photographed were, in fact, operational and ready to fire. As McNamara pointed out, the absence of security guards around the sites made it appear unlikely. But it was apparent that we had to get more photography at once, and the President readily approved all the U-2 flights which might be necessary.

Then we turned to the central question: What should we do to meet this sudden threat of Soviet nuclear power in Cuba? Secretary Rusk posed the alternative courses of action with which we were to be confronted during the next few days: a surprise air attack against the missiles and associated military targets, or a sequence of political actions leading, if necessary, to a blockade and air strikes in conjunction with other appropriate military measures, such as partial mobilization and the reinforcement of Guantanamo. If the first course were chosen, Secretary McNamara emphasized the need to conduct air strikes before the missiles could become operational and to include among the targets military aircraft and any nuclear storage sites which could be discovered. Thereafter, we would have to be prepared to invade Cuba if necessary. Douglas Dillon pointed out the disadvantage of preliminary political moves which would give the USSR time to utter threats from which they might find it difficult to withdraw. I supported a surprise air attack but pointed out that we should not be talking about a single air strike but a series of air strikes to assure that no additional offensive weapons would be emplaced after the destruction of those which we knew to exist. Also, we would have to blockade Cuba to prevent the further introduction of war materials.

Thus, in a short period of time, we had before us a rough outline of the options available and had laid out an outline for the work ahead. The President summarized the immediate issues as being (a) whether to attack

265

only the visible missiles or the broader target system mentioned by Secretary McNamara, (b) whether any such attack should be accompanied by a naval blockade, and (c) whom we should consult before acting.

As he set us to work, the President indicated his intention to limit his advisers generally to the small group present which was later formalized as the Executive Committee of the National Security Council (EXCOMM). It consisted of Vice-President Johnson, Secretary of State Rusk, Secretary of the Treasury Dillon, Attorney General Kennedy, CIA Director McCone, Under Secretary of State Ball, Deputy Secretary of Defense Gilpatric, Ambassador-at-large Thompson, Special Counsel Sorensen, Mac Bundy, and myself. These men, joined occasionally by nonmembers such as Adlai Stevenson, Dean Acheson, Robert Lovett, and John McCloy, lived and worked together almost around the clock throughout the secret crisis. We assembled surreptitiously two or three times a day, slipping in the southwest gate of the White House to avoid notice and hiding our cars in the State Department basement when we met there in preparation for a session with the President. While this procedure may seem an odd perversion of the National Security Council process which was established for dealing with crises of this sort, it was the way that came naturally to President Kennedy. He wanted the men of EXCOMM not so much because of their official positions as for his confidence in their judgment and reliability. He also wanted to avoid the inevitable leaks which he would expect from a large National Security Council meeting on the pattern of those of the Eisenhower Administration. He judged it of the highest importance to regain the initiative from the Soviets by presenting his discovery of their treachery and making his response thereto with the full benefit of maximum surprise. To do so, there must be no leaks or visible signs of extraordinary activity.

As we settled down to our tasks, there was no doubt about our mission. It was to find a way to remove the threat of a nuclear weapons base on Cuba and to prevent, in the words of Theodore Roosevelt at another historic juncture, "the strategic abuse of the island." As the debate developed during the next few days, it became clear that there were, in the last analysis, only three courses open to us, already partially identified in our first meeting. We could try to talk the Soviet weapons out, squeeze them out, or shoot them out, employing persuasion, inducement, or coercion singly or in any combination. Persuasion could take the form of a direct appeal to Khrushchev, Castro, or to both. Inducement might include threats of the use of force, efforts to split Castro from Khrushchev or offers of compensation for Soviet accommodation, using as *quid pro quo* such counters as the U.S. missiles in Turkey or our naval base at Guantanamo. Coercion might be achieved through a surprise air attack on the known missile sites or on a broader target system including aircraft, SAM's, and heavy ground equipment. A lesser form of coercive action could be some form of naval blockade, either one which undertook to bar all shipping or a partial one concentrating on some special class of ships, such as those capable of transporting offensive weapons or oil tankers. There was general agreement that some form of coercion would be necessary with the air attack alternative attracting the most supporters in the beginning, only to lose many of them after the first few days. The proponents of the surprise air attack were the original "hawks," so named to differentiate them from the "doves," who advocated a less drastic solution, usually some form of blockade supplemented by political actions.

The arguments for an air attack were based on the assumption that the Soviet missiles could become operational and ready to fire in a few days and that, being mobile, they were capable of rapid dispersion from their photographed positions either before or after firing. For the moment, they were unaware of their danger and enjoyed only limited protection from the Cuban air defense system. The latter did not appear to be wholly operational since the SAM's and MIG's comprising it had apparently not detected our U-2 overflights. One of the unresolved mysteries of this period was why the Soviets did not fully install their SAM's before moving in a single offensive weapon and then deny us overhead photography by shooting down our U-2's as they had Major Powers over the USSR in 1960. The SAM's were always a troublesome factor in our planning as we were never sure whether their inaction reflected a policy decision or merely lack of readiness.

Viewing the situation in this light, it seemed essential to me to attack massively all known offensive weapons before they could fire, obtain better protection from their air defenses, or disperse into the forest and jungles where they could never be rooted out except by an invading army. It was true that no matter how heavy the air attack some weapons would escape, but there was reason to hope that this demonstration of American determination, followed by a blockade of Cuba and preparation for invasion of the island, would bring Khrushchev to his senses and induce him to liquidate this rash venture.

The opponents of this approach were convinced that an air attack would lead Khrushchev to escalate, as we would now say, and that he could never tolerate such a reaction without doing something in kind, perhaps some offensive move against Berlin, Turkey, Italy, or Iran. If he attacked a NATO target, all the NATO nations would blame us for having brought the alliance to the threshold of World War III for an island in the Caribbean which meant nothing to them and little to us, and we would have to go to the help of any ally threatened in Europe with severely curtailed forces because of our involvement in Cuba. Also, Castro had to be considered. He might attack Guantanamo in spite of such reinforcements as we might send in, and his MIG's were capable of bombing targets in our southeastern states. Finally, there was the moral issue, raised eloquently by Bob

Kennedy, that a surprise air attack had all the connotations of a Pearl Harbor with ourselves in the role of the perfidious aggressor. Those who aligned themselves with him against a surprise attack eventually rallied behind the alternative of a limited naval blockade, given the less provocative title of a quarantine, for the purpose of keeping out further shipments of offensive weapons and associated equipment. They were ready to concede that this initial measure might prove inadequate and that it might be necessary to enforce a complete blockade or even go to the extreme of invading Cuba. It was not clear to me, however, what we would do if the Soviets stayed outside the blockade zone, opened a vituperative propaganda campaign against the United States, called for negotiations, and continued to develop their weapons systems in Cuba. While stalling, they could complete the construction of the missile launching sites but hide the missiles and related equipment where they would be safe from attack. No one knew at this time whether or not all the essential equipment had already arrived on the island and, hence, whether a partial blockade would seriously impede the Soviet program. We found out later that the 2,000-mile Intermediate Range Missiles (IRBM's) never got into Cuba, only some of the support equipment which preceded the missile shipments.

Hawks and doves changed sides frequently during the six days of debate so that it is impossible in most cases to classify the participants in neat categories. I was a twofold hawk from start to finish, first as the spokesman for the Joint Chiefs of Staff, then from personal conviction. But the confrontation was not on military versus civilian lines—most hawks were necessarily civilian, since I was usually the only military man present in the EXCOMM discussions. Another important point was that neither hawks nor doves took their perches in the aviary for the same reasons. Personally, I was much concerned over the possible development of a situation which would require the invasion of Cuba, something the United States could not afford either politically or militarily. Moreover, I felt that the quarantine alternative was more likely to develop into a choice between invading Cuba or backing down than was the seemingly more violent alternative of the air attack. I was never particularly afraid of either side using nuclear weapons unless through some hideous miscalculation and, if it came to a confrontation with nonnuclear weapons in the Caribbean, Khrushchev was at a hopeless disadvantage. Bob Kennedy's Pearl Harbor argument did not carry much weight with me since President Kennedy in the preceding weeks had explicitly warned the Soviets and Castro of the dire consequences of undertaking to establish an offensive military base in Cuba. If we wished to be impeccably scrupulous, it would be possible, I thought, to give Khrushchev and Castro some limited warning, provided it was not long enough in advance to allow the missiles to hide.

During the years following the missile crisis, there have been efforts to depict the Joint Chiefs of Staff as having been hard-nosed warmongers during the crisis, clamoring for air strikes and invasion and rejecting the more moderate proposals. As Chairman, before every EXCOMM meeting I prepared myself to represent the collective view of the Chiefs by prior discussion with them of the issues coming up. I stress collective view because that is what should be meant when one refers to the position of the Joint Chiefs of Staff on an issue. It may well be and often is the case that individual Chiefs hold views on a given subject well beyond the bounds of corporate agreement but these are individual opinions and should not be charged to the Chiefs as a body. For example, the Joint Chiefs of Staff as a body never recommended the invasion of Cuba, merely the preparations for an invasion that would reinforce the President's hand in his dealings with Khrushchev and keep the option always open to him. That is not to say that none of the Chiefs felt an invasion was desirable or would eventually become necessary as a way to get rid of Castro once and for all.

On two points only can I recall the corporate position of the Chiefs to have been extreme among the hawks. The most eloquent and effective spokesman for the surprise attack alternative, Dean Acheson, supported only an attack on the missiles themselves whereas the Chiefs wanted a massive attack by several hundred aircraft to do maximum damage not only to the missiles but also to the IL-28 bombers and the entire air defense system. Convinced that after the initial attack we would have to dominate the Cuban airspace more or less indefinitely, the Chiefs emphasized, properly I thought, the need to exploit the surprise of the first attack to get maximum effect. As to a blockade, the Chiefs argued for a complete blockade rather than the partial one finally approved. They were particularly anxious to embargo petroleum products because of the dependence of Castro's economy on this import.

Following each EXCOMM meeting, I returned to the Pentagon, reported to the Chiefs the events of the meeting, and set in motion any actions devolving on the Armed Forces from the decisions taken. When these decisions did not accord with the Chiefs' views, I was always cross-examined to see whether I had been sufficiently vigorous in defending their position. Occasionally, in the face of obvious skepticism as to the quality of my efforts, I would turn on them and offer to arrange for them a meeting with the President to present their views directly. I do not recall their seeking such a meeting (at which I promised to hold their coats), but on October 19, at my suggestion, the President invited them to meet with him and thus offered them the opportunity to give full expression to their individual opinions. As there were about as many gradations among their individual views as among an equal number of his civilian advisers, the meeting may not have been particularly helpful to the President, but it certainly made the Chiefs feel better.

The President participated in most of the EXCOMM meetings, generally missing only those which conflicted with speeches and other publicized appointments which had to be kept to preserve the secrecy of our deliberations. He was much concerned over the passage of time and the ever-present danger of a premature leak. He had hoped to go on national television on Sunday, October 21, to explain the situation to the nation, but was obliged to postpone it until the evening of October 22 in order to provide ample time for State to make all the preliminary diplomatic arrangements.

CHAPTER 21

Cuba Quarantine

It had been apparent after the first day or two that President Kennedy was inclining strongly to the side of the quarantine. He had always been a great believer in keeping his options open, and the choice of the quarantine as a first step left him with all the more drastic ones still available. With nuclear war as a possible denouement of any decision, he was inclined to a gradual application of force offering the smallest risk. Overreaction was a word frequently heard in our deliberations to describe what was not wanted.

In contradiction to the thesis often advanced that military advice normally generates violent solutions, it was probably a senior military officer who tipped the scale in favor of the quarantine over the air attack. On October 21, the President called in Lieutenant General Walter C. Sweeney, Jr., who, as Commander of the Tactical Air Command, would be responsible for any air attack on the offensive weapons in Cuba, and asked him a series of questions about the probable outcome of such an attack. In response, Sweeney readily conceded that any such attack could not guarantee the destruction or neutralization of all the missiles, something which I had also emphasized, but it impressed the President more coming, as it did, from the responsible commander. After that interview, Ted Sorensen, the master speechwriter, was told to adjust his draft to a decision based upon the proclamation of a quarantine.

At 7:00 P.M. on October 22, President Kennedy made the historic television address which broke the news of the threat to peace resulting from the nuclear weapons in Cuba and notified Khrushchev that he was caught red-handed. It moved the secret crisis within the White House on to the international stage. It set into visible motion the innumerable plans which had been drawn up and, in some cases, covertly initiated during the preceding days.

271

In illustration of the manifold activities which went on within the government before and after President Kennedy's announcement, I would mention only a few of the measures which had to be prepared and then executed with carefully orchestrated timing. First, our ambassadors abroad had to be prepared for the President's speech and furnished guidance as to how to present our case to the governments to which they were accredited. Ambassadors Stevenson and Finletter had particularly important tasks in their respective roles as spokesman for American policy before the United Nations and the North Atlantic Council. As it would be most important to obtain an endorsement of the President's action by the Organization of American States (OAS), the State Department was charged with calling a meeting for that purpose on October 23, the day following the President's speech.

On the domestic front, lawyers at the Justice Department had to draft a blockade proclamation which would define precisely the scope and conditions of the quarantine and be ready for promulgation by the President following his speech. The President himself had certain personal tasks which he could not delegate, such as informing the full National Security Council and selected Congressional leaders of his decision before the public announcement. The Armed Forces and the CIA had a long list of duties, many of which had to be planned and, in some cases, performed with particular care to avoid attracting attention before the President's announcement. Immediately after seeing the first missile photographs, President Kennedy had directed increased U-2 overflights of Cuba and, later, low-level reconnaissance flights to begin on October 23. He also ordered the appropriate alerting of the Armed Forces but imposed stringent limitations on the depth to which information of the situation could be disseminated in the military structure. The Joint Chiefs had the duty of contacting the senior commanders most affected and giving them the necessary instructions, often orally, to avoid possible compromise through normal electronic transmission. The commanders involved were numerous. There was Admiral Robert Dennison, Commander in Chief of the Atlantic in Norfolk who, as a unified commander, was charged with planning and executing, if directed, the invasion of Cuba. Since 1961 he had kept in readiness plans for the use of air power to eliminate any threat which might arise in Cuba and for a ground invasion in case of a large-scale revolt in Cuba or an attack by Castro against Guantanamo. For this contingency planning, Dennison's Army colleague was General Herbert B. Powell, commanding the Continental Army Command at Fort Monroe, Virginia, and his Air Force colleague, General Walter C. Sweeney, Jr., already mentioned, whose Tactical Air Command would provide most of the air support for any Cuban operation. To try to account for the activities within Admiral Dennison's command during the next few weeks would require a thick volume in itself. They may be suggested by a few topical headings, such as the prepositioning of supplies in Florida, the evacuation of dependents and the reinforcement of Guantanamo, the establishment of a communications net linking his forces at sea and ashore, and preparations for the quarantine which the President was about to declare.

Another commander deriving a mission from our White House deliberations was General John K. Gerhart, commanding the Continental Air Defense Command in Colorado Springs, Colorado. Gerhart was responsible for the air defense of the threatened southeastern states if Castro should elect to use his aircraft against targets in the United States. To meet his threat, he was authorized to move additional air defense squadrons to fields in Florida and to deploy there the very limited number of surface-to-air missiles which we had available for defense against bomber attack.

General Thomas Power, commanding the Strategic Air Command in Omaha, Nebraska, had the task of providing the strategic shield under which our conventional forces could mobilize and operate with minimum danger of a strategic attack by the USSR. To provide this protection, he put one-eighth of his strategic bombers in the air and kept that number aloft throughout the crisis while maintaining the rest of his command, including his strategic missiles, in a high state of readiness. At the same time, Admiral Dennison put several Polaris missiles submarines on alert to strengthen the strategic deterrent.

In brief, the President's decision announced in his speech of October 22 initiated a vast concentration of ground, air, and amphibious forces complete with the supplies necessary for an invasion of Cuba. At the same time it initiated actions to protect the continental United States from air attack; to deter a possible nuclear strike on the United States or our allies; and to mount a blockade of Cuba on the terms laid down by the President. In the course of discharging these tasks, the responsible commanders established and maintained a partial blockade of Cuba from October 24 to November 20. They assembled invasion forces totaling roughly a quarter million men during the period from October 17 to October 31, held them in readiness to invade Cuba until November 31, and thereafter held them in stand-by readiness until December 20. After that date the invasion forces returned to their stations of origin.

The Joint Chiefs of Staff learned a great many things during the crisis, which was the first major test of that body as an operational headquarters since the Korean War. One of the weaknesses of the organization of the Joint Chiefs of Staff had always been the difficulty of directing the day-to-day operations of a war by a committee. The missile crisis presented this problem to the Chiefs in a particularly acute form.

An operational staff makes plans, obtains decisions from higher authority, issues orders to implement these decisions, and then follows up on their execution. The Joint Chiefs were reasonably well organized to perform the first three of these functions, but how does a committee make the

273

kind of on-the-spot verification of the execution of orders which every military man knows is essential to success? We met the problem in part by designating each Chief to act as the representative of the entire body in supervising the activities of his service in the preparations against Cuba. Thus, General Wheeler kept a close eye on the airborne activities; Admiral Anderson did the same for the blockade of Cuba and the defense of Guantanamo; and General LeMay for the air defense of the southeast. Additionally, the Chiefs as a body had frequent sessions in Washington with Admiral Dennison and the senior commanders.

The foregoing is a bare outline of the tremendous world-wide activity which was generated by the President's decision of October 22. On November 26, when the crisis was over and the pressure off, President Kennedy visited the forces assembled in Georgia and Florida just before they reduced their state of readiness. On this trip he took the opportunity to see a U-2 which had been flying photographic missions over Cuba, and he expressed to some of the U-2 pilots the depth of his admiration and gratitude for the men who flew these fragile, glider-like birds repeatedly over Cuban SAM sites, never knowing when they might become the target of a missile. He had similar praise for the pilots of the Tactical Air Command, whose low-level photographs had been invaluable in checking the operational readiness and later the removal of the Soviet offensive weapons. Over-all he was frankly amazed and, I think, somewhat sobered by the evidence he saw of the military power at his disposal and the military consequences of his decisions.

As I regarded the night following the President's speech a very critical period, I slept that night in my Pentagon office for the only time in the crisis. It was not that I feared that we were on the brink of nuclear war but I still harbored a feeling that Khrushchev had some card up his sleeve that he was holding in readiness, which he might play at this time. As I was still apprehensive of a move to hide the missiles, I awaited eagerly the results of the first series of photographs which would show their condition following the President's speech. These were not available until October 24 and 25. To my relief, these photos showed no sign of a move to disperse the missiles; instead, they gave evidence of ineffectual camouflage. By October 25 there were clear signs that the work on the missile sites was being expedited presumably to advance their time of operational readiness.

In the meantime, the OAS gave unanimous approval for the use of armed force to enforce the quarantine which went into effect at 10:00 A.M. on October 24. On the previous day Khrushchev, in a letter to President Kennedy, had condemned the U.S. action in establishing the quarantine, and both parties appealed to the U.N. Security Council. Suddenly presented with this international crisis, acting Secretary General U Thant called on Khrushchev to suspend arms shipments to Cuba for two to three weeks and on President Kennedy to suspend the quarantine. Khrushchev accepted U Thant's proposal, but Kennedy, while willing to negotiate, would not agree to suspend the quarantine as long as the offensive weapons were still in Cuba.

The low-level photography of Soviet shipping on October 24 and 25 brought the EXCOMM the first indication that Khrushchev might be about to break. While work on the missile sites proceeded at top speed, three Soviet ships suspected of being missile carriers en route to Cuba seemed to alter course on October 24. On the following day, they turned and steamed eastward toward the USSR as did several other Soviet freighters in mid-Atlantic. There was an air of quiet satisfaction within the EXCOMM as we bent over the pictures displayed on the cabinet table and saw this first evidence of Khrushchev's retreat.

The crisis, however, was far from over, as Khrushchev still made many turns and twists before finally capitulating. On the night of October 26, President Kennedy received that strange, disjointed letter from Khrushchev which has often been mentioned but never published. I would agree with those who have described it as the letter of a man either drunk or distraught, or both. After long meanderings, the writer, who could hardly have been anyone other than Khrushchev himself, proposed a solution that appeared acceptable. The USSR would cease the introduction of weapons into Cuba and would destroy or withdraw those presently on the island in exchange for our raising the blockade and agreeing not to invade Cuba. That proposition looked promising to the EXCOMM, but I must say that the language of the letter caused me uneasiness, suggesting as it did a disquieting instability on the part of the Soviet leader whose rationality was so essential to world peace.

The hope that a settlement was at hand was dispelled by Khrushchev's letter of the following day which probably was the authentic voice of the Politburo trying to repair the damage done by Khrushchev's personal initiative. It modified the first proposal by making the removal of the Soviet offensive weapons from Cuba conditional upon our removing U.S. missiles from Turkey. This day, October 27, was probably the most discouraging point in the crisis. Not only had Khrushchev's second letter dampened our hopes of a prompt settlement, but we had the report that a U-2 had probably been shot down by a SAM battery of the Cuban defense system. This loss was subsequently verified by Cuban statements regarding the discovery of wreckage and recovery of the body of the pilot. He was Major Rudolph Anderson, Jr., who had piloted the plane that had provided the first photographic evidence of the presence of missiles in Cuba.

Another cause for gloom was the continuing work on the missile sites, five of which now appeared to be fully operational with a sixth approaching that condition. This meant that the Soviets would soon be capable of launching twenty-four 1,100-mile missiles in six to eight hours after a decision to do so and could fire a second volley a few hours after that. In view of this intelligence, the Joint Chiefs urged an air strike against them not later than October 29 unless clear evidence of dismantling the missiles was received in the interim. Meanwhile, President Kennedy chose to disregard Khrushchev's second letter and responded only to the first, insisting that work on the Cuban bases stop, the offensive weapons be removed under international inspection, and the further shipment of weapons be halted. In exchange, he repeated his willingness to lift the quarantine and to give assurances against an invasion of Cuba.

The Communists have a way of looking most unyielding just before taking a step backward. In a clash of wills such as the Berlin blockade, the Austrian peace treaty, or Khrushchev's threat of a unilateral peace treaty with East Germany, the Soviets never appeared more intransigent or talked tougher than just before they lifted the blockade, signed the treaty, or extended the time limit for recognizing East German sovereignty. With equal suddenness Khrushchev reversed his position on October 28 and, in a letter to President Kennedy, stated that he had ordered the dismantling of the arms "which you described as offensive" and their return to the USSR in exchange for Kennedy's pledge not to invade Cuba. The President welcomed publicly Chairman Khrushchev's "statesmanlike decision," and the Thirteen Days were at an end.

But there still remained two unresolved issues: the international verification of the removal of the missiles and the inclusion of the IL-28 bombers among the weapons to be evacuated. Khrushchev had accepted United Nations verification of the dismantling, but he had not consulted Castro, who violently rejected any form of foreign inspection on Cuban soil and refused to be mollified by U Thant, Mikoyan, or anyone else. In the end Khrushchev could not deliver on this part of his bargain, and we were obliged to satisfy ourselves with the photographic inspection of outgoing weapons exposed on the decks of the departing freighters and by continued U-2 overflights of the island. This arrangement did not allay apprehension in the United States, fed by rumors of missiles hidden in caves and clandestine submarine base construction. President Kennedy sought partial compensation for the loss of international inspection in his statement of November 20 by qualifying somewhat his no-invasion pledge.

> As for our part, if all offensive weapons systems are removed from Cuba and kept out of the hemisphere in the future, under adequate verification and safeguards, and if Cuba is not used for the export of aggressive Communist purposes, there will be peace in the Caribbean. And as I said in September, "We shall neither initiate nor permit aggression in this hemisphere."
>
> We will not, of course, abandon the political, economic and other efforts of this hemisphere to halt subversion from Cuba, nor our purpose and hope that the Cuban people shall some day be truly free. But these policies are very different from any intent to launch a military invasion of the island.

While Castro was the villain in the verification squabble, Khrushchev teamed with him in making trouble over the removal of the IL-28's. Castro claimed that they were his and not for Khrushchev to take away, and Khrushchev was glad to support his disgruntled ally. John McCloy and Adlai Stevenson argued for days with Kuznetsov in New York, and, on his visit to Cuba, Mikoyan tried to soften up Castro but to no avail. In the end, it was not diplomatic persuasion which broke the impasse but the growing impatience of the President backed by his formidable invasion force ready to strike. On November 20 Khrushchev, rather than risk the consequences of an invasion, yielded a second time, agreeing to withdraw the IL-28 bombers within thirty days. On December 6, American pilots checked off the last of the bombers on the decks of the cargo ships carrying them back to Russia. Thus ended the missile crisis, but the United States still had a dangerous neighbor in Castro.

Throughout the crisis and, indeed, ever since its termination, there have been two intriguing questions, often posed and as yet never satisfactorily answered: Why did Khrushchev embark on this disastrous course? And why was he surprised by the American reaction?

As to Khrushchev's motives in introducing nuclear weapons into Cuba, there were several answers of varying plausibility that suggested themselves at the time. There was no doubt that he wanted to strengthen the defenses of Cuba to the point of discouraging the United States from invading the island and overthrowing Castro, but this level of protection could have been attained without nuclear missiles and bombers. Also, in strengthening the defense of Cuba he was building up his bully-boy, Castro, and increasing his potential for subversion in Latin America. Both of these achievements would further diminish American prestige, which had not yet recovered from the effects of the Bay of Pigs, by adding the humiliation of a Soviet military presence in the Caribbean almost within sight of American shores.

But, even if this reasoning were accepted, it still left unanswered the question of why the offensive nuclear weapons, since conventional weapons in sufficient quantities could have accomplished these two results without the mortal offense given President Kennedy by the introduction of the medium range missiles and bombers. The only explanation of this point I found convincing was that Khrushchev wanted to increase on the cheap the coverage of American targets by his strategic weapons. Did he believe that this increase would make any significant difference worth the risk he was running? It seemed hard to believe that he was really concerned about the strategic imbalance since we had never tried to exploit our superiority aggressively even when we enjoyed a complete or virtual monopoly of strategic weapons. So this motive did not seem plausible unless the Soviet strategic weapons on Russian soil were considerably less numerous or reliable than we thought.

277

As a political counter for use in maneuver in the Cold War, it was another matter. There would be many appealing possibilities open to Khrushchev if he succeeded in installing and retaining these offensive weapons in Cuba. He would have made what the airborne troops call a vertical envelopment of the forward bases of the United States and its allies which ring the borders of the Soviet Union and would have gained something to trade for their removal. The American press has frequently called attention to the analogy of the Cuban base with those we maintained on the Russian frontiers in such places as Turkey and Iran. If Khrushchev finally had to give up his Cuban foothold, it would not be unreasonable for Khrushchev to expect some kind of payoff to recompense him.

Commentators have often looked to Berlin to find an explanation for Khrushchev's acts in Cuba. If the Cuban ploy was intended to divert the United States from the defense of Berlin, it was successful to the extent that it made Cuba the number one issue in Washington for the moment, but President Kennedy and his advisers never took their eyes off Berlin, where they always feared a countermove. However, this concern did not prevent them from preparing to invade Cuba, even though the commitment of the necessary forces to that operation would have seriously diminished our immediate capability for military action elsewhere.

Beyond these possible motives there was always the possibility of something in the personal relationships within the Kremlin which provided the impetus for this misguided adventure. Khrushchev might have felt a compelling need for some kind of triumph to confirm his right to hegemony among his fellows of the Politburo. But how could he expect a triumph under the circumstances? That was the second question which intrigued me.

The best answer I could advance on this point was that Khrushchev had grievously underestimated President Kennedy, possibly because of impressions received at their meeting in Vienna in June of the previous year, but more likely because of the débâcle of the Bay of Pigs. To Khrushchev, the American leadership must have appeared weak, vacillating, and disorganized during and following the abortive landing. It must have seemed strange to him that the government leaders would have indulged in such public lamentations over the loss of a little prestige and 1,300 mercenaries. This national hand-wringing magnified a defeat which the Soviets would have written off with a shrug, covering their retreat with a propaganda blast claiming victory and later conducting a quiet purge of the bunglers responsible for the failure.

If the Bay of Pigs could produce such shock and consternation in Washington and throughout the United States, could not Khrushchev hope for something approaching paralysis of decision and action if these same American leaders found themselves suddenly looking at the nuclear warheads of missiles in position capable of destroying any American city within 2,000 miles of Havana? If this was the hope, it explains to some extent the great pains to deceive Kennedy about Soviet intentions while bringing in the weapons with the utmost secrecy. But, on the other hand, it leaves unexplained the failure to emplace the SAM's and clear the Cuban skies of U-2's before introducing the missiles and bombers.

As we now know, it was Khrushchev who was caught by surprise and who exhibited symptoms of shock while the American President seized the initiative and coolly proceeded to implement a carefully thought-out plan. Why Khrushchev did not disperse his missiles, conceal them, demand negotiations, and then stall while threatening or carrying out reprisals in Berlin or elsewhere—in short, resort to some or all of those dirty tricks which I expected from him—remains an enigma. Was he so sure of success that he had no plan to extricate himself in case of failure? It seems improbable but his behavior after the President's speech strongly suggested that such was the case.°

It is unfortunate that no after-action analysis of the missile crisis similar to the Cuba study of the previous year was ever undertaken to assess the performance of the government in coping with this situation. Those books and articles that have been written on the subject suffer like mine from being parts of a whole which has never been assembled *in toto* by impartial historians. This is regrettable because the episode is rich in valuable lessons.

The presidential decision-making process has been criticized after the event as having been a disorderly improvisation with no one in charge. There is a certain truth in that description. However, in contrast to the Bay of Pigs affair, which was conducted by virtual strangers, this time the crisis was managed by a group of intimates working together for a President who gave them his complete confidence in exchange for their complete loyalty. Whether or not the method employed violated a textbook view of the right way to deal with a crisis, it conformed to the President's way and got the job done. Structured, orderly procedures are all very well, in fact indispensable, in linking the subordinate elements of the executive branch to the White House, but there the President is in his own house where the organization and procedures must fit the style which is peculiar to him.

Whatever the informality of the method, I would say that it achieved the purpose of producing for the President a timely set of reasoned alternatives from which to choose, based upon the best available intelligence. Each al-

---

° Presumably we now have Khrushchev's own explanation of these events in his memoirs, *Khrushchev Remembers*. While he justifies his actions largely on the need to forestall an American invasion of Cuba which he considered inevitable after the Bay of Pigs, he leaves unexplained many of the questions I have raised. His description of Robert Kennedy's conversations with Ambassador Dobrynin relating to President Kennedy's fear of a military coup touches on the fantastic.

ternative blended political, military, and psychological components in a way designed to concentrate the necessary pressure on Khrushchev and Castro to induce or compel the removal of the offensive weapons from Cuba—as such, each constituted an example of the integration of power derived from several sources for a political purpose.

In making his choice among the alternatives presented to him, President Kennedy behaved as any responsible world leader is likely to do in a crisis in the nuclear age. He wanted to run minimum risks while acting promptly and decisively enough to avoid a dangerously prolonged confrontation. But of these two *desiderata*, it was the concern for caution that predominated because of the disastrous consequences which could result from uncontrolled escalation. This consideration led him to adopt a gradualist approach, starting with the minimum step, the limited blockade.

Once this decision was made and implementation began, the same considerations that made him cautious in picking his first option made him wish to control personally the key actions of his military forces. He had tried to do this in the Bay of Pigs episode and had failed miserably. This time, however, he was better served by an established communications and command structure which enabled him to move naval units about the Caribbean almost by hand. This personal intervention was offensive to many of my military associates who regarded it as unwarranted civilian interference, but I did not agree with the criticism. The quarantine was a political gambit in a deadly serious game, and the master player on our side had every reason to keep his hand on the pawns. It was a classic example of the use of military power for political purposes which, after all, is the prime justification for military power.

The episode was filled with lessons for the military, most of them of such a professional or technical nature that I shall not discuss them here. In the broad domain of strategy, the crisis exposed the fallacy of a shibboleth of the previous decade that it would be impossible to have a nonnuclear conflict between the United States and the USSR. While not a shot was exchanged during this confrontation, it was quite apparent that had there been, neither side would have responded with an immediate nuclear exchange. In effect the strategic forces available to both sides neutralized one another and allowed the play of political and military forces to proceed with little preoccupation over nuclear consequences.

Khrushchev eventually retreated not because of SAC aircraft aloft and Polaris submarines on station in European waters but because Cuba was beyond the range of support of his conventional forces and Kennedy had called his bluff. The decisive factor was our conventional military forces in Florida, which convinced Khrushchev that his opponent was quite serious about invading Cuba if he did not yield. Once convinced of that fact, it was interesting to see how little diplomacy was needed to obtain his retreat and how little the concern over loss of face seemed to motivate him. I

280

never sympathized much with those of my colleagues who, on occasions, have been reluctant to press Communist opponents hard for fear of facial damage to them. A few days after his discomfiture, Khrushchev was posturing unabashed as the great friend of world peace who deserved the praise and thanks of all right thinking people for his magnanimity in taking home his weapons. Those who need a formula to save face can usually find one.

CHAPTER 22

Limited Test Ban Treaty

As the missile crisis receded, the members of EXCOMM were able to resume their normal duties and look again at the world beyond the Caribbean. In the ensuing months, I found my attention engaged principally with matters arising from the continuing debate over NATO strategy, with discussions of a limited test ban treaty with the USSR, and the perennially troublesome situation in South Vietnam.

On the NATO front, we Americans continued to try to convince our European allies that, in proposing a shift in the emphasis of NATO strategy, we were moved by sincere concern for the safety of Europe and the well-being of the alliance rather than by national self-interest. We argued that a credible forward strategy capable of assuring the Germans a quick reaction to a violation of their frontiers required strong conventional forces east of the Rhine. If the conventional defense failed, there would be thousands of relatively low-yield tactical nuclear weapons ready for use and behind them the vast strategic nuclear power of the United States committed to the defense of NATO.

This concept of defense seemed reasonable to most senior U.S. officials but it ran afoul serious obstacles when it was advanced in discussion with our NATO colleagues. The most serious objection was financial because the U.S. thesis implied a substantial increase in military expenditures by the European countries; but there was also an undertone charging that Americans wanted the Europeans to provide the cannon fodder for a conventional war which would create no risks for the American homeland. This suspicion created a growing uneasiness over the reliability of the U.S. nuclear shield. To allay this feeling, we Americans proposed a number of actions designed to permit greater European participation in nuclear matters. An attempt was made to agree on the conditions under which nuclear weapons would be used and the procedures by which they would be released from U.S. custody for use by field commanders. But while we were generally forthcoming in our efforts to meet the desires of our European colleagues, few changes of consequence were made. In the first place, the Europeans could not agree among themselves as to the changes desired; secondly, the President's veto power on the release or use of U.S. nuclear weapons put a definite limit on the European participation in the nuclear decision-making process. In the end, the only real progress made toward greater European participation was in giving the NATO staff access to more information on nuclear weapons effects and an enlarged role in nuclear planning and targeting.

The MLF issue remained unresolved while the over-all strategy was under debate. The crisis in Anglo-American relations in December 1962 occasioned by our decision to cancel the Sky Bolt air-to-ground missile project had an unexpected influence on this question. To quiet the uproar in the United Kingdom over what was regarded there as an abrupt and arbitrary action on our part, President Kennedy and Prime Minister Macmillan met in Nassau from December 18 to 21 to repair Anglo-Saxon fences and to work out an amicable settlement. Macmillan came supported by Foreign Minister Home and Defense Minister Thornycroft; Kennedy by Under Secretary of State Ball and Defense Secretary McNamara. It was indicative of the lack of military importance attached to the meeting that neither side had representation from its Chiefs of Staff.

The basic purpose of the meeting was to permit McNamara to propose several alternatives to the British that might allay the criticism being directed at Macmillan over the cancellation of Sky Bolt and provide a way to extend the British strategic capability, which was fading with the obsolescence of their bomber force. McNamara first offered to continue the Sky Bolt development as a joint venture with the British in which both sides would share the cost but from which we would withdraw when the missile was ready for procurement. This offer was politely declined as was an offer to the British of the Hound Dog missile which had an air-to-surface capability similar but inferior to that sought in Sky Bolt. In the absence of anything better, the President and the Prime Minister ended by agreeing to join in creating at once a NATO-controlled nuclear force consisting of contingents drawn from U.S. strategic forces, from the U.K. Bomber Command, and from the tactical nuclear forces of both countries stationed in Europe. As a longer-term measure, they agreed that the United States would make available Polaris missiles without warheads for new British submarines which, along with a number of American nuclear submarines, would eventually be incorporated in a multilateral NATO nuclear force. It was recognized that to provide these missiles to the British was likely to offend the French, as it did, so President Kennedy broadened his offer to include France. But de Gaulle, unmollified, rejected the offer and vented his displeasure on the British by blackballing their application for membership in the European Economic Community.

The U.S. Chiefs, like their British counterparts, sat at the end of the Nassau cable and followed the negotiations from Washington with growing concern as the discussions ranged widely into strictly military matters. Unfortunately, the distinguished principals in Nassau did not speak the NATO military jargon, with the result that their joint communiqué was filled with ambiguities which required clarification after the party ended and the principals had returned home. Personally, I was rather pleased with the proposal to improvise a NATO nuclear force out of national contributions from existing forces. It avoided the mixed-manning of ships by crews drawn from several nations, a procedure which was anathema to naval commanders forced to contemplate the tasks of training and fighting a polyglot force. A multinational force composed of units from different nations retaining national crews looked much more feasible, and its success, I thought, might lead to shelving the controversial MLF project. It did indeed contribute to that end; the heat over the MLF issue subsided after 1963 without any formal show of hands ever being taken in NATO.

As the senior military spokesman for the U.S. strategy in NATO, I used the annual meetings of the NATO ministers and Chiefs of Staff as occasions to probe the thinking of my foreign colleagues and to argue with them the military logic of the American position. To extend these contacts made on European soil I invited, during the year, a number of the Chiefs of Staff to visit some of our military installations in the United States, particularly SAC at Omaha and Commander in Chief, Atlantic (CINCLANT), in Norfolk, where the visitor could receive a vivid impression of the strategic power of our forces. Following such a trip about the country, our visitor usually joined the Joint Chiefs of Staff in the Pentagon for a kind of NATO strategic seminar.

Our first visitor was Admiral Lord Mountbatten, my counterpart in the British Chiefs, who always impressed me by the breadth of his political and military views as well as by his personal charm. I found him valuable as a colleague throughout my term as Chairman and always enjoyed our brisk exchanges of view on the defense of Europe. After Nassau, we had a great deal to do in clarifying the meaning and intentions of our civil masters whom we resolved never to let stray abroad again without at least one qualified military adviser in their entourage.

Other visitors included General Foertsch from Germany, Air Marshal Miller from Canada, and General Ailleret, the French Chief of Staff. Because of the widening rift between the United States and France, I made an especial effort to understand Ailleret's position since he was evidently de Gaulle's military spokesman. On the occasion of his visit in September 1963, the Chiefs had a full day of discussion with him in a relaxed and friendly atmosphere. As one might expect, most of the talk centered on our conflicting concepts of the defense of Europe against limited and major attack. Ailleret argued that the Soviets would never make a move across a

284

frontier unless they ware going all the way and, hence, only a trip wire of forces would be needed at the frontier to verify that enemy forces regardless of size had crossed into NATO territory. The establishment of that fact would justify an immediate large-scale response with nuclear weapons since it must be assumed that the survival of Western Europe was threatened. However, Ailleret did not propose limiting NATO ground forces only to a trip wire. He conceded the need for a reserve of divisions capable of blocking the advancing heads of enemy columns while the main bodies behind them were being destroyed by nuclear weapons. A significant point arising in our discussion was the French insistence on treating all aggression as major aggression warranting the immediate resort to nuclear weapons. We asked Ailleret whether, if the East Germans suddenly seized Hamburg, France would support a response with nuclear weapons which could lead to reprisal nuclear attacks on Paris. He had no answer other than to say that the risk had to be taken. Like most European generals, he showed little appreciation of the effects of nuclear weapons and seemed to have given little thought to the consequences of a nuclear exchange upon Western Europe.

Meanwhile, on the domestic front the Joint Chiefs of Staff were intensively engaged in appraising the proposed limited test ban treaty which, after long preliminaries, was reaching the point when a governmental decision was imminent. While it was a pallid substitute for the comprehensive test ban treaty barring all nuclear tests in all environments which Kennedy had originally hoped for, it seemed the most he could get from the Soviets and probably from the U.S. Senate at the time. On July 15, Under Secretary of State Harriman with a team of experts opened final talks on the proposed treaty with the Russians and British in Moscow, and soon reached an agreement with them on prohibiting all testing except underground. The agreement was then referred to the Senate for ratification.

The Joint Chiefs of Staff had watched closely the development of this issue from its inception to the time of its submission in treaty form to the Senate. We had opposed the previously proposed comprehensive test ban treaty, largely on the grounds that it could not be enforced without on-site inspections which the Russians refused, and we regarded this new proposal with controlled enthusiasm although it took into account some of our previous objections. However, we knew the importance President Kennedy attached to the treaty and agreed among ourselves to make a sincere effort to examine the new text with unbiased minds purged of the memory of the Soviet mendacity and double-dealing a few months before at the time of the Cuban missile crisis.

In mid-June, in anticipation of having to take a position on the proposal, we began a round of consultations with officials and scientists qualified to advise us on political and technical aspects of the issue. Unfortunately, the scientists were far from unanimous among themselves so that eventually we had to pass judgment on highly technical matters about which the experts were divided. But these consultations were helpful and gradually we identified the key issues, examined and debated them, and progressively developed a corporate position regarding them.

President Kennedy knew of our deliberations and was very much interested in their outcome, as he knew full well that our position would carry much weight in the Senate where the critics of the treaty were many. He talked to me individually and to all the Chiefs as a group about the great store which he set on the adoption of a treaty as a means to check the nuclear weapons race and the spiraling cost of armaments. At first, some of the Chiefs were inclined to fall back on the old argument Kennedy had rejected in 1961: that they were his military advisers and should limit their examination to the military aspect of the treaty, leaving the political and economic considerations to the officials responsible to the President in these fields. Knowing that if our considerations were limited to the purely military facts we would probably conclude that the treaty showed a net disadvantage, the President eloquently appealed to us to look at the issue in its total aspect in the way that he would have to judge it, and we all agreed to try.

To guide our judgment of the treaty, we first established four criteria which we felt an acceptable treaty should meet and then measured the proposed treaty against them: (1) we decided that we should not accept limitations on testing if they would permit the Soviets to achieve or retain a significant advantage in important nuclear technology; (2) if the Soviets should indulge in clandestine testing, this kind of cheating should not be able to affect seriously the relative balance of military power; (3) there must be some simple, uncomplicated way of withdrawing from the treaty for due cause; and (4) if the first three criteria could not be entirely met, the treaty should offer adequate compensating advantages outside the military field to justify accepting the risks. In the end, it was this last condition which eventually allowed the Chiefs to support the treaty.

Applying these yardsticks to the evidence they had received, the Chiefs concluded that the Soviets were probably ahead of the United States in high-yield technology and, if the treaty were adopted, that lead could not be overcome. On the other hand, the United States was probably ahead in the low-yield field but, by underground testing under the terms of the treaty, the Soviets could probably catch up. Both sides could obtain an anti-ballistic missile under the constraints of the treaty.

The Chiefs recognized the possibility of clandestine testing by the Soviets but felt that the danger of detection would deter them from large-scale cheating. Also, remembering Khrushchev's sudden breach of the testing moratorium in August 1961, we foresaw the possibility that at any time the Soviets might abruptly abrogate the proposed treaty and resume atmospheric testing. These two possibilities were not inconsiderable risks to take.

286

In deference to the President's view of our responsibility to consider all factors before reaching a final judgment, the Chiefs tried to evaluate the probable effect of the treaty on international relations and world peace. After listening to the views of the State Department, we concluded that the treaty offered some promise of restraining the further proliferation of nuclear weapons and of reducing world tensions. If both of these results did, in fact, ensue, they would contribute importantly to the deterrence of war and the maintenance of peace on honorable terms. These possible advantages, we believed, were of such potential importance as to offset to some extent the technological disadvantages which appeared likely.

On balance, the Chiefs decided that they should support ratification of the treaty provided that it included certain safeguards. These safeguards were that following the treaty the United States would conduct and maintain a vigorous underground testing program, would be ready on short notice to resume atmospheric testing, would continue to maintain modern nuclear laboratories, and would improve the national capabilities to detect treaty violations. As a final word of warning, the Chiefs stated that their most serious reservations regarding the treaty arose from "the fear of a euphoria in the West which [would] eventually reduce our vigilance and the willingness of our country and of our allies to expend continued effort on our collective security."

I must say that I was surprised by the outcome and rather proud of the Chiefs for overcoming their instinctive opposition to a testing agreement with a dangerous, distrusted adversary in the hope of gaining important but uncertain advantages in nonmilitary fields. If I was surprised by the consensus achieved, the Senate was incredulous and suspected that we had been the victims of the presidential rack and screw. I appeared on successive days as a witness before the Stennis Preparedness Subcommittee and the Senate Foreign Relations Committee chaired by Senator Fulbright. I read a carefully prepared statement of the Chiefs' position, agreed to by us all, and then answered questions regarding it for several hours. A few days later, the other Chiefs were called to testify as a panel and were similarly crossexamined. We all staunchly denied that we had been exposed to undue pressure and confirmed that we did indeed consider the treaty in the national interest if, but only if, our four safeguards were met.

With the support of the Chiefs a matter of record and with presidential assurance to the Senate leaders that our safeguards would be respected, the Senate ratified the treaty on September 24 without further serious opposition.

CHAPTER 23

The Autumn of Disaster

As I mentioned earlier, the implementation of my 1961 Vietnam report got off to a slow start in 1962 and made irregular progress throughout the year. However, In January 1963, General Wheeler, returning from his first trip to Vietnam, submitted a relatively favorable report to the Joint Chiefs of Staff on the accomplishments of the preceding year. In this period American planners in Washington and Saigon had worked out a blueprint, called the U.S. Comprehensive Plan, which undertook to estimate the requirements in Vietnamese contributions and in U.S. military assistance on the assumption that the insurgency could be brought under reasonable control by the end of 1965. Concurrently, General Harkins' staff had developed a National Campaign Plan setting forth a concept of coordinated political, economic, and military operations to be undertaken in order to attain the 1965 objective.

General Wheeler and his party reported a number of favorable developments which encouraged the hope that the 1965 objective was not too ambitious. American military advisers had tripled during 1962, reaching a strength of over 3,000. Nearly 300 American-operated aircraft, largely helicopters and transports, had reached Vietnam and were already giving greater mobility to the Vietnamese forces. The latter had grown from about 300,000 to 385,000 and were showing more aggressiveness and less inclination to static defense. The impression was that this strength should be sufficient to cope with the Vietcong threat as it existed at that particular moment. The intelligence available had improved largely as a result of an extensive American advisory effort generated during 1962. In particular, there were encouraging indications of a growing willingness of the country people to provide information on the Vietcong as military successes created confidence in the protective power of the government forces.

Of course, there were also adverse factors to report. There remained a

288

serious shortage of junior officers and of noncommissioned officers in Vietnamese units. Senior officers often lacked professional training and were more interested in covering up their deficiencies than in correcting them. The most disquieting aspect in the situation was the continuous build-up of the Vietcong in strength and in the quality and quantity of the weapons with which they were equipped. Their expanding military radio nets provided some measure of the growth of their force structure and area of operations.

Wheeler had good things to say for Ambassador Nolting and General Harkins, who, in combination, appeared to be integrating the American effort well. However, Wheeler noted the difficulties that Diem was having in coordinating the military, economic, and political programs of his government. Even so, the strategic hamlet program, aimed at protecting the country people and insulating them from the Vietcong, was moving forward, at least in terms of reported numbers of completed hamlets. Throughout the country there were signs of increased economic activity, although it was obvious that the economy could not become self-sustaining for a long time without extensive American assistance.

Among the recommendations of the Wheeler report was the maintenance of U.S. military support at existing levels and acceptance of the Comprehensive Plan as guidance subject to semiannual reevaluations of the situation. Because of the evidence of continued bad relations between the American press and the Vietnamese government, Wheeler urged a press orientation program consisting of sponsored visits to Vietnam by mature and responsible American correspondents and executives. The report ended on the note that unless the Vietcong chose to escalate the conflict further, the principal ingredients for eventual success seemed present in Vietnam.

The course of events in Vietnam in the months following Wheeler's return generally confirmed his evaluation. However, the slowly growing optimism arising from the indications of progress evaporated a few months later with the outbreak of the Buddhist revolt led by Tri Quang, the adroit and unscrupulous leader of an extremist wing of the Mahayana sect based in Hue. While it was no secret that a large part of the Buddhist majority in the country resented the preferential treatment accorded the Catholics by the Diem government, most observers were not prepared for the emotional explosion which took place in Hue on May 8. There government forces reportedly fired on a crowd of Buddhists who were demonstrating against a government prohibition against flying the Buddhist flag in public, and eight or nine persons lost their lives. I say "reportedly" because to this day the facts are in dispute, although there is no doubt that there was a clash involving Buddhists in which some lives were lost. Tri Quang, aided by lurid press reports, proceeded immediately to exploit the Hue incident as a means of charging the Diem government with religious persecution. As we now know, there never was anything truly involving religious persecution in these incidents; rather, there was a conflict of the political Buddhist "outs" trying to replace or at least gain parity with the Catholic "ins." But so commonplace a motive was hard to accept when shocking photographs of monks burning themselves, presumably in protest against governmental repression, began to appear in the world press and on the TV screen. Subsequently, the evidence became pretty clear that at least some of these immolations were contrived by Tri Quang and his henchmen to discredit Diem, but that suspicion was not voiced audibly at the time.

The clash in Hue inspired widespread antigovernment demonstrations in many parts of Vietnam to which the police responded with force, and at times with brutality, thus playing into the hands of the anti-Diem foreign press. Within our Embassy, the rift widened between Nolting and Harkins, on the one hand, both of whom discounted the charges of religious persecution against Diem, and certain second echelon officials, on the other hand, who were violently anti-Diem. On this side of the water the events in Hue incited Diem's critics to redouble the volume of their chant, "We can't win with Diem." As a result, there was soon a growing loss of public confidence in our policy of backing Diem and the credibility gap began to emerge, resulting from the contrast between the situation in Vietnam as reported in the press and the official assessment of it.

President Kennedy was deeply alarmed over this sudden turn which exposed him to sharp attacks from the anti-Diem wing at home and to pressures from many quarters to take reprisals against Diem for his repressions. In seeking guidance in this crisis, the President found his associates divided along much the same lines as the Embassy in Saigon. The anti-Diem faction was centered in the State Department but did not include Secretary Rusk. The objective of its members was to force Diem to a reconciliation with the Buddhists and to a separation from his brother Nhu, using as a sanction the withholding of military and economic aid for his government. If he did not respond, they favored a coup to oust him. The pro-Diemists were generally among the senior officials in the Department of Defense, the Joint Chiefs of Staff, and the White House staff. They certainly did not approve of much that Diem was doing, particularly his increasing dependence on his dangerous and unpredictable brother, and they supported carefully applied economic sanctions against Diem provided they would not hurt the war effort. They opposed any action that might lead to an overthrow of Diem as long as no one knew who might replace him.

As the summer dragged on, although the military situation continued to show slow progress apparently unaffected by the Buddhist issue, the internal situation grew steadily worse. Diem continued to resist American urging to conciliate the growing opposition to his government and listened more and more to the counsels of Nhu and his wife to take harsh action

290

against the Tri Quang Buddhists and the pagodas in which they were plotting against the government. Some of his generals were growing restive for fear that the Buddhist issue would undermine the unity and morale of the armed forces and set back the prosecution of the war. Coup rumors were rife as always, but far from consistent as to form and content. There was talk of a coup to replace Diem with Vice-President Tho, of a plot by Nhu to seize power, and of a takeover by a military junta of unidentified generals. This situation reached a flashpoint on August 21 when Diem's police, supported by elements of the Army Special Forces under the control of Nhu, raided several pagodas including the Xa Loi pagoda serving as the command post of Tri Quang's political bonzes in Saigon. There the police arrested several hundred priests, nuns, and other antigovernment suspects and caused numerous casualties in so doing. In the following days, Saigon was the scene of violent clashes between Diem's opponents and the police which provided topics for the agenda of repeated White House meetings in Washington.

The first problem for the President's advisers was to establish the facts and that was not easy. There was, and still is, uncertainty as to who was responsible for the pagoda raids and the subsequent declaration of martial law. Diem had the ultimate responsibility, but who had put him up to it? Nhu was the prime suspect, but Diem had received a delegation of senior generals on the previous day and some reports indicated that they had counseled a crackdown. A more pressing question was who was in control of the government? It looked to us in Washington as if Diem were playing off his generals against one another and in so doing was apparently succeeding in fragmenting the only group with the power to stabilize the situation.

Because of the importance of knowing the attitude of the generals, I sent Harkins a private cable asking for his assessment of this crucial point. His reply pointed out that although Diem knew that senior officers such as "Big" Minh, General Don (the newly appointed Chief of the Joint General Staff), and some of the corps commanders were among his critics, he had made no move to replace them with hand-picked officers, not even General Dinh, the Military Governor of Saigon, upon whose loyalty the safety of his government depended. A military coup appeared easy to engineer, but Diem seemed to trust the officers best situated and most likely to carry one out, and Diem was not inclined to be overtrusting. Meanwhile, Harkins reported that the events of the previous days had not affected operations against the Vietcong and that, within twenty-four hours after the raids on the pagodas, the military had restored order with little violence. The overall impression was that the generals were thus far responsive to Diem's orders and had the situation in the streets pretty well in hand. Unanswered was the role which Nhu had played and was continuing to play.

While we in the Pentagon were viewing the situation with concern but with comparative calm, elements of the State Department were deeply agitated by what they viewed as the repressive actions of the Diem government in blatant defiance of U.S. advice urging conciliation. As if some of the conspiracy-laden atmosphere of Saigon had found its way back to Washington, a small group of anti-Diem activists picked this time to perpetrate an egregious "end run" in dispatching a cable of the utmost importance to Saigon without obtaining normal departmental concurrences, an action which created extremely hard feeling among President Kennedy's advisers at a time when he badly needed their harmonious cooperation. In the course of Saturday, August 24, the group, later identified as having involved Under Secretary of State Harriman, Assistant Secretary of State Hilsman, and White House staff member Michael Forrestal, drew up this cable, cleared it with Undersecretary George Ball on the golf course, and obtained a telephone clearance from President Kennedy in Hyannisport. It was then dispatched without the concurrence of the Secretary of Defense, the Deputy Secretary of Defense, or the Joint Chiefs of Staffs, all of whom had a vital interest in its contents. It was significant that in addition to the President, Rusk, McNamara, McCone, and McGeorge Bundy were all out of Washington at the time and Nolting had left his post in Saigon where he had just been replaced as Ambassador by Henry Cabot Lodge.

I first heard of the incident in the early evening of August 24 when Deputy Secretary of Defense Gilpatric telephoned me at my quarters at Fort Myer, Virginia, from his Maryland farm, where he was spending the weekend. He told me that Forrestal had informed him by phone of the substance of the message for his information but not for Defense concurrence, as it had already received presidential approval. Gilpatric then outlined the content to me, and I expressed great concern, in which he joined me, over the substance of the message and the way of handling such an important matter. Upon hanging up, I called the Pentagon for a copy of the message and, in response, General Krulak of the Joint Staff brought a copy of the dispatched message to my house later in the evening.

On reading the cable, my first reaction was that the anti-Diem group centered in State had taken advantage of the absence of the principal officials to get out instructions which would never have been approved as written under normal circumstances. In terms of content it was not an easy cable to understand, and, had I received it, I would have had to request clarification from Washington on many points before initiating action. For example, Lodge was told that the U.S. government could no longer tolerate Nhu in the government but that Diem was to be given a last chance to get rid of him. Presumably, the Ambassador was to convey this point as a kind of ultimatum prior to moving against Diem himself. However, the cable contradicted this concept of the sequence of events elsewhere by stressing that immediate action must be taken to prevent Nhu from further consolidating his position; hence, Lodge was authorized to inform key Vietnamese officials at once that the U.S. government could not accept the repressive actions of Nhu and his collaborators and that prompt remedial action must be taken to repeal martial law and to release the arrested bonzes. Concurrently with this approach to the civilian officials, Lodge was to inform key generals of our position and to point out that, while we wanted Diem to have reasonable time to remove Nhu, we could no longer support him if he proved obdurate. If at any point the generals took action against Diem, they were to receive "direct support" from us, although the cable gave no explanation of what "direct support" meant. The cable ended with instructions to Lodge to draw detailed plans to bring about Diem's replacement and with an assurance of complete Washington support for actions taken under this cable.

In summary, as I read the cable, our Ambassador was to serve an ultimatum on Diem while, at the same time, establishing a conspiratorial relationship with Diem's officials and generals to whom he would make clear our disenchantment with the regime and would promise our active support to Diem's overthrow, if it were undertaken. Thus, even if Diem should make an honest effort to comply with the ultimatum, action directed by the cable would reveal our unhappiness with him in a way which gave open-ended encouragement to plotters to move against him at any time.

In the absence of senior officials from Washington, I had all of the following Sunday to meditate on the situation and the probable consequences of the cable. On Monday morning I had my first opportunity to discuss it with Secretary McNamara and the other Chiefs and found them all pretty much in my frame of mind as to its significance. At noon, McNamara, Gilpatric, and I adjourned to the White House to attend a meeting on the subject with the President. Rusk, Ball, Harriman, and Hilsman represented State. I do not know what discussions, if any, Rusk and McNamara may have had with the President in advance of the meeting, but Kennedy was obviously aware of the unhappiness of several of us around the table. Hilsman explained the cable and described the plan as he conceived it for contacting such generals as Minh, Khanh, and Khiem and responded to questions about the intended meaning of "direct support." This term he explained as being logistical support of the South Vietnamese forces through a port other than Saigon so that supplies would not pass through the hands of Diem's government. To the President's query about my views, I replied that I had never had experience in turning over the choice of a head of state to local generals and doubted that it was the way to proceed. As to furnishing "direct support" without the use of Saigon, it would involve major changes in our logistical system which would take considerable time and impose delays. Before giving a final answer on that point, I asked for time to make a study of it, as the Chiefs had never before considered such a contingency.

There was a general discussion of other questions the cable raised. How were Lodge and Harkins interpreting "direct support? Who did Lodge think could replace Diem? What was he to say to Diem when he offered him the last chance mentioned in the cable? It was obvious that no one had thought through these points, so the President adjourned the meeting and directed us to reconvene the next day when we were better prepared. Since former Ambassador Nolting had reached Washington on his return trip from Saigon, I suggested that he be invited to attend. To the objections from one official that Nolting's views were colored, the President observed, "Maybe properly colored."

It was unfortunate that these events were taking place just at the time of a change of ambassadors. Nolting's departure from Saigon on August 15 had been the result of a long-standing request for relief, and Lodge was a popular choice as his successor, not only because of the bipartisan political flavor he brought to the Vietnam policy, but because of his many friends in American military circles. Another point in his favor was a long acquaintance with General Harkins reaching back to military service together at Ft. Bliss in 1929. In the course of Lodge's briefings in Washington prior to going to Saigon, the Chiefs had him to luncheon at the Pentagon where we had a long and, I thought, very satisfactory discussion of the military problems in Vietnam. We told him about our concern over the impetuosity of Diem's American critics and our opposition to ousting him without a replacement in sight. Lodge did not resist this line of reasoning and gave us the impression of carrying an open mind to the scene of action. But, upon his arrival in Saigon, he quickly showed himself in alignment with those who insisted, "Diem must go."

As a consequence of this uncoordinated and ill-advised start on a vastly important change of policy, the Kennedy team did not look its best during the critical period from August 24 to 31 which, in its demand on the time of the President and his advisers, was comparable to the period of the secret crisis the previous October. As then, the President's principal advisers met each noon in the White House, usually with him, to talk over the information or lack of information from Saigon. The first important news was that Lodge, immediately upon receiving the August 24 cable and without seeking further clarification, had set about implementing his instructions. Using CIA officers rather than military in order to conceal the U.S. hand (a purpose reminiscent of the Bay of Pigs), he established contact with General Khiem, the Chief of Staff of the Joint General Staff, who seemed reasonably receptive to the American advances. However, General Khanh, the II Corps commander, felt the time was not right to mount a coup, and the most important military figure of all, General "Big" Minh, avoided contact with the Americans on the ground that he was under constant surveillance. Meanwhile, there had been no approach to Diem to give him that last chance to rid himself of Nhu which was to precede sanctions against him.

Back in Washington there was ample time for us to have second thoughts about this venture, and we did. The President and his advisers began to make a serious evaluation of the feasibility of the kind of coup they wanted, one which would put a better man than Diem in the presidency with little bloodshed and minimal effect on the war. Nolting, who was the best judge of the generals at our meetings, was openly skeptical of their ability to execute a successful coup, and he warned us that, in his opinion, there was no one who could hold the fragmented country together if Diem were overthrown. The President began to see that he was involved in anything but a sure thing and that his ability to control events from Washington was going to be minimal. So we began to argue among ourselves over the merits of several alternatives. Should we build a fire under the generals who were showing so little alacrity, energize them by additional offers of support, and prepare to take an active part in the coup ourselves? Or should we merely wish the generals well and accept whatever they could accomplish by themselves? Or, finally, was it still possible to withdraw from the enterprise without too great a loss?

Lodge and Harkins united in rejecting this last alternative as being completely destructive to our future relations with the generals who were essential to the prosecution of the war. They were divided on the desirability of having a face-to-face last-chance confrontation with Diem—Harkins was for it, Lodge against. It never took place. Both felt that Harkins should now approach the generals, even though it exposed the American hand, to reinforce our covert approaches and bolster with his prestige their confidence in the American *bona fides*. Also we hoped that he might get a look at the coup plans which we assumed the generals were devising. When Harkins made his approach, he got a clear indication that there were no plans being formulated; the generals were not about to accept the risks implicit in a coup for which they had so little time to prepare.

So one week after receiving the bristling cable from Washington, our Embassy in Saigon conceded that the coup was a nonstarter if left to the generals, and no one was inclined to propose that the United States should take over the job. Our only immediate fall-back was to try to reopen communications with Diem in full knowledge that he was probably aware of our plotting against him. In the end this was the course adopted, embarrassing though it was to the would-be king-makers in Washington. Having been opposed to the program laid out in the August 24 cable, I did not feel too badly for them but I was sure that our bungling had deprived us of most of our remaining leverage on the Diem government.

Our policy planners were sent back to their work bench for new ideas but, though they toiled mightily, they produced little in September which looked either new or promising. It was decided that our public attitude would be one of dignified displeasure with Diem, while privately we would continue to urge him to free his political prisoners, lift martial law,

295

and separate himself from Nhu. Seeking to find some way to influence Diem, we slowed down the commodity import program that constituted most of the economic aid which we were supplying to South Vietnam. President Kennedy, on television, publicly indicated his disapproval of the actions against the Buddhists and expressed regret that the Vietnamese government had gotten out of touch with the people. While publicly opposing an interruption of aid to the Diem government because of its adverse effect on the war effort, he indicated sympathy with Senator Church's resolution calling for an end to American aid and for the withdrawal of our personnel if repressive acts continued. In Saigon, our Embassy showed where its sympathy lay by giving asylum to Tri Quang, the ring leader of the militant Buddhists, and to two of his companions and by rejecting the request of the government to give them up. Madame Nhu made virulent attacks on the Kennedy Administration and the American press to which the latter replied in kind. Meanwhile, reports proliferated regarding possible coups and the machinations of cliques within our Embassy in Saigon. The President's uncertainty about what was really going on in South Vietnam was further increased by flatly contradictory reports brought back by Joseph Mendenhall of State and Lieutenant General Victor Krulak of the Joint Staff, who visited Vietnam at the same time but went to different places and interviewed different people.

Although the tension eased somewhat after mid-September when Diem lifted martial law, the curfew, and censorship, the President's concern over the situation was far from relaxed. He still wanted to be reassured about the course of the war and to know the truth about the reports that Lodge and Harkins were not communicating with one another and that the CIA was out of control. So he asked Secretary McNamara and me to undertake another trip to Vietnam in the last week of September.

This time we focused our efforts primarily on finding out how military operations were going and in determining what the American attitude should be toward the Diem government. On the first count, we arrived at a conclusion very similar to those of General Krulak, namely, that the military campaign had made and was making considerable progress; hence, when we returned to Washington, we had only a few substantive recommendations to make for military improvement. The most important one was a proposal that, in conjunction with the Vietnamese government, we adopt specific military goals for an agreed time schedule on our midterm economic and military aid programs, and then drive hard for their attainment. Such goals, like those of a fund-raising program, should be high, perhaps a little out of reach, to offer an incentive to the workers to do a little better than would normally be expected. My thought was that such goals would not only stimulate a greater U.S.-Vietnamese effort but could be used as a warning to Diem that, if the programs lagged from his failure to perform, we Americans would not feel obliged to stay in Vietnam indefinitely and wait for him to catch up after doing our part. After checking our judgment against that of many Americans and Vietnamese officers and officials, McNamara and I concluded that, if Diem could succeed in mobilizing Vietnamese resources and in stabilizing the political front, as we thought he could if he really tried, the Vietcong threat could be reduced to a state approximating low order banditry by the end of 1965 as we had assumed in the National Campaign Plan earlier in the year. At this level, we thought that it would be controllable without significant U.S. military aid. To remind Diem that we were serious in taking this goal and would plan to reduce our forces progressively in accordance with it, we recommended by the end of 1963 the reduction of about 1,000 U.S. personnel who were doing work of a kind which could be taken over by Vietnamese.

The socio-political situation was far more difficult to evaluate than the military. There were certainly serious political tensions in Saigon, but there was no solid evidence that a coup was imminent, although the assassination of Diem or Nhu was always a possibility. While Diem had shown few signs of changing his ways as the result of our strictures and the limited economic pressure we had applied to date, it seemed desirable to keep up or increase the pressures, if only to show Diem that we were not resigned to his lack of cooperation. It seemed to us that metering the input of economic aid and suspending funds for long-term development projects offered the best way of showing our dissatisfaction without seriously retarding the conduct of the war or breaking finally with Diem and his government—an ambivalent policy not easy to follow, we were aware. While maintaining this precarious balance, we proposed to watch Diem's reaction for the next few months and adjust our conduct accordingly. In the interim, we saw no advantage in actively promoting a change in government. Indeed, at the time of our visit, Diem's political adversaries seemed to be lying low, and we had no desire to stir them up.

In trying to assess coup attitudes I was very anxious to get the views of General "Big" Minh, the *doyen* of the Vietnamese military, who had avoided American contacts during the coup-plotting of late August. Shortly after my arrival, I got word from an American friend of his that Minh had an important message for McNamara and me which he would like to convey if an inconspicuous meeting could be worked out. After some negotiation, such a meeting was arranged to take place at the Saigon Officers' Club under the guise of a game of tennis, a natural cover plan since I had played tennis with Minh on other visits. The match also provided a reasonable excuse for the presence of Secretary McNamara as an admiring spectator.

But it did not turn out as we had expected. The game took place all right, with McNamara sitting uncomfortably on the sidelines in the sweltering heat, but at no time did we get a serious discussion started with Minh, whose sole interest that afternoon seemed to be tennis. In spite of broad hints of our interest in other subjects which we gave him during breaks in the game, we got nothing for our pains beyond exposure to the sun and a secretarial ribbing for me over the clumsiness of military plotters. Even so, we had reason to conclude that if Minh's eagerness to cultivate the support of American leaders against Diem was representative of military attitudes generally, a coup attempt did not seem to be in the offing.

The most important recommendation which we decided to make on our return was that the President restate his Vietnam policy for the benefit of his official family in such a way as to clear away any doubts or misunderstandings. Such a statement, we believed, should reaffirm our conviction that the security of South Vietnam remained of great importance to the interests of the United States and, hence that our government should persevere in its objective of denying South Vietnam to Communism and of suppressing the Vietcong insurgency. For reasons previously discussed, we should take the end of 1965 as the target date for the termination of the military part of the American task. If a further deterioration of the political situation should occur to invalidate this target date, we would have to review our attitude toward Diem's government and our national interests in Southeast Asia.

After checking our tentative conclusions with Ambassador Lodge and General Harkins, whom we found in substantial agreement, we paid a final call on President Diem. McNamara, with Lodge translating, bore down heavily on the contrast between the progress in the military field and the repeated political setbacks, and on our concern over the political direction of Diem's government. He stressed our confidence in being able to cope with the Vietcong military threat by the end of 1965 if Diem stabilized the internal situation and made a serious effort to accomplish the reforms which we Americans had been urging. McNamara made it clear that the American people and Congress would not continue to support our present policy if the conflict were prolonged by the ineffectiveness of the local government. I expressed confidence in the military feasibility of the 1965 date provided Diem's government did many of the things it had been unable or loath to do in the past: energize all agencies, military and civil; replace ineffective commanders and officials; allay domestic political tensions. I promised to deal with these matters more fully in a letter to him after my departure.*

* The following is an extract from my letter to President Diem, delivered 2 October 1963:

> In closing, Mr. President, may I give you my most important overall impression? Up to now, the battle against the Viet Cong has seemed endless; no one has been willing to set a date for its successful conclusion. After talking to scores of officers, Vietnamese and American, I am convinced that the Viet Cong insurgency in the north and center can be reduced to little more than sporadic incidents by the end of

I wish that I could say that our words evoked some signs of a desire for reconciliation or even of an inclination to accommodation. Our task of bringing him around was made all the more difficult by his undoubted knowledge that we were at least privy to, if not accomplices in, the plotting going on against him. While smoking the usual chain of cigarettes, he defended his acts point by point and was obviously not about to capitulate to this latest delegation of Americans, even though they were from the Pentagon, which he viewed as friendly, and not from State, which he viewed as hostile. Altogether it was a depressing evening, the refusal of this stalwart, stubborn patriot to recognize the realities which threatened to overwhelm him, his family, and his country. Our leave-taking was the last time I was to see him.

We flew back to Washington by way of Honolulu and, on October 2, presented our report to the President and the National Security Council. The subsequent White House press statement announced the approval of our report and gave the highlights of our recommendations, including the restatement of Vietnam policy and the proposed plan for reducing our military contribution. In spite of the widespread criticism of Diem and Nhu in the United States, I do not recall that the reaffirmation of our national interest in the security of South Vietnam aroused any particular comment in the Congress or in the press. However, the target schedule for terminating our military involvement was seized upon by many commentators, some regarding it as encouraging, others as overly optimistic. Unfortunately, although probably inevitably, the qualifying conditions placed upon adherence to the schedule were overlooked or soon forgotten, namely, that the 1965 date was feasible only if the political situation did not worsen and affect the military effort, which it soon did, and if Diem carried out the needed internal reforms, which he did not. Also, in deference to Vietnamese sensibilities, there could be no public mention of the use of the schedule as a pressure device to get better Vietnamese performance. So when the overthrow of Diem a month later completely changed the game, our target withdrawal schedule remained on the books as one more example for the Vietnam critics to cite of unwarranted official optimism and the way the government misled the people about the prospects in Vietnam.

Two matters not mentioned in our formal report were the disunity

1964. The Delta will take longer but should be completed by the end of 1965. But for these predictions to be valid, certain conditions must be met. Your Government should be prepared to energize all agencies, military and civil, to a higher output of activity than up to now. Ineffective commanders and province officials must be replaced as soon as identified. Finally, there should be a restoration of domestic tranquility on the home front if political tensions are to be allayed and external criticism is to abate. Conditions are needed for the creation of an atmosphere conducive to an effective campaign directed at the objective, vital to both of us, of defeating the Viet Cong and of restoring peace to your country.

299

within our Embassy and the lamentable state of relations with the press. The impression I had received in Washington was that Harkins was not being consulted by the Ambassador on many matters in which the military interest was high and, in Saigon, I quickly verified this to be the case. There seemed to be no clash of personalities; it was rather that the Ambassador was inclined to keep his own counsel and not to seek that of others. The same anti-Diemists who had caused trouble for Nolting were still on the Embassy staff, displaying unabated hostility toward Diem and his family. The CIA Chief, John Richardson, had become non grata to Lodge for reasons which I could not assess, but it seemed in the interest of all parties to reassign him elsewhere.

Leaks to the press from Embassy factions were common and the press enjoyed reporting their divisions, usually with a bias favoring those who were anti-Diem. Many of the reporters had long since abandoned any pretense of impartial reporting and had committed their reportorial skills, which were often considerable, to disparaging Diem in the name of religious freedom. Harkins had also become a prime target because of his optimism regarding the course of the war at a time when the anti-Diemist theme was that the oppressive actions of the Chief of State were seriously impeding all progress in Vietnam. Since this kind of reporting was the principal source of public information at home, most of our people pictured the situation as a chaotic mess for which the repressive tactics of a religious fanatic were largely responsible. To me, it was a sobering spectacle of the power of a few relatively young and inexperienced newsmen who, openly committed to "getting" Diem or "getting" Harkins, were not satisfied to report the events of foreign policy but undertook to shape them.

McNamara and I discussed with Lodge and Harkins our view of the seriousness of the disunity in the Embassy and the need to align the American official community in support of the government position on Vietnam. The press problem was far more difficult. Our only suggestion was to repeat the old one that Washington continue to try to get senior media representatives to come to Vietnam periodically and judge the situation for themselves.

During October President Kennedy and his advisers were preoccupied with implementing the recommendations of the McNamara-Taylor report. Public statements by American officials expressing the disapproval of the Diem government continued as did actions to hold back commercial imports. Nhu's Special Forces, having been prominent participants in repressing the demonstrations, were singled out for discriminatory treatment in the allotment of American aid. When Richardson returned to Washington, the press attributed his reassignment to his past associations with Nhu and interpreted it as another rebuke of President Diem. Other events contributed to raise U.S.-Vietnamese tensions. Vietnamese police roughed up three American journalists who, apparently acting on advance information, had assembled to photograph a bonze immolation, and the American press was enraged. Madame Nhu chose October for a trip to America for the purpose of carrying her attacks on the Kennedy Administration to the American people. Coup rumors continued in Saigon, but most ears had become dulled by previous cries of "wolf"—mine certainly had, and so, I believe, had those of most Washington officials. So in spite of some advance indications, when the coup finally took place I was as surprised as anyone.

It was sometime after midnight on the morning of November 1 when I was awakened at my house by a call from the National Military Command Center reporting the start of the coup. It had begun about noon Saigon time, and as usual, the initial reports were very unclear. I dressed and hurried to the Pentagon, where I stayed reading the cables until time to meet with the Chiefs to review the situation. Then, at ten o'clock, I joined Secretary McNamara and drove to the White House for a meeting with the President.

By that time it was fairly clear that a group of generals headed by "Big" Minh, with the support of General Ton Than Dinh, the commander of the Saigon garrison, had launched an attack upon government installations and Diem's palace in Saigon. The palace guard had resisted, but the palace was believed to have been taken. When the meeting opened, the fate of Diem and Nhu was unknown. But, shortly after we had seated ourselves around the cabinet table, a member of the White House staff entered and passed the President a flash message from the situation room. The news was that Diem and Nhu were both dead, and the coup leaders were claiming their deaths to be suicide. Kennedy leaped to his feet and rushed from the room with a look of shock and dismay on his face which I had never seen before. He had always insisted that Diem must never suffer more than exile and had been led to believe or had persuaded himself that a change in government could be carried out without bloodshed.

So far as I know, the facts surrounding the mounting of the coup and the death of the Ngo brothers are not fully known to this day. That they had been shot in the back of the head with their hands wired behind their backs was shown in photographs taken at the time and published in the press. There are several stories as to how it was done—I know of no confirmation of any one of them. The claim of suicide was so ridiculous that it suggested that the generals were caught by surprise without a prepared story.

The degree of American complicity has often been raised, but here again I know of no evidence of direct American participation in carrying out the coup and certainly of none in the assassination. But there is no question but that President Kennedy and all of us who advised him bore a heavy responsibility for these happenings by having encouraged the perpetrators through the public display of our disapproval of Diem and his brother.

That responsibility extends beyond the death of Diem—so bitterly regretted by President Kennedy—to the prolongation of the war and to the increased American involvement of later years, which were among the consequences of the events of this autumn of disaster. Diem's overthrow set in motion a sequence of crises, political and military, over the next two years which eventually forced President Johnson in 1965 to choose between accepting defeat or introducing American combat forces. The encouragement afforded the enemy by Diem's downfall found expression in a massive offensive, political and military, to exploit the removal of their mortal enemy. Taking into account all these effects, I would assess this episode as one of the great tragedies of the Vietnamese conflict and an important cause of the costly prolongation of the war into the next decade.

In the following days, while the population danced in the streets of Saigon, Diem's Vice-President Nguyen Ngoc Tho, with the approval and support of a junta of four generals, formed a government of mixed military and civilian membership. The U.S. government quickly recognized it and announced the renewal of commodity import aid. *Izvestia* expressed satisfaction with the turn of events, and the attention of Washington officialdom drifted away from Saigon as normal life resumed. On November 13 the Black Watch serenaded President Kennedy as he sat on the South porch of the White House and his little son, John-John, played with the huge bearskin of the drum major. I sat behind the President during the ceremony, in attendance on him for the last time.

On November 19, I joined a party headed by Secretaries Rusk and McNamara to rendezvous in Honolulu with Lodge, Harkins, and others from Saigon to exchange views about the situation and to verify that we were all on a common bearing. It was too early to form an impression of the ability of the new government, but its prompt purge of old Diem officials and the dismantling of the Diem police system, while productive of favorable headlines in the United States, had their disquieting aspects. Experienced officials would be hard to find to replace the ousted Diemists, and police experience was badly needed to counter Vietcong agents who were always infiltrating into Saigon and now could be expected at an increasing rate. The new regime was likely to have hard going and I gave it a short life expectancy.

Back in Washington, I completed preparations to receive the visit from the German Chief of Staff, General Foertsch, and his successor-designate, General Trettner. They arrived on the morning of November 22, met with the Joint Chiefs during the forenoon and then joined us at lunch in the Chairman's dining room just across the corridor from my office. After lunch, we broke up to rejoin at two o'clock for a continuation of our discussions in the "Tank."

Taking advantage of the break, I returned to my office and proceeded to indulge in a lazy but refreshing practice to which I had been addicted for years, a short postlunch siesta. I had just locked my door and lain down on the couch in my office when the buzzer of my communications box sounded. It was General Tibbetts, the officer in charge of the National Military Command Center, informing me that the radio was reporting that President Kennedy had been shot in Dallas and was in a critical condition. Unbelieving but obliged to react, I called Bob McNamara in his office above mine and gave him the message which he received with the same shocked disbelief. Then I summoned the Joint Chiefs to my office, sending word to our German guests that we would be delayed.

The Chiefs assembled about two o'clock, and McNamara soon joined us. By that time there was no longer ground to doubt the news or to hope that it was a bad dream. We had lost or were about to lose our President. We quickly considered the possible consequences world-wide, discussed what we should do, and could think of nothing useful beyond repeating what information we had to U.S. commanders throughout the world and urging them to increase the alertness of their forces on the bare chance of an unexpected political or military reaction somewhere. Then we rejoined the Germans.

We broke the news to them that the President had been shot but that we did not know how badly; nevertheless, I proposed that we should proceed with the afternoon session. They seemed reluctant to do so but in response to our urging resumed their seats and our discussions of NATO matters. The next hour seemed endless as we tried to talk calmly and sensibly while thinking about what had happened in Dallas. In the midst of the session an aide passed me a note that the President was dead, which I circulated surreptitiously under the table to my colleagues without interrupting the discussion. When it finally came to an end, I broke the tragic news to the Germans. I have rarely seen such ashen faces or heard such words of spontaneous grief as those with which they reacted to the loss of a man who meant almost as much to them as to us.

CHAPTER 24

Chairman JCS under President Johnson

On the day following President Kennedy's funeral, the Joint Chiefs addressed a note to President Johnson requesting permission to pay their respects and to receive such guidance as he might desire to give them. The note also reminded him that they should discuss with him at an early date his emergency duties in the case of an outbreak of nuclear war.

We Chiefs had known President Johnson both as senator and as Vice-President, and I had always found his views on matters of defense extremely sound. I had been pleased with his quick statement of intention to continue President Kennedy's Vietnam policy, which he confirmed in a National Security Council Memorandum. In it, President Johnson retained the target date of 1965 for the withdrawal of most of our military personnel and called upon all officials to unite behind U.S. policy in support of the new Vietnamese government.

President Johnson responded to our request for an interview with an invitation to meet with him on November 29. He welcomed us with an expression of his confidence and his desire to keep us in our assignments. His thoughts that day ran not so much to strategy as to the level of readiness of the Armed Forces and the budgetary costs of that readiness. Regarding the first point, each Chief assured him that his service was in a high state of readiness and stronger than at any time since the Korean War. The President then expounded his views concerning the need for frugality and thrift in administering the Armed Forces and his desire that the Chiefs seek ways to save money and watch over contracting procedures.

After some discussion of the economics of defense, I called the President's attention to the National Security Memorandum in which President Kennedy, following the Bay of Pigs, had set forth his concept of the responsibility of the Chiefs to provide him broad advice transcending purely military considerations. I told him that the Chiefs had attached great importance to this interpretation of their advisory relationship and I recommended that the NSC Memorandum be retained or be reissued in his own name. His eventual decision was to retain it as issued so that it remained binding on the Chiefs throughout his Administration.

Time that day did not permit us to explain in detail the decisions which he would be obliged to take in a nuclear emergency. But I assured him that his two aides, General Clifton and Captain Shepard, were well acquainted with all the procedures and would always be at his side. A few days later I got the opportunity to sit down with him at leisure and carefully went over these vastly important matters, reflecting while doing so on the tremendous responsibility this man was obliged to carry and hoping that he would never have to avail himself of the information which I was conveying.

In December the President asked me to pay a visit to India and Pakistan after the winter meeting of the NATO Chiefs of Staff in Paris. As usual, feelings were running high between the two countries over the perennial Kashmir issue, and the United States, in trying to maintain a stance of impartiality, had succeeded in offending both parties. The Indians, badly frightened by the Chinese offensive in the fall of 1962, were not satisfied with the limited assistance that the United States was providing to improve their air defense and were turning more and more to the Soviets for help. The Pakistani considered that the aid we were giving India was, in effect, strengthening the Indian threat to them, and they had turned to Peking for arms—indeed, Chou En-lai was about to arrive in the country on a state visit. The White House thought that it would be well for me to visit both countries in the hope that my past associations with President Ayub might be of some use in Pakistan.

While I cannot say that my trip did much to improve the situation, it was most instructive to me in regional national attitudes and allowed me to make an air reconnaissance of the mighty barrier of the Himalayas, an experience which brought the feasibility of military operations along that frontier into perspective. My conversations with the leaders of both countries impressed me with the difficulty—indeed the impossibility—for a great power like the United States to stand completely aloof from any important world problem involving third parties. India was maneuvering to get additional American support against China, Pakistan to get our help against India, and both were holding in the background the threat of turning to the Communist powers if we failed them. Having been unimpressed with the effect of past military aid as a means for creating durable political ties with recipient countries, I was not particularly enthusiastic about the

305

prospect of competing with either Russia or China for the role of arms supplier of South Asia, and I so reported on my return.

In Pakistan, I found Ayub in a highly emotional state over what he viewed as the growing Indian military threat and the abandonment of Pakistan by his American friends who refused to give him weapons, particularly tanks, to offset the Indian superiority. I had only two placatory offerings for him: (1) the suggestion of a combined maneuver of Pakistani and U.S. forces in Pakistan provided it would not appear to be aimed at India; (2) a personal letter from President Johnson, couched in the most friendly terms, expressing his hope for continued cordial relations. Ayub showed little enthusiasm for the maneuver proposal but received the President's letter with visible pleasure. This reaction afforded me the opportunity to express regret over the downward trend of governmental relations when the person-to-person friendship between the heads of state was so genuinely warm. I urged that we cease recriminations over past disagreements and resume the kind of friendly cooperation which had marked our relations in former years.

We discussed frankly the new relationship of Pakistan with Red China which was creating a bad impression in the United States and, I reminded him, would probably adversely affect Congressional attitudes toward aid to his country. Ayub tried to portray this liaison as purely platonic which, in opening a new means of access to Peking, would be of actual help to the West. Also, it would allow him to keep tabs on Chinese moves to help India, a contingency which he anticipated at any time. In further support of his case, he underscored the domestic problem of explaining to his people the aid which the Americans were giving his enemies in India. When I returned to the idea of a U.S.-Pakistani military exercise he remained wary of the proposal, possibly for fear that an exercise demonstrating the rapid introduction of American forces into Pakistan might be used as an argument against the need to strengthen his own forces. We parted without reaching any important conclusions but with renewed expressions by Ayub of his esteem for President Johnson.

As I looked over my office agenda for the first half of 1964, I found two predominant activities, those related to the improvement of the quality of the work of the Joint Chiefs of Staff and those arising from continuing supervision of our military programs in Vietnam. Typical of the first was a determined effort to make a more useful document out of the Joint Strategic Objectives Plan (JSOP). This is a thick study produced annually by the Joint Chiefs of Staff which defines and describes the military threats confronting the nation, sets forth the strategy to counter them, and proposes the force levels deemed necessary to support the strategy. In a perfect world this document would have served as the point of departure of all defense planning; in fact, it had never achieved anything like this status over the years of its existence.

There were several reasons for this failure. The first was the chronic absence of authoritative political guidance setting for the goals of our future foreign policy and the obstacles that we might expect to encounter in achieving them. Without such guidance, the Chiefs were left to develop their own concept of future policy and of the form, time, and place of international obstacles which might have to be overcome by the use of military force. They also had to use their own judgment in determining such critical matters as the reliance to be placed on getting authority to use nuclear weapons in an emergency, a matter which would have an important bearing on the strength of the military forces required. Another reason was the absence of agreed criteria for the sufficiency of various categories of forces, the old question of how much was enough. Such criteria were particularly elusive when one sought to measure a subjective quality, such as the deterrent effect of military power on a potential aggressor. Without guidance from on high, the JCS fell back on their individual judgments of what forces would be necessary, a procedure which produced widely varying estimates of force requirements, any one of which always exceeded the limits of budgetary feasibility. These excessive estimates had a way of leaking out into the press and thus tended to discredit the judgment of the Chiefs in the public mind. They also created many "splits" in the JSOP which invited the intervention of the McNamara cost-effectiveness experts whose computers could always produce figures more acceptable to the decision-makers than those generated by the pencils of the Chiefs.

In the spring of 1964 the Chiefs attacked the perennial problem of the JSOP, determined to make it more effective in the decision-making process of the Department of Defense. In this effort, we had Secretary McNamara's encouragement but little guidance as to standards of sufficiency. Such standards are not too difficult to establish for strategic weapons, the requirements for which can be directly related to the numbers and kinds of targets and the level of destruction desired for them. But it is a different matter to justify the so-called general purpose forces needed to meet limited contingencies arising in situations such as we had faced in Korea and later in Vietnam.

To form a basis for their judgments on force levels, the Chiefs directed the Joint Staff to draw up a series of politico-military scenarios, depicting plausible situations that might arise around the world. Then, using wargame techniques, the staff was to develop an estimate of the forces which would be necessary to cope with the early stages of hostilities in each hypothetical situation. I found this kind of analysis useful but certainly not fully effective in producing unchallengeable force requirements. No one would ever propose that the United States maintain in being all of the forces necessary to meet simultaneously all possible contingencies worldwide. In the end, the Chiefs still had to use common sense and some feeling for budget feasibilities before making their force recommendations in the JSOP. But these contingency analyses were useful as a means of rebutting some of the cost-effectiveness arguments derived purely from the abstractions of computer models.

I can not say that the JSOP of that year was a great success but it was an improvement over the past. My involvement in it convinced me that the strategic analysis approach and the cost analysis technique of Dr. Enthoven's analysts should not be rivals but allies of the Chiefs, and that the Joint Staff must become fully aware of the possibilities of systems analysis and the applicability of its techniques to their problems. Ideally, it seemed to me that the Systems Analysis office of the Secretary of Defense should be available for use by the Joint Staff just as were the budget experts of the Department of Defense in dealing with budgetary matters. However, at the same time, the systems analysts should be kept out of matters of strategy and recognize the limits of the competence of their methodology.

Vietnam returned front stage on January 30, 1964, when, after two months of comparative quiet, a new and unexpected coup occurred, unwanted by anyone of my acquaintance in Washington or elsewhere. General Khanh, the I Corps Commander, who had played some part in the anti-Diem coup, found himself outside the ruling junta and excluded from the spoils of victory. Unwilling to accept this depressed status, he mounted a coup of his own which succeeded with amazing ease and no bloodshed. Suddenly the generals we knew best—Minh, Don, Dinh, and Xuan were out and General Khanh was in, largely because of the help of General Khiem, who had succeeded Dinh in command of the critical III Corps surrounding Saigon. Khanh's stated reason for the coup was his conviction that the former junta chiefs were contemplating the neutralization of South Vietnam in accordance with the plan put forward by de Gaulle a few months before. He justified his suspicion by pointing to the pro-French background of several of the generals, notably Don. As an immediate step, he put Don, Dinh, Xuan, and Le Van Kim in house arrest in Dalat while their conduct was under investigation but preserved "Big" Minh as an ornamental Chief of State for the new government while he himself became Prime Minister. The Khanh government was installed on February 8 and the United States avoided the embarrassment of having to recognize it by adopting the fiction that the continuity of the regime in Saigon had not been interrupted by the coup.

Khanh's coup caused a brusque awakening of those in Washington who had believed that all our political troubles in Vietnam had ended with Diem. It reminded us that there was a lot we did not know about personalities and motivations in Vietnam politics and that among the unknowns was Khanh, the man with whom we now had to deal. Along with this turn in internal politics, there was a sharp rise in Vietcong activities which demonstrated a new and ominous trend toward terrorism directed at Americans. The day after the installation of the Khanh government, the Vietcong exploded bombs in the Saigon sport stadium, killing two U.S. servicemen and wounding a score. This was the first of a long, bloody series of terrorist attacks on Americans which extended over the ensuing years.

Apart from this anti-American turn in the war, there were signs of a general deterioration in security throughout the country since the New Year. The Vietcong were boldly attacking the strategic hamlets and in Binh Dinh province alone had severely damaged seventy-five in the first three months after Diem's fall. Governmental control of rural territory was diminishing and with it the freedom of circulation without armed escort. However, our Embassy made generally favorable reports on Khanh, who seemed to be performing as well as could be expected in view of his inexperience with the governmental problems he had to face.

Because of the uneasy feeling that the whole situation was slowly unraveling, the President decided on another McNamara-Taylor expedition to Saigon in mid-March. A few days before our departure, he talked to the Chiefs about the trip and asked our opinion about what we should do next in South Vietnam. I replied that our military program should consist of two parts, an intensified counterinsurgency campaign in the south and selective air and naval attacks against targets in North Vietnam. The other Chiefs expressed general agreement, but, perhaps thinking of the Bay of Pigs, they added that if our government embarked on such a program, we must carry it out successfully regardless of cost. The President did not contest this view but, faced with the twin necessity of neither losing Vietnam nor expanding the war before the November 1964 elections, he was not inclined to accept our advice on the spot. He was, however, very clear in expressing his opposition to any more coups; his feeling was that we must support Khanh as the new national leader and establish that fact openly to deter all potential coup-plotters. For this purpose, he said he wanted to see Khanh on the front pages of the world press with McNamara and Taylor holding up his arms.

With this presidential injunction, the Secretary and I took off again for Saigon on March 8 and returned four days later. We concentrated first on appraising Khanh, then on surveying the general situation. With regard to the first point, we found Lodge quite high on Khanh but concerned about his hold on the Army and his vulnerability to the coup-plotting which had become the national pastime. This activity was so general that our people in Saigon were unable to keep track of the plotters and offered no hope of being able either to detect preparations for a coup or to prevent it if detected.

When we called on Khanh, the Secretary raised his spirits visibly by a strong affirmation of the American intention to support him. After expressing his thanks, Khanh gave us a well-phrased evaluation of the situation and an explanation of his plan for mobilizing the resources of his government. When we sounded him out with regard to possible air and naval retaliation against North Vietnam, to my surprise, he showed no particular eagerness for such action. Rather, he emphasized that his primary concern was to establish a firm military and political base in the South. The general impression he made during our interview was one of intelligence, energy, and good sense.

With the official calls completed, our party, accompanied by General Khanh, made a quick tour of the provinces partly to get a feel of the rural situation, partly to show ourselves before the Vietnamese public in company with Khanh. From Bac Lieu in the south to Hue in the north, we produced repeatedly that picture for the press which the President wanted: Khanh on a platform in some town square with McNamara holding up his right hand, me his left in a posture befitting the victorious finale of a prize fight or of a party convention. When it was all over, there was no doubt that he was the "American boy," at least for the time being.

The politico-military situation was more serious than I had appreciated in Washington. The enemy was clearly making the most out of the political turbulence and reduced military effectiveness resulting from the November and January coups. The political structure linking the central government with the provinces had virtually disappeared. Thirty-five of the forty-one province chiefs were new appointees, and most of the senior military commands had changed hands twice since the previous October. The desertion rate in the South Vietnamese forces was high and increasing, while confidence in their ability to provide security was decreasing proportionately throughout the countryside. There was corresponding evidence of a growth of strength on the part of the Vietcong derived from local recruiting and added assistance in equipment from North Vietnam. General Harkins called our attention to the appearance of heavy weapons of Chinese origin among those captured—recoilless rifles, heavy machine guns, and mortars. The boldness of the Vietcong attacks attested to their growing confidence and rising morale.

To cope with this situation, a number of possibilities were open. If we were convinced that the situation was hopeless or nearly so, we could offer to negotiate on the basis of de Gaulle's vague neutralization proposal, but it was obvious that neutralization on terms satisfactory to Hanoi could only end in a Communist take-over of South Vietnam. At the other extreme, we could initiate military actions against North Vietnam in the form of bombing strikes and commando raids. But measures of that kind encountered the objection which Khanh had raised, the lack of a firm political and military base in the south capable of supporting serious action against the North. Sandwiched between these extremes was a long list of short-range remedial actions which were feasible and clearly desirable: a further increase in Vietnamese forces, improved aircraft for their air force, the creation of a civil administrative corps to improve leadership in the nonmilitary programs, higher pay for the paramilitary forces, and certain economic measures such as an expansion of the fertilizer program.

Upon returning to Washington, Secretary McNamara prepared a memorandum for the President summarizing his conclusions and recommendations from our latest trip. It reaffirmed the validity of our current policy of assisting South Vietnam to defeat the Vietcong by methods short of the use of American combat forces. It rejected neutralization and proposed the remedial actions mentioned above. It recommended against direct military actions against North Vietnam at this time but did favor making preparations to permit the initiation of such actions on relatively short notice. After consideration by the National Security Council, the President approved these recommendations on March 17. While supporting this action, the Chiefs expressed serious doubt that the McNamara program would be enough to reverse the unfavorable trends without taking offensive action against Hanoi at an early date.

One of the facts of life about Vietnam was that it was never difficult to decide what should be done but it was almost impossible to get it done, at least in an acceptable period of time. Regardless of the alacrity of American actions in implementing McNamara's recommendations, the governmental machinery available to Khanh was totally incapable of doing its part. During the latter half of March and April, it was obvious, as we watched the reports come in from Saigon, that very little new was happening and some things which did happen were not good. Vietnamese military strength did not rise; instead, it continued to drop as desertion rates rose. To achieve the established strength targets for the end of 1964 would require raising 140,000 men, a figure which was clearly beyond the capability of the rickety recruitment system. In the field, Vietnamese units were taking heavy losses and accomplishing little in finding and destroying the enemy.

On the political front there were signs that the militant Buddhists were warming up for a test of strength with Khanh, whom Tri Quang had publicly branded as a lukewarm Buddhist. Khanh himself was beginning to reveal a trait which we found later was cardinal to his nature, a propensity to abandon a course of action as soon as an obstacle was encountered and to start something new and less demanding. Shortly after our return from Saigon, in apparent frustration over the hard going of his military and political undertakings, Khanh startled Washington by making public statements urging attacks on North Vietnam, a complete reversal of the attitude he had displayed a few weeks before to McNamara and me. Watching these events was an impatient President unable to understand the lack of visible progress resulting from his recent decisions. So in mid-May, Bob McNamara and I found ourselves back again in Saigon.

This time there was little to do but verify what I already knew, namely, that we were expecting too much too fast from Khanh. Khanh himself confessed that he had been so harassed by internal problems, especially those arising from the tugging and hauling of Buddhists and Catholics, that he had been obliged to neglect military matters and his National Pacification Plan. To make the latter move at an acceptable rate, he had concluded that we must hit the head of the enemy in Hanoi. He recognized that the solid base in the south desirable to support such action could hardly be achieved before the end of 1964. However, he thought it might become necessary to strike anyway to compensate for some Vietcong victory in the south which might occur at any time.

We tried out Khanh's views on Lodge, Harkins, and Westmoreland, who had become Harkins' deputy in the preceding January. They were unanimous in feeling that the National Pacification Plan could not get under way before September, but Harkins thought that it could probably show enough progress by the year's end to warrant operations against the North. Westmoreland thought that the necessary progress would require considerably more time. Neither felt that there was any urgency which justified initiating these offensive air operations prematurely as they might have the effect of distracting Khanh and his generals from the decisive battlefield in the south. We concluded that we should use the possibility of attacking the north as an incentive to get Khanh to work harder at pacification and adjust our future decisions to his accomplishments.

The Secretary and I returned to Washington this time with no new ideas to translate into programs but with a more realistic appreciation of what we could reasonably expect from Khanh. We had little to allay the impatience of the President, who had hoped for solid evidence that our policy was indeed on the right track.

For all the high-level visits, the situation in Vietnam continued to resist stubbornly the prescribed course of treatment. The end of May found the American principals back in Honolulu for another conference to find out what was wrong: Rusk, McNamara, Taylor, McCone, Felt, Lodge, Westmoreland (who replaced Harkins in April), and Ambassador Martin from Thailand. Lodge and Westmoreland considered that the Vietnam situation had ceased to deteriorate, and might even begin to improve during the last half of the year without resort to strikes against North Vietnam. Neither felt that we were racing the clock or that we needed to take action against Hanoi until the time was ripe. McNamara and McCone, impressed by indications of low Vietnamese morale, the high desertion rate, and the large number of weapons lost, were considerably less sanguine than the Saigon visitors. I was inclined to side with the latter for no better reason than an ingrained belief that the front-line units usually have a better sense of how the battle is going than the senior headquarters to the rear.

Westmoreland outlined an emergency program which would concentrate our efforts on eight critical provinces, each of which was to receive a strong supervisory team composed of Vietnamese and Americans. Lodge urged the establishment of an antiterrorist organization throughout the provinces based on a cellular police structure. Both Westmoreland and Lodge opposed a measure which the President favored, an extensive incorporation of American officials into the Vietnamese administrative structure. We did not have qualified people for this purpose, and most of us doubted that, if we had them, it was the right way to bolster the administration.

As usual, we talked about the problems incident to air attacks against North Vietnam: the need to prepare public and Congressional opinion for such an action, logistical factors involved in an air campaign, and the desirability of designing a war-game to bring out any hidden problems. The military representatives present felt that these preparations could be completed by about November 1. Everyone agreed that when the time came for offensive action, operations against North Vietnam would have to be taken with due regard for the situation in Laos which, as always, was precarious.

I got back to Washington from Honolulu just in time to set out for Paris to attend the midyear meeting of the NATO Chiefs and returned to Washington by way of Geneva. Home, I was plunged into the discussion of Ambassador Lodge's successor in Saigon.

It had been apparent for some time that the President would have to release Lodge to allow him to participate in the presidential primary campaign. The urgency of this step increased with Lodge's victory in the New Hampshire primary and the clear need for his active participation with liberal and middle-of-the-road Republicans if they were to block Senator Goldwater's nomination. I became privy to this matter early in May, as I recall, and suggested one or two names for consideration as Lodge's successor. Many of the President's senior advisers announced their willingness to undertake the task, men such as Rusk, McNamara, and Bob Kennedy. Shamed by their demonstration of devotion to the public weal, I also put my name in the hat.

To my considerable consternation, I found upon returning from Europe that I had become the leading candidate. For a variety of reasons, it was about the last job I would have chosen. I had lived abroad for a good part of my service in the Army, spending five years away from my family in World War II and the Korean War. While my wife could accompany me to Saigon, she was by now entitled to live in a home of her own and enjoy her friends. Also, I was responsible for my widowed mother in Washington who could not be moved. Finally, I was enjoying my job at the top of the military profession. The aggregate seemed to me a lot of good reasons for not going to Saigon.

But when Bob McNamara broke the news to me that I was the President's choice, I accepted. Feeling somewhat as I had in 1961 when President Kennedy asked me to return to active duty, I told Bob that I could

313

never turn down the request of a President to do a job which obviously needed doing. However, for personal reasons, I would have to insist that the duration of the assignment to Saigon be limited to about one year. He transmitted my reply to President Johnson, who then called me to the White House to make formal tender of the assignment. I accepted with the condition of the one year tenure, and the President's decision was announced on June 23. A week later I appeared before the Foreign Relations Committee which confirmed me with only one negative vote, that of Senator Morse who could see no good in sending Taylor to Saigon. When reporters asked me what I had to get this assignment ahead of such formidable rivals as Rusk, McNamara, Kennedy, et al., I could suggest only one reason—expendability.

CHAPTER 25

Saigon Kaleidoscope

When I arrived in Saigon on July 7, 1964, to take over as the American Ambassador, I felt that there were at least three circumstances favorable to the success of my mission. The first was the quality of the American officials with whom I was going to work, particularly my deputy, U. Alexis Johnson, General Westmoreland, and William Sullivan. Alex Johnson had been a close friend since our days together as Japanese language officers in Tokyo before World War II. In the course of the following years, he had risen to the top of the Foreign Service and was occupying the position of Deputy Under Secretary of State at the time he accepted assignment as my deputy in Saigon. He already occupied the highest post a career diplomat can normally attain, so his new job was a hierarchical demotion, and his acceptance of it was an act of abnegation for which I was deeply grateful. During our association in Saigon he was an able and loyal colleague, always calm and infinitely patient, whose wisdom and experience were invaluable to a soldier suddenly turned diplomat.

I have mentioned elsewhere my first meeting with Westmoreland when he was a lieutenant colonel commanding an artillery battalion on the battlefield of Gela, Sicily. I had renewed acquaintance with him in Korea, where he was an airborne brigade commander. When I became Army Chief of Staff I selected him to serve as Secretary of the General Staff, a traditional stepping stone to senior rank. After he had spent about two years in that position I reluctantly released him to command my old division, the 101st Airborne. Later he was Superintendent of West Point, and then, as a three star general, he went to Vietnam as Harkins' deputy. He succeeded Harkins shortly before my arrival as Ambassador, and I had the pleasure of pinning on his fourth star in August.

As for Bill Sullivan, I had observed his alertness, initiative, and ability during my days as Military Representative of President Kennedy. Hence,

315

when President Johnson indicated that I could have anyone in Washington for my Saigon staff, I put him high on the list of those whom I desired from State. Unfortunately from my point of view, I was allowed to enjoy his services only for a few months as he was soon offered the ambassadorship to Laos, and I could interpose no objection to this merited promotion.

A second asset was the fact that I had a reasonably clear understanding of the American objectives in Southeast Asia and was deeply convinced of their soundness. It is an enormous advantage for a missionary to be a true believer, and I was. Unhappily, during the Johnson Administration, there were many supporters of the President in key positions related to the Vietnam policy who were not true believers, and both the individuals and the policy suffered from that fact.

Finally, to reinforce my position in Saigon President Johnson had given me an unusually broad grant of authority. In addition to the usual duties of an Ambassador, the President specifically charged me with responsibility for the whole military effort in South Vietnam and authorized the degree of command and control which I might consider appropriate. This directive might have caused trouble as it could be interpreted to conflict with the responsibilities of Commander in Chief, Pacific (CINCPAC), Admiral Sharp and the Joint Chiefs of Staff for the conduct of military operations, and thus would have put General Westmoreland in the unhappy position of having two military masters. Actually, it produced none of these effects. In Washington and Honolulu, I had frank discussions of the directive with the Joint Chiefs of Staff and with Admiral Sharp, then with General Westmoreland in Saigon. I assured them that I had no intention of getting into MAC/V's day-to-day business. However, I would expect Westmoreland to clear with me all policy cables going back to Washington through military channels. If I concurred, all well and good; if I did not, I would report my views to Washington through State channels and so inform CINCPAC (Sharp) and the Joint Chiefs of Staff. Largely because the parties involved were reasonable people, this arrangement worked well, although I would not defend the propriety of the arrangement as a matter of organizational principle. But at the outset of my ambassadorial stint, it gave me a feeling of confidence to alight in Saigon with such a paper in my pocket.

As our party arrived on the scene, we might well have asked ourselves, as I asked myself in later times, how our mission fitted into the stream of events which had arisen out of the Geneva Accords in 1954, and how our immediate efforts might affect the subsequent course of history in Southeast Asia. The hostilities going on since the 1954 Accords grew out of a conflict of international objectives: those of the Communist alliance formed by the Vietcong and North Vietnam in the forefront with Red China and the USSR in the background, bent upon unifying both Vietnams in a single

Communist state and eradicating American influence in Southeast Asia; those of South Vietnam and the United States, determined to repel the aggression from the North, to defend the principle of self-determination for South Vietnam, and to restore peace and stability to Southeast Asia. Since 1954, both sides had adhered stubbornly to their respective objectives without essential change, although both had made repeated changes in the politico-military strategy by which they pursued them.

In 1954 and subsequently, Ho Chi Minh undertook to gain the Communist objectives by means of political subversion conducted by cadres of trained Communist organizers and supported by supplies of arms left behind at the time of the regrouping of the population north and south of the seventeenth parallel under the terms of the Geneva Accords. President Eisenhower had responded to this strategy by giving support to the government of President Diem despite its inauspicious prospects for the purpose of "developing and maintaining a strong viable state capable of resisting attempted subversion or aggression through military means."

Although at the outset Diem looked like a frail champion with little chance of overcoming the dragons in his path, he turned out so well that, by 1959, the North had despaired of overcoming him by subversive means alone. Ho Chi Minh was obliged to make a drastic change in his strategy, the passage to a War of National Liberation supported by a massive infiltration of armed men and military equipment into South Vietnam. As noted elsewhere, President Kennedy countered this act of Communist escalation with the programs agreed upon following the Taylor-Rostow mission of 1961 which were succeeding reasonably well until the events leading to the overthrow of Diem. Hanoi, enormously encouraged by Diem's fall and the evidence of critical internal weakness in South Vietnam, initiated an all-out effort to exploit these favorable circumstances in the hope of administering a *coup de grâce* to the weakened state in the south. My colleagues and I arrived on this scene in the summer of 1964 with the task of repelling this threat and of restoring enough stability in South Vietnam to weather the storm and eventually pass to a counteroffensive.

In accordance with the prevailing views in Washington, my instructions were to place the initial emphasis on stabilizing the government as a preliminary to any military action against the North. The government which we inherited was that of General Khanh, the Chairman of the Military Revolutionary Council, whose principal assistants were four generals, Tran Thien Khiem, Do Mau, Pham Xuan Chieu, and Nguyen Van Thieu. General "Big" Minh was the Chief of State, but he had had no real authority since the seizure of power by Khanh.

My first efforts after settling into place were directed at strengthening the American organization in Saigon and then encouraging Khanh to set up a counterpart with which we could mesh our activities. Our part was easy. We accomplished it on the afternoon of my arrival by formally establishing a mission council chaired by the Ambassador and composed of the chiefs of the various mission components and General Westmoreland. It met at least once a week as a miniature National Security Council advisory to the Ambassador in the same way that the National Security Council in Washington is advisory to the President. Throughout my tenure, this body dealt with all substantive matters of interest to more than one component of the mission and made recommendations regarding them to the Ambassador. It was understood that any member might appeal to Washington any decision I made with which he disagreed, but this contingency arose only once. As I remember, the issue involved the desirability of introducing public television into South Vietnam to improve the ability of the government to communicate with the public. This action was favored by all but one member who felt that substantial expenditures for TV were incompatible with an appropriate wartime austerity.

To get the Vietnamese organized in a similar way took several weeks, but eventually General Khanh formed a Vietnamese National Security Council, which provided a weekly forum for joint discussion and consultation with the Americans. In practice, I always tried to reach prior agreement in private with Khanh and his successors on controversial matters before the joint meeting and thus avoided sharp debates in plenary sessions.

A primary purpose in these early days was to establish close relations with the "American boy," General Khanh. Having demonstrated our support for him the previous March and having exchanged friendly greetings with him by cable after the announcement of my appointment as Ambassador, I had anticipated no particular difficulty in working with him. However, I soon learned that he harbored a deep suspicion of me because of my well-publicized tennis matches with General "Big" Minh on previous visits. Although Minh now had little power, he was Khanh's nominal superior and the two were constantly sniping at one another, thereby creating a crossfire to which I was soon exposed. While I found Minh far more likeable and a much less complicated personality than Khanh, the latter was far more astute and enterprising and, hence, appeared to offer greater hope of providing some of the leadership which the country so badly needed. I tried conscientiously to mediate some of the differences between the two, whose mutual hostility typified the tragic factionalism which plagued the entire country, but I achieved no enduring success. I discovered early that there was no way to translate directly into Vietnamese or French Ben Franklin's saying about hanging together or hanging separately.

The most dramatic event of the summer was the Tonkin Gulf incident in early August when North Vietnamese PT boats attacked U.S. destroyers in international waters off the coast of North Vietnam. Two things surprised me in this incident, first, Hanoi's error of judgment in attacking our naval forces on the high seas apparently without expecting a counterblow, and, second, the failure of the United States to retaliate immediately after the

318

first attack. If Hanoi had not obligingly repeated the attack two days later and thereby provoked our belated response, American prestige in Asia and especially in Vietnam would have been seriously damaged. As it was, our South Vietnamese allies were greatly encouraged by the subsequent American air attacks on North Vietnamese targets and Khanh urged tit-for-tat bombings as a regular response to Hanoi's provocations. I was left wondering about the soundness of judgment of the decision-makers in Hanoi, whose imprudent actions reminded me of Khrushchev's rashness in introducing missiles into Cuba and worried me for similar reasons. One likes to feel able to count on the rationality and good sense of a dangerous opponent.

About this time, Khanh broached a plan that he had been drawing up for restructuring the Vietnamese government. While his alleged reason was to achieve greater efficiency, it was readily apparent that one reason, perhaps the prime one, was to reorganize Minh out of a job. Another was probably to take advantage of the excitement over the Tonkin Gulf affair to tighten his political controls. At any rate, in mid-August he showed me a draft of the so-called Vung Tau Charter which was to serve as the basis for the new government. It eliminated Minh's position as Chief of State and established an all-powerful President as chief executive, to be elected by a Military Revolutionary Council composed of the senior generals. Obviously the President was to be Khanh. Although there was also to be a legislative assembly, most of the members were to be appointed by the generals and the executive branch was to have concurrent authority to legislate by decree.

Without going into the specific merits of his plan, I expressed concern to Khanh over the renewed instability which would result from such sweeping governmental changes with no visible promise of compensating gains. But if he were determined to pursue this course, I urged him to explain what he was about to the individuals and political groups whose support he would need and then do the same for the general public. It was important for him to make clear that there was a national emergency which justified such a concentration of power in the President.

Unfortunately, Khanh did nothing or at least not enough to conform to my suggestions. Once he became aware of what was taking place, Minh was enraged at this move to oust him. The old troublemaker, Tri Quang, with his Buddhist cohorts and student allies who for some time had been watching Khanh with suspicion, condemned Khanh's grab for power as a threat to them and as an indefinite postponement of civilian government. Incited by Tri Quang and encouraged by Khanh's failure to act against recent student demonstrations against the French Embassy, the students began to demonstrate against him. Although the pressure from this Buddhist-student coalition did not look very formidable, Khanh soon collapsed. On August 24 he sent a messenger in the middle of the night to

319

bring Alex Johnson and me secretly to his office at the General Staff Head-quarters. There he informed us of his intention to yield to his critics and to repeal the Vung Tau Charter. Johnson and I urged against this capitulation, pointing out Tri Quang's known voracity for power and the likelihood that this humiliating concession would only generate new demands. But Khanh would not be moved; after two stormy sessions with the Military Revolutionary Council, whose members seemed to feel the stigma of defeat more than he, Khanh withdrew the charter on August 27. Not only were many of his fellow generals humiliated by this action, but they resented the fact that it had not been approved in advance by the full Council. A first-class row ensued, in the course of which Khanh felt obliged to offer to resign. However, the offer was declined, probably because of Khanh's reputation for being the "American boy."

The consequences of the Vung Tau Charter incident were numerous and important. Khanh lost face by yielding to Tri Quang, who in turn gained in prestige and in potential for harm. Khanh's hold on the generals was weakened and with it his base of power. To fill the void created by the revocation of the Charter he was obliged to improvise an interim government, which in turn would phase into a provisional government, eventually evolving into a constitutional civilian government. A triumvirate consisting of Minh, Khiem, and Khanh would supervise this metamorphosis, with Minh acting as Chief of State and Khanh as the Prime Minister. Additionally, Khanh proposed to establish a so-called High National Council of elders to design first the provisional, then the constitutional, government. I suspected that Khanh hoped to bewilder or perhaps to lose his adversaries in this political maze which he was setting up. Whatever his motive, I acquired my second government since arriving two months before and developed a growing conviction that Khanh was far from being the strong man we had been seeking to lead South Vietnam out of the wilderness.

Before leaving Washington, I had obtained agreement from President Johnson that I should return to Washington approximately every other month to report on the situation and to meet in person with him and his principal advisers. I made my first return trip early in September and found our leaders as dubious as I about Khanh's capacity for leadership. In the discussions about what to expect from our Vietnamese allies, I pointed out that the recent fracas over the Charter gave us a pretty good understanding of how little progress in administrative improvement we could expect in the short run. I estimated that any new government which Khanh might contrive out of the wreckage of the Vung Tau Charter would be strained to conduct even a holding operation against the Vietcong and would need considerable luck and strenuous American efforts to achieve a modicum of progress in rehabilitating the provinces. It certainly could never carry out Khanh's ambitious plans for mobilizing the national resources. At best, Khanh and his associates might be able to improve the security in the zone around Saigon, maintain order in the cities, and steer an unsteady political course over the next few months. But I viewed it unlikely that they could ever establish that solid political and military base which we all wanted in South Vietnam before taking military action against the North. If they could not, we would be faced with the question of whether we could wait for the desired stability before taking action. I was inclined to think that we could not wait beyond December 1, as we were playing a losing game which had to be changed shortly before the political situation fell apart again.

The senior officials in Washington accepted my pessimistic evaluation of the situation with little debate, but they were not ready to make hard decisions at the moment. There was a wide range of opinions as to the proper timing of either tit-for-tat reprisal bombing or the initiation of a sustained air campaign to induce Hanoi to cease its aggression against the South. In the end, the only decisions of importance reached were a resumption of some of the clandestine naval activities along the North Vietnamese coast which had been suspended following the Tonkin Gulf incident, and an expansion of antiinfiltration measures. The consensus remained that the emphasis should be placed on actions to strengthen the political and economic structure of the Vietnamese government and that air operations against North Vietnam should await success in these nonmilitary fields.

One of the advantages of my trip was the opportunity it afforded to brief Congressional leaders whom I found surprisingly patient and uncritical in view of the recent turn of events. I appealed to the party leaders to restrain congressmen from visiting Vietnam in these troubled times and, in exchange for such restraint, I promised to return frequently to report personally on the situation to the appropriate committees. To my surprise, they agreed to this procedure and adhered to it faithfully during my tenure as Ambassador.

On my return flight I was greeted in Honolulu with the unwelcome news of an attempted coup in Saigon led by a relatively obscure Brigadier General Lam Van Phat. Fortunately, it fizzled almost at once, and Phat went into hiding without leaving behind clear evidence of his motivation or backing. At least two things accounted for his failure: the leak of his plans into the rumor stream and the absence of any suggestion of American encouragement. If one counts the Vung Tau Charter episode, this was the second time that the presumption of American support had saved Khanh, but I was becoming convinced that he was not worth saving much longer.

Upon returning to Saigon, I began a round of meetings with Vietnamese officials, military leaders, and newspaper editors for the purpose of describing to them how recent events in South Vietnam looked in the United States and the dismay felt there by their staunchest friends. The attempted coup by Phat was an added blow to American support and understanding which, I warned, could not survive much more of the disunity which was crippling our joint effort. My hearers seemed to understand the points made, but I must say that I saw little change in their subsequent conduct.

However, the Phat episode did have a chastening effect on Khanh, who was rapidly losing the cockiness that normally characterized him. His tribulations since the Vung Tau Charter affair seemed to increase his suspicions, always deep, of his Vietnamese associates and particularly of the Americans. He began leaking anti-American accusations to the press, alleging that the United States had been behind Phat's coup and was also responsible for a very ugly revolt of some of the Montagnard tribes which took place in the Darlac-Quang Duc area in mid-September.

Khanh's political base was shaky and he knew it. It consisted of a loose coalition represented on one flank by Tri Quang and his Buddhist faction and on the other flank by the so-called Young Turk officers headed by Generals Thieu and Ky, who had come to his rescue during the recent coup. He knew Tri Quang to be a political opportunist and an unreliable ally, and he recognized that Buddhist support was offset by the hostility of other groups, including most of the Catholics and an important element of the officer corps. For the moment, however, his support in the army seemed adequate because of the continuing impression of American backing and the absence of a strong rival. With all these causes for worry, it was not surprising that Khanh became lonely, isolated, fearful for his life, and apparently anxious to find some graceful way out of his job. Nor was it surprising that American confidence declined in his ability to carry on until the installation of the provisional government which the High National Council was designing.

As always, the question was: If not Khanh, who? This time there was again the possibility that "Big" Minh might do. He had been behaving quite well and had done some very useful work in preparing the provisional government. The hope of getting it established and working by the end of the year rested largely on him, and it was just possible that he might be able to pull it off. In any case, as I reported to Washington, if we were to adhere to the objectives of our Vietnam policy—an independent Vietnam free from attack—in spite of discouragement, we must hang on, keep up the war effort, and play for the breaks. This meant that we should support and expedite the work of setting up the provisional government, be ready to switch our support from Khanh to Minh if the former stumbled again, and continue to prepare for an air offensive against North Vietnam by the end of 1964.

In setting up the High National Council, Khanh had given Minh the task of selecting its members and of putting the Council to work at drafting a charter for the provisional government. I was surprised that Khanh had given this responsibility to his rival unless Khanh did not expect much to come from the Council. As it got under way in early October, it soon became clear that the Council was in for trouble. Its members, all selected by

Minh, soon indicated a preference for a Gaullist form of government with an all-powerful Chief of State, the position which Minh expected to hold. They wanted a civilian Prime Minister and hoped, nervously, that Khanh would be willing to step down to the position of Defense Minister or Commander in Chief. These pro-Minh machinations were foolhardy since Khanh, who controlled all or most of the military forces, would never allow such an accretion of power by Minh, and we Americans would be loath to encourage it because of our doubt concerning Minh's ability to handle such a job. Hence, we used all our influence on the High National Council to get it to deflate the authority which was proposed for the Chief of State, and we urged Khanh to accept the position of Commander in Chief, which he seemed inclined to do. In the end, the draft constitution was revised as we had suggested but Minh declined to be Chief of State, ostensibly because under the governmental charter he could not hold the position as an active officer in uniform. A respected if incompetent elder statesman, Pham Khac Suu, was selected Chief of State and a former Saigon mayor, Tran Van Huong, became Prime Minister. Khanh agreed to become Commander in Chief with the understanding that the Army would keep aloof from domestic politics.

Huong was very highly regarded by most of us who knew him. A former school teacher and well-known *Sudiste* (native of Cochin-China), he was widely respected for his integrity and courage but was handicapped by poor health and by a highly developed bump of stubbornness. In spite of these liabilities, I came to regard him quite highly during the tribulations which brought us closely together in the subsequent months.

That Huong could expect trouble was soon demonstrated by his difficulty in forming a government. Many of the men he sought were reluctant to sever their business connections to enter a government with such uncertain life expectancy. His difficulty was augmented by the fact that the Tri Quang Buddhists were dead set against him from the start and brought pressure on cabinet prospects to decline office under him. The shadow of Khanh and the generals, in spite of their protestations of sincerity about their withdrawal from politics, hung over the new government and did little to brighten its attractiveness to new leadership. Nevertheless, Huong eventually filled out his cabinet slate with well-intentioned though inexperienced ministers, and his government got off to a slow, uninspiring start to the sound of Buddhist sniping from the pagodas. The consensus of the Embassy council was that it would take three to four months before we could expect anything like an effective government—if Huong could last that long.

Early on the morning of November 1, I was awakened with the news that the American air base at Bien Hoa, fifteen miles northeast of Saigon, had received a heavy mortar attack which had caused numerous casualties and considerable damage to planes. When it was fully light, I helicoptered to the field in a heavy rain to inspect the scene of the incident. The vicinity of the main runway had been sprayed with mortar shells fired from positions a few thousands yards away near the bank of one of the many streams which intersect the area. Apparently during the night, a Vietcong detachment had come down the stream in sampans, bringing their mortars to a previously reconnoitered site on the shore. Judging by the accuracy of their fire, I guessed that the exact range to targets on the airfield had probably been paced off by Vietcong posing as local farmers. After firing their shells with maximum speed, the gunners had reloaded their equipment on their boats and disappeared in a matter of minutes without ever being seen. Fortunately, loss of life on the field was light, but a squadron of B-57 light bombers stationed there was virtually wiped out.

The attack on Bien Hoa marked a turning point in Vietcong tactics. While small attacks on American personnel and equipment had not been uncommon in the past, they had almost always occurred under circumstances related to the day-to-day operations in which Americans participated as advisers and took their chances along with the South Vietnamese whom they were advising. In this case, a major U.S. installation was singled out as the target for deliberate attack in a way that suggested analogies with the Tonkin Gulf incident. The principal differences were that at Bien Hoa the enemy were the Vietcong rather than the North Vietnamese; the attack took place on land rather than at sea; and the U.S. forces suffered losses without being able to exact a toll from the enemy who escaped unscathed. I felt that such a significant change in Vietcong tactics, undoubtedly instigated and approved by Hanoi, warranted immediate retaliation against North Vietnamese targets to show that we would not put up with such tactics without making Hanoi pay an appropriate price.

With the unanimous support of my colleagues, I fired off a recommendation to Washington for immediate retaliation of the kind which we had often discussed with Washington in the abstract. But this time the abstraction was an unwelcome reality on the eve of the American presidential election, an event that Hanoi had not overlooked in timing this affair. Without mentioning this political factor, the Washington response was negative, arguing that it was impossible to portray the Bien Hoa attack to the public in a convincing way as a significant act of enemy escalation warranting a violent reaction from us. A second point, more valid in my judgment, was the undesirability of making so significant a change of tactics in retaliation for purely American losses. But while rejecting retaliatory action, Washington asked for comment on the desirability of assigning American ground troops to the defense of our principal bases, Bien Hoa, Da Nang, and Nha Trang, reminding us that we might expect a hostile reaction against such targets if we ever decided to attack the north. I replied quickly that, at least for the time being, we did not want U.S. ground forces for the close defense of bases unless needed as an accompaniment of a program of air pressure against North Vietnam. I was greatly surprised that the offer of ground troops was made so casually, as it seemed to me a much more difficult decision than the use of our air forces against military targets north of the seventeenth parallel.

While disapproving our proposal for retaliatory action, Washington did not reject the general scenario which we advocated for planning our immediate future: several months of intensive effort with the Huong government to achieve a few modest goals in improved governmental performance in the fields of organization, greater mobilization of manpower, police expansion, and rural pacification, accompanied by preparations for more ambitious projects which might include air attacks against North Vietnam. We took February 1, 1965, as the target date for the completion of this phase, although I warned Washington that I was doubtful of its feasibility unless we found some way in the immediate future for reviving the flagging Vietnamese morale and lifting the chronically low spirits of the Huong government. The only means we could conceive for this purpose was the long-debated, long-delayed use of air power against targets in North Vietnam and the infiltration routes in the Laotian corridor.

My pessimistic evaluation of the future of the Huong government was unhappily justified by the events of November. Throughout the month, Huong was in rough weather in both a political and meterological sense. Demonstrations by minority groups, instigated by Tri Quang and possibly by Khanh, kept Saigon in a state of political unrest. Khanh was maneuvering to find ways to free himself as Commander in Chief from subordination to the Prime Minister. At one time he suggested to me that it would be a good idea for the armed forces to report directly to Chief of State Suu in the way the Japanese armed forces had reported to the Emperor prior to World War II. Suu himself repeatedly displayed signs of disloyalty to his subordinate, Huong, and of sympathy for the minority groups who were bedeviling his government.

To add to Huong's problems, a mighty typhoon hit the Da Nang area causing disastrous damage and creating thousands of refugees. Shortly after it struck, Huong and I traveled together through the ravaged area, checking the progress of the clean-up which was taking place under the direction of the local officials. I was surprised at how well they rose to the crisis in a display of unity and team play which I would have liked to carry back to Saigon. Washington, impressed by the extent of the disaster, inquired if we needed American logistical troops to help in flood relief, supported by U.S. combat forces to give them local protection. This was essentially the proposal which I had made to President Kennedy in the wake of the Mekong Delta flood in 1961 and which he had not approved. This time I declined the proposal on about the same grounds as Kennedy had —the lack of clear need justifying a course of action difficult to control or to reverse.

The bearer of increasingly bad tidings, I returned again to Washington at the end of November. In my round of discussions with the President and his principal advisers I tried to summarize my impression of the situation in Vietnam a year after the Diem coup. The record of that year was not encouraging. The counterinsurgency program was bogged down except immediately around Saigon where the special resources accorded the so-called Hop Tac pacification plan for the capital area had permitted some limited progress. While the Vietnamese army had increased in strength and competence, the Vietcong seemed able to replace their losses as needed from local recruiting and increased infiltration from the North. Their operations in the northern provinces of South Vietnam had expanded and had achieved significant gains in several provinces such as Quang Ngai and Binh Dinh. In this area, there was serious danger that they might drive a salient reaching to the sea. In their offensives the enemy were using three new, or newly expanded, tactics: stand-off mortar fire against important targets as in the attack on Bien Hoa, economic strangulation of limited areas by guerrilla interdiction of the roads, and stepped-up infiltration from the north. These tactics employed against the background of political deterioration were a serious menace to the rehabilitation program in the provinces and to the safety of important military bases.

There was little need to expatiate in Washington on the dismal governmental picture in Saigon. While Huong was showing commendable courage and had an able colleague in Deputy Prime Minister Vien, his government was highly vulnerable to the malcontents and might collapse momentarily. Without an effective central government with which to mesh, the U.S. effort was a spinning flywheel, unable to transmit impulsion. In the provinces, the weaknesses of the capital were compounded by the dearth of competent provincial chiefs and supporting administrative personnel to carry forward the complex programs involved in successful pacification.

In essence, the record of the last year showed that the enemy drive for victory in exploitation of Diem's overthrow was succeeding and that we Americans were playing a losing game which it was high time to change before it was too late. We had to find ways to establish some minimum level of government which could at least communicate with its own people, maintain order in the cities, protect vital military bases, and gear its efforts with those of the United States. While striving to attain this modest but difficult objective, we needed to prepare plans to drive Hanoi out of its supporting role to the guerrilla insurgency.

The preparation of such plans with the South Vietnamese could have several valuable ancillary effects. It would encourage their leaders to learn that at last the United States was willing to contemplate military action against North Vietnam, the source of all their miseries of recent years. Additionally, we could make the actual initiation of such a program conditional on improved performance by the South Vietnamese in fields where past performance had been poor, in such matters as the replacement of incompetent generals and province chiefs, the improvement of mobilization procedures, and better protection of American nationals and installations. Also, it would provide an opportunity to get agreement on alternative ways of ending the war, a sensitive matter never yet broached in a serious way because of the ever-shifting Vietnamese leadership.

My audience in Washington was generally sympathetic to such ideas but still not ready to bite the bullet and face the inevitability of either taking military action against North Vietnam or running the very real risk of failing disastrously in Southeast Asia. No one was yet prepared to abandon the dictum that stable government in the south must precede military action in the north despite the improbability of ever getting stable government without the lift to the national spirit which military action against the homeland of the enemy could provide. But I did return to Saigon with authority to plan military action against the North with our allies but with the understanding that the United States was not committed to execute the plans.

I have often been asked why, in view of the demonstrated inability of the South Vietnamese to pull themselves together in this critical period and cease the suicidal feuding among themselves with the enemy on their doorstep, I did not recommend that we give up and go home. We had made an honest effort to save this little country and had found it apparently incapable of self-defense and self-government. No one could charge us with failing an ally who seemed determined to fail himself.

In response to this valid question, I must in honesty reply that it never occurred to me to recommend withdrawal. There were too many good reasons for not thinking about retreat. In the first place, we had not exhausted our alternatives or made inroads into our vast resources. We could still try a number of things which might supply the new ingredient we were seeking to reverse the adverse trend. There were many ways in which we might make use of American air and ground forces in North Vietnam, in South Vietnam, or in the cross-border sanctuaries. We could use our Navy to blockade the enemy coasts. We could make changes in our relationships with our South Vietnamese allies; conceivably we could take operational command of their armed forces and even control of all their war-making resources. Some of these possibilities had serious objections, but others should certainly have been tried before we thought of quitting.

Furthermore, we had every reason to keep up the American will to persist in Saigon following the expression of national determination after the Tonkin Gulf affair. Had not the Congress declared with only two dissenting votes that "The U.S. regards as vital to its national interest and to world peace the maintenance of international peace and security in Southeast Asia"? With this authoritative confirmation of the essentiality of our mission, no senior official could in conscience harbor thoughts of retreat.

Then there was the memory of Diem to haunt those who were aware of the circumstances of his downfall. By our complicity we Americans were responsible to some degree for the plight in which the South Vietnamese found themselves. That thought gave pause to any consideration of abandoning them.

Finally there was concern over the safety of Americans, particularly of our dependents, if a wave of violent anti-Americanism swept the country. Early in the year I had made a study of the problem of evacuating our people under such conditions and was sobered by the dangers to which they would be exposed. At that time we had no large American units to protect our dependents who generally lived intermingled with the local population. If the American government suddenly withdrew support from South Vietnam and ordered our people home, we could expect an outraged feeling of betrayal on the part of our allies which could express itself in many ways endangering our citizens. Under such circumstances I certainly did not aspire to the role of an American Xenophon leading our citizens, harried by our late allies, in a retreat to the evacuation ports and airfields of Vietnam.

CHAPTER 26

Playing a Losing Game

On my return to Saigon on December 6, I conducted another round of talks with senior Vietnamese, beginning with Huong, Vien, and Khanh. Only to these three did I communicate the good news, as they viewed it, of the authorization to initiate joint planning for air action against North Vietnam, and I did so only after another blunt talk about the unfavorable Washington view of the recent events in Vietnam. While the United States government was prepared to render any help necessary which could be effectively used, I pointed out that it regarded political stability as essential to any further commitments beyond present levels—indeed, to the maintenance of existing levels. To be sure that my words of warning reached deeply into the ranks of the military, General Westmoreland gave a dinner at his house to which he invited a score of senior generals whom I exhorted with all the eloquence I could muster to rally around the Huong government in a display of national unity. Otherwise, there was no counting indefinitely on American aid.

General Khanh was always a source of concern, but now he had become increasingly so because of the unstable relations between him and the other generals. He was often too clever for his own good and had alienated his colleagues by his sudden turns and dodges. He was clearly not succeeding in unifying the armed forces, the primary task he claimed to have set for himself upon assuming the position of Commander in Chief. But he was a skillful if unscrupulous croupier in the political roulette as played in Saigon, one who knew how to give the wheel a new spin whenever the ball seemed about to settle on the wrong number. He gave it such a spin on December 20 when he induced his generals to abolish the High National Council and to jail many of its members.

Since the formation of the High National Council, many of the generals, particularly the so-called Young Turks, had developed a number of griev-

329

ances against it. In the first place, it symbolized the movement toward civilian government, a goal to which many gave lip service but which they inwardly distrusted and resented. Khanh was ever mindful that its members had been picked by General Minh, and they were consequently suspect. But the immediate issue which caused the eruption was the refusal of the High National Council to support the mandatory retirement of all officers of twenty-five or more years of service, a measure by which the Young Turks hoped to eliminate some of their superiors. In particular, Khanh wanted to get rid of the four "Dalat generals" who since early in the year had been enjoying something like house arrest in that pleasant mountain resort. The High National Council, showing more boldness than judgment, curtly rejected the proposal in a way which enraged the young generals. They responded by bursting in upon Chief of State Suu and Prime Minister Huong in the middle of the night of December 19–20 and informing them that the armed forces had dissolved the Council.

Alex Johnson and I had had no warning of the generals' intentions and had to get the facts the next morning by calling on Huong whom we found clearly shaken by the violence of his nocturnal visitors. I then telephoned Khanh to obtain his version but he preferred to send four emissaries, Generals Thieu, Ky, Thi, and Admiral Cang, to face the music which he expected me to provide. Prior to their arrival, Johnson and I compared views on the significance of this event and on the way to receive our visitors. While the High National Council had no great value as a political institution, the action of the generals in dissolving it was quite serious for other reasons. As the deed of men who only a few days ago at General Westmoreland's dinner had joined in pledging themselves to work for Vietnamese unity and to support the Huong government, it was a flagrant violation of their assurances. It was a reversal of the well-publicized plans to "civilianize" the government and thus was sure to frighten away qualified civilians from participation in this or any future government. Finally, it was a fatal blow to Huong, who could hardly be expected to display much leadership and initiative while in constant fear of violent military intervention.

Alex and I saw the situation alike and I decided to deal with the representatives of the generals with calculated asperity. As they entered my office with shame-faced grins, we greeted them coldly, offered them seats, and asked for an explanation of the recent events. As they had little to add to what we already knew, I then launched into what they later described as a rude tirade over the irresponsible behavior of the generals at this critical time in the history of their country, behavior which alienated their American friends who were indispensable to its salvation. Devoted as we were to the cause of Vietnam, I assured them that we were not prepared to take more of this suicidal nonsense. I stated that I regretted having to speak in this way, but they would have to excuse an older man who was deeply committed to the liberation of their country and who was dismayed by the unnecessary dangers to which their conduct exposed the common cause. They had little to say at the time, and upon breaking up, we shook hands in apparent amity. However, after reporting back to Khanh, and, I suspect, instigated by him, they let it be known publicly that I had insulted them and the armed forces by treating them like American puppets.

For the next few weeks, there was a three-cornered conflict, most of it unfortunately public: the Huong government versus the generals, the generals versus the American Ambassador, and the Buddhists versus the government and the Ambassador. On the first front, I urged Huong to drive a hard bargain with the military: to refuse to recognize the validity of their abolition of the High National Council, to insist on the release of the prisoners taken at the time, and to make a public declaration of military support for his government. Huong had considerable leverage through the threat of resignation which would have forced the military to take responsibility for their actions, something they were not ready to do.

I kept my feud with the generals one-sided by holding my peace and leaving the public acrimony to them. Khanh we found belligerent and completely unrepentant when Alex Johnson and I called on him the next morning. He accepted responsibility for the action of the generals, which he said was taken to "limit the deterioration of the situation," and stated that the armed forces were again ready to retire to the political wings. I recalled our recent conversations after my return from Washington regarding the importance of governmental stability and the American need for a loyal ally with whom we could work in mutual trust. I told Khanh that frankly I had lost confidence in him as such an ally. While his continuation in office as Commander in Chief was an internal Vietnamese decision, I gave him my personal view that his withdrawal from the public scene would be good for the common cause.

Khanh quickly grasped the possibility of utilizing this dispute with the Americans to strengthen his hold on the generals, since it allowed him to pose as a valiant nationalist resisting the puppet role which an arrogant American ally wished to impose. He spread abroad the details of the quarrel which, in the interest of both our countries, should have been kept quiet, and in so doing, he received considerable support for his position from the American press in Saigon. But while achieving some short term success in rallying the generals, Khanh necessarily revealed to them that he was no longer the "American boy," and hence he lost the immunity from attack by his rivals which his privileged position with the Americans had formerly conferred. In the circumstances, I felt that we had only to wait in silence until the other generals cooled off and had time to reflect, feeling sure that eventually Khanh would fall to his colleagues.

During the remainder of December and the first week of January, the political situation remained stalemated. A break occurred on January 9 when, after much parleying, the government and the generals came to a compromise agreement which they announced in a joint communiqué. The High National Council was left in the limbo to which the generals had consigned it, but the prisoners taken at the time were released from arrest, and the armed forces agreed to provide four ministers to the Huong cabinet as a token of their support. Chief of State Suu held a reconciliation tea-party for all the recent contestants and Khanh and I were photographed amicably shaking hands. However, Khanh let it be known to Alex Johnson that he still viewed the armed forces as the true guardians of the nation's anti-Communist spirit with responsibility to intervene if any undesirable elements worked their way into government.

It would be pleasant to be able to report that we all lived happily ever after following the tea party, but unfortunately such was not the case. On January 19, just before the presentation to Chief of State Suu of the new cabinet, Khanh, speaking for the Armed Forces Council, called everything off and threw the entire matter of cabinet membership into renegotiation. The generals had decided that, whereas they were contributing four of their best officers to the cabinet, Huong had not purged any of the ministers whom they viewed unfavorably. After a great scurrying about Huong agreed to replace two of his civilian ministers, and the new cabinet was presented to Suu on the following day amid sighs of relief.

One day in early January I was sitting at my desk at the Embassy when I received a long distance call from Bob and Ethel Kennedy in Washington. It was a particularly poor connection with the conversation constantly interrupted with squeals and squawks. Through the static I gathered that they were telling me about the birth and christening of a son whose arrival I had known to be imminent. Pleased but somewhat perplexed that they were taking this trouble to inform me, I mumbled conventional congratulations and hung up still mystified. Almost at once, a local pressman called to ask my comment on having had Matthew Maxwell Taylor Kennedy named after me. Then the enormity of my apparent ingratitude to Bobby and Ethel hit me like a bombshell, from which I revived to curse alternately my bad "artillery ears" and the quality of the trans-Pacific telephone service.

The distracting politicking, so detrimental to the direction of the war, had been punctuated by the Vietcong bombing of the Brink officer billet in Saigon on Christmas Eve. It happened as I was meeting Bob Hope and a troupe of his entertainers who had just arrived at the Ton San Nhut airport. When Bob reached his hotel, which was just across the street from the Brink, he found the square lit up by towering flames rising from the billet and filled with police, soldiers, and fire equipment. He commented imperturbably, "I never had such a warm reception in my life."

While the loss of life was light, the bombing of the Brink, like the attack on Bien Hoa, was an act of terror directed at Americans which, I thought, required quick retaliation. I cabled to Washington a recommendation for an immediate air strike against an appropriate North Vietnamese target, but, as in the case of Bien Hoa, my request was rejected for reasons which seemed quite persuasive in Washington but not in Saigon. There was the old argument that the political turmoil in Saigon made retaliation unwise. Then there was a question as to the adequacy of the evidence that the Vietcong were the perpetrators of the bombing. While the radio of the National Liberation Front had loudly claimed the credit, maybe they were bragging. Finally, President Johnson remained dead set against widening the war while dependents were in South Vietnam.

Other points in the cable further revealed the Washington state of mind. There was doubt expressed as to whether we had done enough to protect our installations and intimations that perhaps our carelessness had invited terrorist attacks. It was evident that our repeated recommendations for air attacks against North Vietnam were causing no joy at home, where they were regarded in some quarters as an effort to find a military panacea to avoid the drudgery incidental to making progress by more plodding means. I knew from discussions in Washington that the President himself could not understand why we had not been more successful in the conciliation of political groups and in the use of man-to-man appeals to bring together the leaders of the many minorities.

Although negative on the matter of air strikes, the cable again encouraged us to ask for American ground forces, particularly for Rangers and Special Forces who had particular aptitudes for counterinsurgency. I recognized this suggestion as a reflection of the President's conviction, which I shared, of the importance of the ground operations in South Vietnam over anything which could be accomplished by air power in North Vietnam. However, I felt that there was an important secondary role for the air campaign in supplementing and advancing our efforts in the South.

As the cable obviously reflected the President's views, Johnson, Westmoreland, and I put our heads together to draft the most convincing reply possible to the principal points raised. We reiterated our view of the seriousness of the deteriorating situation on all fronts in South Vietnam and forecast increasing anti-Americanism, further civil disorders, and possibly the eventual installation of a hostile government in Saigon unless we found a way to reverse the trend. We conceded the difficulty in finding short-term solutions for long-term problems grounded in historical causes of the remote past. We doubted that much could be accomplished with more advisers than the 30,000 already in Vietnam. We were against the introduction of American ground forces at this time for fear that their presence might lead the South Vietnamese to slacken their efforts. The Washington view that we should have American guards to protect all our people and establishments was not feasible when one calculated the troop requirement. To keep all Vietcong mortars out of range of one airfield like Bien Hoa would require about six American battalions of infantry, and we estimated that similar protection for all our facilities would demand over 75,000 troops.

We were a bit hurt by the implication that we had not been working hard enough on our local political contacts. Alex Johnson, with the authority of his long diplomatic experience, contributed the view to our reply that there was not a country in the world in which the United States representatives had closer communication with the government and the people. In Saigon we had over fifty Embassy officers for this purpose and in the provinces hundreds of civilians and military officers in daily contact with their Vietnamese counterparts. This was a far cry from the situation which I had found in 1961. While we would never have all the information we would like, more personnel was not the answer.

With this dearth of promising alternatives for the short run, we could only revert to our old recommendation, a program of graduated air strikes against North Vietnam. Among the advantages of such a program, I pointed out to the President that it would permit the evacuation of our dependents—something he had long wanted—without it looking like a retreat. If carried out simultaneously with air attacks on the North, it would have the appearance of clearing the decks for action and would encourage our allies, whereas otherwise it would frighten and dishearten them. Our cable produced no immediate modification of policy in Washington but did result in a directive to me to convey to Prime Minister Huong our readiness to resume the discussions, interrupted by the rumpus over the High National Council, of possible air reprisals for unusual acts of violence committed by the enemy.

But hardly had the message been delivered to Huong than the project was set back by another Khanh power play—fortunately his last. It had been no secret for some weeks that he was making common cause with Tri Quang and his Buddhists in undermining the Huong government. The Buddhists repeatedly demonstrated against Huong and me in Saigon, Da Nang, and Hue while the generals criticized Huong for his inability to maintain order although they themselves were its ultimate custodians. Possibly timing their action with my absence in Bangkok, on January 27, the Armed Forces Council withdrew confidence from Prime Minister Huong and charged Khanh with solving the resulting political crisis. At first Khanh seemed inclined to set himself up as a de Gaulle-like chief of state, but I passed the word to selected generals that the U.S. government had lost confidence in Khanh and could not work with him in such a capacity. Eventually, he was obliged to back away from his original plan; he contented himself with retaining Suu as Chief of State, and naming Jack Oanh, a Harvard-trained economist, Acting Prime Minister while he looked around for a prime ministerial candidate of some stature who would be amenable to his control.

As the American Mission viewed this new development, it amounted to a dangerous Khanh-Buddhist alliance which might eventually lead to an unfriendly government with which we could not work. Tri Quang's animosity had again been manifested in a series of anti-American activities. These had been particularly violent in the Hue area, where on January 23 a mob had burned the U.S. library, raising renewed concern in the Mission Council over the safety of American dependents.

Our political preoccupations were interrupted on February 7 by the Vietcong attack on the American base at Pleiku where eight Americans were killed, over a hundred wounded, and several aircraft destroyed or damaged. By good fortune, having been sent by the President in response to my suggestion of early January, McGeorge Bundy was visiting us at the time. Together we examined the reports from Pleiku, got the views of Alex Johnson and Westmoreland and then agreed to call Washington and recommend retaliatory air strikes. Telephoning from Westmoreland's command post, we got Deputy Secretary of Defense Cy Vance on the phone and presented our views as to the importance of retaliation and the recommended targets. He asked time to seek the necessary presidential approval which he obtained with surprising promptness. I hurried to Acting Prime Minister Oanh's house and obtained his concurrence in the strike. This celerity at both ends of the line and the preplanning of the military made possible a strike on that same day by forty-five U.S. Navy planes against military facilities in Dong Hoi just north of the Demilitarized Zone (DMZ). A second strike by twenty-four South Vietnamese aircraft was made on the following day against the Chap Le barracks in the same area. The inhibitions which had restrained the use of our air power against the enemy homeland were finally broken, and a new phase of the war had begun.

In the midst of dealing with the Pleiku incident, I received a letter from Bob Kennedy telling me that he detected efforts in Washington to make me the scapegoat for the deterioration of the situation in Vietnam and warning me that I had better protect my rear. Although deeply appreciative of his warning, I had no clear idea of what I could do about my rear if, indeed, it was threatened. It was quite natural that the Ambassador should be criticized, at least in anti-Administration circles, for the low ebb of our fortunes and the only way I knew to respond was to return to Washington to confront the critics as soon as I could feel easy about leaving Vietnam. It was perhaps surprising that the wolves had not been after me sooner. I was inclined to attribute my past immunity to the personal appearances I had made before the press and the Congress and the opportunity they afforded to explain what was happening and why. Now, with

335

events moving much more rapidly, the requirement for explanation at home had increased, but the urgency of the situation held me close to my post. As a consequence, I did not know until several years later that parts of the American press had interpreted our struggle with the generals and the Buddhists as the ill-advised efforts of missionaries of American-style government to impose a civilian regime prematurely against the will of the local military. Actually, whatever our other faults, the American mission was completely free of any doctrinaire political bias, and we would have supported any government which could have run the country reasonably well and cooperate effectively with us. Since the armed forces were the only component of Vietnamese society which could serve as a stabilizing force, we were thoroughly aware of the importance of having them either as participants or loyal supporters of any government. It was due largely to our urging that we had got four able generals into Huong's second cabinet in the hope that their presence would assure the backing of the Armed Forces Council. It was a good idea but it did not work because of Khanh's inveterate refusal to play on any team of which he was not the captain.

Often events seem to pile up in a logjam behind retarding obstacles and then rush forward in a torrent when the jam is suddenly broken. Such a torrent burst upon us in the weeks after Pleiku. Our first task was to evacuate our dependents within ten days in an orderly fashion and with minimum discomfort as I had promised the President. Concurrently, we had to adjust ourselves to a new government headed by Dr. Phan Huy Quat, who, after several other prospects had failed, succeeded in passing inspection both by the generals and the Buddhists and assumed the premiership. We Americans had known Quat fairly well from the time when he was Foreign Minister in Khanh's government the previous year. We rated him high in ability and intelligence but suspected him of being under the thumb of Tri Quang. Although his government was sure to be highly sensitive to the vicissitudes of military-Buddhist relations, we welcomed the opportunity to work with him and exploit the wave of hope in the south growing out of the recent air attacks on North Vietnam.

Another sudden development was the final undoing of Khanh. Hardly had the Quat government been installed when an inconsidered, ill-timed coup attempt against Khanh was made by a group of officers headed by Brigadier General Lam Van Phat, the leader of the previous unsuccessful attempt against Khanh in September 1964. Phat should have done better the second time around, but he failed again primarily because he misjudged the temper of the military commanders with effective strength in the Saigon area. But in failure, he still accomplished his purpose because Khanh's fellow generals were by then fed up with the troublemaker who had so entangled them in political toils as to render them impotent as military leaders. While I never knew the details of what occurred at the meeting of the Armed Forces Council on February 20, the upshot was that the generals voted to unseat Khanh as Commander in Chief, obtained his appointment as Ambassador at Large, and on February 25 shipped him off to the United States and Europe in indefinite exile. In this status, he joined his old rival "Big" Minh, who had left the country several months before and had settled in Bangkok. Khanh was a great disappointment to most of us who knew him well because, with some character and integrity added to his undeniable ability, he' might have been the George Washington of his country.

There was a mountain of pressing business awaiting Quat's government. Vietcong incidents were 60 percent higher than a year before. Their main forces were estimated at over 40,000, and there was an ever-increasing proportion of North Vietnamese among them. Vietcong activity in combination with the Da Nang typhoon had created an enormous refugee problem which had been neglected during the political broils. The main lines of coastal communications from Saigon to the north, primarily Highway 1 and the railway, were cut in many places and could not be restored for lack of security forces.

We agreed with Quat that the situation was dark but, nonetheless, not without hope. Several new factors were working in our favor. We had Khanh out of the country, a clear gain. The principle of air retaliation for unusual terrorist attacks had been established by our response to the attack on Pleiku and, a few days later, to the bombing of an American billet in Qui Nhon. A further extension of the use of air power occurred at the end of February when CINCPAC was authorized to initiate the so-called Rolling Thunder air operations against North Vietnamese targets, not for retaliatory purposes but as a deliberate application of force to induce Ho Chi Minh to desist from supporting the aggression against the South. The program was to consist of measured and limited air action jointly with the Vietnamese Air Force against selected military targets in North Vietnam south of the nineteenth parallel, that is, about eighty miles into North Vietnam. The tempo was to be limited to one or two days of operation a week and to two or three targets each day. Concurrently, we were to intensify the ground action in South Vietnam while proclaiming to the world our readiness for negotiations to bring an end to the conflict. I was told to assure the Vietnamese leaders that, during any talks or negotiations which might ensue, military operations would continue until Hanoi stopped the aggression. These were gallant words which we chose to forget when negotiations eventually started in 1968.

In spite of the limited scope of the authorization for air strikes, we of the American Mission were elated over the approval of a policy which we had been urging for months. Rolling Thunder got under way on March 2 when 160 U.S. and South Vietnamese planes attacked an ammunition depot and a naval base north of the seventeenth parallel. An even more significant event occurred a few days later when two U.S. Marine battalions landed at

337

Da Nang on March 8 and 9 to strengthen the defense of that vital air base. All of these actions were most encouraging to the South Vietnamese, and it behooved Quat, I urged, to take full advantage of this lift in the national morale to press hard on his many stalemated civil programs.

It was curious how hard it had been to get authority for the initiation of the air campaign against the North and how relatively easy to get the marines ashore. Yet I thought the latter a much more difficult decision and concurred in it reluctantly. It was my acceptance of General Westmoreland's assessment of the precariousness of the security of the Da Nang and Bien Hoa bases which caused me to agree. The subsequent enemy offensive in the northern provinces showed that Westmoreland had been right and that the decision had been taken none too soon. However, as the marines were landing I cabled the President my devout hope that we were not about to rush in and take over the conduct of the war from the Vietnamese. I pointed out that, since President Kennedy's decision in 1961 to increase aid to South Vietnam, our help had been predicated on the principle that we should assist the Vietnamese only to do those necessary things which had to be done and which they could not yet do for themselves. It was the time factor, I thought, which justified our change in policy at this juncture. The South Vietnamese simply could not create the additional forces fast enough to offset the mounting strength of the enemy. But while our increased involvement in the air and on the ground would have many short-term benefits in raising morale and restoring a balance of force, in the long run we would have the continuing problem of preventing the Vietnamese from feeling that the American participation reduced their responsibility for making a maximum war effort. We would also have to be constantly aware of the danger of dissipating our available military strength and thus exposing our interests in other parts of the world.

CHAPTER 27

The New Strategy

At this juncture, President Johnson called me back to Washington from March 28 to April 5, my first visit home since the previous December. In Washington, I made the usual status report to the President and his chief advisers and appeared in two sessions before the combined Foreign Affairs and Armed Services Committees of the Senate and House. Although sharply questioned by the congressmen, I found no particular evidence of ill will toward the Ambassador but rather considerable sympathy for the official nearest the stove in a remarkably hot kitchen. As a matter of fact, I was encouraged by my visit although unhappy with the number of new programs which I carried back to try out in Saigon. When I got home and counted old and new tasks, I found that there was a total of fifty-four nonmilitary programs which we were to ask the new Quat government to conduct, and General Westmoreland had about as many military ones to work out with the Vietnamese high command.

This may be the place to comment on a serious problem which I have not mentioned up to now—the danger represented by the excessive good will of our friends in Washington and their ever burgeoning crop of new ideas. With a critically sick government on our hands in Saigon which had not responded to previous treatment, there were always panacea peddlers in Washington who wanted to try some new prescription on the grounds that the patient was *in extremis* anyway, and a new pill might do some good. The result was that the feeble government was in constant danger of being overfed, overphysicked, or constipated by the excessive zeal of his American physicians.

It may surprise some to learn that in this period most of the programs on the books of the American Mission were nonmilitary in character. I have a spread sheet showing Mission tasks in early 1965 which indicate that of about sixty programs, only nineteen had a direct military component. Most

339

of the money spent by the agencies of the Mission and certainly most of their efforts expended in 1964 and 1965 were directed toward the solution of political, economic, and social problems rather than military. The security sought by military means was primarily to provide protection and to guarantee permanence to the nation-building activities which were the core of the nonmilitary programs. If we made a mistake this period, it was in trying too much in the civil field before an adequate level of security was reached. We should have learned from our frontier forebears that there is little use planting corn outside the stockade if there are still Indians around in the woods outside.

The magnitude of the nonmilitary programs never got through to the American public primarily because of the difficulty in interesting the press in anything but the violent aspects of the conflict. For example, I was very proud of a pig farm program sponsored very successfully by our economic mission and often tried to get reporters to accompany me on inspection trips to see samples of it. But although they would queue up in a moment for a helicopter ride to a combat area, they showed no interest in accepting my invitations, apparently believing as one of them put it, "There is no headline appeal in a pig's squeal." Similarly, after American troops arrived and entered action, it became almost as difficult to get reporters to visit Vietnamese combat units as pig farms, since editors at home wanted news about American military operations and little else. Thus the impression grew at home that only the Americans were fighting the war in Vietnam, that the Vietnamese did not really care about the outcome, and that neither Americans nor Vietnamese worried much about the political and social problems of the country.

Returning from this digression, I can only say that in my ambassadorial role I protected the Vietnamese government as best I could from the excessive weight of the programs pressed upon it. While it was hardly possible to reject out of hand a new proposal from an earnest well-wisher in Washington, I could always accept it with the understanding that it would have to receive a priority rating in competition with other programs awaiting attention. In spite of such protective efforts, I am sure that we often asked the Vietnamese to do much more than they could have been reasonably expected of them to the detriment of their net useful output.

As we set about our new programs we worked in a bombed-out Embassy building, the work of Vietcong terrorists during my absence. On the morning of March 30, a small sedan of the kind which fill the streets of Saigon had pulled up alongside the Embassy building and stopped, apparently because of motor trouble. Actually it was loaded with explosives with the fuse burning. Before the police could intervene, the heavy charge went off, killing two Americans and a score of Vietnamese while wounding nearly 200 persons. Within the building, most of the damage was done by pieces of glass which, flying from the windows with the velocity of shell fragments, penetrated flesh, blinded eyes, and imbedded themselves in the walls and furniture of the Embassy. Most of the furniture in my office was so badly gashed that it had to be replaced. Alex Johnson, who was in charge during my absence, received cuts about the face, and few of our staff escaped without some scars to record the incident. I returned to the blasted building more than a little ashamed at having been away a third time when a crisis had occurred in Saigon. The other two times had been the abortive Phat coup in September and the anti-Huong coup in January. I told Alex Johnson that I wasn't sure whether it was my absence or his presence that stimulated trouble.

Alex and I often had occasion to smile at the mystification among the Vietnamese over our respective roles in the Embassy. Some Vietnamese interpreted our relationship as a case of the Pentagon keeping an eye on State or the reverse. During my recent troubles with Tri Quang, some believed that I was pro-Catholic and hence Alex must be pro-Buddhist to give balance to the Embassy. The last thing Vietnamese would have suspected was the prevailing harmony between us.

When I left the President in Washington, I had not realized that he had made up his mind on a number of important subjects, of which the reprisal bombing for Pleiku and the landing of the two battalions of Marines were only the first on the list. During our White House meetings on April 1 and 2, some of the President's advisers had proposed the deployment of two American divisions to Vietnam, but the President only approved two additional Marine battalions for the protection of Da Nang-Phu Bai and a 20,000 increase in logistical troops. He gave me the impression of a President exercising restraint in increasing the American military involvement. But shortly after arriving in Saigon, I soon sensed that, having crossed the Rubicon on February 7, he was now off for Rome on the double. His speech at Johns Hopkins on April 7 outlined much but not all of what he had in mind. Abandoning the condition that Hanoi must halt the aggression before negotiations could begin, in his Baltimore speech he indicated his readiness for "unconditional discussions" at any time. But while offering as an inducement for peace talks the inclusion of North Vietnam in a billion dollar economic program for Southeast Asia, he asserted in strong terms the American resolution never to be defeated, never to grow tired, and never to withdraw from Vietnam before the goal of an independent Vietnam had been achieved. Having spoken thus, he then proceeded to take far-reaching actions to show that he meant what he said. Critics who later blamed the President for concealing from the public his intentions to "escalate" should review his public statements and actions at this time.

I first became aware of the President's new mood from a series of cables which began to arrive following my return. They indicated growing concern over the military situation and a desire to accelerate deployments beyond the schedule approved during my visit. There seemed to be an

341

eagerness in some quarters to rush in troops now that the initial official reluctance had been breached. These indications led me to cable on April 14 a restatement of my reservations about additional deployments until their need was uncontrovertible. I wanted more time to learn from the experience of the Marine battalions in the Da Nang-Phu Bai area before deciding on brigade and division deployments. My concern was further increased by a cable of April 15 which informed me of a plan to introduce a brigade in the Bien Hoa-Vung Tau area to provide security for those bases and also to participate in counterinsurgency combat operations. Additionally, battalion or multibattalion forces were to be put ashore along the coast with similar missions. These steps were viewed in Washington as experiments which, if successful, could justify requests for additional troops. The cable noted other possible innovations such as stiffening Vietnamese military units with American soldiers, providing advisers to improve Vietnamese recruiting techniques, utilizing mobile U.S. medical dispensaries in the countryside, introducing U.S. Army civil affairs personnel into the provinces, and distributing food directly through American channels to Vietnamese military personnel and their families.

It was quite a cable, particularly significant to me because few of these proposals had originated in the Embassy. They were the product of Washington initiative flogged to a new level of creativity by a President determined to get prompt results. It was a reminder to us in Saigon that the conduct of U.S. policy would be taken over by Washington if we were not careful. I countered the cable of April 15 by urging that all action on these matters be held in abeyance pending a full discussion of them with McNamara, Wheeler, and Sharp in Honolulu at a meeting scheduled for the following week. To this request for time, the President consented.

When we gathered in Honolulu on April 20, our agenda included three principal items: the bombing campaign, additional ground force deployments, and the innovative measures mentioned above. As for the bombing, all of us were in agreement that what we were doing would never have a decisive effect in itself; however, we felt that it should be continued for its value in bringing pressure to bear on Hanoi. While most of the Joint Chiefs of Staff favored a rapid increase in the scope and intensity of the bombing, the Honolulu conferees believed that if the already approved target system were only moderately extended to the north our available aircraft would have all they could do without going as far as the Chiefs wished. I felt that the extent of the target system was not so important in producing the desired psychological effect in Hanoi as an inexorable continuity of attack repeated day after day without interruption. I am afraid, however, that despite repeated efforts, I never convinced either the proponents of massive bombing or the partisans of frequent bombing pauses of the validity of this concept.

As for the need for additional combat troops, we concluded after much discussion that they were necessary to give the required impetus to the ground campaign in South Vietnam where the decisive action lay. For maximum effectiveness in breaking the will of Hanoi, we needed concurrent success on all fronts: in the military operations on the ground, in the civilian programs, and in the air operations against North Vietnam and along the Laotian trails. To compensate for the inadequacy of Vietnamese forces available or to become available in 1965, we agreed to recommend to the President an increase during the summer of about nine U.S. battalions, a reinforcement which would bring the American total to 82,000, to which would be added about 7,200 third-country troops furnished principally by Korea and Australia. These numbers, we thought, would be sufficient for the next increment. But as always, it was impossible to say that this force would be sufficient to see us to the end. Too much depended upon the unpredictable performance of the enemy and our allies. As for the so-called innovations, we thought well of all those proposed except the incorporation of American soldiers into Vietnamese units and the use of U.S. Army civil affairs teams in the provinces. We recommended that these two proposals be dropped and they were.

The President was inclined to accept our troop recommendations but first wanted to get the reaction of Quat's government since the Prime Minister on one occasion in the past had expressed a reluctance to accept foreign ground forces. Alex Johnson and I broached the matter with Quat on April 24, explaining to him the reasoning behind our conclusion as to the need for a substantial increase of U.S. and third-country forces. We told him that these additional units were necessary to give greater security to such places as Bien Hoa and the new airfield construction at Chu Lai and to increase the central reserve now reduced to four battalions. Quat received our exposé calmly, showing none of his former reservations regarding foreign reinforcements. He expressed his personal concurrence in principle but asked for time to consult with his principal colleagues. A few days later, he informed us of the approval of his government to the introduction of the forces recommended.

Meanwhile, Quat was showing considerable finesse in steering his government through the rocks and shoals of Vietnamese politics. For instance, he persuaded the generals to dissolve the Armed Forces Council which, as long as it existed, provided a ready means for the generals to toss a monkey wrench into the machinery of government whenever they were of a mind. He also got military agreement to relieve General "Little" Minh from the position of Commander in Chief and to leave the post vacant. He was successful in conducting municipal and provincial elections in which, despite Vietcong harassment, about 70 percent of the eligible electorate voted. He showed an early appreciation of the ineptitude of some of his ministers and made plans to get rid of several of them. While he was the target of a feeble coup attempt on May 20 and 21, he reacted quickly and soon rounded up the conspirators, a riffraff of Catholic and southern extremists (Quat himself was from North Vietnam) led by a professional coup plotter, Lieutenant Colonel Pham Ngoc Thao.

He survived this coup only to fall into a trap of his own contrivance. In reshaping his cabinet, he dropped two ministers for incompetence but failed to obtain their resignations before presenting the new cabinet to Chief of State Suu. When he did so, Suu challenged the constitutional right of the Prime Minister to hire and fire ministers without the approval of the Chief of State. In spite of Embassy efforts to smooth things over, the issue soon reached an impasse as the result of the ambiguity of the constitutional charter which provided no legal way to resolve the conflict. Quat's enemies began to line up on Suu's side with the obvious hope of overturning Quat, while the generals on the sidelines grumbled over the impasse and the inability of the civilian politicians to overcome it.

Because of the possibility of a new military intervention, I delayed a pending trip to Washington for several days but eventually felt obliged to leave on June 8 to take part in an important debate over the proposed year-end strength for U.S. forces in Vietnam. The military authorities were recommending the deployment of an air-mobile division and a total strength of 116,000 whereas Secretary McNamara's view, which ultimately prevailed, was to add only five battalions. When I got to Washington, there was a spat going on between the press and the Administration as to whether or not the mission of our American ground forces had been changed. When the first Marines landed, Administration statements had emphasized their security mission in protecting bases, and, indeed, that was the primary purpose at the time of their landing. But no military man could visualize our troops remaining indefinitely in tight defensive positions such as Da Nang and Bien Hoa—at least, I could not. Even if their mission remained primarily defensive, the best defense of the bases would be a mobile one which would seek to find and destroy threatening enemy forces before they could attack. Regardless of the formal statement of their mission, our forces would be obliged to patrol vigorously outside their defensive positions and engaged in combat as necessary. Beyond this, it is a fact of military life that soldiers do not thrive on a continuous defensive; the fine edge of their training becomes dull, and the aggressive spirit and morale decline. In the present case, if our troops remained on a static defensive we would lose the benefit of the mobility and fire power conferred upon them by the quality of their equipment. It was inevitable that, considering the desperate shortage of a central reserve, sooner or later General Westmoreland would want to use the American ground forces on mobile strike missions without any restrictions. That this evolution of mission was taking place soon became apparent to press observers and, during my visit to Washington, the White House Press Secretary George Reedy was being asked about it. While denying a change, he justified the expanded mission about as I had done but indicated that the mobile strike mission would be authorized only by General Westmoreland when urgently necessary. This formula was ample for the moment, but the restrictions had to be progressively relaxed in subsequent months to meet the changing situation.

When about to return to Saigon, I was surprised to learn that since Quat had been unable to reach an understanding with Suu, the former had decided to return the political power to the military, thus bringing the government around a full turn to the pre-Vung Tau Charter days of the previous summer. The eventual outcome of their action was a government supervised by a ten-general National Leadership Council, with General Thieu acting as the Chief of State and General Ky, the *de facto* Prime Minister, who presided over a cabinet largely civilian in membership. This was the origin of the Thieu-Ky team which soon became well known to the American and world public and which displayed surprising political viability during the following years. Ky was the fifth prime minister with whom I had worked as Ambassador, and I must say that, at the start of our relationship, there was little to justify the hope that he would be the last. But as it turned out, the accession of this government marked the end of the vertiginous rotation of generals and politicians in and out of the seats of power and the beginning of stable government as that term may be applied in Vietnamese politics.

I must say that when I returned to Saigon on June 14 and surveyed the scene I had no reason to believe that the political situation had turned such a decisive corner. While Thieu in the past had showed himself a man of considerable poise and judgment, Ky was known primarily as a gallant, flamboyant airman with a well-developed penchant for speaking out of turn. An American officer who knew him well, and on whose judgment I relied, described him as proud, sensitive, and courageous but a naïve politician and an inexperienced administrator. As the quality of the government would depend very much on Ky's performance, there was not much cause to hail his advent to the premiership with excessive optimism.

Once in office, Ky displayed an almost frightening zeal in setting about his proclaimed task of awakening an apathetic nation to its peril and getting it on a true war footing. He promptly formed a cabinet which looked quite good by Vietnamese standards and announced an ambitious "revolutionary" twenty-six–point program. He seemed to have learned the Washington game of measuring progress by the number of programs on the government ledger, an aptitude which caused me to worry that he would attempt too much without regard for priorities. Hoping to direct his energies into the most useful channels, I wrote him a long letter pointing out the need to concentrate on such bread-and-butter problems as the improvement of security, the restoration of combat effectiveness in the many understrength units of the Army, the elimination of incompetent military officers and civil officials, the punishment of profiteering and hoarding, and the reform of the tax-collection system. One simple action I urged as a way to improve national morale and self-respect—a clean-up of the rubbish stacked in the streets of Saigon and other cities—but this was too prosaic to interest him.

In the end, it was the pressure of events, largely the doings of the enemy, which established Ky's priorities during the following months. His government arrived on the scene at a critical juncture in a long struggle. Hoping to cripple the Vietnamese combat units and make important territorial gains before the effect of the presence of American forces could be felt, the Vietcong, reinforced by at least one division of the North Vietnamese Army, had launched a summer offensive which was achieving considerable success. They were now attacking in regimental strength and showing a high degree of professional competence in handling such units. Largely as a result of combat attrition imposed by the enemy, about 20 of the 137 South Vietnamese infantry battalions were rated as combat-ineffective, and many other combat units were badly understrength. The unfavorable balance in ground forces had forced the Vietnamese to abandon six district capitals since May. While the military strength on our side was declining, the Vietcong seemed to have little difficulty in replacing their own very considerable losses, and there were increasing reports of the presence of North Vietnamese units in the northern provinces. As we learned later, North Vietnamese units had been infiltrating since about November of the previous year.

Ky was reasonably well equipped to understand if not to solve these military problems, but he faced many perplexing difficulties of an economic and political order for which he was totally untrained. The war was disrupting rubber production, rice distribution, and the coastal fishing industry and thus sharply reducing foreign exchange earnings at a time when the demand for imports was increasing. There were warnings of severe inflation in the economic indicators. Rising prices and labor shortages were creating popular unrest. While Ky was quite capable of shooting a black market profiteer in the Saigon market place from time to time, a firing squad was no final answer to his domestic problems.

Like his predecessors, Ky could never afford to forget the fragility of his political base. It depended largely on the unity of the armed forces behind him which, fortunately, seemed reasonably solid for the moment. However, he knew that General Nguyen Chanh Thi, commanding the I Corps in the north, might at any time join with Tri Quang in making common cause against the government, using as a prime target General Thieu whom Tri Quang had already branded as a Catholic Diemist. If Ky's program should falter, all of these political elements could quickly coalesce against him, reinforced by out-politicians and businessmen who were frightened by his pronouncements on austerity and the repression of corruption.

Taking all of Ky's assets and liabilities into account, I reported to Washington in mid-July that his government could probably last out the year if the top military leadership remained united and if, with American help, he succeeded in blunting the current enemy offensive. To do the latter, he would have to have more American ground forces for use both in general reserve and in offensive roles until the new Vietnamese units in training were ready for the field. The strength of the enemy offensive had completely overcome my former reluctance to use American troops in general combat. Also, I thought that, since the limited air attacks against North Vietnam had failed thus far to produce any evidence of inclination on the part of the enemy to negotiate, for psychological effect we would have to raise the level of our air efforts over North Vietnam at the same time that we increased our strength on the ground. I had become convinced that we were going too slow in the application of military power, air and ground, to accomplish our intended purposes.

CHAPTER 28

End of a Mission

By this time, the end of my agreed one-year tour as Ambassador was approaching. During my last two visits to Washington I had discussed my relief with the President, Rusk, and others, and, while willing to extend my tour to facilitate the transfer of duties to a successor, had politely insisted that my assignment terminate essentially as agreed. In due course a schedule was drawn up which called for an announcement on July 8 that Henry Cabot Lodge would succeed me at the end of July and that Secretary McNamara, accompanied by Wheeler and Lodge, would visit Saigon before my departure. The primary purpose of this visit, obviously not made public, was to discuss troop requirements for the remainder of 1965 and the expectations from them if provided.

On July 16 McNamara, accompanied by Lodge, Wheeler, and Goodpaster, arrived and spent five busy days with the Mission. The basic issue was whether to approve the request of the American military authorities to increase the foreign troops in Vietnam to 175,000 men by the end of 1965, a strength which would provide thirty-four infantry-type battalions. This goal was arrived at by considering the South Vietnamese troop contribution in the period, the likely enemy build-up of strength, and the estimated force ratios believed necessary to accomplish the regional missions throughout South Vietnam. Because of the importance of the impending decision, Secretary McNamara had cabled ahead of his arrival a long list of questions which he wished the Mission to answer during his stay with us.

The answers which McNamara got from us were not always precise or completely reliable, as the Mission members who produced them were quick to concede. There were always two important unknowns in an estimate of future events, the performance which we could count on from our Vietnamese ally and the reaction of the enemy. In later years, a third unknown of even greater importance entered into the equation, the reaction

348

of American public opinion to Southeast Asia policy, but in mid-1965 the crucial significance of this third factor had not yet been fully recognized.

The fundamental question which McNamara posed at the outset was whether the requested increase in U.S. military strength would force the Vietcong to a settlement on our terms. Our answer to it was negative. By the arithmetic of this irregular war, one fresh, combat-ready guerrilla introduced into operations in South Vietnam required the addition of four to eight soldiers on our side to compensate for him, a disadvantage which we shared with the police of any city in rounding up the criminals in their jurisdiction. Hence, we recognized that the Vietcong and Hanoi could always make a compensating increase in their forces and would probably continue to do so until they became convinced by some combination of factors—the air campaign, American, Chinese, and Russian governmental attitudes, the combat performance of the Vietnamese forces, or the resulting balance of power in South Vietnam—that they could not hope for victory and must sue for peace from self-interest. Since we could never be sure when this turning point might come, we could not base our plans on quick results but had to be prepared for a long campaign of uncertain duration.

A similarly imprecise answer had to be given to questions regarding the effect in South Vietnam of the presence of such large numbers of foreign troops. While a let-down in South Vietnamese efforts and an adverse popular reaction to so many white faces about the country were possible, we could only say that the quadrupled American presence during the past year had thus far produced no such results. There was no question that increased numbers of American troops would increase troop-civilian incidents, would raise the prices of certain commodities, and in the end distort to some extent the social and economic structure. But by a nation-wide program to inform the Vietnamese public of the reason for our presence and by the intensive instruction of our troops in civilian relations, it should be possible to attenuate these adverse effects. In any case, they did not seem to us sufficiently important to warrant rejecting the proposed troop augmentation.

Some officials in Washington remained apprehensive concerning possible Chinese reactions to such reinforcements. We in Saigon conceded that the Vietcong might at any time publicly invite volunteers from North Vietnam, and, if they were provided, the Hanoi leaders could henceforth acknowledge the presence of North Vietnamese in South Vietnam which thus far they had felt obliged to deny. A similar invitation might go to North Korea. But we doubted that either Hanoi or the Vietcong would ever request or accept Chinese combat forces in their country. For centuries the Chinese had been regarded as hated, foreign oppressors by all Vietnamese, North and South, and that historical attitude was not likely to change.

The subject of command arrangements, often debated in the past, arose again during our meetings. Many leading American officials, including some senior military officers, had thought from the beginning of the U.S. troop build-up that General Westmoreland should receive operational control over the South Vietnamese forces, as the American Eighth Army commander had controlled the Korean forces from 1950 to 1953. However, in Korea the American commander was a representative of the United Nations, and he exercised operational control of all U.N. forces in that capacity. In South Vietnam, no such U.N. authority existed and a demand for operational control by the Americans would be likely to raise serious resistance among the Vietnamese whose nationalist pride was an intense as their repugnance to the charge of being American puppets. Westmoreland was firmly against such an action and strongly recommended that command relationships be regulated by the principle of cooperation and mutual support, a view which eventually prevailed.

After dealing with ground force matters, the conferees turned to a consideration of Rolling Thunder, the air campaign against the North. As always there were differing points of view. One favored raising the tempo of the Rolling Thunder attacks during the next few months in the hope of compensating for the relative lack of success in South Vietnam. The stimulus to South Vietnamese morale resulting from its initiation in March was wearing off, and signs of war-weariness were returning. Furthermore, critics of the bombing were beginning to appear in the United States. Most of them were united in charging that it was ineffective, but some wanted it increased while others wanted it stopped. In our conference in Saigon, it was pointed out that the bombing could be stepped up by increasing the rate of attack, the intensity of attack, or the territorial limits within which targets could be struck. I favored any combination of the three which would convince Hanoi that we meant business and that we would progressively and inexorably destroy everything of war-sustaining value if the aggression against the South continued.

Those supporting the current tempo argued that no level of air attack could in itself bring Hanoi to its knees; to do so would require the simultaneous peaking of pressures from many sources. It would be psychologically wrong to let the air campaign run away from the ground campaign and exhaust prematurely the limited number of military targets. Many of these targets, it was argued, should be preserved to permit greater climactic effect when the timing was right for a maximum combined effort. In the end the latter view predominated, although it was conceded that we might wish to mine Haiphong harbor or destroy the bridges on the main railway lines leading from China during the latter part of the year.

Another subject discussed, inadequately I would say in retrospect, was the need to impose some kind of press censorship on the reporting of military operations. At the time, a system of voluntary censorship was being worked out with the foreign press in Vietnam to protect military information which might be of value to the enemy; such matters as operational plans, troop movements, friendly casualties, and information regarding certain special weapons. Sanctions against violators would be loss of accreditation or expulsion from the country. As this system was just going into effect, it was too early to evaluate it, but everyone hoped it would be sufficient and eliminate the need for formal governmental censorship which was sure to cause many difficulties. The prevailing opinion was that censorship would have to be imposed by the government of Vietnam, which had a well-established reputation for callous and unsympathetic treatment of the press, both domestic and foreign. It was easy to predict an even more hostile reporting of Vietnamese news by a press corps which worked under a Vietnamese-administered censorship. The latter would call for a new governmental mechanism for the control of telecommunications and for a large corps of multi-lingual translators, all operating under a competent management familiar with the working of press, radio, and TV. The very thought of undertaking to create such an organization in any short period of time made those of us who knew the limits of the local bureaucracy recoil. So we crossed our fingers and put our hopes for the moment in the voluntary ground rules.

Thus far I have withheld comment on the heightened diplomatic activity which accompanied the increased military build-up. When President Johnson took the decision in February to introduce American forces into combat, he undertook simultaneously a renewed drive for peace negotiations. In mid-March, he welcomed the initiative of seventeen nonaligned nations who appealed to the belligerents in Southeast Asia for negotiations without preconditions. In his Johns Hopkins speech the following month, he expressed his willingness to participate in "unconditional peace discussions." On July 31, Washington invited all members of the United Nations to use their influence to bring about negotiations, only to be rebuffed by the U.N. reply that the Security Council "has absolutely no right to interfere in the affairs of Indochina." In the succeeding weeks and months, the air was filled with negotiation, proposals, and rumors emanating from Washington, from nonaligned governments and from well-intentioned individuals and private groups.

From the outset I had grave misgivings about this vast effort sponsored and led in person by the President. While it might alleviate some of the domestic and international criticism, that uncertain gain appeared slight in comparison to the clear disadvantages which an overzealous pursuit of negotiations would entail. In the first place, our peace efforts were premature and had been from the start. There was nothing in the military or political situation to bring Communist negotiators to the table in a frame of mind conducive to a settlement which would be other than a sell-out of South Vietnam. We had every reason to know from past diplomatic confrontations with the Communists that they regard a negotiation as another form

351

of international conflict to be waged with all the determination and ruthlessness of a military campaign. Until they were convinced that they could not take South Vietnam either by force of arms or as the result of a collapse of the American will, it would be a mistake, I was sure, to expect reasonableness from them at the conference table. Furthermore, they would interpret the excessive eagerness which we were showing as evidence of our lack of confidence in ultimate success rather than as evidence of an honest desire for a just peace, a motive probably beyond their comprehension anyway. Finally, premature negotiations would detract from the effectiveness of the military campaign directed at bending the will of Ho Chi Minh—the sword must appear inexorable and inescapable to produce a change in the enemy's conduct. Under the circumstances, our peace-making efforts offered no prospect other than a repetition of the wrangling stalemate which had lasted over two years at Panmunjom. In a similar way, a stalemated negotiation on Vietnam would offer the Communists a priceless sounding board for propaganda and recriminations while carrying on the war at their leisure.

There were other reasons for my coolness toward negotiations at this time. Their initiation would be interpreted at home as an indication that "peace is just around the corner" and, as in the case of Korea, would raise a popular cry for a cessation of offensive military activities to avoid needless loss of life with the war almost over. It could lead to demands to reduce the war effort and to "bring the boys home" after the disastrous fashion of 1945.

My last reason for opposing the peace drive was that our government was not ready for negotiations in the unlikely event that the other side should make a favorable response. During the last year, the senior members of our Saigon Mission, particularly Alex Johnson, had given much thought to ways of terminating the conflict without sacrificing our basic objective of an independent South Vietnam free from Communist aggression. The first extended treatment of this complex problem of which I am aware was contained in a Saigon cable to Washington in late January 1965, which Alex had prepared. It discussed the preferred objectives of peace negotiations and the play of the counters, the so-called blue chips, which each side would bring to the table to exchange with maximum gain.

The cable pointed out that in this play of the blue chips, our side would want North Vietnam to stop the infiltration of men and supplies into the south and to bring about a cessation of the Vietcong insurgency. Since the Vietnam situation was interlocked with that in Laos, we would also want a restoration of the terms of the 1962 Laos Accords, including the withdrawal of Communist troops and freedom of movement throughout the country for the International Control Commission.

In exchange for agreement on these points, our side should be willing to offer amnesty and civil rights to Vietcong wishing to reenter society and safe passage to North Vietnam for those who wished to go there. We could also offer the progressive reduction of foreign military personnel in South Vietnam to the 1954 ceiling, the restoration of trade relations with North Vietnam, and participation by all parties in an American-sponsored development program for Southeast Asia.

As to the format for such negotiations, we in Saigon thought that they should be conducted preferably as bilateral negotiations between North and South Vietnam in spite óf our doubts about the ability of the negotiators whom our ally might choose. Knowing South Vietnamese sensibilities regarding recognition of the National Liberation Front, we were opposed to accepting it as a legal party to the negotiations.

Obviously there would be many difficulties in carrying out such a program, but we advanced it to serve as a basis for discussion first with Washington and, when appropriate, with the South Vietnamese government. On the critical question of whether we should base our over-all position on a return to the 1954 Geneva Accords or, instead, seek a new international agreement, we were inclined to favor the former course. It was true that the Accords contained much which had lost relevance and that they were distasteful to the South Vietnamese because, in their view, the Accords were a sell-out to Ho Chi Minh over the signature of a French brigadier general. Nevertheless, their legal status and the soundness of many of their principles constituted a strong reason for retaining them, at least as a base of departure.

This cable was well received in Washington and, in due course, we were authorized to open a dialogue on the subject with the Vietnamese. We started such a conversation with the Khanh government but were obliged to break off because of the political turmoil of the early months of 1965. Our first discussion in depth was on May 26 with Prime Minister Quat, Foreign Minister Do, and State Secretary Bui Diem. We discussed common political objectives, negotiation tactics, and our use of the blue chips, particularly our bombing of North Vietnam which, in view of the complaints against it from Hanoi, was plainly our most valuable counter. We were pleased to find that our Vietnamese colleagues recognized that the unification of North and South Vietnam could not be regarded as a feasible political objective for the time being and seemed quite willing to deal fairly with the Vietcong who might apply for readmission to citizenship. As expected, they did not like basing our negotiating position on the Geneva Accords and rejected any role for the National Liberation Front in any future government. They viewed it most important to maintain the bombing of the North and had difficulty in suggesting a *quid pro quo* which we might accept in exchange for its cessation. They made the point that a halt to our bombing could be readily verified whereas the important things we wanted in exchange, such as an end to infiltration and the withdrawal of North Vietnamese units and individuals, could not be verified. Hence, it was hard to find a swap which was both equitable and safe. Unhappily, shortly after this very useful discussion, the progress made was nullified when on June 12 Quat returned his authority to the generals. Thereafter, we had to start all over again with the Thieu-Ky team.

Because of my imminent departure, I had only one major encounter with these new leaders on the subject of war aims. It occurred at the end of July as an outgrowth of President Johnson's decision to increase our troop ceiling to 175,000. Washington had sent me a draft statement which the President proposed to make on the subject and asked me to get Ky's concurrence in advance of its release. It contained a number of important points. It explained that the American forces were to be used by General Westmoreland to fight wherever they were needed; there were no longer to be any strings attached to their mission. At the same time, the President reaffirmed his strong desire for unconditional discussions leading to a peaceful settlement. He cited some fifteen different efforts already made to get discussions started and announced a new approach to the United Nations which Ambassador Goldberg was about to make. The draft also made reference to the American hope that North and South Vietnam could eventually work out a way to reunify the country through free elections under international supervision. It also contained language which suggested that the Geneva Accords of 1954, appropriately strengthened, might serve as the basis for the eventual settlement.

Thieu and Ky were much interested in the language referring to negotiations and postwar measures. They doubted the efficacy of the new approach to the United Nations but accepted it as a means to demonstrate again our desire to exhaust every possibility to open discussions. While they did not object to the reference to reunification through free elections, they made very clear their disbelief that the Communists would ever accept the principle of international supervision of elections. Also, they were uneasy at the thought of tackling the reunification question as soon as the hostilities ceased, because of their lack of confidence in the ability of the fragmented anti-Communist majority in South Vietnam to compete politically with the highly disciplined, unified Communist minority.

There was a long discussion of the validity of the Geneva Accords and the attitude which the Saigon government should take toward them. They eventually agreed that their government should take the position that, while it had not signed the Accords, it had respected, and would continue to respect their principles. However, the generals pointed out that an ending without negotiations whereby the war quietly faded away was a possibility and, in their view, a preferable way to restore peace. I thought that their views were quite reasonable and gave no ground to fear difficulties with our ally as we progressed toward a termination of the conflict.

By this time, my ambassadorial chore had reached its end. I paid the usual departure calls and received a decoration from General Thieu. Just before leaving I boarded a helicopter with my son, Captain Thomas Taylor, who had just arrived in Vietnam for duty, and flew to Cam Ranh Bay to greet the arrival of the 1st Brigade of my old division, the 101st Airborne. It was a moving sight for me to see the Screaming Eagles arriving on a new battleground far removed from the fields of Europe where I had led them in World War II. I was proud to leave Tom among them to become an infantry company commander.

Just before my departure on July 30, I filed a lengthy evaluation of the situation which summarized the gains and losses during the period of my ambassadorship. On the side of accomplishment, I felt that at last our government had adopted a coherent strategy which, if pursued with patience and determination, offered a good chance of attaining our perennial objective of an independent South Vietnam free from attack. That strategy consisted of interrelated military, political, economic, and diplomatic components. By military means, we would blunt and repel the Communist aggression in South Vietnam while directing limited and controlled air strikes against military targets in North Vietnam. The combined ground and air campaigns, if relentlessly and effectively pursued, should convince the Communist leaders that they could not win the military struggle and condition them to accepting a reasonable settlement. This conviction would be speeded and reinforced if on the political and economic fronts we succeeded in fostering a stable government and protecting the fragile economy from disastrous inflation. Success in all these sectors should facilitate peace efforts on the diplomatic front.

On most of these fronts, the record of the past year had been spotty and often discouraging. It was slight compensation for the five changes in government and three attempted coups that such government as had existed had always been cooperative within its limitations and had tried to carry out the programs that we recommended. It was inexperience and weak leadership, not lack of good intentions, which accounted for the absence of progress in most sectors. The team of Thieu and Ky looked mildly promising; at any rate, their presence at the head of the governmental hierarchy provided reasonable assurance of the backing of the generals, the *sine qua non* of any viable Vietnamese government. But the national tendency to factionalism remained a continuing threat to political stability, and there was little we could do about it in the short run.

In retrospect I have often asked myself whether, during this period, my colleagues and I were too reluctant to intervene in Vietnamese internal affairs in order to stabilize the political situation. Personally I avoided excessive interventionist zeal for two reasons. From my Korean experience I knew how sensitive Asian allies were to the charge of being American puppets, and how favorably they responded to treatment as respected coequals. Next, I was thoroughly aware of the limits of our knowledge of the true character of most of the Vietnamese with whom we worked. We were particularly ignorant of the complex relationships which linked individuals and groups within the heterogeneous society. However, such considerations did not deter us from expressing candid views to appropriate Vietnamese officials regarding the performance of duty of military and civilian officers within our range of observation. I had certainly done so in the case of the generals who overthrew the High National Council. After all, the parties to an alliance have pooled their resources in a common cause and have yielded to each other some of their own independence of action. Each has a right and a duty to urge actions on the other conducive to the success of the partnership. So I felt completely justified in pressing for such things as greater use of American advisers, unimpeded access to Vietnamese governmental data, and joint U.S.-Vietnamese supervision of activities in the provinces.

The proper limits on American influence in the choice of the head of the government was another matter. Having observed the disastrous effects of American intervention in the overthrow of Diem, I never authorized any action by Americans in support of a specific change of government or in the selection of a particular official. If our purpose was to prepare South Vietnam for self-government, we Americans had to control our impatience for quick results and allow the South Vietnamese to make progress in their own way. I never sought to influence the choice of any one of the five Prime Ministers with whom I was obliged to work in these turbulent times. However, I did reserve to myself the right to exercise a kind of veto over any senior official whom I knew from experience to be incapable of working harmoniously with the Americans and of using effectively the American aid which was indispensable to success. I used that veto only once, in the case of General Khanh already described. In this instance it was only necessary to pass the word quietly to the senior Vietnamese generals that the U.S. government had lost confidence in Khanh and could not work with him again as the head of the Vietnamese government. As the generals had already reached a similar, independent conclusion, it was not long before Khanh was on his way to exile. If this was imperialist intervention, let the critics make the most of it. I regarded it as the act of a responsible ally, taken to forestall a situation which would be adverse to the success of the alliance.

In spite of the turbulence of the internal political scene, the international support of South Vietnam had increased during the year. There were now thirteen flags flying over as many foreign activities within the country, whereas twenty-three other nations, unrepresented by nationals on the scene, were contributing some kind of assistance. Most of their contributions were minor but were highly important as symbols of endorsement. Korea and Australia had combat troops in the field fighting alongside our own forces and more third-country troops were expected.

The military situation had continued to decline in the first half of the year, but the arrival of U.S. troops in numbers gave hope that the trend might be reversed by the end of the year. South Vietnamese forces of all kinds had increased from about 450,000 to over 580,000 but continued to be plagued by a shortage of leaders, a lack of aggressiveness, and an excessive desertion rate. Despite increases in the South Vietnamese forces, there was reason to suspect that increased infiltration from North Vietnam coupled with local recruiting had resulted in a net gain in enemy strength.

Lack of security and administrative incompetence continued to hold back the many economic and social programs which we were sponsoring throughout the provinces. Inflation remained an ever-present danger but, considering the circumstances, it seemed reasonably under control. There was some evidence of progress in agriculture, education, and public works, but there was a vast refugee problem created by some 700,000 country dwellers who had fled to the cities to avoid the Vietcong, the floods, or the dangers of the battlefield.

I was very proud of the logistic system which was coming into being under General Westmoreland's direction. Despite the repeated augmentations of American forces with little advance notice, our troops had never lacked accommodations upon arrival. Airfields, roads, and ports were expanding on all sides. Particularly impressive was the development of Cam Ranh Bay, which promised to provide the country with one of the best deep-water ports in Asia and a postwar boon to the peacetime economy.

In the field of public information and psychological warfare, I could find no cause for gratification. While we Americans had given technical and training assistance to Vietnamese press and radio, and had provided the beginnings for a limited TV net, it was beyond our power to do much about the quality of the substantive output. Unhappily, local governmental and private agencies in these fields were woefully weak and no leader had appeared with the gift of using the media to communicate effectively with a war-worn people sadly in need of inspirational guidance. I had to admit, also, that American officials in Saigon and Washington had not done well enough in interpreting the situation to our own people and resolved to dedicate myself to this task upon returning home.

I felt sincere pride in the performance of the American Mission in Saigon under the difficult conditions of the past year. We had learned early to work easily together, to respect the importance of the contributions made by the various agencies on the Mission Council, and to integrate these assets fairly well both in Saigon and in the provinces. There had been no feuding among us or leaking to the press for personal advantage. In spite of many discouragements, there were no defeatists among us. I had been most fortunate in the quality of my associates from whom I departed with sincere regret.

CHAPTER 29

Presidential Consultant

In my letter of resignation to President Johnson, I expressed my conviction in the essential rightness of our Vietnam policy and my faith in the ultimate success of our strategy if persisted in with determination. Then, perhaps rashly, I offered myself to further the cause in any possible way when I became a private citizen.

The President took me at my word and set me promptly to work upon my return. While I was still on the rolls of the State Department he sent me on a round of visits to leaders in press, television, and radio to engage in private discussions of the Vietnam situation. One of my first public appearances in what was to be a long series of speeches extending over the next six years was before the Commonwealth Club in San Francisco, an occasion which gave me my first exposure to the antiwar demonstrators who were just beginning to stir.

On the way from the San Francisco airport to my hotel, the club representative who had met me cautioned that there might be some pickets to greet me. Sure enough, as we approached the hotel, we could see figures milling about the porte-cochere carrying placards and banners. At nearer view they turned out to be a sample of the motley, bearded crew which came to symbolize the era of violent dissent. This first encounter seemed fun, so I rolled down the car window and waved a friendly greeting to the boys and girls as we came alongside them. The boys and girls, who included a number of tough-looking adults, responded by throwing a stack of posters in my face which carried a very unflattering picture of "Taylor, War Criminal." They then proceeded to block the driveway and the hotel entrance.

The manager of the hotel was on hand to meet me and help break a way through my admirers to the lobby and the elevators. But the demonstrators were ahead of us and had preempted all the elevators on the ground floor so that we were compelled to fight our way on foot to the manager's mezzanine office, the boys and girls in hot pursuit. We jumped inside just in time to lock the door on which our pursuers proceeded to beat as if to knock it down. At a moment when it was still a question whether the door would hold or not, the manager's secretary called me to the phone to take "an important call from Washington." I could hear on the other end of the line, though only faintly above the pounding, the worried voice of a State Department officer saying, "Mr. Ambassador, you'll be distressed to know there is another student demonstration going on in Hue."

When I formally terminated my assignment in the State Department in mid-September, the President had a new job awaiting me—special consultant to him on a part-time basis. His letter on the subject indicated an intention to give me specific tasks from time to time and directed me as a starter to keep abreast of the situation in Vietnam and to undertake a review of all governmental activities involved in counterinsurgency. He asked that this review include recommendations for assuring our readiness to cope with subversive insurgency whenever it might be in the national interest to do so. As to my commitment of time to these tasks, the President reminded me that I had expressed a willingness to devote half of my time to White House work. In the course of the next few months I discovered that under this arrangement the White House share of my time was the daylight half, and the dark belonged to me.

For a workshop, I set up an office in the same suite I had occupied under President Kennedy on the third floor of the Executive Office Building. My staff consisted of one carefully selected Army officer, who was rotated about once a year, and two secretaries, one of whom was Ray Jones from the State Department, who had been my highly prized secretary in Saigon. Additionally I was authorized, by presidential directive, to call on any governmental agency for information and for personnel on a temporary basis to expand my staff.

I undertook this White House assignment with some reluctance, because from my previous work with President Kennedy I knew much about the strengths and weaknesses of a presidential consultant. In official Washington such a man, particularly one who obviously has the President's ear, is generally unloved. He is viewed by officials on the job as an irresponsible rival who can peddle his advice in high places and then disappear before its flaws appear, whereas the full-time bureaucrat has to stay and live with the consequences of his own acts and with those of the consultant as well. If the latter proffers bad advice, the bureaucrat must devote valuable time to neutralizing its pernicious effects; if the advice is good, it is a reproach to the official for not having thought of it himself. Hence the Pentagon definition of a consultant, "A smart s.o.b. from out of town."

Having myself shared this view in other days, I was never completely at ease in the role of presidential consultant. But I soon found that all the advantages were not with the irresponsible transient. A consultant has his own difficulties which the bureaucrat does not perceive. While a consultant may have ready access to the President and thereby be able to cut corners and red tape, he still has the problem of getting his suggestions carried out even if they gain a favorable reception from the President. The latter is not likely to express his support more forcefully than by a note inviting the attention of an appropriate executive to a promising idea. If the latter is a senior official like the Secretary of State or Defense, the White House staff is unlikely to press for a prompt response, or for any at all—they have too much trouble in getting action taken on their own directives to follow up on the suggestions of a private citizen. So unless the consultant can win allies within the bureaucratic power structure, his brain child is quite likely to end in the limbo of unappreciated ideas which clutter the files of Washington agencies. In the end, a consultant is likely to have only the recourse which I have taken: to write a book to show how much better the world would have been "had they listened to me."

For simplicity, I shall begin by accounting for my second task, the review of counterinsurgency activities which I conducted concurrently with activities related to Vietnam. For this task I had the benefit of the work I had done in this field for President Kennedy, and the additional experience recently gained in the ambassadorial school of hard knocks in Vietnam. Assisted by four committees, each including representation from State, Defense, JCS, CIA, and USIA, I was able to submit my report to the President in mid-January 1966.

My principal finding was that the problem of dealing with subversive insurgency on the Vietnam model was a part of the much broader issue of how to deal with the underdeveloped world in general. The latter task required an intimate knowledge of many countries and a surveillance system to keep watch on their development and to anticipate their troubles. It would need an apparatus to collect this information, sort out the important, and present it in time to the Washington officials responsible to act on it. An organization for this purpose would have to include high-level officials representing the principal departments with capabilities and resources abroad—State, Defense, JCS, AID, CIA, and USIA—in short, a very senior interdepartmental committee. But committees are notoriously ineffective unless something is devised to offset their congenital weaknesses. I thought that much of the curse could be removed if a committee met three specifications: its members would be permanent and always attend in person; it would have a so-called executive chairman with the power to decide split issues; it would report to a senior official who supervised its operation. This line of thinking led to my recommending an organization reaching from the Ambassadors overseas through the regional Assistant Secretaries of State to the Secretary of State for "the direction, coordination and supervision of interdepartmental activities overseas." These functions represented in effect most of the activities of the executive branch involved in carrying out approved foreign policy—one of the responsibilities of the President. Hence, it was necessary for the President, when he approved the concept, to designate the Secretary of State as his agent to discharge these functions since they were additional to the departmental duties of the Secretary.

To assist the Secretary, I recommended a permanent interdepartmental committee called the Senior Interdepartmental Group (SIG) with the Undersecretary of State acting as its executive chairman. Similar committees were to be set up to assist the regional Assistant Secretaries of State in maintaining the countries of their regions under continuous watch to anticipate and prevent trouble endangering the interests of the United States. Thus, in an odd way, the quest for a way to deal with subversive insurgency led to the adoption of a whole new organization for dealing with foreign affairs in general. In discussing the matter with President Johnson I commented that there were at least two things which my recommendations were *not* intended to do: They were not designed to inject an impersonal automaticity into the decision-making process, or to encourage the United States to take a larger share in policing the world. But I did hope that the new procedure would give a President greater protection from unexpected crises and greater effectiveness in concentrating all available supporting resources behind his decisions in overseas matters.

A basic question under consideration from the outset was whether this apparatus should terminate in the President or in one of his subordinates, who would then be responsible to the President for the conduct of overseas affairs. Impressed, as most close observers of the presidency are, with the need to lighten the burdens of the incumbent, I was inclined to the second solution. But to whom should this responsibility be assigned? The choice was between the Secretary of State and some White House official such as the Special Assistant to the President for National Security Affairs, at that time McGeorge Bundy. Disregarding personalities, I felt that it was preferable to give the job to the Secretary because of his primacy in the Cabinet, the fact that he was confirmed by the Senate, and the heavy involvement of his department in foreign affairs. The structure of the State Department offered an existing framework upon which to superimpose the new functions under consideration.

After formal presidential approval in National Security Action Memorandum (NSAM) 341, the new system was launched with considerable fanfare at a White House press conference under kleig lights and with appropriate pronouncements by the President and the Secretary of State. But the shouting died quickly, to be followed by an impressive display of inactivity. There were a number of factors accounting for this bad start. The key figure in making the system work was the Undersecretary of State, but unhappily the plan was initiated just as Undersecretary Ball was preparing to leave the State Department. After his departure there was an interregnum until Nicholas Katzenbach was nominated and confirmed in the post. Thereafter there was an inevitable low level of activity in his office while the new incumbent learned his job. As a result of these circumstances, it was nearly a year before the system got really going and then only in low gear. Because of my parental relationship to it, I watched its retarded growth unhappily from the sidelines but kept my counsel until a year after its birth. Then I submitted a memorandum to the President expressing my regret over the unfulfilled hopes of the NSAM 341 system and cited as evidence of its unproductiveness the fact that the Senior Interdepartmental Group had met only five times in the last nine months. The SIG had played no role in the most serious interdepartmental problem facing the government, our involvement in Vietnam, and it had showed little interest in the counterinsurgency mission which the President had specifically assigned to it.

Rather than allow the NSAM 341 system to die from atrophy, I urged the President to review its utility with his principal advisers and to decide whether to try to vitalize it or to concede its failure and try something else. The result was a White House goading of State officials to inject some life into the system which was doing rather well by the end of the Johnson Administration. Its over-all record, however, was not sufficiently brilliant to save it from liquidation by the Nixon Administration which wished to center the foreign policy process in the White House rather than in State. The leaders of the State Department had missed a great opportunity in failing to exploit the grant of authority given them by President Johnson and had vindicated those who had warned me that State would never rise to the challenge.

While engaged in this review of the foreign policy process I was constantly working on Vietnam matters, the other task which the President had assigned me. Looking over my papers of this period, I would say that these matters could be grouped under four general headings: periodic estimates of the general situation, the conduct of military operations, the quest for peace negotiations, and relations with allies. There were also recurrent discussions of domestic and Congressional attitudes toward the Vietnam policy. In retrospect, however, I would say that there was too much discussion of this latter problem and too little effective action taken to anticipate the mounting opposition to the war. No one in the President's entourage ever seemed to have a feel for this problem, and no one was ever put in charge of doing something about it in all its aspects.

The latter half of 1965 was a period of intensive military activity with American combat forces in Vietnam reaching about 150,000 by late October. As our units arrived on the battlefield they immediately began to make their presence felt, scoring successes at such places as Chu Lai in

August, An Khe in September, Plei Me in October, and Ia Drang in November. Enemy losses rose and a new feeling of confidence began to permeate the northern provinces which the enemy had threatened to overrun a few months before.

The bombing of North Vietnam proceeded slowly—too slowly I thought —under rigid presidential control while a clamor of criticism mounted, first from the Communist countries, then from elements in the United States and in friendly nations. Plane losses increased as the attacks moved slowly northward and began to include industrial targets in the well-defended Hanoi-Haiphong area.

In parallel with these military activities, President Johnson's peace offensive continued unabated but to no avail. There were many reports of peace feelers from the Communist side, but, when investigated, they revealed nothing of substance. Hanoi continued to denounce the President's proposal for "unconditional discussions" without incurring a word of reproach from the war critics at home. Instead, they demanded a cessation of the bombing of the north to allow Hanoi to respond without pressure. When the President declined the demand, he was charged with being insincere about wanting negotiations and with seeking to expand the war while talking peace.

As the end of the year approached, I became increasingly uneasy over the disorderly way in which our war-related programs were progressing in Washington. We needed a strong supervisory mechanism like the Senior Interdepartmental Group which I later proposed to the President. As it was, the programs were proliferating in all directions without clearly defined goals or mutually supporting, synchronized efforts. To provide them coordinated direction I suggested that we establish ambitious but not impossible goals for all our principal programs in 1966 and then use these goals as bench marks against which to measure progress during the year. In setting a goal for ground operations, I proposed its expression in terms of population made sufficiently secure to permit progress of the nonmilitary programs. Terrain in itself meant little to this strange war; there was no Berlin to capture, no Rhine to cross, no Bastogne to defend and thereby establish a claim to victory. Here people were everything—it was they whom we had come to liberate and to shield from the guerrillas who fed upon them and depended on them for survival. At the end of 1965 the secure population was estimated at about 53 percent of the total and I proposed that we should take from 75 to 80 percent as the goal for 1966. Thereby, I hoped that we would avoid dissipating our forces throughout the forests and jungles on remote targets of negligible value and focus on the security of the people in the populated areas. I was especially concerned about the ramifications of the military objective contained in the JCS "Concept for Vietnam," which entailed extending the Saigon government's control over all of South Vietnam. I could anticipate an endless requirement for American troops if we undertook to pursue the enemy into the remote vastnesses of the Vietnam frontier where he would be close to his cross-border sources of supply and where the terrain would be favorable to his hit-and-hide tactics.

Also, I thought that it was timely at the start of a new year to examine the way our troops were being used in combat. It seemed to me that there was a growing tendency for our forces to take over the heavy fighting and allow most of the Vietnamese forces to perform clearing jobs and local defense behind the protective screen provided by our forces. From the beginning, I had hoped that we could depend on the Vietnamese to locate the main enemy units which our better equipped and better trained forces could then help to destroy. If this were to be the division of labor, the Vietnamese would have to assign at least half of their ba:talions to mobile combat roles—another goal I wanted set for 1966.

As for the air campaign, we should start, I thought, by reminding ourselves of the three purposes for which it had been initiated: to raise the morale in South Vietnam; to retard infiltration; and finally, to convince Hanoi that the continuation of the aggression would be increasingly costly. There were indications of some success in achieving the first two purposes, but there was no sign that Hanoi was becoming convinced of the folly of its ways. But, when one reflected on historical precedents, that was not surprising. The Soviet leaders had given no indications of any intention of calling off their Berlin blockade or the North Korean and Chinese leaders any sign of abandoning their effort to take over South Korea until the game had been played almost to the last card. It was far too early to expect our tough adversaries in the north to reveal any evidence of wavering. But that did not mean that they had no misgivings.

In this context, I advocated for 1966 a continuation of air attacks on all targets of any value to the enemy war effort lying outside the heavily populated areas, the interdiction of rail and road movement throughout North Vietnam to the extent feasible, and, after warning, the aerial mining of the principal ports, of which the most important by far was Haiphong. It was important that such a campaign be carried out without interruption and with an air of irrevocable determination to have maximum effect on the will of the enemy—the point I had made repeatedly in the past to no effect.

It was much more difficult to propose concrete goals for political progress, but I suggested one—the holding of elections in the secure areas of South Vietnam during 1966 to choose members of a constituent assembly. For a long time, we had talked with our allies about establishing a constitutionally based government in South Vietnam, but the many difficulties, while the nation was fighting for its life, had discouraged taking the first step in the long process. If everyone resolved to make that start in 1966, I felt that it would have the ancillary benefit of giving a new sense of immediate purpose to many of the lagging civil programs. At the same time, the Vietnamese would demonstrate to the world their dedication to the principle of free elections and their willingness to abide by the results.

In the United States, we needed to set new goals for improving the popular understanding of the meaning and necessity of the events taking place in South Vietnam. In my speaking tours about the country, I had been impressed not only by the general support accorded our Vietnam policy by the substantial people of the country but also by the widespread criticism that the government was not adequately explaining what was going on. There was considerable suspicion that it was holding back or distorting the facts. It was apparent that the antiwar movement would grow in 1966 unless a candid public information campaign were set in motion to forestall it.

Although my memorandum on these matters was rather widely circulated, it received no enthusiastic reception from any one. Before the President's meeting with Thieu and Ky in Honolulu in early February, I raised the matter again as a possible topic for the agenda. I explained that I held no brief for any specific goal in any sector of activity but was absolutely sure of the need for goals if we were to stay on any kind of course and know at any time how we were progressing. Still there was no observable reaction to a suggestion which no one seemed to oppose. In the absence of a supervisory mechanism of the kind I have mentioned to guide and direct the course of interdepartmental programs, there was really no place to refer such a paper as mine for action. Furthermore, there seemed to be little interest in the White House for getting full return from programs once started; it was much more interesting to start something new.

In mid-February I received a vivid reminder of the need to fight for "the hearts and minds" of the people in the United States with at least as much fervor as in South Vietnam. Senator Fulbright opened televised hearings on Vietnam policy which were said to carry the discussion to 50 million people. Although I was no longer an official, I was called to testify and thus had the opportunity to strike a blow for truth as I knew it. The committee was and remained loaded with doves, some bitterly hostile to the Administration's policy and all wanting to look good before the vast TV audience while making Administration witnesses look bad.

As Senator Fulbright and some of his senatorial supporters had made a great point of the difficulty they had in understanding what our government was really up to in Vietnam, I prepared a brief opening statement setting forth in the plainest possible terms our objectives and the strategy being pursued to attain them. I described the situation as a clash of our national objectives with those of the militant wing of the Asian Communist movement represented by the Vietcong and North Vietnam and with China and the USSR in the background. The purpose of the enemy was to impose a Communist regime on the South Vietnamese against the will of the vast majority of the people; ours was to frustrate their purpose and, in so doing, expose the myth of the invincibility of the War of National Liberation and protect Southeast Asia and other underdeveloped areas from being exposed to it later.

I explained that, to attain our ends, we had developed a strategy consisting of four components. The first included the measures taken to increase the effectiveness of ground combat against the Vietcong and the North Vietnamese units in South Vietnam. The second involved the use of air power against military targets in North Vietnam for the three purposes which I have previously enumerated. The third embraced the many political, social, and economic measures described generically as pacification, rehabilitation, or nation-building. The fourth component consisted of our political and diplomatic efforts to initiate the negotiation of a peaceful settlement. In the aggregate, the four constituted a complex but related package of measures to achieve our basic objectives. It was a strategy limited as to purpose, geographical scope, weapons, forces, and targets. All elements were interrelated and indispensable. We must be successful on all fronts; failure on any one would ultimately cause general failure. This strategy could succeed, I told my audience, if we pursued it relentlessly and refused to deviate from the course set. It carried risks, of course, but the risks were justified by the importance of the stake which Congress itself had recognized in the Tonkin Gulf Resolution of August 1964. "The U.S. regards as vital to the national interest and to the world peace the maintenance of international peace and security in Southeast Asia."

Needless to say, my statement drew no applause from the majority of the committee. I was sharply cross-examined during the rest of the day with only a kind word or two from the few senators not of the persuasion of the majority. But while it was a trying session, I left it feeling that some hits had been scored on the vulnerabilities of the inquisitors. My fan mail in subsequent days convinced me that it had not been wasted time to debate these important issues before a national audience. However, for lack of another invitation I was never privileged to use this particular forum again.

CHAPTER 30

Vietnam Preoccupations: 1966

In the course of the Fulbright hearings, the senators had pressed me for an expression of views as to the stability of the current Ky government, but I had avoided any unqualified statement of confidence. By that time it was apparent that Ky was in trouble in a quarter from which trouble had been expected. From the time of Khanh's eviction, it was apparent that Lieutenant General Thi, the warlord of the I Corps area, together with Tri Quang and his political bonzes were likely to make common cause against Ky. Overt political warfare broke out between them in March and continued into June. Ky took the offensive by inducing a directorate of senior generals to dismiss General Thi from his command on the ground that he had been acting independently of the government in Saigon, which indeed he had. But then Ky and his associates made the serious mistake of letting Thi slip out of Saigon and take refuge in his satrapy in the north where, in cooperation with Tri Quang, he established a base for antigovernment operations.

There were three factors involved in this threat of revolt against Ky. One was General Thi's ambition for hegemony among the generals; a second was the traditional Annamite regionalism in the Da Nang-Hue area; and the third was a compulsion on the part of Tri Quang and his Buddhist supporters to destroy any government which resisted their demands. The Buddhists constituted the principal threat as they had demonstrated their skill as wreckers in pulling down the Diem, Khanh, Huong, and Quat governments. Now they were turning against Ky the same tactics that had proved successful against his four immediate predecessors.

Tri Quang had had another advantage, the recollection, which, since the

367

Diem coup, succeeding Prime Ministers had always in mind, of the American reaction to strong-arm measures of the Diem police in putting down antigovernment demonstrators. Recognizing that the loss of American support over this issue had cost Diem his position and his life, high officials who followed him were naturally cautious in resisting challenges in the streets. Their timidity greatly enhanced the prestige of Tri Quang as the unmaker of premiers. Only gradually was this advantage neutralized by mounting evidence that Tri Quang had lost his standing with the Americans, who by now had come to know him as a dangerous conspirator who, if not actually controlled by the Hanoi leaders, often conducted himself in strict conformity with their interests.

At first Ky was as reluctant as his predecessors to come to grips with this threat to his government. During March and April, he took no real action against the demonstrations in Hue and Saigon, and his vacillation caused grumblings within the Army. The prestige of the Buddhist Institute rose in the public eye while that of Ky and the directorate of the generals declined. Signs of renewed factionalism accompanied by increased symptoms of anti-Americanism in Vietnam encouraged critics in the United States to call for another review of Vietnam policy.

The situation took a turn for the better in May. Ky, his backbone stiffened by official American assurances of support for strong action against Tri Quang, sent his troops into Da Nang where they regained control with little trouble. In Saigon, his police broke up the Buddhist demonstrations, which were Tri Quang's response to Ky's action in Da Nang. From that time on, Ky was in charge of the situation which, after government troops had seized the Buddhist Institute in Saigon, ceased to qualify as a crisis.

Throughout this period there was a continuing debate within our government over the way to conduct negotiations with the Communists, if they ever should come to pass. It was easy to agree on the desired outcome, the attainment of our long-time objective, an independent South Vietnam free from attack. But how to reach that objective in the face of the resistance which we were sure to encounter from our adversaries at the negotiation table?

One could foresee many difficulties and make provisions for some of them. One of my fears was that we would allow ourselves to be diverted from our basic objective to some meretricious substitute such as a cease-fire, a de-escalation, a coalition, or a premature peace. It would be so easy to yield to a humanitarian desire to save lives now and unwittingly create conditions which would result in the loss of more lives another day. I recalled how in Korea after the retreat from the Yalu we had made an armistice our objective instead of the prompt defeat of the enemy forces and thereby had paid a heavy price in American lives during the interminable haggle over armistice terms.

If both sides in negotiating adhered in their basic objectives, one could foresee a collision of an irresistible force and an immovable body exemplified by the uncompromising nature of their conflicting purposes. The enemy was bent on imposing a Communist regime on South Vietnam; we were intent on frustrating that effort and assuring a free choice by the South Vietnamese. In the end, South Vietnam would be Communist or would be independent. It was obvious that both sides could not win, and it was difficult to foresee a way to reconcile their divergent objectives through negotiations. Our side must occupy a position of marked superiority at the table to expect any back-down on the major points at issue. But if our primary objective was not negotiable, there were many matters related to it which did offer room for give and take. We Americans were not insisting on any particular form of government or set of officials in Saigon. So far as most of us were concerned, the ultimate government could be neutral or even Communist, but it must be the free choice of the South Vietnamese. A coalition government arrived at by barter rather than by ballots was a traditional Communist device to prepare a way for a take-over and could not be accepted.

If the Vietcong could not get into the government by barter how could we assure them a fair deal in a final settlement? One facile answer was to offer them an amnesty in exchange for putting down their arms along with full civil rights including those of voting and running for office. So far so good, but then the question arose as to whether they could participate in elections only as individuals or whether they might run as a political party. On this point, South Vietnamese leaders insisted that they be limited to individual participation for fear that the unity and discipline of the Vietcong would make them the strongest single party in spite of the smallness of their numbers. My own feeling was one of skepticism over the feasibility of the free election formula to meet the Vietcong problem, unexceptionable as was its principle. I simply could not believe that the Communists would ever participate in an electoral procedure which would assure honest elections on a one-man, one-vote basis. They could never win on such a basis and were not likely to be inveigled into trying.

This consideration and others raised doubt that the war could ever be terminated by formal negotiations. From the outset, the North Vietnamese had stubbornly refused to admit that their troops were fighting in South Vietnam regardless of how many were on display in the prisoner of war stockades. So how could we ever get them out of the country by negotiation? The North Vietnamese also denied the legal existence of the South Vietnamese government and insisted that the National Liberation Front alone could speak for the South Vietnamese people. Such difficulties could conceivably be circumvented if the war were allowed simply to subside with the North Vietnamese fading back to their homeland along with those

Vietcong who did not wish to remain in the south. We could reduce our forces concurrently so that, in the end, each side could claim victory by having driven the other out of the country.

There were, of course, disadvantages to this alternative of peace through the subsidence of war. There would be no certainty as to the future behavior of the opposing sides since neither would have undertaken any precise commitments for which it could be held publicly accountable. There could be no international guarantee of the permanence of the peace, something which the South Vietnamese were most anxious to obtain. The verification of the withdrawal of enemy forces would be difficult whereas our own actions in withdrawing forces and vacating bases would be done under the eyes of the whole world. As to future enemy intentions, we would probably have to hedge against a resumption of hostilities by leaving a residual force of some size or by giving an assurance to the South Vietnamese that we would return to their aid at once if the aggression were renewed.

In this long period of cogitation over ways to end the war, the subject of a cease-fire was often a lively issue of debate. The bombing pauses, which the President reluctantly conceded from time to time in response to the demands of the war critics, were short term cease-fires, which gave us a chance to observe how quickly the enemy took advantage of them to move men and supplies while immune to air attack. The occasional mutual cease-fires at Christmas, New Year's, and Tet were never universally observed and always brought forth charges of violations from both sides. While these experiences were limited, they supported my conviction of the impracticality of a true cease-fire under the conditions of the war in Vietnam. It was all very well to echo the appealing slogan "Stop the shooting and start talking," but unfortunately the cease-fire proponents had no idea of what these words meant in a confused guerrilla war on the Vietnam pattern.

Following the arrival of American combat forces, there were three kinds of ground warfare going on in South Vietnam which had to be taken into account in a cease-fire: a so-called big war between the tactical units of both sides which was quite similar to the conventional combat we had known in Korea; a local war of guerrilla bands whose operations suggested the raids of Quantrill and his men along the Missouri-Kansas border in our Civil War; and finally, what Ambassador Lodge had dubbed the "criminal war" consisting of assassination, kidnapping, and other forms of terrorism as a calculated means of the Communists for intimidating the civil population. Any true cease-fire would have to make provision for stopping all of these forms of warfare as well as related activities which did not involve the firing of weapons such as propaganda, recruiting, the collection of taxes by the Vietcong, and the multiple forms of sabotage which the Vietcong practiced. All these activities went on at varying levels of intensity and in varying combinations at different times of day and night in forty-four different

370

provinces, creating forty-four different situations and, in a sense, forty-four different wars. With such a variety of conditions from province to province, it was almost impossible to conceive of arrangements adapted to all these local situations that would result in a complete and concurrent cessation of the use of weapons and of related forms of violence throughout South Vietnam.

Obviously an armistice on the Korean model had no applicability here. In Korea, with a stabilized, clearly defined fortified front, it had been possible to stop all firing at a prescribed hour. In Vietnam, with no front lines and no secure rear areas, the concept was almost meaningless. If it meant simply that all shooting stopped while other war-sustaining actions continued, it would offer all the advantages to the enemy—something like an armistice between the criminals and police in one of our big cities.

After many discussions over the feasibility of a cease-fire I undertook, for my own edification, to list the preconditions for an acceptable cease-fire. There were such matters on the list as the timing of a cessation of hostilities; the freezing in place of all units of both sides; the supply arrangements for units so immobilized (who feeds the troops?); the relation of the timing of the cease-fire to the opening of political negotiations; and the verification of reported violations of the cease-fire. Any one of these topics could require months of negotiation with the Communists, a fact which led me to conclude that a cease-fire should not be undertaken until a political settlement had been virtually agreed upon. If both sides knew how they were coming out at the end of the negotiation, it should not be too difficult to achieve a cease-fire which would then be a part of the scenario of a total settlement.

These were some of the broad issues in 1966 which bemused government planners concerned with ending the war. In addition, there was a whole bagful of other problems, if one assumed that somehow we had brought the Communists to the negotiating table, an objective which had become almost an end in itself in the minds of many of our leaders in Washington. I was particularly concerned with the way we proposed to use our blue chips and I addressed a series of memoranda on the subject to the President in hope of stirring up official interest in determining how we should play our bargaining counters if we ever got the chance.

The basic issue was simple enough. We knew, or should have known, how we wanted to come out of the negotiations and what kind of agreement would assure our objective. Our most valuable chip, the bombing of North Vietnam, was obviously causing great pain to the enemy. His discomfort was evidenced by the violent propaganda campaign promoted by Hanoi and abetted by American doves at home to make us stop the bombing. There were other blue chips in our bag consisting of other actions that Hanoi wanted us to stop, such as our military operations in South Vietnam and the continuing build-up of our forces and bases. Also, Hanoi probably would want us to undertake certain political commitments to assure just treatment for the Vietcong following a termination of hostilities.

Just as the enemy wanted these chips from us, he had a pile which we wanted from him: an end to the attacks of the big war and the terrorism of the local and criminal wars, a cessation of the infiltration of men and supplies from North Vietnam, and the withdrawal of North Vietnamese units from South Vietnam as well as from the sanctuaries of Laos, Cambodia, and the DMZ. Also, we wanted the safe return of our prisoners of war and the eradication of the clandestine infrastructure which held together the Vietcong political organization in the countryside.

There was a certain symmetry between our mutual desires that suggested reasonable swaps: a cessation of reinforcements by our side for a stopping of infiltration by theirs; the withdrawal of outside forces by both sides; the vacating of our bases in exchange for the evacuation of their sanctuaries; and a simultaneous exchange of all war prisoners. There were asymmetries, too; for example, our use of the air arm against North Vietnam and their use of terrorist attacks against the civil population had no counterparts. But despite the apparent dissimilarity, our bombing and their terror and sabotage had similar purposes—to destroy the enemy morale, throttle his economy, and sap his war-sustaining capability in order to establish a basis for bargaining.

We never reached an agreement among ourselves on the price to exact for a termination of the bombing of North Vietnam. Most of my colleagues favored equating it to a cessation of infiltration, but I found a serious objection to this. Any agreement on infiltration would require international supervision to assure performance, something the Communists would never accept, whereas the whole world would know whether or not we were bombing North Vietnam. For this reason, I favored lumping together our bombing of North Vietnam and our offensive ground action in South Vietnam, and equating the aggregate to all enemy operations of the big, local, and criminal wars, operations which were regularly recorded and tabulated as a part of the data used to measure the course of the war. This pairing had the added advantage of permitting flexibility in raising and lowering the level of our activities in proportion to the enemy's. If the latter rose 10 percent, we could increase our bombing or ground offensives 10 percent or reduce them to zero if the enemy was completely inactive.

I was not able to rally support for this approach. Although most of the President's advisers talked tough about keeping military pressure on the enemy during negotiations and about refusing to accept another stalemated negotiation like Panmunjom, we never got these good intentions recorded in any binding manner. Hence, we were never in a position to prepare public and Congressional opinion for the hard-nosed positions which we would have had to take and hold to achieve the negotiation objectives most of us favored. In particular, we needed to make it crystal clear to the enemy and to our own people that we would never stop the bombing or pay any other price for the privilege of engaging in negotiations and explain to our people why this position was in our national interest. Meanwhile, foreign and domestic propaganda media were telling them that the bombing was illegal, ineffective, and counterproductive in that it was making the enemy tougher and alienating our friends. To this propaganda our government made no effective reply although we had a testimonial to the efficacy of the bombing in the world-wide campaign to compel us to stop it.

CHAPTER 31

~~~~~~

Vietnam: 1967

By the end of 1966, I had begun to feel that my value as a presidential consultant was steadily declining and that after a year and a half of absence from the scene of action in Vietnam I was in danger of becoming an ex-expert. So I asked Walt Rostow to sound out the President's receptivity to my resignation. Getting back a quick rejection of the proposal, I asked and received permission to make a ten-day trip to Vietnam to update my knowledge of the situation.

I returned from it very much struck by the progress which had been made in solving many of the problems I had known, particularly those which had arisen from a lack of military resources. The big war of the search-and-destroy operations was going well, and the enemy was suffering severe losses in the engagements of the large tactical units. Our forces were fighting their way into the formerly inviolate enemy base areas, assisted by B-52 strikes which kept the enemy constantly on the move. From the many prisoners and documents captured, information on the enemy was now forthcoming in quantities so great as to be almost unmanageable. However, it was largely tactical intelligence which threw little light on the long-range plans of the senior enemy leadership.

The military progress resulted in a large measure from General Westmoreland's success and timeliness in providing logistical support for the growing American forces which, by January 1967, had reached about 385,000. They were well equipped and supplied. If there was a fault, it was that, as in Korea, they had brought much equipment not needed in this theater.

As for the local and criminal wars, as well as the pacification activities in the provinces, the situation was much less favorable. The province chiefs were still overburdened by the combined load of their military and non-military responsibilities and harassed by their multiple Vietnamese bosses

374

and American advisers. On our side, we had combined all of our provincial activities into an Office of Civil Operations, but there had not been time for the effect of the change to be felt.

Since the success of pacification necessarily depended on achieving some minimal level of security behind which to work, a decision had been taken to assign roughly half of the South Vietnamese infantry battalions for use in the provinces in local defense. Also our American forces were preparing to support pacification in addition to their other missions of destroying the main units of the enemy, expanding territorial control around their base areas, and reopening rail and highway communications.

The acceptance of this additional mission without definition of limits renewed a concern which I had expressed to President Johnson in the preceding year. In both 1966 and 1967, General Westmoreland had submitted a twelve-month campaign plan to Washington, which set forth his interpretation of the mission of his forces for the next year and described in general terms how he intended to discharge it. It was a most important document because it provided the basis for troop requests during the coming year. Yet, so far as I could see, it was never carefully reviewed and formally approved, disapproved, or amended. I called the President's attention each year to the fact that, under the language of the document, General Westmoreland would be entirely justified to ask for troops to defend all Vietnam to its utmost frontiers and to use American troops to conduct pacification operations to any extent he saw fit. However, I failed to arouse any real attention to this matter of potential troop requirements until it became an important issue in 1968.

As a result of the impressions of my trip to Vietnam, I again urged the adoption of specific goals, this time for 1967 which might conceivably be the year of victory. To have any chance of decisive success I was sure that we must make a maximum, simultaneous effort across the whole front of our activities. We would have to do better in the ground operations in the south, raise the level of air actions in the north, carry through the constitutional program leading to a presidential election, hold the line on inflation, and show greater progress in pacification than in 1966. I told the President that if we could do these things in South Vietnam—and they seemed within the bounds of possibility—while conducting ourselves at home in such a way as to show that, regardless of internal and external pressures, the United States would not change its course, we had every right to anticipate a greatly improved situation by the end of 1967. Even a successful termination was possible if we did nothing to encourage the enemy in the meantime.

As the strength of American forces in Vietnam rose in 1967 and our casualties mounted proportionately, the President was assailed by complaints over the inadequacy of the troop contributions of our Free World allies which, at that time, amounted to slightly more than 50,000. In mid-July he asked Clark Clifford and me to make the rounds of our allies in Korea, Thailand, the Philippines, Australia, and New Zealand for the purpose of exchanging views on the conduct of the war and explaining the need for a greater allied effort, particularly in ground forces. Unfortunately, even before we had left town news of our mission had leaked to the Washington press, which described us as an arm-twisting delegation off to squeeze more troops from laggard allies reluctant to do their fair share. This publicity led President Marcos of the Philippines to decline our visit and caused unhappiness among our other hosts-to-be who were put on an uncomfortable spot vis-à-vis the antiwar elements of their own electorates.

In spite of this bad start, in all the countries visited we received the close and sympathetic attention of our hosts, who seemed genuinely appreciative of the courtesy of President Johnson in consulting them on the conduct of the war, even though the consultation carried with it a reminder of the smallness of their contribution. We visitors, in turn, received insight into their views on the war and the politics of the region. Our Anglo-Saxon friends in Australia and New Zealand seemed to think the strategy of the war being pursued was about right whereas the Asians felt that we were not pressing the enemy hard enough. They urged such things as the mining or bombing of Haiphong harbor and the cutting of the infiltration routes in Laos. Some even talked about an Inchon-type landing on the Vietnamese coast north of the seventeenth parallel. However, our reminder that such operations would require greatly increased ground forces tended to dampen their enthusiasm.

On the sensitive subject of troop requirements no one argued against the increased needs set forth in our strategic presentation. But each country had good reasons why little more could be expected from it. The Thais had a growing guerrilla threat in their northeast; the Australians and New Zealanders pointed to new defense problems arising from the planned British withdrawal of troops from Malaysia and Singapore; the Koreans faced an increase of terrorist infiltration from North Korea. Nevertheless, in no country was the attitude completely negative, and we returned home reasonably confident that the countries visited would respond in due time to our nudging. Eventually this hope was modestly realized as allied forces gradually increased to over 70,000 men in the next two years. While our mission could not claim all the credit it is fair to say that it was a factor in setting this trend in motion. Although the allied troop strength was always less than we Americans wished, we could remind ourselves that in the Korean War the top figure for allied combat strength (less that of the United States) was about 39,000 even though that war was waged under the flag of the United Nations.

Notwithstanding the fact that military operations in 1967 were generally successful in defeating the hit-and-run forays of the enemy from their cross-border sanctuaries into South Vietnam, opposition to the war in the

United States continued to rise at an alarming rate. While prominent politicians were generally reluctant to advocate openly a disengagement from our Vietnam commitment, many were advancing proposals which, if carried out, would eventually have had that effect. I refer to such things as the concept of withdrawing our forces into enclaves along the coast and waiting out the enemy, the various demands to reduce or stop the bombing in North Vietnam, and the proposal to give the Communists some hand in the procedure already underway to establish a constitutional government in South Vietnam. Many of the proponents of such schemes were, I felt sure, the victims of misinformation or lack of information and could be rescued from error, if the truth could reach them. The most common complaint that I heard as I traveled about the country continued to be that the average citizen was confused about the issues and felt that his government was not leveling with him.

Although my field of expertise certainly did not include public relations, I made several ineffectual efforts to get something started in this vastly important and woefully neglected area. Using the experience gained in my trip with Clark Clifford, I reported to the President the concern of our allies over failure to get our message across in international circles and the evidence I saw that we were doing equally badly at home. I suggested that, for the purpose of organizing a common effort with our Asian allies, the State Department arrange periodic meetings of allied Ambassadors in Washington in order to identify informational problem areas and to prepare public statements for joint use.

To assist in coping with the far more serious problem of domestic public relations, I recommended a touring panel of high-level governmental experts to make the round of the leaders of the publicity media as I had done upon returning from Vietnam in 1965. I thought that a national figure such as Cabot Lodge might lead such a party, supported by qualified spokesmen for the political, military, economic, and pacification programs. Not only could such a panel give off-the-record briefings to media chiefs but it could appear before television and answer publicly some of the questions troubling our people. It could also be used on swings through the academic world and assist in allaying the growing discontent on the campuses. These suggestions were generally well received in the White House, but it was felt that an effort such as this should be delayed until after the Vietnamese presidential election in October. Some work was in progress along these lines when the matter received support from another quarter.

On November 2, 1967 the President assembled in the cabinet room a group of distinguished private citizens, later referred to as the Wise Men, to get their views on the conduct of the war. In composition, it was almost the same as that of the more widely publicized meeting in March of the following year and included Dean Acheson, George Ball, McGeorge Bundy, Douglas Dillon, Arthur Dean, Cabot Lodge, Robert Murphy, Clark

Clifford, General Bradley, and Justice Fortas. In sharp contrast to their attitude a few months later, in these discussions they displayed general satisfaction with the progress and conduct of the military aspects of the war. I recall only one visitor who advocated cutting back the bombing; he did so for the purpose of creating an atmosphere favorable to negotiations. There were several who warned against pushing negotiations too hard and raising excessive expectations in the public mind. The theme that dominated the session was the public information problem—how to get a better understanding of the issues and of the situation on the part of the general public and of special groups such as the media and the universities. While none of the specific measures discussed offered the hope of a decisive breakthrough, I was impressed by the unanimity of their concern for this neglected area of governmental effort.

Because of the eminence of this group and the regard of the President for its members, I expected some vigorous action to flow from the meeting. But nothing happened. Indeed, I discovered that no official record had been kept of the discussion at the meeting and that no follow-up action had been undertaken on the suggestions made. After awaiting action in vain for a couple of weeks, I resumed my prodding in a note to the President which urged the drafting of a plan for informing important sectors of domestic and public opinion regarding our objectives in Vietnam. The plan would have provided for special approaches to the media, the opinion molders (teachers, ministers, columnists, broadcasters), political and business leaders, the general public at home, and selected individuals abroad. The means used to reach these groups could have included a variety of devices such as the usual speeches, news conferences, and TV appearances of officials; citizens' committees in large cities supplied by Washington with speakers and literature; White House briefings of the big shots of the political, business, and media worlds; trips to Vietnam by selected senior citizens; a government-sponsored TV program to answer citizens' questions about Vietnam; a Central Information Center in Washington, where the media representatives could get any reasonable questions about Vietnam answered authoritatively in a single place; and an aggressive information program conducted by our embassies abroad.

The question was who should draft such a plan and then who should carry it out? I suggested several alternative means for drafting it and recommended that the White House staff develop their pros and cons for the President. My paper came back approved, but again there was no follow-up action of which I was aware. If anything was accomplished at this period in improving the government's case before the world, such progress was more than offset by the increasing clamor of the opposition.

The end of a calendar year always seemed a proper time to review the situation and reconsider the alternatives available to our Vietnam policy. At the end of 1967, such a review was stimulated by a proposal attributed to Secretary McNamara that we consider stabilizing our military strength in Vietnam by the announcement of a troop ceiling at about current levels. Thereafter, we would continue the war in much the same way as it was being conducted but would make every effort to hold down American casualties and to pass the burden of the fighting to the South Vietnamese. The air war would continue unchanged for a time, but, at some point, we would stop the bombing of North Vietnam except for targets in the DMZ. The purpose of this modified strategy would be to allay apprehensions at home and abroad of a further expansion of the conflict and to increase the pressure in Hanoi to reduce its military activities or to enter upon negotiations. In commenting on this proposal to the President, I found it necessary to compose a rather lengthy estimate of the situation to set forth my views.

Although volumes had been written on our alternatives up to that time. I contended that there always had been and still were only four alternatives, although each had several variants. The basic four in simplest terms were: *all-out, pull-out, pull-back,* or *stick-it-out. All-out* was the solution of the extreme hawks who would increase the military pressure in one or several ways. In the air war, they would remove all restrictions as to targets in North Vietnam (except those in or near the densely populated urban centers) and attack them with maximum intensity in the shortest feasible time. In the ground war, *all-out* usually implied an expansion varying from raids into the cross-border sanctuaries of Laos and Cambodia to various forms of invasion of North Vietnam. Usually the *all-out* partisans also favored a declaration of war and the imposition of wartime controls at home. *Pull-out* meant just what it said, to withdraw our forces from South Vietnam just as rapidly as we could safely do so. In 1967 there were few if any spokesmen for such a measure among men of substance in public life, and as I was unable to advance any arguments to support it, I did not include it among the alternatives worth considering at the end of 1967. *Pull-back* was the de-escalation alternative which usually included a cessation of the bombing of the North, a reduction of offensive ground operations, and some abandonment of forward terrain, which could go as far as the withdrawal of our forces into defensive enclaves along the coast. *Stick-it-out* was the status quo alternative which amounted to continuing the current strategy emphasizing, first, aggressive military operations to increase population security and to inflict casualties on enemy ground forces and, second, air pressure on North Vietnam to limit infiltration, to drain war-making resources, and to convince Hanoi of the need to change the game.

Just as our side had four basic alternatives, so did Hanoi: *escalate, play-dead, protract,* and *negotiate,* which corresponded roughly in character to ours but differed somewhat as to content. Their escalation could take the form of increased infiltration, renewed cross-border offensives, the introduction of new and better weapons, the use of foreign Communist volunteers in North Vietnam or even in South Vietnam, and possibly the opening of a new front in some such place as Thailand, Burma, Korea, or Berlin. The *play-dead* alternative was the fade-away option, avoiding further serious combat losses and giving the impression that the war was ending or, at least, subsiding. *Protract* corresponded to our *stick-it-out* and implied a continuation of the strategy of 1967, although it had proved both costly and unremunerative for them. The *negotiate* alternative was resort to the negotiation table as a new sector of conflict and maneuver after the model of Panmunjom. It offered Hanoi an escape hatch to avoid capitulation if the going got too hard, or a propaganda sounding board to reinforce the escalation alternative. It was a unilateral advantage since we could hardly fail to respond to a call for negotiations after our breast-beating pursuit of a peaceful settlement. They could pick the time to talk; we had no such freedom of action.

After analyzing the probable consequences of any combination of these alternatives, it seemed to me that our best choice was to stay on our present course and *stick-it-out* provided that we could keep the home front intact and contain our burning national impatience for quick results. *All-out* would require more forces than we had available or could raise in short order and would be moderately risky in its foreign and domestic effects. *Pull-back,* of which the proposal attributed to Secretary McNamara was an example, offered nothing beyond a temporary appeasement of some of our critics; it would be read as weakness by Hanoi and thus, I thought, would prolong rather than shorten the war.

Taking all factors into account, I recommended to the President that he continue his current strategy while making every effort to stiffen the backbone of the home front. We should be prepared to meet any of the forms of escalation open to the enemy and make no move of de-escalation without compensatory action by him. As for negotiations, we should always be prepared to enter upon them if the other side appeared to be serious but with the firm resolve not to tolerate a Panmunjom.

I even ventured to indicate what I would recommend to Ho Chi Minh if I were one of his advisers. My advice to him also would be to stay on his present course of military, terrorist, and political action in spite of the disappointments of 1967, at least until he could understand better the situation in the United States and evaluate the staying power of our leaders and people. If he eventually decided that he could not count on us to cave in, he should then propose negotiations and exploit them to gain time, to bruit propaganda, and to divide the Americans from the South Vietnamese.

As 1967 drew to a close, President Johnson seemed to be favorably inclined to my analysis of the alternatives open to our side. As we now know, Ho and his advisers viewed the situation otherwise and would have rejected my gratuitous advice. His choice was for all-out escalation in 1968, preparatory to opening a negotiation on the Korean model.

CHAPTER 32

The Climactic Year: 1968

Since its inception in 1954, the Vietnam War had been a conflict between two sets of international objectives pursued consistently with little deviation by the contending sides: an independent South Vietnam free from aggression on the one hand, or a South Vietnam with an imposed Communist government, ripe for absorption into North Vietnam on the other. But, while their objectives remained remarkably constant over the years, each side repeatedly changed its strategy to meet new conditions. Usually these changes were made necessary either by the actions of the adversary or by evidence of the inadequacy of the current strategy.

Any change on our side, whether in strategy, tactics, or logistics, was usually branded in the American press as escalation, a term which acquired an evil sense in usage roughly synonymous with aggression. Escalation became a word of reproach, used by war critics to describe any action of ours, regardless of provocation, which could be remotely regarded as an expansion of the war. Actions by the other side apparently did not qualify for the term. Actually, escalation was an inherent feature of the strategy of gradualism which our government had pursued since 1965 in deference to fear that over-reaction might expand the conflict to World War III. Our cautious behavior, however, gained little credit for the Administration because each of the many small steps taken to increase pressure on the enemy provided one more instance of escalation for the critics to denounce. Then we would take time out to explain our motives and, in so doing, often revealed our future intentions to the enemy. Under such conditions we were at a serious disadvantage in playing this international poker game, a fact which should not have surprised the country that had invented poker. Had we played our cards boldly and close to our vest instead of playing them apologetically before an audience of kibitzers openly discussing our hand, with our preponderant resources we should have

381

driven our less affluent opponent from the table. Instead, we gave away our blue chips one by one as a price to get into the game and eventually arrived at the negotiation table in Paris practically broke.

I have made the point that the objectives of the adversaries in Vietnam remained constant while the strategies were adjusted frequently. The first important shift was that of Hanoi in 1959 when Ho Chi Minh declared a War of National Liberation against South Vietnam in order to regain the ground lost during the early years of Diem's presidency. The significance of this change from dependence on political subversion to active guerrilla warfare was not fully appreciated in Washington until 1960 and 1961 when the deterioration of the situation caused President Kennedy to change his strategy generally in accordance with the recommendations of the Taylor-Rostow mission. This reaction by our side contained the military threat for the time being but the political situation went from bad to worse until the overthrow of Diem offered Hanoi a golden opportunity to finish off South Vietnam. The Communist passage to the offensive supported by tactical units of the North Vietnamese Army was the next significant modification of enemy strategy, and it would probably have brought them success but for President Johnson's decision to meet the threat by introducing American ground troops and initiating the air campaign against the North.

Both sides slugged it out in 1966 and 1967 with the enemy getting very much the worst of it. As we now know, sometime in the latter half of 1967, Hanoi took the decision which made 1968 the climactic year of the war. That decision was to abandon the strategy of protracted war by which they had hoped to wear down our side and to pass to an all-out offensive under cover of the Tet cease-fire at the end of January. I have never understood why this decision was taken. Clearly Ho Chi Minh had not agreed with the estimate of the situation which I had given President Johnson at the end of 1967 as reported in the preceding chapter. Possibly misled by his own intelligence services or by the auto-intoxicating power of his own propaganda, Ho seemingly came to believe that our forces had really suffered the losses in 1967 which the Hanoi radio and press had claimed and that the South Vietnamese were ripe for revolt against their "American masters." In any event, his troops attacked on January 29 to the slogan "general offensive-general uprising," apparently convinced that they were advancing to final victory.

One must admit that the enemy put on a good show. Over the years I had often wondered why neither the Vietcong nor the North Vietnamese units had never attacked us in several places at the same time, particularly during the lean years when we had few mobile reserves. I eventually concluded that the logistic difficulties of secretly assembling the necessary supplies by bicycle and porter for simultaneous attacks on widely separated battlefields were probably too much for the enemy leaders to coordinate. Hence the real surprise of Tet to me was not the fact that the enemy mounted a big offensive—it had been no secret that they were planning one against the principal cities and towns—but the approximate simultaneity achieved by so many different attacks. In the course of two days they hit five cities, thirty-nine provincial capitals, and many smaller towns. While they secured no lodgment except in Hue, they created scenes of death, fire, and destruction which, as recorded on American TV screens and reported in gory headlines in the American press, scared much of the American public and some of our officials into a funk from which recovery was slow and, in some cases, never complete.

At the time, American military men both in Vietnam and in the United States commented on the analogy between the Tet offensive and the Battle of the Bulge in World War II. Just as Hitler had lost the last of his combat-worthy divisions in the Ardennes, Ho Chi Minh lost the flower of his forces in the Tet offensive and the subsequent operations of 1968. Out of the 84,000 men who, we estimated, were committed to the immediate Tet offensive, over 30,000 were killed in the first two weeks of the fighting. In the first six months of the year, the number of enemy killed in action approached 120,000.

While the enemy was losing the war on the battlefield, he was gaining a valuable psychological victory in the United States and in large parts of the world. The general public was shocked by the unexpected vitality shown by an enemy whom many had supposed to be on his last legs. Convinced that there had been a disaster in spite of official claims to the contrary, politicians, war critics, and news media raised the cry that we had been betrayed. The culprits were presumably the civilian leaders who had concealed the true state of things in Vietnam together with the military leaders who, lulled into a false sense of security by their notorious optimism, had allowed themselves to be surprised. Also sharing the blame were our impotent Vietnamese allies who were incapable of securing even their principal centers of population. Official after-action reports from Vietnam which should have dispelled these misapprehensions were disbelieved, denounced as a cover-up by the guilty, or simply ignored.

In the midst of this hubbub, President Johnson directed the President's Foreign Intelligence Advisory Board of which I was chairman to investigate the charges that American forces had been surprised by the Tet offensive. After going over the available documentary evidence and talking to many officials, we concluded that there was nothing to indicate that a lack of information had caused any American unit to fail to carry out its assigned mission at the time of the enemy attack. That did not mean, of course, that our commanders knew in advance the time, place, and intensity of every attack made. Intelligence is rarely if ever that explicit and, in this case, the indicators had pointed to the period just before the Tet holidays or just after Tet as the most probable times of attack. But a competent commander does not need a precise warning to be ready for an enemy who is known to be poised to attack, and fortunately our commanders in Vietnam were competent.

How is it possible even now to explain the distorted interpretation placed on these events in the United States? There is probably no single explanation, but a number of factors certainly exercised an influence. Since 1965, our people at home had been exposed to a constant flood of information and misinformation on Vietnam from officials, press, radio, and TV. Much in the reports was or seemed contradictory and hence of dubious credibility, although they were not necessarily inaccurate because of the widely differing conditions throughout the provinces. Faced with a mixed assortment of facts, half-facts, rumors, and fabrications, the consumer at home was obliged to make a choice of what to accept as true, and he would have been more than human if he did not select for belief those things which coincided with his own predilections. Thus, most of our citizens constructed in their minds personal mosaics made up of selected bits and pieces of news which depicted, in the aggregate, a situation which was far removed from reality.

In forming the popular concept of what had happened during the Tet offensive, TV was the dominant factor. The picture of a few flaming Saigon houses, presented by a gloomy-voiced telecaster as an instance of the destruction caused in the capital, created the inevitable impression that this was the way it was in all or most of Saigon. This human tendency to generalize from a single fact to a universal conclusion has always been a prime cause for the distorted views regarding Vietnam and certainly contributed to the pessimism in the United States after the Tet offensive in 1968.

I mentioned that even some officials, in spite of having access to government reports from Vietnam, joined the Cassandra chorus bewailing defeat. A partial explanation of their state of mind may be found in the greater impact upon them of the spectacular media reports than the low key official reports which always arrived after those of the media had time to make their effect. Press, radio, and TV can and do report an incident on the spot without waiting to verify or interpret the facts. A responsible official, on the contrary, must at least try to make some verification before firing off a cable to Washington, and he will often feel obliged to add an interpretation to help his superiors understand what is happening. Thus he is usually scooped by the media which have the great advantage of forming the first impression in the governmental mind, which the follow-up official report, if at variance, will find hard to set straight.

Another point is that the official reports from Vietnam passed through several intervening headquarters on their way to destination, where their contents were often reworked and summarized before being forwarded. This processing had the effect of bleaching out the news and removing the vividness imparted by the original composer who was under the influence of the actual event. This phenomenon, I believe, caused many Washington officials to miss the urgency of the pre-Tet reporting from Saigon which should have put everyone on notice that something extraordinary was about to occur. As a result, many in Washington were psychologically unprepared when it did occur and thus fell an easy prey to despondency.

The burning question before the President in February and March was the probable course of military events in South Vietnam during the rest of the year and how to prepare for them. Should we expect further attacks on the Tet pattern and get ready to defend ourselves against them or was it time to pass to the offensive to exploit the demoralization of the enemy as the result of his losses? In either case Westmoreland would need more troops to achieve maximum effect, as he was quick to point out.

It took several weeks to form a reasonably clear picture in the White House of the actual conditions in Vietnam in the immediate post-Tet period. There were certain obvious things, notably the fact that the enemy had brought the war into the cities and towns for the first time and had inflicted heavy casualties on the civilian population. In so doing, he had dealt a blow to the prestige of the Saigon government, exposing it to the charge of impotence in defending its people. Indeed, many Vietnamese units, heavily hit in the provinces, had withdrawn into the towns and cities, thus rendering up rural territory to the enemy. Other matters were less clear—the degree of the setback to pacification, the effect on the national economy, and the degree of loss of combat-readiness among Vietnamese units. But by mid-February it was evident that the enemy had failed to occupy and hold any important towns except Hue or to damage seriously any important airfields, communications, or other military facilities. They had not destroyed any major Vietnamese units or stirred up anything which even enemy propaganda could call an uprising among the population.

While the enemy had failed to achieve his broad objectives and had not been able to sustain his attacks, Westmoreland in his reports conceded the Communists' capability of mounting another round of attacks although probably not of Tet magnitude. Westy was particularly uneasy about a renewal of the campaign in the northern provinces abutting on the DMZ in the area where the Khe Sanh outpost of the Marines had been under heavy pressure for several months. To prepare for such eventualities, as well as for a passage to the counteroffensive, on February 12 Westmoreland requested the immediate deployment of an airborne brigade and a Marine regiment to Vietnam and asked to have the remainder of the two divisions from which these units came ready for deployment if requested at a later date. So far as I ever knew, these were the only reinforcements which he ever requested as a direct result of Tet, a matter which soon became the subject of much debate in and out of government.

The confusion over what reinforcements Westmoreland had requested was a by-product of a review of our strategy directed by President Johnson after the Tet offensive had demonstrated the drastic change which the enemy had made in his. It looked as if he might try to continue his winter-spring offensive with diminished strength at a level at least sufficient to make headlines in the American press. Thereby, he might hope to create conditions favorable to opening negotiations with a concurrent cessation of the bombing of North Vietnam. Hanoi leaders would hardly overlook the possible advantages in negotiating with an administration facing presidential elections in the fall, and, for that reason, might wish to open talks with President Johnson's Administration. On the other hand, they still had formidable manpower reserves in the north and might decide to try again to gain a decisive victory before diplomatic overtures.

As I saw the possibilities, we had three alternatives worth considering if we continued to adhere to our long-term objective of an independent South Vietnam free from attack. We could provide limited reinforcements consisting of those Westmoreland had requested for immediate delivery and the few additional American units which could be ready in time to take part in the 1968 campaign. These units would permit a limited offensive to exploit the weakened condition of the enemy, regain the initiative, and thus might create conditions favorable for negotiations. A second alternative would be to withhold further American reinforcements, conduct a mobile defense in South Vietnam limited to protecting population centers, and thus provide a low-cost protective screen behind which to build up the political and military potential of the Vietnamese government. The objective in this case would be a military stalemate favorable to the uninterrupted development of indigenous strength; "Vietnamization" it was to be called in the Nixon Administration. A third alternative would be an all-out escalation well beyond the existing ground rules, expanding the ground war into the cross-border sanctuaries, and removing most or all the limitations in the air war. However, since American reinforcements of the necessary magnitude could not reach Vietnam in time for use in 1968, this strategy could not have been put into effect until the following year, even if the President had been willing to approve it.

Reverting to my former definitions, the first alternative would be a variant of the *stick-it-out* strategy, the second of the *pull-back*, and the third of the *all-out*. Regardless of the choice of alternatives, the facts were that Westmoreland could not receive a fresh unit before about June or significant numbers before the end of the year, and then at the cost of draining the strategic reserve in the United States to the vanishing point. In order to maintain any kind of reserve for world-wide contingencies, in all three cases it would be necessary, I thought, to call up reserves at home.

In response to the President's desire to review the alternatives before making new decisions, other studies like mine were floated about the senior executive offices, and General Wheeler at the President's instigation encouraged Westmoreland to prepare one showing what might be done with a substantial increase in strength beyond the current manpower ceiling of 525,000. The plan Westy eventually developed was designed to show the troop requirements for an *all-out* strategy similar to the third alternative outlined above. It was a contingency plan based on the highly pessimistic assumptions that the South Vietnamese troop contribution did not increase as planned, that the enemy was reinforced heavily by further infiltration, and that the Koreans, alarmed by the seizure of the *Pueblo* in January and by recent North Korean raids, would shortly withdraw all or part of their forces from South Vietnam. Being a study of the forces needed to support an aggressive strategy under very adverse conditions, it is not surprising that the estimated cost was high. Under these assumptions, it indicated a need for additional infantry battalions by the end of 1968 which with air, navy, and supporting forces would have amounted to 206,000 men and would have required a large call-up of reservists.

General Wheeler visited Westmoreland from February 23 to 25, went over the contingency plan with him, and brought its contents back to Washington for consideration. After hearing Wheeler's report at a White House breakfast on February 28, the President directed Dean Rusk and Clark Clifford, who was to succeed McNamara as Secretary of Defense on the following day, to develop recommendations by March 4 that would take into account the situation as reported by General Wheeler and alternative courses of action. It was agreed that Clifford would host the effort at the Pentagon.

The first meeting of the working group assembled the same day in Clifford's dining room. The principals, as I remember them, were Rusk, Katzenbach, and William Bundy from State; Clifford, Nitze, Warnke, and Goulding from Defense; Wheeler from the JCS; Fowler from Treasury; Helms from CIA; and Rostow and myself from the White House. With slight shifts in individuals, we met for nearly a week preparing a recommended course of action to cover the remainder of 1968.

Under Clifford's direction, the members were formed into groups and assigned papers to prepare on the principal issues which the President should take into account before making a decision: the ground reinforcements needed for the short and midterm, the air and naval campaigns to be conducted against North Vietnam, the need for a call-up of reserves, the cost of the various programs under consideration, and the domestic impact of decisions arising from them. As the drafts were prepared and submitted to the committee of the whole for review, it became clear to me that some of the civilians in the Department of Defense were taking a new tack which caught me by surprise. Apparently, they were interpreting the events of Tet and its aftermath in quite a different way from the rest of us. Rather than regarding these events as a net victory which should be exploited if the resources could be made available, they appeared to feel that

Tet had proved that success in Vietnam could never be attained by military means. Hence, we should cease sending reinforcements, minimize our losses, try to stalemate the situation with the resources presently committed, and hope for a break. Also, they seemed to have missed the distinction between what Westmoreland was specifically requesting, about 25,000 men, and the requirements of his contingency plan, about 206,000. In the course of our discussions, their gist was leaked to the press in a distorted form, and the 206,000 figure was publicized as a firm request for reinforcements, one which demonstrated the endless character of the war as it was being waged and the urgency of revising a costly, hopeless strategy.

If a simple explanation exists for this confusion, it may be the fact that some of the individuals involved in the Clifford study were not initiated into the jargon of military planners. To the latter, a requirement is an estimate of resources which may be needed to meet a contingency arising under certain assumed conditions. Every contingency plan includes a requirement and the Pentagon is chock-a-block with contingency plans and hypothetical requirements. If the troop requirement of all these plans were added together they could be used to prove that the military could put every able-bodied citizen into uniform and would still lack manpower to meet their needs.

While some public commentators on these discussions, often without ever having been present, seemed able to summarize for publication the views expressed by those who were present, their reportorial skills far exceed mine. By the nature of these meetings they were a rather disorderly crossfire of individual expressions of opinion with no official record kept. About all that I can state with reasonable certainty is that there was no audible opposition to sending Westmoreland at once the force of some 25,000 men which he had requested and that no one recommended sending him the 206,000 men contained in his contingency plan. The real debate was whether we should readjust our strategy and, if so, the new direction to give it.

I had no difficulty in deciding my own position. I favored giving Westmoreland at once the 25,000 men requested, but merely noting his contingency figure of 206,000 as illustrative of what might be needed under one rather extreme set of circumstances. Its principal utility was to remind us how weak was the pool of ready forces at home to meet contingencies not only in Southeast Asia, but in Korea, Europe, and the Middle East as well. I strongly supported General Wheeler in urging a call-up of reserves to add a three-division balanced force to strengthen our strategic reserve at home. Not only was such a call-up justified by military considerations, but it would have a useful political value in demonstrating to our friends and enemies alike that we meant business and did not consider turning back. Particularly, it would remind our own citizens that, though technically not at war, we were in a situation of emergency which placed on them duties and responsibilities analogous to those of a state of declared war.

As to the conduct of the war in South Vietnam, I took advantage of the occasion to repeat my former recommendation that General Westmoreland be sent fresh strategic guidance. As I mentioned in Chapter 31, Westmoreland had adopted the practice of sending an annual campaign plan to Washington which described how he intended to carry out his mission as the field commander during the following year. He had submitted such plans at the end of 1966 and 1967. His language in the plans suggested to me that he placed a very broad interpretation on his mission, one which could justify troop requests far beyond current ceilings, and I called the President's attention to the fact. Nevertheless, insofar as I know, the plans were accepted without comment, a fact which gave Westmoreland the right to assume that his view of the mission was correct. Hence at the time of crisis in 1968, it was not surprising to detect in the language of some of his cables a feeling that, by national policy, he was responsible for evicting the enemy from all South Vietnam, something which clearly exceeded the strength he had at the time or ever might be expected to have. In fairness to him, I thought he should be told that, in this phase of the conflict, remote terrain along the frontiers of South Vietnam meant nothing in itself insofar as Washington was concerned, that the President and his advisers looked with favor on the avoidance of combat close to the cross-border sanctuaries of the enemy where he had the advantage of short lines of communications, and that they saw no advantage in paying a high price to hold exposed outposts like Khe Sanh. Apart from other disadvantages, such border operations offered the enemy the opportunity of gaining cheap, minor successes which propaganda and our own media would then blow up into a major victory for them and a disaster for us. I felt sure that if the Khe Sanh outpost were lost the event would be heralded world-wide as another Dien Bien Phu.

New guidance should make it clear that Westmoreland's mission was primarily the suppression of attacks on the cities, the restoration of order in the areas attacked at Tet, and the creation of a mobile reserve ready to pass to a vigorous offensive with the resumption of favorable weather in the spring. As to the air campaign, I felt that it should be conducted at maximum levels of effort during this period, leaving immune from attack only urban centers and the heavily defended localities where our plane losses would be prohibitively high.

As an unattached bystander, I did not participate in the drafting of the final recommendations at the end of the meeting, but they were generally in accord with what I had supported. Westmoreland should get the troops immediately needed and available but action should be deferred on the 206,000 increase. The general reserve should be augmented to meet world-wide contingencies as well as those which might arise in Southeast Asia. The necessary actions to effect a call-up of about 250,000 reservists should be taken to provide the additional man power required. There should be a continuation of intensive bombing in North Vietnam, but views were divided about mining Haiphong harbor. There was recognition of the need to review political and military guidelines underlying the approved strategy. That was about all of substance coming out of the conference which I recall, and it was my impression that the President accepted the recommendations without approving them pending a further study of costs.

The internal debate over the proper course of action continued until mid-March. As it became evident that the post-Tet situation was in no danger of getting out of hand, the recommendations reached in the Clifford review lost much of their urgency and I had a growing feeling that most of them were about to be shelved. The press leak regarding the planned 206,000 increase in our Vietnam forces achieved the purpose probably intended of stirring up Congress and the public against any such escalation to save a cause generally presumed to be lost. In such an atmosphere, there was little likelihood of a call-up of reserves. More likely was some action to placate aroused public opinion and to recast the President in the role of seeker after peace.

On March 25 and 26, the President reconvened the Wise Men who had met in the preceding November to advise him further on Vietnam. Essentially the same men were in attendance as before. They received briefings on the general situation in Vietnam from Dr. George Carver of CIA, on the military situation from Major General William De Puy of the JCS, and on the political situation from Mr. Philip Habib of State. I had heard Carver and De Puy make similar briefings many times in the past and found nothing unusual in what they said on this occasion. I had heard Habib's views less frequently, but, while he seemed slightly more pessimistic about the political situation than I had expected, he too made a temperate, thoughtful presentation.

I make these comments on the briefings because the President was at first inclined to blame them for the unexpected reaction of his guests. Whereas only a few months before they had generally supported his policy and concentrated their attention on ways to obtain better public understanding for it, this time they arrived apparently convinced in advance that the policy was a failure and must be changed. After two sessions of sharp debate, they met with the President and expressed their views with the utmost candor. The President polled the meeting for individual views and received highly pessimistic replies from such stalwarts as Acheson, Vance, and McGeorge Bundy. Only three men—Robert Murphy, Abe Fortas, and I—advocated following a course of action similar to the one laid out in the recommendations of the recent strategy review. The majority were for change, although far from united as to its form. A small group in the middle were unhappy about the situation but noncommittal as to a preferred course of action. This dramatic and unexpected reversal of position on the part of so many respected friends made a deep impression on the President and probably tended to confirm his decision to withdraw from the forthcoming presidential race.

What accounted for this change in so short a time? As I have mentioned, the President suspected the quality of the briefings and had two of them repeated privately for himself. I could not fault the briefers and defended them to him. For what it is worth, my own explanation was based on my estimate of the effect of media reporting of the Tet offensive on many of our visitors. Most of them lived in the news enclaves dominated by *The New York Times* and *Washington Post*, both of which were strongly anti-Administration with regard to Vietnam. It is all very well to say that intelligent sophisticates of the Eastern Establishment would be immune to the effects of media bias, be it ever so subtle. But I had lived in Japan before the war under conditions of governmental press censorship and often confessed later, only half in jest, that by the time I left Japan, I had lost most of my skepticism about the kinship of the Emperor to the Sun Goddess.

Also I strongly suspected that the Pentagon doves with whom I had become acquainted during the recent strategy review had got to some of the visitors and had impregnated them with their doubts. In the discussions of the Wise Men, there were familiar references to the futility of seeking a military victory, a strawman which, then and later, was a favorite target of the opponents of the Vietnam policy. I had never heard the term "military victory" defined but supposed it meant the imposition of our will on Hanoi largely by military means and the termination of the war in a surrender on the model of Yorktown or Appomattox. Throughout the years, I never heard any authentic spokesman for our Vietnam policy express any such concept of the nature of the victory sought. Rather, the emphasis was always on the need to blend many sources of power to achieve our political purpose of an independent Vietnam free from attack.

The guests departed, leaving the President to carry out his bitter decision to withdraw from public life in the hope of uniting a divided nation which the divisions among his friends typified. I can contribute little to the question often raised as to who or what decided the President to follow the course he chose at this historic juncture. I attended some of the discussions regarding the content of his speech of March 31 and was surprised to find Dean Rusk advocating a bombing pause north of the 20th parallel for incorporation in it. Of all the President's advisers, Rusk had been the most steadfast in adhering to an unyielding pressure on the enemy so that his change on this point should have alerted me to the probability that something unusual was up. I was still unconvinced of the wisdom of this new concession, feeling that, in the existing climate, it would be impossible to resume bombing if the pause elicited no response from the enemy. I played no part in drafting the President's speech beyond reviewing an early text before the critical final paragraphs had been added. So I was unprepared for the climax when I listened on March 31 to the President on television. I was deeply moved by the sacrifice which he was making for national unity but also greatly apprehensive over the uncertainties injected into our Asian policy by his withdrawal from public life. Who among his possible replacements could lead the country in such difficult times? Could he himself lead it in the long lame-duck period extending until January 1969? How would the enemy react to his withdrawal and to his unilateral concession in cutting back the bombing? Would the effect not be to prolong rather than to shorten the war? Clearly we were entering a new period of crisis, and the auguries were not good.

CHAPTER 33

Lame-duck Consultant

The period from President Johnson's speech of March 31 to the end of his Administration was devoted to an increasingly frantic chase after the will-o'-the-wisp of negotiations, a changeling objective which was progressively replacing the freedom and security of South Vietnam as the controlling objective of American policy. From the time of the introduction of our forces into Vietnam in 1965, the President had made it a point of honor to counterbalance new military measures with new diplomatic initiatives despite the obvious danger that the enemy would interpret his desire for negotiations as a sign of weakness. His eagerness worried many of us who had some knowledge of Asian psychology and who felt that it would make Hanoi harder to bring to the table than would a posture of stern determination, maintained quietly and without fanfare. While it could be argued that this pursuit of negotiations was necessary to demonstrate to our own people the sincerity of the desire of the government for peace, it had the adverse consequence of encouraging a belief among them that negotiations were tantamount to peace and that peace alone was the objective of our policy. Thus we were gradually shifting away from our original objective, although we still talked of seeking an honorable peace which presumably would take into account our obligations to our Vietnamese ally.

As the negotiation fervor waxed, our leaders progressively relaxed the conditions previously asserted to be essential preliminaries to discussions with the enemy. We foresook the good resolutions often expressed in the early days to heed the lessons of Panmunjom and to keep the military pressure on the Communist enemy both before and during negotiations. Forgotten also was the need to prepare carefully for negotiations and to rehearse the play of our blue chips in advance to be sure of getting a maximum return from them. Into the same limbo went our oft-repeated resolve not to pay a price of admission for sitting down at the table with the representatives of Hanoi.

393

There is no need to review here the many preliminaries to the negotiations in Paris or the negotiations themselves after they finally got under way, except to remind ourselves how we squandered many of the hard-won gains achieved in Vietnam since 1965 and even before. The President himself started the series of concessions when he offered in his speech of March 31 the cessation of bombing north of the 20th parallel. The promptness of Hanoi's reply in April was encouraging, but we should have been warned by the terms of their acceptance, namely, that they would discuss only "the unconditional cessation of bombing and all other war acts by the United States against the Democratic Republic of Vietnam." In any case, we were shortly disabused of any premature optimism by the prolonged stalling over the site of the first meeting and by the absence of any military restraint on the part of Hanoi to match our reduction of the bombing. In point of fact, there was a prompt increase in infiltration and enemy attacks on urban centers in South Vietnam. Not only did the enemy take military advantage of our restraint, but they showed no intention of entering into productive discussions, thereby providing us with good reason to reconsider the wisdom of unilateral concessions. But the Washington mood opposed any caviling at the opponents' conduct, which might delay the missionaries of peace waiting to set out for Paris.

When our negotiators, Averell Harriman and Cyrus Vance, finally reached Paris, they soon found that nothing had been gained by the President's concession on the bombing except the privilege of listening to Communist invective directed at "American aggressors" who presumed to ask for reciprocal actions in reducing the violence in Vietnam. The Communist delegates threw back reciprocity in our teeth as an unclean word to use in their presence, and the mildness of our reaction appeared to accept the rebuke. We also appeared to accept as a matter of course the renewed shelling of Saigon shortly after the meetings opened, for which there was neither reprisal nor any really strong protest. At all times in these negotiations, we had two powerful weapons capable of influencing the behavior of the other side, a resumption of the bombing at some appropriate level or a break-off of the negotiations. But in this period we never had the will to use either or even to threaten their use convincingly. At White House luncheons we repeatedly discussed resuming the bombing at least to the twentieth parallel, but in spite of repeated provocations by the enemy, it remained halted at the nineteenth parallel until completely stopped on November 1.

The main point argued in Paris during the summer and early fall was the cessation of all bombing in exchange for some assurance of moderated behavior by Hanoi. For our part, if we were to cease the bombing, we wanted to know what they would do about such things as refraining from further attacks on South Vietnamese cities, respecting the DMZ, accepting the participation of the South Vietnamese government in the negotiations, and admitting the National Liberation Front to participation without recognizing it as a diplomatic coequal of South Vietnam. Harriman and Vance worked diligently and patiently to move the other side to reasonable discussion but were frustrated by Hanoi's absolute rejection of the concept of reciprocal concessions. The only commitment which they ever got was an affirmation of readiness to move to substantive negotiations immediately following a full cessation of bombing.

In the end our negotiators became convinced, and they eventually convinced the President, that the impasse could only be broken by ending the bombing completely, subject to certain unilateral understandings on our part which Harriman and Vance would convey privately to their North Vietnamese counterparts. The understandings were that, shortly after our ending the bombing, substantive talks would start between "our side" and "their side" (so described to allow the South Vietnamese government and the National Liberation Front to participate without legal identification); that the demilitarized status of the DMZ would be restored and respected; that there would be no further indiscriminate attacks against major population centers such as Saigon, Hue, and Da Nang; and that our reconnaissance planes would not be attacked when flying over North Vietnam. It was understood that the North Vietnamese delegates would probably never give any indication of accepting these understandings, but, if they did not reject them and if they knew that we would resume the bombing if the understandings were not observed, Harriman and Vance felt the step worth taking.

There were a number of arguments in support of this point of view. If we took this initiative, it might deter the enemy from launching new offensives which were believed to be in preparation in South Vietnam. If new offensives took place, the increased casualities accompanied by a continued stalemate in negotiations would produce adverse effects on public opinion at home at a time when the Democratic convention was in the offing. In Administration circles, such considerations argued for a new initiative in Paris in hope of breaking the deadlock.

On the other hand, this proposal to stop the bombings in exchange for the understandings was based on several questionable assumptions. One was the assumption that a new enemy offensive was against our interest, whereas I was sure that our military leaders would welcome another opportunity to inflict additional casualties on the enemy in the interest of shortening the war. A more critical assumption was that the other side would observe the understandings either out of good will, out of fear of reprisals, or out of consideration for world opinion. But the past showed that they had taken advantage regularly of the various partial bombing halts despite the existence of these same restraining factors, and there was no reason to expect the restraints to be more effective under a complete bombing halt. I doubted that Hanoi believed that we would ever resume bombing if the understandings were violated. I myself was doubtful. A third assumption was that a cessation of the bombing would create an atmosphere conducive to substantive discussions once the talks got under way. I felt it far more likely that the removal of the pressure of the bombing would encourage the kind of stalling and maneuvering which had characterized past negotiations with the Communists.

President Johnson was fully alive to the pitfalls which the understandings presented, and cross-examined Harriman and Vance in great detail before acquiescing. He canvassed his principal advisers as to their views and to my surprise met with a consensus favorable to making the proposal in Paris. However, my impression was that the concurrence of the Embassy in Saigon and of our military leaders was predicated on the assumption that the understandings would be observed or the bombing would be resumed—a very shaky assumption as they soon found out.

We still had the problem of aligning the Saigon government with the Washington position. This proved difficult as Thieu and Ky were distrustful of the Paris arrangements which the United States proposed, particularly those relating to the participation of the National Liberation Front in the negotiations. Also they probably wanted to stall for time to see who the winner would be in the impending American presidential election. In any event, the South Vietnamese played hard to get, and caused lights to burn long and late in the White House and the State Department before accepting on November 27 the reassurances which President Johnson eventually gave to allay their concern.

About all that remains to be said on this subject is that, by the end of the year, the four parties representing the two sides finally got together in Paris at a table of acceptable configuration and proceeded to pursue their divergent purposes. Our purpose was to persuade and induce the other side by appeals to logic, reason, and international opinion to enter upon substantive discussions. Theirs was to frustrate substantive discussions, to drive wedges between the Americans and the South Vietnamese, and to make noisy propaganda while continuing to strive for military successes which would support their claims of victory. It was soon clear that the "understandings" were a hoax, largely self-perpetrated I must admit. The Communists never admitted that they existed, and we had nothing in writing to gainsay them. So our negotiators, first Johnson's and then Nixon's, were condemned to sit indefinitely listening to Communist insults and propaganda. For this privilege, our government had ceased the bombing of North Vietnam, ended naval actions against the coast of North Vietnam, halted the reinforcement of our troops in South Vietnam, and had accepted the presence of the National Liberation Front in the negotiations. In return we had got next to nothing. The enemy still fired mortars and rockets into the South Vietnamese towns; they continued to violate the DMZ; they fired on and sometimes shot down our reconnaissance aircraft; and they steadily refused to engage in substantive discussions. By closing our eyes to repeated violations of the understandings, we soon convinced the enemy that they had no need to fear an abrogation of our unrequited concessions and that American government was quite reconciled to accepting the principle of no reciprocity.

As the end of the Johnson Administration approached, I viewed the future of our Asian policy with increasing forebodings. Having had the opportunity to observe the President from close range during many of his trials, I had developed a great admiration for his fortitude in resisting the many pressures converging on him. Although as time went on he had yielded against his better judgment on some points, in general he seemed to believe that he had set his government on the right course in 1965 and that any departure from it would be an encouragement to the enemy rather than an act conducive to peace. Would his successor be willing to hold the line as well in the face of the kind of criticism which President Johnson had endured?

In overcoming obstacles and averting defeat in Southeast Asia, Lyndon Johnson had accomplished many admirable things but had acquired few admirers in so doing. When he authorized the air campaign against North Vietnam and introduced our combat forces into the south, he took the most difficult presidential decision since that of Truman in sending American forces into Korea. He deserved much credit for the vast program to expand the military, paramilitary, and police forces of South Vietnam, the success of which allowed his successor to embark on the so-called Vietnamization program in 1969. The American forces which he sent into Vietnam had established a vast net of airfields, roads, and ports in an underdeveloped country to support the needs of war, which later would be capable of serving the purposes of the national economy in peace. The combat forces for which he was responsible as Commander in Chief had arrived in Vietnam magnificently equipped, trained, and led. They had adapted themselves quickly to the difficult conditions of the jungle battlefield and in hundreds of combats with a tough, war-hardened enemy had never suffered a military reverse worthy of the name. Yet we Americans at home, never unduly modest in boasting of our personal or national achievements in ordinary times, had been strangely reticent in expressing pride in what our citizens, military and civilian, had done to turn the tide of Communist victory in 1965, and to convert impending disaster into the relatively favorable situation of January 1969. Far from giving appropriate honors to the departing President responsible for these things, a segment of our people took perverse enjoyment in defaming him and, at his departure, had few kind words even for his renunciation of power in the interest of national unity.

It was a great disappointment to me that more good did not come from the President's decision of March 31. On the day following his speech, I

397

sent him a note suggesting that the effect of his act could be deepened if the leaders of both parties would unite in a joint statement endorsing the peace overture contained in his speech and announcing their continued support of the war if Hanoi rejected the offer. If senior Republicans and Democrats had aligned themselves publicly behind President Johnson at that moment, I felt that it could have had an important effect at home and abroad as a demonstration of national unity. I later learned that Walt Rostow had made a similar suggestion but, as was so often the case with such proposals, no action was taken on it.

So President Johnson retired to private life, unhappy at having left the nation at war in spite of his unceasing efforts for peace. I suspected that he regretted the unilateral concessions he had made to Hanoi in deference to the urging of most of his advisers, but that he had felt obliged to run the risks of trying them for the sake of national unity. In any case, he had left the seeds of victory implanted in the soil of Vietnam for cultivation and harvesting by his successor—if Mr. Nixon could hold the country together for the time required for the reaping.

CHAPTER 34

Lessons from Vietnam

Regardless of one's attitude toward the wisdom or folly of our Vietnam policy over the years, it should not be difficult to agree that it is an historical episode worthy of careful study and review after a decent time has elapsed to permit an adequate degree of objectivity. It contains a wealth of material bearing upon the capababilities and the limitations of our power to influence the course of world events and to shape the international environment in a sense favorable to our interests. It demonstrates the many difficulties of leading a strong-willed democracy impatient of discipline and resentful of authority in a prolonged, frustrating effort on behalf of a complex cause not readily understood.

But such a study will not be easy to carry out. For maximum value, it should include as participants the principal decison-makers responsible for Veitnam policy, a participation which may be difficult to obtain, particularly since the admission that a lesson exists is often tantamount to an admission of erroneous judgment. Even after a possible lesson has been accepted for study, it will be difficult to reach agreement as to the facts involved. What took place, why, how, and with what consequences? It will be even more contentious to attempt conclusions as to what should be done in the future to avoid repeating the same mistakes.

In spite of the traps involved in such a procedure, I shall venture to single out certain aspects of the Vietnam experience which strike me as clearly worthy of post-mortem examination. For present purposes I shall omit matters which are of a specialized nature or of limited professional interest and shall concentrate instead on a few subjects of general interest.

The first point which seems to qualify under this guideline is in my view one of the outstanding lessons of Vietnam: the high cost of fulfilling a foreign commitment when it falls due for payment. Our commitment to Vietnam was one of a series undertaken with countries on the periphery of the

399

Sino-Soviet bloc following World War II. Except in Europe these commitments generally involved small states united to us by a kindred fear of expansive Communism but capable of contributing little to the common cause beyond serving as friendly outposts along the Iron or Bamboo Curtains. Most of them had weak governments and shifting leadership of untested ability. While the Korean War had given us some intimation of the cost of fulfilling a commitment under such conditions, that experience did not prepare us for the surprisingly high cost of redeeming our promises to South Vietnam.

That the Vietnam commitment has been costly beyond anyone's expectation is hardly open to debate. By mid-1971, it had cost more than 45,000 American lives in combat and on the order of 100 billion dollars. Additionally, there were the costs to Vietnam which, though not accurately known, were far greater in relative terms than our own. Finally, we had paid a price for the war in terms of disunity at home, in loss of freedom of action in dealing with other pressing foreign and domestic issues, and in the exposure of our internal weaknesses to the world community.

How were we trapped into such a costly venture? Who or what was responsible for this miscalculation? These are valid questions for the historian to raise, but I know of no completely satisfactory set of answers although I can advance a partial one. For one thing, by the nature of the undertaking it was never possible for Presidents Eisenhower, Kennedy, or Johnson to have in time all the facts necessary to permit an accurate estimate of what we could expect either from our Vietnamese ally or from the enemy. More important, even though we Americans had exhibited certain traits in the Korean War that might have served as a warning, our leaders in Washington did not anticipate the reaction of important segments of the American people after they began to feel the crunch of the Vietnam policy. Uncertainty or lack of anticipation regarding these crucial points made impossible any reasonably valid estimate of what it might cost to attain our objectives as the need for new decisions arose. Also, as we became more deeply involved, there was little thought given to the additional cost we would have to pay if, after trying, we then failed. This cost of failure increased as time went on.

Such an explanation would seem to convict our decision-makers of having committed the country to a disastrous course of action on the basis of insufficient information, but in fairness to them, one should recognize that the requirement for a decision always preceded the availability of most of the needed information. After our visit to Vietnam in 1961, Rostow and I warned President Kennedy of the inadequacy and inaccuracy of much of the information on Vietnam which our government had received up to that time. Nevertheless, we urged that he approve our recommendations for increased American support as necessary actions under any circumstances if we were to adhere to the goals of our Southeast Asian policy:

an independent South Vietnam free from attack. In the interim, we proposed to improve our intelligence in South Vietnam while working on the job. We felt reasonably comfortable in proceeding on that basis since Diem's over-all performance in coping with the Vietcong threat had been quite good up to that time and his government appeared capable of assimilating the additional aid we proposed to give. What we could not know was that an American-supported coup in 1963 would remove Diem, and with him the lid from the political Pandora's box in which Diem had confined the genies of political turbulence. When freed, these forces tore South Vietnam apart in 1964 and 1965 and presented us with a completely different set of political problems. But, in 1961, Kennedy could not wait two years for events to expose these weaknesses. He had to proceed on the information he had or concede victory to the War of National Liberation initiated by Hanoi in 1959.

President Johnson had a similar need for timely information about the North Vietnamese before making his critical decision to introduce American air and ground forces into combat. In 1965 we knew very little about the Hanoi leaders other than Ho Chi Minh and General Giap and virtually nothing about their individual or collective intentions. We were inclined to assume, however, that they would behave about like the North Koreans and the Red Chinese a decade before; that is, they would seek an accommodation with us when the cost of pursuing a losing course became excessive. Instead, the North Vietnamese proved to be incredibly tough in accepting losses which, by Western calculation, greatly exceeded the value of the stake involved. Nor did we foresee in time that the conduct of American war opponents at home would provide encouragement to the enemy to prolong the war.

Much as we may regret our lack of foresight in evaluating the probable conduct of the two Vietnams, the failure to foresee the internal difficulties at home is much harder to excuse. Indeed, our understanding of our ally and the foreign enemy, defective as it was at the outset, developed more rapidly than did our appreciation of the emergent domestic reactions. The Tonkin Gulf resolution, passed by Congress in 1964 with near unanimity, seemed to indicate such extensive support for our policy as to allay concern for the home front. It was not until 1967 that President Johnson and his advisers became deeply alarmed by the growth of antiwar agitation and by evidence of a widening communication gap between the Administration and the public. Somehow we had failed to observe the philosopher's injunction "Know thyself," and for this failure we were to pay a heavy toll in loss of national unity.

Closely related to the high cost of fulfilling a foreign commitment is its sequel, the even higher cost of failure once the effort at fulfillment has begun. The bill for failure is largely additive to the expenditures for achieving success. In the case of Vietnam, if, in addition to the lives lost, the billions expended, and the violence done the social and political fabric at home in the effort to succeed, we then fail, the additional consequences would be disastrous. These would include the reprisals of the victorious enemy against our former friends in South Vietnam; the exposure of Cambodia, Laos, and Thailand to further Communist aggression; and encouragement to the use elsewhere of the War of National Liberation technique. At home, the humiliation of failure, when once recognized as having been largely self-imposed, would deepen internal divisions and create irresistible demands for the punishment of those scapegoats thought responsible for the disaster. Abroad, there would be yet another price to be paid—a decline of confidence in the United States on the part of our allies and thereby a loss in the effectiveness of our Armed Forces in deterring war, particularly nuclear war. Deterrence depends upon a belief approaching certainty that our leaders and our people will risk war and even survival to aid an ally who is the victim of attack. A self-inflicted defeat in Veitnam which carries with it the destruction of our Asian ally would create understandable doubts everywhere as to our dependability in greater crises.

A third Vietnam lesson arises from the many limitations and inhibitions placed on the use of our national power in the course of the struggle. When one considers the vast resources committed to carrying out our Vietnam policy, the effective power generated therefrom seems to have been relatively small.

This conclusion should not surprise us because inefficiency in the use of national power is pretty well built into the American system. There is nothing in our past history which would justify the assumption that in a crisis we will find experienced, tough-minded operators at the control points of the governmental power train, individuals capable of getting the maximum horsepower from the machine. Experience indicates the contrary to be likely. For one thing, our political system makes it reasonably certain that, for one or two years out of every eight, the operators at the switches will be for the most part inexperienced newcomers in a new administration which, in the American political tradition, has just tossed out the key figures of the preceding regime. Regardless of how able these new men may be, when they first settle at their desks they are neophytes in the most complex business in the world, unacquainted even with the telephone numbers of their equally inexperienced colleagues. Though they may prudently try to avoid making critical decisions during their apprenticeship, crises are no respecter of official convenience, and any new administration will be just as vulnerable to disaster through miscalculation as were the Kennedy officials at the time of the Bay of Pigs.

Not only are the leaders likely to be new and untrained, they are likely to be timid as well. Many Americans have an inbred bias against the premeditated use of power as being an exercise in power politics which, like secret diplomacy and clandestine intelligence, is offensive to the virtue of a respectable democracy. The bias is strongest against resort to military power; this is repugnant even to those who are not averse to power in general. This prejudice leads to questioning the efficacy of military force as an instrument of policy. During the Vietnam War, it was not unusual to hear the argument that the use of military force, bombing in particular, makes an enemy stronger and more determined to resist rather than inclining him to submission. Unfortunately, Hanoi and the Vietcong were not aware of these alleged counterproductive effects of violence and resorted to it in all forms against us without our ever feeling stronger for it.

Attitudinal biases against the use of military power contributed to restrictions upon it which will long be a source of debate and hence deserve special attention in any evaluation of the Vietnam experience. In this conflict, the traditional reluctance to resort to military force except in direct self-defense was reinforced by the fear of overreaction in a world living precariously under the threat of possible nuclear war. The Korean experience and the injunctions of respected military leaders against a land war on the Asian continent added to the disinclination for American military involvement. President Kennedy's success in dealing with the Cuban missile crisis by low-order military action seemed to confirm the view of those officials who wished to go slow in utilizing our military strength in Vietnam. Even after President Johnson decided that there was no way to avoid defeat other than through the introduction of American combat forces, the strategy adopted was one of gradualism, the piecemeal employment of military force at slowly mounting levels of intensity.

There was a certain logic in this gradualism if not carried to excess. The purpose of rational war is to break the will of the adversary and cause him to adjust his behavior to our purposes, not necessarily to destroy him. In World War II, the demand for the unconditional surrender of our enemies provided a powerful incentive to their leaders to hold out to the last, a mistake we did not wish to repeat in Vietnam. Instead, we wanted Ho and his advisers to have time to meditate on the prospects of a demolished homeland in the hope that, from self-interest, they would mend their ways and seek a peaceful accommodation. Thus, in bombing North Vietnam we limited our operations to low-intensity attacks on targets restricted as to type and location, and in the ground campaign we increased our troop strength slowly and deliberately after experience had demonstrated the need for reinforcements. The over-all purpose was to apply limited force with limited means to gain limited results.

While this carefully controlled violence may have had some justification at the start, it ended by defeating its own purposes. Designed to limit the dangers of expanded war, it ended by assuring a prolonged war which carried with it the dangers of expansion. The restrained use of our air power suggested to the enemy a lack of decisiveness. The repeated bombing pauses, designed to allow Hanoi the opportunity to give us a signal, were taken by the enemy as an indication that our leaders were not sure of themselves and were unlikely to continue the bombing in the face of domestic and international pressures. So gradualism encouraged the enemy to hang on until his hopes were fulfilled in 1968 by a collapse of the American will to persist in the bombing. It may well be that Ho knew Americans better than Americans knew themselves.

If gradualism worked against the political purpose of inducing the enemy to seek an accommodation, it also violated the military principles of surprise and mass as means to gain prompt success with minimum loss. Our pilots were required to return through increasingly heavy enemy defenses to repeat attacks on targets deliberately hit previously by aircraft insufficient in number to assure their destruction in a single attack. This was a misguided attempt to translate the principle of gradualism and limited violence from the strategic to the tactical realm—a fallacy which ignored the fact that for the soldier or pilot in the presence of an armed enemy any war is total since his survival is at stake. No one, not even the President, has the moral right to put a man on the battlefield or in hostile air space and restrict him from taking all the measures needed for his survival and the execution of his mission. So in a variety of ways, gradualism contributed to a prolongation of the war and gave time not only for more men to lose their lives but also for the national patience to wear thin, the antiwar movement to gain momentum, and hostile propaganda to make inroads at home and abroad.

If these were some of the consequences of gradualism, what should one conclude from this experience? As I see the lesson, it is that our leaders of the future are faced with a dilemma which raises questions as to the continued feasibility of a limited war option for future Presidents faced with a compelling need to use military force in support of a national interest. Should such a President employ military force swiftly and decisively and risk the international consequences, or should he proceed tentatively and incrementally and risk a prolonged war on the Vietnam model? Neither is an attractive choice, but the only other is the do-nothing option which offers the prospect of a progressive attrition of our interests. The lesson of Vietnam is the need to recognize the uncertainties involved in a resort to limited war and, before deciding upon that step, to take all possible precautions to avoid re-creating the conditions which worked against the success of our military efforts in Vietnam.

Closely related to this dilemma of limited war is the requirement for greater attention to domestic attitudes in planning and guiding our foreign policy. In the course of the Vietnam tribulation, we have discovered within our society attitudes and weaknesses which we never knew existed or which perhaps we had not wished to recognize: a growing polarization of social groups, multiplying extremists on the right and left, increasing disparagement of our institutions and of the symbols and substance of conventional patriotism, loss of pride in America and its accomplishments, and unashamed defeatism in time of national crisis as soon as the going becomes hard. I would be inclined to date many of these changes in the national mood and behavior, or at least their visible manifestations, from the death of President Kennedy and to attribute much of the change in mood to the despondency generated by his loss. Without the hope which his leadership had inspired, the appeal of former national goals steadily waned, and nothing replaced them to provide a national unity of purpose. This void has been particularly noticeable in foreign policy, where old slogans in support of the containment of Communism and the principles of the Truman Doctrine are no longer sufficient to rally public support for actions entailing public sacrifice. The same could be said about the loss of vitality in our domestic life of honored principles such as peaceful reform through the ballot, equality before the law, advancement by merit, and respect for majority rule. The American melting pot seems no longer to fuse the disparate elements of our multiracial society but rather to accelerate their coagulation into blocs which resemble the proliferating power centers of the multipolar international world.

Such new factors as these added to the difficulties which President Johnson encountered in rallying support for his Vietnam policy and in obtaining and retaining the backing necessary for its successful prosecution. Under the most favorable circumstances, it was a policy difficult to explain amid the conflicting interpretations advanced by officials, pundits, and media. Even if all such sources had been dedicated to impartiality and exactitude in reporting, it would have been difficult to avoid confusing the public. There were forty-four provinces in South Vietnam, and the situation in one province was quite different from its neighbors. Thus two reliable and conscientious observers in two different provinces could file completely contradictory reports and both be right. But whatever the causes, a large majority of our population never understood the meaning and importance of the Vietnam policy, and if in spite of their confusion they continued to support it, it was out of a sense of loyalty to a President who was in deep trouble rather than from conviction as to the inherent rightness of the cause.

The gradual erosion of public support for President Johnson should remind any future President of the many factors he must take into account before deciding to lead the American people into another intervention like Vietnam. Before charging up the hill, he had better be sure that his troops will follow. He should be certain that the cause at stake is of clear, unchallengeable importance which can be explained in simple terms. He should verify that there is a high probability of attaining his objective in a short time well within the probable limits of the national patience. If it requires the use of armed force, he will be well advised to obtain Congres-

405

sional approval before committing himself and then to seek a declaration of war or emergency to silence future critics of war by executive order. To be perfectly safe from adverse public reaction, his military objective should be attainable without large scale resort to conscripts or reservists. While circumstance may oblige him to deviate from some of these criteria, he should know that when he does so he is acting counter to the lessons of Vietnam.

A point not to be omitted from these warnings relates to our governmental ineptitude in the Vietnam negotiations. We should have learned from two frustrating years of wrangling at Panmunjom what to expect from Communist negotiators in terms of stalling, bluffing, propagandizing, and avoiding substantive discussions. After the Korean Armistice, Admiral Joy, one of the principal negotiators, wrote an excellent book on the subject which should have been required reading by all the members of the delegation which we sent to Paris. Before departing, they should have war-gamed the negotiations in the presence of senior officials with past experience in negotiating with Communists. By this device, they could have prepared themselves to meet the important issues which they could expect to face in Paris and they could have tested alternative means of dealing with them. Unfortunately, I have encountered few officials out of uniform who believe in the need for such thoroughness, and the outcome of our past negotiations results at least in part from our tendency to take such preparations lightly.

Our mistakes in the Vietnam negotiations began in 1965 when President Johnson resolved to display the same energy in the search for peace as he did in striving to coerce the enemy into better behavior. The record of the following years is replete with American and third-party overtures, first, to get a meeting of interested parties, then, to get substantive discussions started. While our diligence in pressing for talks sprang from laudable motives, in the early years it was premature since the military situation was not yet sufficiently unfavorable to the Communists to offer us any hope of serious negotiations. As noted earlier, our concessions to get negotiations started, like the cessation of the bombing, were probably read as signs of weakness and worked against our sincere desire to end the fighting promptly but without sacrificing our over-all objective.

Notwithstanding the oft-expressed resolve on the part of Johnson officials never to pay a price for the privilege of sitting down with the Communists, in the end we did just that, and it was an exorbitant price. First, President Johnson offered up his political career and a partial concession on the bombing of North Vietnam to restore national harmony and to get our delegates to the table. Once they got there, the talks promptly bogged down over the Communist demand for a complete cessation of bombing to which we finally acceded at the end of October. In exchange for this major blue chip, we got the so-called understandings that the enemy would not attack urban centers in South Vietnam, would not violate the DMZ, would permit aerial reconaissance of North Vietnam, and would enter at once into productive negotiations. The enemy never complied with these understandings, and soon were claiming that they never existed.

So it was that we were ingloriously bilked in spite of the fact that our fighting men by the end of 1968 had gained a military superiority which our government should have been able to exploit. Instead of passing to the diplomatic offensive, we required our diplomats to sit passively at the table for over three years under a hail of Communist diatribes and propaganda unalloyed by any trace of serious negotiation. We always had powerful trumps to play such as the withdrawal of our unilateral concessions and a suspension of the negotiations. But we did nothing of the sort, a fact which makes the record of Paris considerably inferior to that of Panmunjom, where through a last-minute display of determination, we did score a victory on the critical issue of the voluntary repatriation of enemy prisoners of war. President Nixon, upon succeeding President Johnson, spoke eloquently about ending the era of Cold War confrontation and of initiating an era of negotiations. Our experience in Paris makes one wonder if the United States is ready for the transition to this golden age.

In reviewing these lessons of Vietnam, one is bound to be impressed with the fact that we Americans created many of our own problems and thereby contributed to the prolongation of a war which everyone detested. Few of us escape some responsibility for this disservice. The leaders of our government contributed insofar as they shared in the responsibility for the overthrow of Diem without making preparation for the consequences. It is true that even if no American had lifted a finger against him, Diem's compatriots might have eventually deposed him with roughly similar results. But in that case it would have been purely the doing of the Vietnamese, and American officials would not have shared culpability with the coup leaders for the disastrous events of 1964 and 1965. In the post-Diem period when the political turbulence in South Vietnam offered the United States an excuse to withdraw from its involvement, the realization of our role in creating the Vietnamese predicament was a strong deterrent to anyone inclined to make such a proposal. Our leaders were responsible for prolonging the war also through the indecisive use of our military power and through their attitude toward negotiations, both points already discussed. Even President Johnson provided unintended encouragement to the enemy when he withdrew from the presidential race and agreed to reduce and later to end the bombing of the North.

Elements of the information media contributed to prolonging the war by their manner of reporting the news. It required only selective reporting, not deliberate fabrication, to create the impression that we Americans were the prime aggressors bent on expanding the war to avoid impending defeat, and that our alleged successes were really defeats which officials were trying to hide from the American public. Biased reporters found no good to say about our Vietnamese allies, whom they held up to scorn in a way which led the American people to believe that our allies were not worth the sacrifices we were making in their behalf. Such selective and slanted reporting spread defeatism among the tender-minded at home and provided enormous encouragement for Hanoi to hold fast and concede nothing.

Of course, the media did not have to manufacture dissent and antiwar feeling in the United States; there was enough of the real article to provide them with legitimate subject matter. Every war critic capable of producing a headline contributed, in proportion to his eminence, some comfort if not aid to the enemy. Unfortunately, from 1967 onward there was no shortage of eminent figures among the opponents of the war willing to make this contribution.

Notwithstanding the many antiwar demonstrations during the Johnson Administration, we probably misled ourselves as to the strength and depth of the antiwar movement. From early 1968 on, many of the advisers around President Johnson displayed a demoralization and loss of confidence in the Vietnam policy which was unjustified by the public attitudes which I encountered on my numerous speaking tours about the country. There was really such a thing, I felt, as a silent majority in support of the President, stout citizens who, though confused about the issues and worried by the Tet offensive, were not about to flee the battlefield. But even the President allowed himself to become convinced that nothing short of the sacrifice of his political career could save the internal situation from disintegration. If this tough-minded leader reached such a conclusion, how much easier must it have been for Ho Chi Minh—viewing the same situation, hearing the same American voices, and reading the same American news—to believe in the imminence of an American collapse and the certainty of ultimate victory.

We are carrying into the next decade many unresolved problems raised by Vietnam. How can a democracy such as ours defend its interests at acceptable cost and continue to enjoy the freedom of speech and behavior to which we are accustomed in time of peace? To a Communist enemy the Cold War is a total, unending conflict with the United States and its allies —without formal military hostilities, to be sure—but conducted with the same discipline and determination as formal war. Unless we can learn to exercise some degree of self-discipline, to accept and enforce some reasonable standard of responsible civic conduct, and to remove the many self-created obstacles to the use of our power, we will be unable to meet the hard competition awaiting us in the decade of the 1970's.

CHAPTER 35

Adjustments to Declining Power

The unifying theme of these memoirs has been the use of American power in its various forms for the purpose of protecting or advancing our national interests. The obstacles and threats to our interests in the span of time reviewed have been both external and internal in their origins and to overcome them has required a heavy expenditure of national resources including, in four cases, the resort to arms. Twice we have participated in world wars in which the survival of governments and political systems were at stake, and in which both sides used their resources without stint to destroy the war-making power of the enemy. Since World War II we have been involved in the nonmilitary hostilities of the Cold War which, on two occasions, erupted into limited war.

Having recounted my personal participation in various episodes of this period and having described my reaction to them, I feel that I owe a few general remarks bearing upon the defense and enhancement of our national interests in the post-Vietnam years. My over-all conclusion is that we are entering the decade of the 70's in a condition of declining power while facing increasingly difficult and complex problems of foreign and domestic policy that will challenge our claims to world leadership.

This belief derives in part from the weaknesses revealed in the Vietnam conflict which, as I write, is still in progress. At this moment President Nixon's Vietnamization policy holds promise of achieving our main objectives provided those Americans who appear dedicated to its failure do not find means to salvage defeat from the costly achievements of past years. But even in victory we cannot completely redeem the unheroic image created by many aspects of our behavior in the course of the con-

409

flict. The record of our violent internal divisions, our loss of morale, and our psychotic inclination to self-flagellation and self-denigration justifies serious doubts as to the performance to be expected from us in any future crisis—an uncertainty which will becloud our prestige and diminish our ability to influence world events as long as it lasts.

In regard to the Vietnam War, I have noted many examples of our ineffective use of available power arising from the bias or inexperience of officials, from self-imposed restrictions on the use of military power, and from the ineptitude of our diplomacy in exploiting military success. Although such defects are in part at least correctable, until there is evidence that correction will be undertaken, it is only prudent to assume in estimating our future power position that the deficiencies are likely to remain. In particular, the limited war dilemma as to whether to use military power decisively and risk World War III, to use it incrementally and risk a Vietnam, or not to use it at all will continue to plague decision-makers.

In the immediate post-Vietnam period, a revulsion against any form of military intervention anywhere seems likely to be a prevailing national attitude. The antimilitary bias which has followed all our wars will be accentuated in the present case by the ever-increasing need for resources to cope with our domestic problems. In this climate military budgets and force levels will tend to decline, and with them our capabilities to deal with troublemakers abroad. Our Armed Forces, regardless of their size, will have limited effectiveness in advancing our interests until there is new evidence to demonstrate an American will to use them decisively if required. To be convincing, such evidence must include indications that we have regained a sense of national unity and purpose and have outlived the morbid excesses of self-criticism which now afflict us.

These are some of the most cogent reasons for my feeling that we face the new decade in a condition of declining power. Unfortunately, that decade promises to be one of increasing dangers. The possibility of nuclear war remains despite the unlikelihood that any nation will embark upon it from choice. The Soviets continue to display a disquieting willingness to sacrifice human comforts to achieve nuclear supremacy over the United States, whatever supremacy may mean in such a context. For our part, we are increasingly reluctant to spend the vast sums necessary for the maintenance of modernized strategic forces even though the deterrent effect of those we have has been impaired by our disunity at home.

In the coming decade the need to wage limited war may arise under a wide variety of circumstances. We have many interests abroad which are vulnerable to foreign predators. They include the lives and interests of our citizens, our trade and investments, and our Armed Forces and their bases. Each of our many allies constitutes a possible target which, if attacked, might involve us in limited war. We may be obliged to respond to mini-aggressions by weak powers wishing to demonstrate their lack of fear of the

American colossus. Our overseas intelligence sources may be a target for attack, as was the *Pueblo* in 1968 by the North Koreans. We could be drawn into military operations arising from peace-keeping missions or from third-party wars. The current Arab-Israeli conflict illustrates this possibility. We should bear constantly in mind that we may have limited war forced upon us whether we choose it or not.

Just as the threat of limited war will always be with us, it is also an unpleasant truth that we must be prepared to wage the Cold War whether we like it or not. One sometimes hears the view that with the rift in the Sino-Soviet bloc, the moderated tone of Soviet Communism, and the new hope for accommodation with Peking, the Cold War is over. Anyone differing with this comforting assessment is apt to be regarded as an unregenerate Cold Warrior bent on perpetuating a past which is happily gone forever. Unfortunately, the Cold War is not a form of hostility in which only Russians can indulge. It comprises a technique available to any troublemaker clever enough to advance his interests by bluff, propaganda, falsehood, and subversion, while avoiding open hostilities. The earlier techniques of the Cold War have been refined in recent years and now are assuming new forms which permit their application even against the United States.

When in 1961 President Kennedy recognized the War of National Liberation as a Cold War threat to emerging countries, I doubt whether he or any of his associates anticipated that its methods might be employed against an advanced country like the United States. But the central feature of this form of Cold War aggression is the erosion of the sources of power of a state—its leadership, institutions, economy, and national unity—and any country is vulnerable if hostile weapons can reach such targets. Lin Piao warned us in 1965: "Everything is divisible and so is the colossus of U.S. imperialism. It can be split and defeated." This effort to split and defeat us is now in progress, based not on guerrilla warfare but upon the exploitation of our own internal weaknesses coupled with the abuse of such revered democratic practices as freedom of press, speech, and dissent.

The forces of division have received powerful support from the publicity provided by the information media. It is the support of the media which has made possible the campaign of defamation which is now directed at virtually every institution of government and society. The Presidency, the Congress, the Courts, the church, and business have all been vilified for their stupidity, cupidity, or immorality. The Armed Forces and police have been depicted as brutal, venal, and oppressive. Such propaganda, repeated in many forms and contexts and seldom refuted, has created an atmosphere of suspicion and cynicism destructive to national unity and morale. The feeling is that somehow we have been betrayed by our leaders.

In making this contribution to the subversive campaign, it has not been necessary for the media to intend the consequences of the support they

411

render this movement. It has only required adherence to certain time-honored practices to produce most of the results I have mentioned. The first such practice is the standard traditionally applied to what is newsworthy and what is not. The long-standing view has been and remains that the tragic, the sensational, and the criminal are news; the heartening, the normal, and the wholesome are not. By this criterion, extremist radical attacks on authority, demonstrations against the war, the views of draft-dodgers in Sweden, and the Calley trial receive the undivided attention of press, radio, and television. On the other hand, a speech by a responsible official in support of the Vietnam policy, the uncomplaining performance of duty by millions of soldiers, and the activities of the American government to repair the ravages of war in Vietnam do not qualify as news and are barely reported, if at all.

An attitude of the media which has had similar effects is that their primary role is to expose the rascals in government and thus protect the public from stupid or dishonest officials. This was a potential public service which undoubtedly loomed large in the eyes of the authors of the First Amendment. But the pursuit of rascals produces unintended results in a time of armed hostilities as in the case of Vietnam. In this conflict, the only officials within range of the critical eye of the reporters have been Americans or their allies, and thus the only breed of rascals which could be exposed. Those who might have qualified for the title on the Communist side operated under the protective covering afforded by a closed police state. As a result, media coverage of the war created an impression that it was the Americans or the South Vietnamese who committed all the stupidities and the brutalities, that our side's actions in the waging of war were immoral, and that it was the enemy who deserved the sympathy of right-thinking people.

This uneven treatment of the news has been exacerbated by the increasingly common practice of selective reporting in accordance with the personal bias of the reporter. Once considered contrary to professional ethics in the era of "all the news that's fit to print," selective reporting has now become accepted behavior. It is not necessary to do violence to the truth to create biased news. It suffices merely to suppress parts of the whole truth or to present parts as though they constituted the whole. This distortion of reality may then be abetted by the reader or viewer himself who indulges in the human frailty of jumping at general conclusions from limited evidence.

The media are not alone in contributing to the forces which enfeeble us. We have national habits which play into the hands of those seeking to erode our power. For instance, as a people we are inclined to talk too much for our own good. Sometimes this talking has a legitimate purpose—after all, a leader in a democracy must explain his motives and intentions if he is to get the popular support necessary to get and stay elected. But this obligation to inform the public does not extend to the release of valuable secret information to reinforce an argument or to gain a political advantage. Yet responsible officials have been known to indulge in that practice and thereby supply our enemies with information of the kind for which we spend billions of dollars in a vain attempt to get from them. If the Soviets wish to learn about the size, location, and characteristics of our strategic missiles, they have only to read the official data published in the open press.

Another trait which works against our interests is our national impatience for quick results. A persistent adversary soon learns that to get what he wants, all that is necessary is to wait out the Americans. Unfortunately the important objectives of a great nation are not of the kind which can be achieved by "a heart unfortified, a mind impatient." Perseverance is still an indispensable virtue for pretenders to world power.

Faced with this evidence of declining American power and of the erosion of its sources, may we not find ways to forestall the misfortunes which may flow therefrom? Certainly some of these shortcomings are correctable and such remedies as are possible should be undertaken at once.

A first step is to recognize the new Cold War technique directed against the sources of our power as a formidable threat to our national security. This form of attack is not new in its weapons—propaganda, subversion, power seizures by minorities. But the acuteness of the threat is new because of the increasing strength and boldness of the internal revolutionary movement and the mind-numbing power of press and television in their effect on the critical judgment of the public. This threat strikes at the roots of national power, particularly at our national unity without which we are an easy target for all enemies, large and small, foreign and domestic. To cope with it, we need a new concept of national security broad enough to assure that defensive measures are taken against subversion in this form. Surely the defense of our national unity merits a dedication of effort at least equal to that which we have lavished in the past on the protection of our overseas possessions, our coast lines, and our air-space from overt foreign foes.

I am reasonably optimistic about our ability to make procedural improvements for greater governmental efficiency in the use of our power. We can certainly bring more method into the determination of our national interests and thus avoid premature commitments from which it may be difficult to withdraw. The approach I have suggested in earlier chapters is to test the validity of the national interest of an issue in four aspects: the gain to be anticipated from its success, the probable cost of achieving this success, the probability of failure, and the additive cost which failure would entail. The cost of success would have to include consideration of both the cost of overcoming enemy resistance and the loss in power due to internal friction and waste in the governmental power plant. The cost of

413

failure after trying would have to include such things as loss in reputation, damage to allies resulting from our failure, and the domestic effects of the humiliation of defeat. The probability of failure would have to depend not only on the inherent difficulty of the task but also on the adequacy of available resources and the likelihood of gaining and retaining popular support for the effort. While such a validation process for a national interest contains many unknowns, for example, the future behavior of adversaries and allies, it does represent a rational approach to a problem of the utmost importance. With such a process in effect, it should be possible not only to avoid gross errors in choosing new policies but to have an accepted means to revalue old policies which may have outlived their usefulness. Thus we would achieve one of the requirements of a period of declining power, the assurance that we are expending our limited resources for something of real and continuing value.

Let me illustrate the working of this approach by using it to answer the highly controversial question: All things considered, is our current Vietnam policy in the national interest? While the final outcome is still uncertain in mid-1971, the decline in intensity of enemy military operations and the steady reduction of American forces afford strong reason to believe that we are in the final phase at least of the military hostilities. Sufficient reliable data are now available to permit a fair estimate of the gains and losses of our Vietnam policy to date. But since we are still not sure how it will terminate, whether in victory or defeat, we should evaluate the policy under both cases.

But what is victory or defeat in this contest? It is certainly not an Appomattox or a Waterloo; the concept of a classic military victory for either side has never had relevance in Vietnam. I would contend that victory for us is to accomplish what we set out to do, namely, to assure South Vietnam the possibility of choosing its own government, free from the danger of having a Communist regime imposed by force. Victory for Hanoi would be the reverse, success in imposing such a regime or at least creating a terminal situation which would assure a Communist regime in a reasonably short time. So I propose to use these definitions in projecting the gains and losses in the event, first, that the Vietnam War ends in victory and second, that it ends in defeat.

If we leave Vietnam with our objective achieved, we will have demonstrated loyalty to an ally to whom we were committed by treaty and governmental assurances, and, in so doing, we will have diminished the threat of further Communist aggression to neighboring countries. We will have exposed the myth of invincibility in which the Communist world leadership has sought to drape the War of National Liberation. We will have avoided the costs of failure which would be very high. Finally, in the course of the conflict we have acquired a better understanding of ourselves and the limits of our capabilities as a great power. It has been a painful way to gain wisdom, but the aftermath of victory should provide a favorable climate in which to reflect upon the lessons learned. If we succeed in identifying and in correcting our past mistakes, even if only in part, we should be better prepared to face future challenges.

The losses sustained in achieving victory are still uncertain as they depend on the time and terms of the outcome; however, they will of necessity exceed somewhat the current costs to date in lives and resources. The revelation of our internal divisions has created doubts abroad as to our future reliability, doubts which will remain until dispelled by evidence of improved conduct following Vietnam. Even in victory our ability to deter war will remain curtailed until we demonstrate convincingly that we have regained our national poise and unity of purpose.

So much for the debits and credits of victory. What are they likely to be if we accept defeat? The gains will necessarily be few, but at least we will have tried in the name of principles formerly held in high esteem—resistance to aggression, the right of self-determination, and loyalty to the pledged American word. Some credit will surely be due for the costly though futile effort made. Also we should benefit from the same gain of increased self-knowledge as in the case of victory, although the postwar atmosphere following defeat is not likely to be conducive to temperate analysis of our mistakes. The costs of defeat will necessarily include the heavy losses suffered in seeking victory and the additive consequences of defeat —enemy reprisals against South Vietnam; dangers to Laos, Cambodia, and Thailand; doubts raised about American trustworthiness; and loss in the peace-keeping effectiveness of our Armed Forces. The damage to the sources of our power, particularly to our democratic institutions, our Armed Forces, and our national unity are sure to be serious if not in some cases irreparable.

If it were possible to assign numerical values to these items in the gain and loss columns, we could strike a balance and thus determine whether it is in the national interest to pay the additional cost for victory or to accept defeat with no further effort. Unfortunately, it is not possible to quantify and computerize such value as human casualties, international reputation, and national unity; hence, in the end, like our decision-makers we must depend largely on human judgment to weigh the pros and cons of the alternative courses of action. Personally, I would expect the probable gains of victory to exceed its anticipated costs by a substantial margin. However, agreement on this point is not particularly important since the costs of defeat are so prohibitive by this time that the net balance of the gains and costs of victory is comparatively inconsequential. Whatever one may have thought about the Vietnam policy at various times in the past, defeat today would constitute a national disaster of such proportions that it must not be accepted if it can be avoided. Fortunately, it can be avoided since most of our disabilities have been and remain self-imposed. We have it in our power to make an honorable and successful ending to this struggle which should redeem much of the feckless and unheroic in our past conduct.

Related to better methodology in determining national interests is the need to learn to integrate the forms of power found in various governmental departments. Having commented on this problem in an earlier chapter, I will only reaffirm my conviction of its continuing importance and my uncertainty as to the adequacy of the organizational changes made by the Nixon Administration to correct deficiencies demonstrated in the past. The changes made seem to stress timely planning and the development of policy alternatives for the President. Both are indispensable components of the integration process, but they are not designed to remedy our greatest weakness. In past practice, our failures have been mostly in the assignment of clear missions to executive departments to carry out a presidential decision once made, and in the establishment of an effective supervisory system to check on progress and performance in execution.

Procedural improvements should also be possible in establishing national priorities among the foreign and domestic issues which compete for national resources. The demands of the Vietnam War and the cost of such expensive programs as those for the exploration of space, for ballistic missile defense, and for a supersonic transport have stirred a nation-wide debate over priorities, one which is likely to increase in intensity as our domestic needs become more sharply defined. Thus far the requirements of programs related to national security have had a clear organizational advantage over domestic programs. In spite of the imperfections of the national security process, the NSC mechanism with its basis in law has provided a forum to deal with national security issues. There has been no comparable machinery to deal with important domestic programs, a deficiency which has given rise to recurrent complaints that domestic policy cannot compete on equal terms with foreign and security policy.

The procedural measures which I have discussed thus far have been for the purpose of obtaining a greater output of usable power from available resources. But it should be possible also to use the power output to better advantage, particularly the military power which has proved disappointingly indecisive in the Vietnam conflict. The basic problem here is to assure the President the option of using or threatening to use limited war in support of national policy, an option which the Vietnamese experience has rendered uncertain.

In the previous chapter we left any President wishing to exploit military force as an instrument of policy impaled on the three-horned dilemma: risking World War III if he uses military power decisively, another Vietnam if he uses it timidly, or the attrition of our world-wide interests if he relies only upon nonmilitary forms of power. The first requirement for getting out of this dilemma involves the President himself. He must be a man of character who refuses to be intimidated by his fears while, at the same time, avoiding undue risks. Future Presidents can profit from a study of President Kennedy, who was not made timid by fears of escalation when he caught Khrushchev with his missiles in Cuba; rather, he did what he could to control the risks and then did what had to be done to remove the missiles. He had the advantage of geographic position over his adversary and the possession of a clear and vital cause which assured the support of his people. Also, he was sure of the adequacy of his nuclear forces for deterrence. Finally, he knew how to exploit these advantages.

The choice of the cause is of the utmost importance in avoiding future discomfitures of the Vietnam kind. To gain initial popular support, the issue must offer a clear promise of important national gain at tolerable costs and thus qualify as a valid national interest. Made confident in the soundness of his cause, a President can then present its requirements to the people bluntly and without embellishment setting forth the need for unity and sacrifice—no promises of guns *and* butter. If convinced that his cause warrants a resort to arms, a President needs to assure himself on two points before making a final decision: (1) he needs to be reasonably sure that he can not only gain but also retain popular support for the duration of hostilities; and (2) to avoid a prolonged war, he must verify that the Armed Forces are capable of carrying out a strategy which will attain its ends rapidly and decisively before the national patience becomes exhausted. To the first point, he must address all his talents of imaginative leadership to assure an understanding of the nature and importance of the cause and to anticipate the discontent which is sure to arise from the unequal burdens of a limited war. To achieve a short war, he must be willing to provide ample resources and concede wide freedom of action to the ablest military commanders he can find.

He will be well advised at the outset, I believe, to seek a declaration of war which, if obtained from Congress, will provide indisputable evidence of a popular mandate for the course of action he is pursuing. A declaration of war will have other advantages. We Americans are accustomed to thinking of war as a condition quite different from peace, one in which we expect to make unpleasant sacrifices and recognize the need to comport ourselves in accordance with standards of conduct far more demanding than those of normal times. President Johnson hoped that the Tonkin Gulf Resolution would serve this purpose, but to the American people it was not the same as a declaration of war. The latter, I believe, would have had far greater impact and would have served to restrain some of our domestic activities which aided the enemy and prolonged the war.

Some form of national service would assist a President in broadening the popular base of participation in a limited war and, if properly administered, it could serve as a unifying factor in peace as well. National service could provide manpower to work for the domestic welfare—antipollution, slum clearance, low-cost housing, conservation of natural resources—while selective service, its military component, produced manpower for the Armed Forces. The nonmilitary activities would provide useful employment for conscientious objectors, a growing problem at the end of the Vietnam War. An absence of academic deferments from some form of national service would involve the young early in a common effort and thereby create a universality of obligation which should mitigate the discontent over the inequities of the draft responsible for much of the campus unrest during the Vietnam War.

In seeking a military strategy which will assure a short and successful war, a wise President will forego the piecemeal commitment of military resources and gradualism in their use in coercing the enemy. He will abjure the concept of limited war as a conflict fought with minimum forces, using minimum violence to achieve carefully circumscribed results. A proper concept of limited war is one in which the objectives are limited to something less than the total destruction of the enemy but which carries no implication of curtailed resources or restricted tactics. The resources allocated and their use in combat should be limited only by the requirements of prompt victory.

To be effective in minimum time, the military strategy pursued must stress surprise, maneuver, and massed strength at the decisive point—the historic formula for quick success. The same history which validates this formula bears ample evidence to the failure of incremental and intentionally moderated violence. War casualties are far more a function of the duration of exposure to enemy action than to the intensity of combat at the decisive point of contact. Whatever prolongs war increases its cost in lives, treasure, and national will; whatever shortens the war decreases these costs. The saying has been attributed to Samuel Johnson that "the King who makes war on his enemies tenderly distresses his subjects most cruelly." A President contemplating limited war should ponder these words.

While impressed with the obstacles to limited war as a policy option, I would emphasize the need to be prepared constantly to wage it. For one thing, our preparations will have some deterrent effect on troublemakers, one which will wax and wane with the impression of strength or weakness of the American character. Moreover, an adversary can force a limited war upon us whether or not we retain the option of resorting to it voluntarily. Then again, a wave of national hysteria can sweep us into a situation where we may be obliged to use limited force whether or not it is in the true national interest. The record shows that we are a volatile people, and, while we may not rise again to the slogan of "Remember the *Maine*," there may be a temptation to "Save Israel," "Free Biafra," or "Chastise South Africa."

This concern over the ability of a democracy to resort to arms for reasons other than survival may be offensive to readers who will view it as the desire of a militarist to keep war alive, whereas all right-minded people should be working to eliminate war as an instrument of policy. I have been reproached for having been an advocate of the military strategy of Flexible Response which, as adopted by President Kennedy, resulted in the creation of many of the forces used in Vietnam. Hence, it is felt that in some degree I must be held responsible for the war. I have heard arguments in Congress against providing the Armed Forces with fast ships and transport aircraft because the availability of rapid transport might encourage military interventions abroad. Without them, an impetuous President would be restrained from involvement in rash military ventures.

It is quite true that a government will probably not undertake a course of action for which it clearly lacks the means. However, the trouble is that the military forces necessary for a Vietnam-type intervention are similar, if not identical, with those necessary to defend the existence of Israel, to maintain the balance of power in the Mediterranean, to assure access to West Berlin, and to participate in peace-keeping operations under the aegis of the United Nations. They are also the forces which back up the police power at home and provide the ultimate guarantee of the defense of the Constitution and the institutions derived from it. If we drastically reduce our limited war forces because of discontent over our Vietnam policy, we shall be obliged to accept impotence in many fields where most of our citizens, including the Vietnam critics, will consider that we have important stakes that they may wish to defend with something more substantial than a diplomatic protest.

The fact is that, without the limited war option and the forces that go with it, we have little of substance with which to defend our interests. If we look to nonmilitary means, the record shows that we have never been able to develop much dynamism from them in the past. The members of our diplomatic service perform well their traditional representational functions abroad, observing and reporting the world scene to Washington in well-written appreciations. But such functions, important as they are, do not require and rarely develop officials of the take-charge type capable of holding their own against tough-minded, well-trained adversaries. By temperament and training our diplomats are rarely experienced executives and it is probably unfair to expect them to change.

With the world's strongest economy, we have had but limited success in harnessing economic power in support of foreign policy objectives in time of peace. Dollar diplomacy has become as opprobrious a term as gunboat diplomacy. The tools of economic power are numerous and have been used effectively by other countries to support their foreign policies—loans, grants, economic aid, tariffs, subsidies, boycotts, and the like—but we have not found them easy to exploit for gaining international advantages. For one thing, their use is likely to produce unintended side effects upon the

419

domestic economy or stir up reprisals abroad, and thereby raise a storm of public and Congressional censure. In any case, the use of the full range of our economic weapons has normally been reserved for wartime; in times of peace they have been used very sparingly.

If we examine our use of propaganda as an adjunct to foreign policy, as do our adversaries, we find little encouragement in the past record. Propaganda, like power politics, is an unclean word in the American lexicon, although as a form of publicity it draws upon many of the advertising skills which are so much a part of our daily lives. For whatever reasons, its practitioners have received little encouragement to take an aggressive part in selling the American political case abroad nor, I must admit, have they displayed talents warranting much encouragement. There is no evidence of which I am aware that any foreign power has ever been deterred from taking an action inimical to the United States for fear of the reaction of American propaganda.

This brief review of the nonmilitary means which may be available to cope with future threats convinces me that they will not be sufficient without the support of a limited war option. There must be a big stick somewhere in the background to assure a hearing for the American voice in international debate. It is an unhappy fact of history that noncoercive means have not been sufficient to allay for long the fear, acquisitiveness, or ideological fervor of peoples and governments—the driving forces which have provided the motivation for most international violence. The tools of the diplomat, financier, economist, and molder of public opinion have not been enough to carry the day without the reinforcement of military power when important interests have been at stake. For this reason, I feel it of the utmost importance to maintain a limited war option for the President despite the discouragement provided by the Vietnam experience.

If despite corrective action doubt still remains as to our ability to curb the erosion of our effective national power, that doubt constitutes a strong admonition to review our goals and programs for the coming period to see whether they are consistent with the power likely to be available to back them. The only official intimation of the future requirements of foreign policy with which I am acquainted is the so-called Nixon Doctrine. While it conveys our intention to assume a low posture abroad, particularly in Asia, and concurrently to cut military expenditures, there is no intention indicated to reduce our formal commitments in phase with the reduction in means. The language fosters an uneasy feeling that we will move into the post-Vietnam period retaining high-posture obligations but with low-posture means, an imbalance which augurs trouble. We may reflect with profit on the fate of our enemies in World War II, Germany, Italy, and Japan, all victims of ambitions unsupported by adequate means. On the other hand, we have the contrasting example of Britain, whose postwar leaders had the wisdom to make the painful but necessary adjustments to foreign policy as British power declined. If, as I believe, we too are a power with declining means in relation to our goals, now is the time to recognize the fact, unpleasant though it may be to the national self-esteem, and make the necessary adjustments.

But we should not forget that while our available power may be declining in absolute terms, the controlling factor in the end will be the relation of our power to that of our potential adversaries. It is the net differential which counts in international competition, and there are important variables that will influence that differential. What will our adversaries, actual and potential, be doing while we are trying to correct our shortcomings and increase the effectiveness of our national power? At the moment, the Soviet Union is indulging in a new display of expansionism under the protection of its increased nuclear armament that now rivals or exceeds our own. The Soviets apparently aspire to become a global power capable of challenging the United States in the Mediterranean, of threatening Europe's oil reserves in the Middle East, and of flying the Russian flag on any ocean. This outward thrust may be interpreted either as evidence of a new self-confidence derived from increased power or as an ill-advised dissipation of resources that may be needed to cope with a hostile China, discontented satellites, or unrest within the Soviet Union itself.

If our principal Cold War rival may be living beyond its means, certain of our allies, notably Western Europe and Japan, have accumulated reserves of resources which are available to support goals as yet unrevealed. How these countries decide to use their affluence in pursuit of the foreign objectives eventually chosen will exert a strong influence on the balance of power, particularly if, in the meantime, the present leaders, the United States and the USSR, have exhausted themselves in unproductive competition.

So the future depends not only on what we do but on what other powers do. Will they join in the nuclear arms race or save their resources for later, more remunerative uses? Will they increase their productivity while we succumb to inflation and its social and economic consequences? Will they live in harmony at home while we remain riven by factionalism and terrorized by crime? Most important of all, will they choose their goals wisely and pursue them relentlessly while we flounder in aimlessness or exhaust ourselves in internecine struggles? These matters are quite as important as the decline in absolute American power in determining the equilibrium of international relations in the 1970's. One thing is sure: the international challenge tends to merge more and more with the domestic challenge until the two become virtually indistinguishable. The threats from both sources are directed at the same sources of national power which provide strength both for our national security and for our domestic welfare. It is clear, I believe, that we cannot overcome abroad and fail at home, or succeed at home and succumb abroad. To progress toward the goals of our security and welfare we must advance concurrently on both foreign and domestic fronts by means of integrated national power responsive to a unified national will.

Index

423